# THE
# ARCHITECTURE
# BOOK

# Norval White

# THE ARCHITECTURE BOOK

Alfred A. Knopf   New York   1976

The author wishes to give credit to the following photographers and institutions for pictures in this book on the pages listed:

20 L. Bezzola; 23 Edmund Bacon; 24 J.A. Vruhof; 27 Armando Salas Portugal; 30 Belgiojiso-Peressutti-Rogers; 42, 47, 194, 217, 262 Ezra Stoller; 44 Norman McGrath; 56 Bob Serating; 65 Karl H. Riek; 71 Frank Lotz Miller; 85 Robert Gray; 88 American Institute of Architects; 96, 102, 271 German Information Center; 101 Simon Scott; 113 Gottscho-Schliesner; 123 Elsam, Mann and Cooper; 127 Bill Engdahl, Hedric, Blessing; 128 Museum of Modern Art; 136 David Hirsch; 138 Lawrence Halprin; 140 Man Ray; 150 Greek National Tourist Office; 160 Balthalzar Korab; 185 George Cserna; 212 drawing by Mark Livingston; 215 John Hill; 240 Long Island Historical Society; 276 Max Dupain; 279 Havas; 284 Ivan Pinter; 291 John Donat; 325 Giuseppe Maestri; 335 Lisenti; 341 Archie Handford

THIS IS A BORZOI BOOK
PUBLISHED BY ALFRED A. KNOPF, INC.

**Library of Congress Cataloging in Publication Data**

White, Norval.

 The architecture book.

 1. Architecture—Dictionaries. I. Title.
NA31.W45  1976    720'.3    76-13713
ISBN 0-394-49326-5

Manufactured in the United States of America
First Edition

## INTRODUCTION

To relish architecture is both an intellectual and intuitive emotional affair. Delight can rise from casual visual sensualism as one can admire and be excited by a beautiful woman; but knowledge of her and commitment to her can raise experience to an exalted plane. Art collector Vincent Price said succinctly: "I like what I know." Know architecture, both in mind and feelings, and your experience of it may become exalted. The beginning of such understanding can be gained through knowledge of the words and people of architecture. This book contains my thoughts and feelings about those words and people.

We use words as decoration, flags of special knowledge. At best they are rich and economical tools for communication; at their worst, so special as to be a code intelligible only to an inner circle. Even the names of those connected with architecture are sometimes no more than slogans, cartoons of the reality. Such is a pity, and it is to restore humanity that, at least in part, this book has been written. You can here share with me the economies and savor the richness of the best of the words, discover the significance of those who are (in my opinion) the most important figures.

If, for example, crenelations, crepidoma, and a rusticated archivolt sound as if they might be, respectively, a special dessert at Harry's Bar in Venice, a crawling thing, and a rusty machine for hurling medieval arrows, fear not. All are needed, and will be explained within, with love and delight in their use, their texture, their expansion of that best of all languages, English. From Imhotep to Robert Gwathmey, moreover, the people-cartoons have been discarded, and an attempt made to replace them with a sense of the architect's attitude, his special role, his human achievement.

The selection of what to include, which words and which architects, is mine, and the act of inclusion as much a statement of opinion as the entries themselves. Words so obscure that their use is limited to archaeologists or obscure technicians are omitted, for they are not the language of architecture but rather the archaeology of language, interesting to excavate but not useful in the real world. The collective result is meant to form a bouillabaisse of a book, a great mess of pottage where the carrots, peas and potatoes (words), and dumplings (architects) stand out within a common cookery (architecture). As in cooking, the parts are both bland and spicy, a bite here setting the mouth afire, a bite there bland reality.

Forgive my omissions of architects of merit who ought to be here, for there will be some overlooked through ignorance. The scope of the book is limited by—deliberately—my own knowledge, my own opinions, my own attitudes.

NORVAL WHITE

*New York City*
*May 1976*

# THE
# ARCHITECTURE
# BOOK

# A

**AALTO, ALVAR (1898–1976)** *Finnish Architect* A lusty Finn who graced modern architecture (1920s to now) with a hardy romance of timber, wood, brick, concrete, and stucco. Original, without eccentricity, he rises from history rather than confronting, challenging, and/or ignoring it.

Aalto is the norm from which abnormality might be measured. His library (1935) at Viipuri (pronounced Vee-pooh-ree) in Finland, burned during the Soviet-Finnish War (1940), was the source of the modern undulating, floating ceiling. (It has been largely restored in what is now part of the U.S.S.R.)

Senior House (1949; now Baker House) at M.I.T. (Cambridge, Massachusetts) is an undulating brick building (a frozen flag waving), stairs applied pendant at its rear, like closed fire escapes.

The village center (1951) at Säynatsälo (Soon-yat-say-loh) is a classic, informal contained space, a miniplaza at the scale of a village population, surrounded by the varied village functions, each with articulated forms and spaces.

Aalto's work is prolific, adorning not only Finland and the United States, but also Germany (apartment house, Hansa district, Berlin) and France (Carrée House). He was a humanist, concerned as much with the human needs and scale of his building program as with architectural distinction. This is in contrast to his late peers Le Corbusier and Mies, who more frequently than not subverted the interests of the human user to the strength and monumentality of their architectural ideas and talked a lot about scale (see also *Modulor*) because they knew, deep in their hearts, that they had lost it

AALTO *Village Center, Säynatsälo, Finland*

(compare, particularly, Le Corbusier's Voisin plan for Paris, 1925).

**ABACUS**   The shim that spaces a column capital both physically and visually from the structure it supports: a pancake of appropriate size and shape. (Some were 6 feet in diameter.)

**ABBEY**   A monastery, or place where workers for the church, in spirit and/or matter, live; particularly, one in the charge of an abbot. Monastic life includes self- and religious contemplation, aid to those in need (food, medicine, nursing, brandy via Saint Bernard dogs), and work: monasteries make wine, beer, cheese, liqueurs, sold to the world outside for the support of monastic good works.

The church (building) of an abbey is sometimes called *an* abbey, particularly by the romantic middle-aged tourist (blame *Ivanhoe* and the Gothic novel).

**ABRAMS, CHARLES (1901–1970)** *Polish American Lawyer, Planner, and Urbanist*   A classy name in American planning history, Abrams wrote much of both federal and New York City housing policy and law; later, books to record the wisdom so learned (cf. *The Future of Housing,* 1946; *The City Is the Frontier,* 1965). What he didn't write he taught to students at M.I.T., University of Pennsylvania, and Columbia. At Columbia he was chairman of the planning department.

Abrams dabbled in real estate: he was client for Frederick Kiesler's one real-world building, the Eighth Street Playhouse (1929, New York), where simultaneous slide showings could straddle the film on view.

**ABUTMENT**   Structure placed to support the weight and thrust of an arch, vault, or dome; most often masonry (brick or stone) in the arched architecture of Rome, the Romanesque, or Middle Ages; sometimes steel or concrete in modern times.

**ACANTHUS**   More verdant in stone architecture than real life, this thistle-like source plant (perennial herb) for carved stone foliage is native to Asia Minor (Turkey). Such foliage enriched capitals (caps or tops) of Greek and Roman columns (particularly that "order" or set of column proportions and parts termed Corinthian). Cast-iron architecture, the economical substitute for stone carving,

ACANTHUS *Leaf drawn by John Ruskin*

brought more acanthus to New York streets than the Mediterranean basin has ever seen.

**ACOUSTIC**   Relating to hearing or sound.

**ACOUSTICS**   Qualities of hearing and sound in a place; particularly, a built place. Sound bounces back and forth (reverberates) and becomes blurred and unintelligible in ill-designed places. (Medieval cathedrals, e.g., Chartres, were reverbatoriums, having been created for ceremonies of vision, with gross sound. When preaching overcame, they proved disastrous places for communication.)

**ACOUSTIC TILE**   A soft but rigid square or rectangle (wood, glass fibers, or asbestos) designed to absorb sound and diminish bounce (or reverberation). Usually used for ceilings, either glued to plaster or hung (suspended) in frames that leave space above through which pipes, wiring, and ductwork can pass, to do their work invisibly.

**ACROPOLIS**   Top of the city, a special place for special events, raised on a natural platform overlooking the city's body below. In "ancient" Athens (ca. 500–400 B.C.), the Acropolis was the stand of Greece's most famous complex of buildings, if not the most famous in world history: the Parthenon, the Erechtheum, and the Propylaea jointly served the gods, in and around the plateau-plaza, which was and still is *the* Acropolis itself.

ACROPOLIS *Acropolis of Athens*

**ACROTERION**   Finial-like, it articulates the apex and edges of a pediment. Strictly speaking, the term describes both the statues and/or ornaments *and* their leveling bases at the peak of a pediment or at its eaves.

**ADAM, ROBERT (1728–1792)** *Scottish-English Architect*   While the rude colonies in America were revolting, the Adam brothers were raising the architectural standards and taste of Mother England (and Scotland). Ceilings loom large in our remembrance of things Adam. The brothers are remembered more for their interiors (and in copy or surrogate form) than for their great English country houses or Scottish Gothic-novel castles. An Adam ceiling brings visions of low-relief plaster decoration, an English Rococo, without the unseemly exuberance (and naked bodies) of French cherubs or

5

Italian putti. The colonists, then citizens, of Boston and New York and Philadelphia brought civilized copies (or imagined copies) of Adam ceilings to brick and brownstone interiors.

Their splendid illustrated book *The Ruins of Spalato* (1764) describes verbally and pictorially Diocletian's Palace, built by the retiring emperor in this then-Roman colony, his home town (and now the Yugoslav Dalmatian coast port and resort of Split). The palace was, and is, a mine of bold urban archaeology, a huge, rectangular micro-city, a single fortified place infilled with houses, housing, public buildings, and spaces that were to serve the emperor's needs and desires, and those of his retinue. It was a great souce of, and inspiration to, the Classical Revival.

The Adelphi (1768–72), a massing of private houses creating an architecture larger than the sum of its parts, was both an architectural apex and economic disaster to Robert's (and his brother James's) London period, a time most marked by large interior alterations and additions, such as Syon House, Osterley Park, and the Royal Society of Art.

Robert Adam shared the teachings of Clérisseau with his brother James, William Chambers, and sometime president Thomas Jefferson.

**ADLER, DANKMAR (1844–1900)** *German American Engineer* Louis Sullivan joined him, needed him, and honored him through their prolific glories in Chicago's late nineteenth century: special remembrance is the Auditorium Building (1887 +) and the Carson Pirie Scott Store (1899).

**ADOBE** Homemade sun-dried brick. In arid climates, materials soluble in rain often become (naturally) the principal building material: mud, daub, rammed earth, adobe. Sometimes exported to rainy climates, architecture developed umbrellas to shield its own flanks (Northern California houses, brought from the arid Spanish south, developed great hipped and verandaed roofs over their adobe bodies). Where water can dissolve and make earth viscous quickly, all the builder needs is a desert and water (well, river, or oasis).

**AESTHETICS** The happy but superficial satisfaction of the senses by architecture, painting, music, and/or the natural world. In architecture, aesthetics is usually separated from the functional

ADOBE *Leonis Adobe, San Fernando Valley, California*

body that it serves, so that a lovely façade that conceals a messy place behind is still considered successful architectural aesthetics, while a happy, working housing project, bringing delight to the daily lives of its inhabitants, may not even be listed on an aesthetic balance sheet. Aesthetics tends to be the province of the expert and esoteric, rather than the real world confronting the art of life; or alternately, it may be considered the separated parts of music (an aria), a painting (the brushwork), or architecture (a court or room or stairway concerned with high moments in a building or the work of an architect).

**AGGREGATE** Cement is the glue, aggregate the body, and concrete the generic name for any strong, hard, durable, man-made, formable, moldable, or pourable building material. The most common variety is Portland cement concrete, the stuff of which skyscrapers are made (forming, with the aid of steel reinforcing bars, columns, beams, and floors). Aggregate as bulk and body is bound into a monolithic form by formwork that constrains its watered Portland cement fluidity until chemistry (not drying out) converts all to the ultimate cake.

With an appropriate aggregate, other species of concrete can be produced using asphalt, clay, or even, in theory, Elmer's glue as binder.

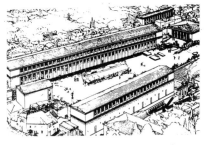

AGORA *A reconstruction of a Greek agora*

**AGORA** Place of outdoor public assembly in pre-Christian Greece, contained by buildings that create an outdoor room. The forums of Rome (and Roman territories), and the plazas (piazzas) of the Italian Renaissance particularly, are the comparable outdoor urban turf of those later cultures.

The urban visual delights of plazas are reclaimed in shopping-center "malls" (a "mall" could or can be a linear plaza) or, unhappily, in overblown modern attempts that curdle in their disuse (Perret's vast plaza at Le Havre, enough to lose the French army).

The secret of the agora (or any public urban space) is in the buildings that form and surround it, combined with its appropriate size and use by people in an active and lively way.

**A.I.A.** *American Institute of Architects, founded 1857* The Establishment.

Any establishment tends toward reaction in its literal sense: *re-*acting against change and directing its efforts toward the status

AISLE *Romanesque aisle*

before quo. A gentlemanly profession holding the hands of corporate and private wealth through the later nineteenth and early twentieth centuries, the profession grew into a new social responsibility in two waves: that of the depression thirties, and then again in the great poverty–race equalization process of the sixties.

Founded under the leadership of Richard Morris Hunt (architect of the dominant central portion of the Metropolitan Museum of Art), the A.I.A. was W.A.S.P., its members posturing as members of an exclusive club until the Second World War. Never politically powerful, as is the American Medical Association, it wishes it were, and, as corporate America absorbs the design process into its conglomerate structure, the single gentlemanly professional fades into unimportance, or into an esoteric archaism. Johnson, Pei, Niemeyer still exist, and others yearn to fill their shoes (Meier, Gwathmey, Soleri, Stirling); but the promise of the future lies in the organization architect who, in concert with industrialization and prefabrication, can have a large quantitative and qualitative impact on mass urban environments. Single and separate monuments will continue to blossom, the unique or bizarre or magnificent, in a beach of well-formed but consistent granules; but the real work will be in the beach and its well-designed total form, its shore, dunes, and bluffs, not in the ever-relentless virtuosity of its grains.

**AIN, GREGORY (1906–     )** *American Architect*  His Dunsmuir Flats (1941, Los Angeles) step stuccoed two-storied units down the hills; handsome and functional Cubism, late-blooming in this garden-desert of a city.

**AIR**  The gas ocean, at the bottom of which we all ply, is air, three-quarters nitrogen, one-quarter oxygen, with a dash of carbon dioxide and a lot of gratuitous pollution. Plant's leaves "breathe" in carbon dioxide, the effluent of humans, and breathe out oxygen, one of the happy symbioses that make life on earth possible. If we eliminated all the plants, the people would quickly follow.

Air inflates rubber tires, tensing them, in effect an early variety of prestressing that can produce air "beams." Advanced thoughts for air in urban society include air-propelled transit vehicles (in a tube, with air behind, and a vacuum before the vehicle); air-cushioned vehicles (cars and even trains, on the principle of the Hovercraft boats).

More prosaic air is dried, heated, cooled, and tubed around a built place, to provide air *conditioning.* Air can be breezes, wind, gales, or hurricanes; can sail boats; allow planes to fly; create waves; change climates; flap flags; and whistle in the windows.

**AIR CONDITIONING**   Frequently and incorrectly thought of as merely air cooling. Air may be hot or cold, moist or dry, static or moving. Its conditioning may modify any one or set of these characteristics. Warm air heating is air conditioning in that it takes cold air and heats, moves, and distributes it; or conditioning may be merely involved with the removal of moisture from the air (dehumidification).

**AIR RIGHTS**   Where building is restricted by local laws, usually called zoning, maximum quantity, size, and shape of buildings are constrained. When built to a lesser size, there is legally vacant air, rights to which have a value and can sometimes be sold, leased, or borrowed by a next-door neighbor.

A new city school rarely uses the maximum legal zoning (i.e., permitted quantity of building) available. New government efforts have been aimed at consuming that unused volume by adding desperately needed housing over or adjacent, allowing the land cost to be distributed (in value and credit) between both school and housing.

ALBERTI *S. Andrea, Mantua*

**AISLE**   Space in a line. A place to walk from here to there within a building, defined by building parts (say columns) or furnishings (say pews). "Down the aisle," where brides move to grooms, is a phrase from post-reformation and counter-reformation Protestant and Catholic liturgy; the new component of preaching generated chairs, then pews, the linear space between which, to the chancel and/or altar, was an aisle.

**ALBERTI, LEONE BATTISTA (1404–1472)** *Italian Architect*
Both a Renaissance and a renaissance man, the former because he lived during its initial flowering chronologically, the latter because of his diverse interests and talents: architect, painter, musician, mathematician, even athlete.

Architecture was a sometime and theoretical pursuit for Alberti. Not faced with detailed or pragmatic problems of building, he devoted himself to principals of proportion and codification for reuse of classical building parts.

9

Most noted buildings include a new façade for the Gothic space of S. Maria Novella in Florence, contributed by the Rucellai family, for whom he had designed a palace façade (Palazzo Rucellai, 1446–51) and the Tempio Malatesta at Rimini, converted from an existing church.

**ALBINI, FRANCO (1905–    )** *Italian Architect* His elegant Italian museum interiors cross the spare luxury of rich materials with dramatic lighting. Exhibits are sparse, widely spaced, with drama of presentation, rather than the encyclopedic approach one would find, say, in the British Museum. The "treasury" (1956) of the Cathedral of S. Lorenzo (Genoa) is non-architecture (and contains the reputed Holy Grail!); no volume, just space in a subterranean cellar beneath the cathedral's plaza.

He also built an elegant branch for the Rinascente Department Store in Rome: highly articulated exposed steel.

**ALCOVE** Small space off a larger one, but open into it. A closet would be an alcove, save for its door. Originally alcoves were the bed-niches of a bed-room.

**ALEXANDER, ROBERT E. (1907–    )** *American Architect* Sometime partner of Richard Neutra and, with Clarence Stein and others, architect of the "experimental" garden city Baldwin Hills Village (1942, Los Angeles), a wood, wartime cul-de-sac place on the Radburn, New Jersey, model (see Stein's book: *Toward New Towns in America*, 1951).

**ALLÉE** A landscaped street, grown or carved from vegetation, limiting the view to a distant vista that the designer wishes to emphasize. Seventeenth- and eighteenth-century gardens, as at Versailles, present allées as the armature of their designs (and pedestrian circulation systems).

**ALLEY** A verbal put-down of a narrow, usually short, secondary access to city buildings and their outbuildings (carriage houses and garages, for example). Nostalgia and a search for venerable charm in this usually aseptic, bland world have returned repute to the alley. Now the wealthy urban dweller may be found in converted (and gas-lamped) carriage houses in Grace Court Alley (Brooklyn), Mac-

AMMANN *Bronx-Whitestone Bridge, New York*

Dougal Alley (Greenwich Village), and so forth, where the alley cats have been displaced by Siamese and Persians.

**ALTAR**   The joint between man and his god(s). An object or surface, often a table, where, originally, physical offerings—such as lives to be sacrificed—were placed, or merely symbolic ones; and, most recently, ones verbal.

Altars varied from that eyrie, a stone slab atop the House of the Magician at Uxmal (of eighth-century Mayan, Yucatán, Mexico), to that under the *baldacchino* by Bernini at St. Peter's (Rome) where popes give homage to Christ.

**AMBULATORY**   Literally, "a built place to walk," usually in a direction, so that it is, or has, an aisle. Commonly it describes the semicircular arc of passage surrounding the sides of a church's chancel, away from the nave (and congregation), and often separating that chancel from a series of radiating chapels, particularly in High Gothic French cathedrals.

The walkways around a cloister are also ambulatories.

**AMENITIES**   The dessert, salad, and wine of environmental design. Amenities are the plazas, fountains, boulevards, vistas, sculpture, painting, paving, curbs, and light standards that separately and together add to and enrich the basic architectural shells of an urban place.

**AMMANATI, BARTOLOMMEO (1511–1592)** *Italian Architect and Sculptor*   He completed the Pitti Palace as conceived by Brunelleschi, but added a garden façade (facing the Boboli Gardens) that was the apogee of Florentine Mannerism. Rustication of mathematical regularity here forms sharp contrast with the Pitti's rock-faced street façade.

**AMMANN, OTHMAR H. (1879–1965)** *Scandinavian American Engineer*   Engineer of elegant steel suspension bridges, particularly the Bronx-Whitestone Bridge (1939, New York City; consulting architect, Aymar Embury II).

**AMORTIZATION**   The process of paying off the principal of a mortgage incrementally, usually with interest attached and, most often, in constant payments. (Borrow $80,000 for 20 years at 9%,

AMBULATORY *Ambulatory around cloister, Rommersdorf Abbey, Germany*

and pay back at the rate of $720 a month; in the first years, most of the $720 is interest, and part is principal, or amortization; in the last years, most is amortization.)

**AMPHIPROSTYLE**  Like Doctor Doolittle's Pushmi-Pullyou (a llama with heads at both ends), an amphiprostyle temple has porticoed pediments at each end.

**ANCHOR**  A fastening to hold down a building, to connect its parts, or to affix accessories. Bolts anchor wooden buildings to concrete foundations to prevent movement (displacement) in wind or hurricane. Lead cylinders, called shields, anchor screwed-in furnishings (e.g., bookshelves) to the plaster walls of a modern room. Ancient anchors laced masonry together to prevent shifting and provide alignment.

**ANDERSON, LAWRENCE (1906–  )** *American Architect and Educator*  Sometime head, then dean, of the School of Architecture at M.I.T. With his partner and fellow faculty member Herbert Beckwith, he built the M.I.T. pool's (1940) cubic space. Unlike other vintage pools, it is above ground, south-lit, served by a garden where one can stroll nude (at least on monosexed days) like a Scandinavian sun-worshipper.

ANDERSON *M.I.T. Pool Complex, Cambridge, Massachusetts*

**ANGLE IRON**  The simplest rolled steel form, a junior member to the I- and wide flange beam, which can be a do-it-yourselfer's or small contractor's piece of steel.

**ANNEAL**  To relieve internal stress by heating: metals, particularly steel, are annealed after being squashed, pressed, rolled, and pummeled into a desired artificial shape: to relieve the internal torment thus caused (in the metal's crystalline structure), and allow it to flex without snapping thereafter, it is annealed.

**ANODIZE**  Electricity and chemistry combine to hard-coat aluminum in gray to brown colors, protecting it from aging by oxidation and giving it permanent color.

**ANTEFIX**  The ornamental eave-blocks of a Classical temple that cover the ends of roof titles.

**ANTEROOM** Architectural preview of coming attractions: the room anticipating the main event. It is also any subordinate room in a grand set or suite.

**ANTHEMION** Honeysuckle stylized makes this another naturalistic source material (see also *Acanthus*) for the decoration of discrete units and/or bands in Greek architecture.

**ANTHEMIUS OF TRALLES (d. A.D. 534)** *Colonial Greek-Roman Architect* With Isidorus of Miletus he built the church of Hagia Sophia (Divine Wisdom; 532+) for the late Roman emperor Justinian, whose capital was Constantinople (modern Istanbul). See also *Isidorus of Miletus.*

**APARTMENT** A place apart for private use: in a palace, the rooms of an individual; in a city or structure, the separate dwelling quarters of an individual or family. An apartment house is merely the multiple-tenanted dwelling that replaced an individual's house.

**APRON** The board that covers the wall beneath a windowsill, as if the sill were a belt and the wall below its aproned belly.

**APSE** A half-cylindrical, half-domed space attached to the east (or altar) end of a church.

**AQUARIUM** The salt- or fresh-water world held captive for private inspection or public exhibit. Fish, shellfish, crustaceans, plants, coral are all separately and jointly candidates for an aquarium.

**AQUEDUCT** Leader of water: the conduits, channels, and canals that bring water from wherever it collects naturally from rain and flow of tributaries to wherever it is needed, usually an urban place (like ancient Rome). Aqueducts made cities possible in the desert, as at Baalbek (Roman colonial city in what is now Lebanon); and irrigation became possible far from lake, stream, or river.

**ARABESQUE** Decoration from the Arabs: intricate, incised surface geometry that enriched the architecture of Islam (representation of people or Allah was and is forbidden, as it is in Judaism). The Renaissance developed its own European decoration in the same spirit and name.

ARABESQUE *Early 16th-century Italian terra-cotta panel*

**ARBOR**   The formal orchard of the grape, architecturally used as a canopy or sunbreak, an umbrella of filtered light and pendant fruit that hovers over diner and sitter on an armature of slats or trellis.

**ARCADE**   Columns and arches in joint venture, numerous and forming a line. In our decadent language and architecture, *arcade* came to mean continuously spaced columns without the arches, and then without the columns: ergo, the penny arcade, a tawdry collection of amusement machines in any old space (and scarcely accepting any penny).

**ARCH**   Arches spring (and sometimes leap); arcs of masonry parts (brick or cut stone) that prop each other in a semicircular or elliptical arc across an open space. Wide (or thick) arches are vaults (vaulting, springing, and leaping).

The arch has always been a symbol of cultural change to the archaeologist: belittled by the Greeks, who used it for concealed work (function), not visual display. The Romans, entrepreneurs and economic imperialists, spread their power through urban organization across Europe, Asia Minor (Turkey), and North Africa; their proudly displayed arches (carrying aqueducts) made cities possible a hundred miles from potable water.

An arch is all of a piece, the whole far more than the parts, only possible when the whole is made one by the last stone or brick (keystone). While under construction it requires support from below, usually called centering. Once complete, the arch can stand on its own, and the centering is removed.

**ARCHAIC**   Reactionary, where applied to architecture, since it is use of earlier forms and/or ideas, as opposed to those currently in favor.

**ARCHED CORBEL TABLE**   One of those obscure and enriching elements of the architecture of a particular period and place that fascinates the dilettante. A flat relief of arches (usually of brick) in small scale follows the rake of a gabled church façade; found mostly in the northern Italian province of Lombardy in the eleventh and twelfth centuries.

**ARCHITECT**   Chief workman, master builder. Now corrupted to mean the office-bound designer and documentor of buildings. The

ARCH *Arch of Septimus Severus, Rome*

group-led mass culture of the so-called Dark and Middle ages failed to identify architects. The Renaissance (of individual creativity) not only sought the individual work of an architect but honored and identified it.

In ancient Egypt (2700 B.C.), Imhotep, to the extent that any words can be literally translated, was first an architect (of Pharaoh Djoser's pyramid-tomb), then a physician, and finally, happily for the future public relations of the profession, a god.

In pre-Christian Greece, architect-sculptors were cited for individual buildings: e.g., the Parthenon was the work of Ictinus and Callicrates. And their role and importance in society was equivalent to that of a priest or politician.

But from A.D. 200 to 1400, there was scarcely one individual honored, or even reluctantly cited, as author or architect of anything. Master builders (*architects* could be so translated and so appear in historic documentation) led guilds that built buildings in joint ventures, and their product was (and still is) superior. The lack of ego-identity did not diminish, and possibly improved, the quality of the product.

But then the Renaissance flowered: Bramante, Brunelleschi, Alberti, Michelangelo, Sangallo, Mansart, Le Vau, Wren, Vanbrugh, et al. The cast of characters is large; the product is debated and discussed; theories are published; buildings are honored in competition with each other.

**ARCHITECTONIC**  Usually applied to non-architecture to suggest it has architectural qualities, as a painting or a girl.

**ARCHITECTURAL REVIEW**  The British magazine that turned the attention of those concerned with the urban environment to the space between buildings and the enrichment thereof: paving, graphics, signs, curbs, drains, bollards, fencing, light standards—"street furnishings" of a city. The *Review* has seemed to some, and particularly in retrospect, effete and concerned with trivia, whereas the competing *Architectural Design* has, supposedly, faced the basic issues of our times: of bold or brutal or "pop" architecture, of creative academicism and its written theories.

**ARCHITECTURE**  The environment(s) man makes to house and/or surround his activities: " . . . music in space, as it were a frozen music," said von Schelling (1775–1854).

ARCHED CORBEL TABLE

ARCADE *Decorative arcade choir, Lincoln Cathedral*

15

Man's mechanical needs for shelter, warmth, cooling, arranged in sub-facilities for sleep, play, cooking, study, work, and commerce, are architecture only when they cause—and are—delight in each man's daily life. Architecture also exists without necessary assistance from an "architect"; and architects sometimes create buildings which are not architecture.

In primitive societies, the choice of materials and structural systems was narrow, if choice existed at all. That fact, overlaid with an ordered, socially monolithic group of citizenry, caused a natural architecture evolving over generations that was largely created without aid of "professionals" (cf. Greek island towns, as at Míkonos; African villages; southwestern U.S. cliff dwellings; and so forth).

In our confusing and confused twentieth century, the choices of materials are endless, those of structural systems many. Society is neither monolithic nor orderly. As a result, the contemporary architect is asked to be technician and tastemaker, leading his client through the jungle of technical and aesthetic decisions that confronts us all. The burden on the architect is, therefore, more staggering, and the opportunity for error immense. Thus we perceive the environment that surrounds us to be of erratic quality at best, of overwhelming bad taste at worst.

**ARCHITRAVE** "Chief beam." The lowest layer of a Greek or Roman entablature, that set of laminated parts crowning the columns of a public building. Together, columns and entablatures form an order, the most common of which are Doric, Ionic, and Corinthian.

The architrave, at the bottom, looks, seems, and usually is the spine that supports the parts of the entablature that are subsidiary structurally but visually important: frieze and cornice.

**ARCHIVOLT** Carved or planted molding around the curve of an arch to enrich, emphasize, and articulate it.

**ARCUATED** The general term for buildings based on arches and vaulted construction, as opposed to post and beam (or trabeated) construction. More a term to separate the sheep from the goats than to give any more detailed explanation.

**AREA** The quantity of surface (usually floor or ground) of a building or the ground(s) on which it rests; or a piece of land defined by

ARCHIVOLT *S. Giovanna, Lucca, Italy*

or assigned to a single particular purpose (e.g., the sports area).

**ARENA** A "sandy place" that served as the stage of an amphitheater for combat of gladiators, lions, and, sometimes, Christians on their way to martyrdom. Later, and more loosely, a place where the action is: the "arena of politics."

The sand suggests vigorous sport, and conflict in man and animal; to soften a fall and sop the blood.

**ARM** The crossmember that makes a pole a cross and bears the arms of one crucified.

**ARMORY** A building to store the weapons of war. Armor, the artificial human carapace made obsolete by firearms, became armor, the guns and tanks, the modern group carapaces of personal battle. An armory now is a place for sometime warriors (the National Guard), who parade, exercise, and party in its vast reaches, often constructed for the exercise and charge of horses or, later, the restricted rumblings of tanks and ancillary vehicles.

One of the last great sets of semipublic spaces in American cities has been the armories (clung to and preserved after the railroad stations have gone), often crenellated medieval-revival forts, where mass activities from flower shows to track meets have found a happily appropriate environment.

**ARNOLFO DI CAMBIO (1232–1302?)** *Italian Sculptor and Architect* His fat brown and beige Gothic nave for the Duomo (Cathedral) of Florence was finished by Talenti, domed and lanterned by Brunelleschi, with a campanile by Giotto.

**ARRIS** The edge between two surfaces, as in the flutes of a Doric column: their knifelike joining is an arris.

**ARTIFACT** Any man-made remnant of someone else's time, place, culture, or geography. *Artifact* is the word of archaeologists and paleontologists for the ordinary implements of a civilization that they have unearthed and are discussing: the daily paraphernalia of life.

**ART NOUVEAU** French: "new art." The Parisian shop l'Art Nouveau, before the turn of the century, gave name but not content

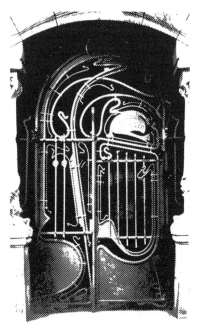

ART NOUVEAU *Gate by Hector Guimard*

17

to the movement: for the shop was a negative idea, breaking with the past and presenting a variety of newly designed wares (as of 1895).

It *came* to mean that sinuous naturalistic ornament and form of furniture, furnishings, and architecture that led the avant-garde (avant-avant) in the 1880s and '90s and continued up to the First World War: Tiffany (Louis Comfort Tiffany) glass and lighting fixtures, in particular; the architecture of Hector Guimard (designer of the Paris Metro's "street-gates," as at the rue de Rivoli near the Palais Royal [1900]); and the buildings of Victor Horta (Belgian architect of the House of the People [1896+] at Brussels).

The extraordinary Scottish architect Charles Rennie Mackintosh tapped and contributed to Art Nouveau but more in drawing and superficial decorations than building.

**ARTS AND CRAFTS**   English neo-medievalism at first, based on William Morris, and extended into architecture by C. R. Ashbee, C. F. A. Voysey, W. R. Lethaby, George Walton, and E. L. Lutyens. Lutyens was its sublime missionary, particularly at Tigbourne Court (1899).

**ASAM, COSMAS DAMIAN (1686–1739) and EGID QUIRIN (1692–1750)** *Bavarian Architects*  The Bavarian Asam brothers brought to the Church of Rome Baroque stagecraft enriched with trick lighting, spatial illusions, and sheer acrobatics. If the Counter Reformation was a Catholic (Jesuit) attempt to round up the flock released by the Reformation's fervor (i.e., Protestantism), through a counter-fervor of Jesuit preaching and Baroque architectural histrionics, the Asams must have been aiming at the rustler himself (Martin Luther).

The church at Rohr has a life-size Virgin climbing (more likely being pulled or hoisted ) to Heaven, a Heaven bathed in light from mysteriously concealed sources. At the abbey church of Weltenburg, a sterling St. George rides at us out of a blazing apse of light; and at St. John Nepomuk in Munich (an annex to C.D.'s house) sensation is rampant; sculpture, painting, light, all intermingling and overlapping, competing for dominance.

**ASBESTOS**   A natural material of high insulating properties: fibrous and pressable into hard (annealed) cemented sheets that serve as fire shields; or merely the inert skin of buildings. Corru-

ASHLAR *Foundation of warehouse, Brooklyn*

gated for stiffness, and impervious to rain or rot, it roofs a million tropical buildings. Made into cylindrical pipe, it drains storm water. Like cast iron, it is brittle (in similar uses it serves well and provides one additional benefit: noncorrosion).

**ASHLAR**  Cut stone, installed in a wall. If "random," stones of varying sizes interlock, with no continuous vertical or horizontal courses. "Coursed" ashlar is that of regular sizing, like concrete block or brick, but of a rougher or less finished surface.

**ASPHALT**  Black butterscotch. It melts with heat, shatters when cold and hard. A tough plastic material that can be melted and poured and acts as a cement in the making of asphaltic concrete paving. Asphalt may be natural, dug from the ground, or created as a petroleum refining by-product.

**ASPLUND, GUNNAR (1885–1940)** *Swedish Architect*  Remember the Forest Crematorium (1940, Stockholm): grass-covered and flowered meadows breasting to a spare Neoclassic colonnade hover in the back mind of every modern architect. (One of the few modern buildings accepted by old *and* avant-gardists.)

His earlier Stockholm Exhibition (1930) was a radical glassy place with multicolored taut canvas-framed awnings, precursor of the later Mendelsohn (and Chermayeff) at the de la Warr Pavilion (Bexhill).

**ASSEMBLY**  A gathering of people for a joint or public purpose. A putting together of parts that make a desired whole.

**ASSESSMENT**  An evaluation of a situation and, particularly, of the value of a building or property. Used especially by towns in defining the value of a building for tax purposes. Assess*ors* make an assess*ment*.

ASPLUND *Crematorium, Stockholm*

**ASSYRIA**  Ancient Kingdom (3500 B.C.+) on the Upper Tigris River (Iraq today) of fierce and fiercely sculpted warriors: elegant cartoon bas-reliefs telling of great victories and conquests over Babylon (thirteenth century B.C.) and Egypt (seventh century B.C.). Assyrian architecture is intermingled with that of Babylon: mud-bricked ziggurats, temples and palaces.

**ASTRAGAL**   Half-round molding or bead (cut or formed from the surfaces it enriches). Corrupted, the word means a cover strip closing the joint between double doors, where they meet.

**ASYLUM**   Sanctuary. A place, built or natural, for refuge of those pursued (criminal or political refugees). Then broadened to include the infirm, the insane, the aged, and the physical institutions that house their pseudosanctuary (more a societal sump, for sanctuary implies a vigorous refugee, self-motivated; the insane "asylum" implies deposit by others of the mentally inert or confused).

**ATELIER**   Workshop of a craftsman or artisan. In architectural jargon, those workshop-studios of, particularly, French architects party to (and clinical faculty of) the École des Beaux-Arts, where students registered worked on their private projects under the atelier-architect's aegis. Like acolytes they served and were wired with the armature of their master.

**ATELIER 5** *Swiss Architectural Team*   These meticulous craftsmen brought an Italian hilltown to a Swiss river valley near Bern (Halen housing project, 1963), with forms in concrete worthy of Le Corbusier and an urban understanding that Corbu never achieved: low-rise, high-density, closely packed housing in rural surrounds, a scheme analogous to those of their medieval town-building ancestors. Le Corbusier's ideas of monumentality gave way here to practical Swiss execution: real houses, real people, real scale, theory taken to a state of human and humane delight.

ATELIER *5 Apartment House, Berne, Switzerland*

**ATLANTES**   Male caryatids. Columns sculptured in the form of male figures, supporting an entablature above.

**ATRIUM**   The courtyard of a Roman urban house: in effect, its open space, since houses, back to back and cheek to cheek, offered no other. A water sump at its center (the Roman *impluvium*) collected water tilted inward by sloping, tiled roofs. All can be seen in faithful restoration at Pompeii, near Naples, where lava froze the culture in time and preserved it for our careful study.

Later, the courtyard in front of a church where parishioners assembled became known as an atrium: see S. Clemente (Rome; small) or St. Paul's Outside the Walls (outside the "Roman" walls of Rome; huge).

**ATTIC**   Strictly speaking, a story above the cornice line of a Classical or Classical Revival building, low functional extra space rising above the visual crown (i.e., cornice). Our modern attic is a loose version of the same piece of hierarchy, but in any style or period.

Parkinson's Law by inference decrees that debris accumulates to fill the space available for it (in an attic), and it is, therefore, filled with grandmother's trunks, diaries, clothes, and plain junk. Its archaeology usually stops there, for there was no room left after grandmother was through (cf. Parkinson). Certainly the architecture of the flat or shed roof, or "cathedral" ceiling, allows for no accumulation, and is a severe drag on future country auctions based on the grandmother culture.

The low-pitched trussed roof of speculative builders (actually cheaper than the flat or shed roof and, usually, cooler) constricts the attic use: too low and cluttered with the braces of the trusses.

ATTIC *Arch of Trajan, Benevento, Italy*

**AUDITORIUM**   A space for group hearing—of speakers, in particular. Music is usually presented in a *hall*, opera in a *house.* An auditorium is commonly termed a place of public assembly: but no assembly is meaningful without talk to the auditors.

**AVERY** *(Architectural) Library, Columbia University*   The bank of American architectural knowledge, founded and given in memory of Henry Avery by his parents (1890), and an adjunct to the Columbia University School of Architecture. Every seeker after architectural truth ends up at the Avery. Whether he finds his grail there is moot; for of all disciplines, architecture is based on opinion and judgment more than fact, and truth resides more in the eyes and mind of the beholder than it does for a doctor, lawyer, engineer, or accountant.

**AVIARY**   A place for keeping birds, at the scale of a building, not a cage.

**AWNING**   A temporary shelter from sun or other weather, made usually of fabric, at first canvas, hung in and over windows, sloping to dump rain and supported by gravity and a metal frame.

**AXIS**   The imaginary line around which a mass, force, place, set of decoration, or movement of rotation is disposed. It is neutral in

21

that, as the line around which any planet, star, sun, or top rotates, it is the only stationary place.

**AXONOMETRIC**   A three-dimensional representation of a building showing the plan and elevations and how they appear and join, but not presenting the building as seen by the human eye, which would be a *perspective.*

Dimensions of the plan and elevation are true and measurable in an axonometric, a useful tool for a designer in working on, developing, and refining a building in drawn form.

**AZTEC**   The final conquerors of Mexico, before the coming of the Spanish, who overran the decaying Toltec civilization concurrent with French High Gothic times (ca. 1250–1325). For almost 300 years, Toltecs had modified Mayan urban centers, at Chichén Itzá, Uxmal, Palenque, Kabah, and the earlier culture and buildings at Teotihuacán (near modern Mexico City). The Aztecs inherited (or took) all, and were in turn destroyed by Cortez.

# B

**BACK HOE** Man's mechanical paw that digs hole and trench in dog-fashion: a tractor bearing a jointed steel arm and claw-toothed bucket grabs earth toward itself and then spoons it into a container or onto a pile.

**BACON, EDMUND (1910–    )** *City Planner and Architect*  Bacon's fulfillment was as executive director of the then avant-garde Philadelphia City Planning Commission (1949; and continued with it until 1973). He was a product of citizen concern and revolt (led by Dean Holmes Perkins of the University of Pennsylvania School of Architecture). His plans for Philadelphia are the first since Burnham's for Washington to suggest a cohesive physical system of streets, boulevards, buildings, and places. His reliance on historical precedent (articulated in his book, *The Design of Cities*, 1967) is an unnecessary and redundant crutch to the smashing ideas he presented through consulting architects Kling, Giurgola; Skidmore, Owings and Merrill; and Louis Kahn.

**BACON, HENRY (1866–1924)** *American Architect*  He won the Lincoln Memorial commission in competition, an American Doric (neo-neo-Greek) design to appeal to bureaucrats who could not believe in American "culture" and needed imported parts of renown to convince themselves that the honor they hoped to bring to Lincoln was culturally acceptable. Bacon did his work well, although the homespun Lincoln (by sculptor Daniel Chester French) must be uncomfortable within all that white, pristine marble. Bacon's varied

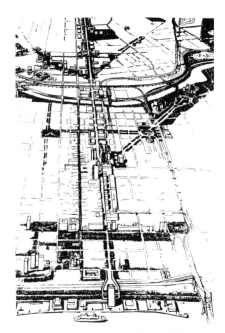

BACON, EDMUND *Plan for Philadelphia*

23

BAKEMA *Church, Nagele, Holland*

other work included the "Eclectic" (fraternity) House at Wesleyan University, a handsome brick and limestone neo-neo-Greek "country house."

**BAFFLE**  A diverter of air, view, or mind. Grills, louvers, and mazes are all baffling devices.

**BAILEY**  The space around the keep (English) or *donjon* (French) within the walls of a castle.

**BAKEMA, JACOB (1914–    )** *Dutch Architect* Bakema and J. H. van den Broek brought elegant urban design to bombed Rotterdam's Linbahn Shopping Center (1951), a massive injection of environmental spirits to the tottering place. One of the first post-World War II adventures into commercial pedestrian places.

**BALCONY**  A leaf of space hanging from a building (as opposed to a terrace, cut into the building's mass, or on it). Balconies are to view, or be viewed, more than they are generous rooms for outdoor activities. A nation's leaders appear on them, mostly to cheering crowds and for formal purposes: the pope at St. Peter's, Hitler, royalty everywhere—those who shouldn't or won't be touched for reasons of security, fear, or symbolism.

The French balcony is subtle, a narrow and railed edge of floor protruding past *French* doors (floor-to-ceiling double casement windows) that allows a garret sixth-story dweller to breathe, view, and participate in the smell, sound, and life of the city around him without much cost or need for furnishings (or collection place for soot).

**BALDACCHINO**  A permanent indoor freestanding canopy, symbolically sheltering the altar of the Christian God in a Catholic Church. *The* baldacchino is that by the great Baroque architect-sculptor Bernini, over the altar of St. Peter's.

**BALLOON FRAMING**  Vigorous invention, vast timber stands, and the industrial revolution combined to make America's greatest contribution to the new architecture of the nineteenth century—the balloon frame. Relatively small sticks regularized in size, easily transportable, became the ribs of buildings, skinned with wood boards that clad them (like a kite more than a balloon). Skin and stick reinforced each other, making the total structure plausible (ergo the 2-by-4 and 2-by-10).

Freed from the post and beam's demanding, regular, rigid plans, American craftsmen discovered a plastic architecture of curved forms and jigsaw detail, light, freely formed ribbons of walls that, tied in turn to each other, created house structures more akin to shells than to wall-roof-beam-post. The Shingle Style, Queen Anne, and the monster-inhabited Mansarded palaces of Charles Addams are all aspects of this structural game.

**BALTARD, VICTOR (1805–1874)** *French Architect* Les Halles in Paris, built for the prefect Baron Haussmann, were the great cast-iron market sheds, early and elegant skylit examples of the new industrial technology (1852+); now demolished.

**BALUSTER** The uprights supporting a handrail.

**BALUSTRADE** The whole assembly of balusters, railings, and banister that serves as protection and hand-guide at the edge of a building or terrace, and on a stair.

**BAND SHELL** An acoustical object more than a building. A backup form and screen that directs sound at an outdoor audience.

The band*stand*, centrally located in myriad small American towns, was centered in the casual sitting—even strolling—evening life of post-dinner summer evenings. When bands came to cities, the bandstand became an outdoor concert hall with accompanying large-scale acoustic problems: hence the band *shell*.

**BANISTER** Railing (of a balustrade), particularly on a stair.

**BANK** A natural or artificial sloping pile of earth, as the edge of a river (the banks of the Wabash), or an artificial berm.

**BAPTISTERY** The building of and for baptism. In the Catholic Renaissance, baptisteries were frequently separate buildings, rather than separate functions within the principal church. Most famous is that of the Cathedral (Duomo) of Florence, by Arnolfo di Cambio. A competition held in 1401 for the sculpted doors (on four of its eight sides) is an art historian's landmark, the springboard of the

BALDACCHINO *St. Peter's, Rome*

25

Renaissance (human form and its literal representation rather than the formalistic forms of the Middle Ages).

**BAR** America's first built-in furnishing. Bars in superlative became goals of earnest tavernkeepers: the longest, deepest, most expensive and/or ornate.

Bars for liquor were later subverted for the dispensing of oysters, clams, fruit juices, and health foods.

**BARGEBOARD** A major piece of trim, covering the construction edge of roofs and revealing only the roofing itself: shingles or metal. The bargeboard became another decorated strip in "Carpenter Gothic" times and was jigsawn in elaborate ways.

**BARJOIST** A minitruss, prefabricated and light in weight, that affords maximum ability to support a load with minimal material by spreading it about in space (like a spider's web) to the points where it is needed. *Bar-*, because it is stamped and stretched or bent and welded from steel bars; *-joist*, because that denominates a small beam.

**BARN** A rural warehouse for the storage of animal food, farm equipment, and, occasionally, the animals themselves. Necessarily of large volume, barns give the possibility of great space, when co-opted for non-barn use (remodeled into New England houses in modern times, 1920+).

An English, French, Italian, or Rumanian barn is of stone with timber roof-span construction. The American is usually all timber (except in Pennsylvania), sheathed and clad, rarely balloon-framed, as the bracing partitions integral to a balloon-frame construction are not possible in an open stick and post structure.

**BARNES, EDWARD LARRABEE (1915–    )** *American Architect*
Barnes (like Harry Weese) is an architect of understatement. Simple houses and summer camps of wood and shingles are done with elegant nonchalance (seemingly) that covers true sophistication.

His recent work (larger commissions for institutional clients) is of brick in the same genre, a happy event for the world overstressed with architectural virtuosity on the one hand, drudgery on the other. Hooray.

**BAROQUE** The Church used the new architecture of the late Renaissance (overgenerously 1600–1750) to melodramatize the liturgy of Christianity through a spectacle of light, sound, and dramatic form. (On occasion the real clergy mingled with sculpted life-size forms that confronted them, peered from or into adjacent spaces, and confused the real and the imaginary, the person and his sculpted image, even the sculpture and its painted image.) All was in counterpoint to the Baroque organ and preaching, Baroque clerical activities projecting sound and ideas into the form and light which surrounded them.

(Sample and special Baroque architects include Bernini, Borromini, Guarini of Italy; the Asam brothers of Bavaria; Wren, Hawksmoor, Vanbrugh of England; Le Nôtre of France.)

Baroque architecture is usually a sequential spatial experience, dramatized, with a piling-up of forms and visual events.

**BARRAGÁN, LUIS (1902– )** *Mexican Architect* Barragán's own house gives modern form and space to traditional Mexican materials: a private "urban" courtyard confers a sense of place to a simple earth-stained stucco box. His cantilevered wood "ribbonstair" inside is unique. Concern with natural and traditional laborintensive materials restricted his practice to wealthy clients.

**BARRY, (SIR) CHARLES (1795–1860)** *English Architect* If you applied Classical orders to the Seagram Building, it would be as appropriate as Pugin's veneered façade (Gothic detail) over Charles Barry's Classically planned Houses of Parliament (officially Westminster Palace). Fancy dress has, however, been an elitist element in many cultures, and fancy dress it was to Barry, who was forced by the politics of style to hire Pugin's decoration, a curious victory of political power over architectural consistency. In fact, Barry's best works are a series of pseudo-Italian palazzi in London (neo-Renaissance), turned to the purpose of men's clubs (Travellers', Reform, et al.).

BARRY *Cliveden, Buckinghamshire*

**BASE** From one viewpoint, the lowest (and most despicable) member of a building or its parts. From the other, what holds everything up.

**BASEMENT** The base space; livable, semi-underground, as opposed to a cellar. *Basement* is often applied, in grand architecture, to

27

the first, but subsidiary, floor under the stairs (or stoop) even though all are above grade. Fontainebleau, Blenheim, and Caprarola are cases in point.

BASILICA *Roman Basilica*

**BASILICA**  A barn-like building form, where a central long space is flanked by side aisles, narrower, usually lower, parallel to and serving the main space as circulation corridors.

The basilica was the Roman law court or, better still, the place of public affairs. Left-over examples were converted to churches by the early Christians and became, therefore, a whole stylistic incident: Early Christian architecture (i.e., A.D. 200–1000).

**BAS-RELIEF**  Low relief: sculpted images rising lightly from a flat ground (of stone, wood, terra cotta, etc.). The rise or relief is accomplished by the negative action of cutting away the field surrounding.

**BASTION**  A look back. At the corner or bend in a fortified wall, it looks back over adjacent surfaces for surveillance.

**BATH**  Liquid meets body and may involve soap, scent, or merely the soothing warmth of liquid.

The act of bathing can, however, become important, if not exalted, socially. Baptism and anointment are gestures from liquids, but the Roman baths made water and its use—hot, cold, warm, frigid—a major element of life. Roman baths, such as those of Caracalla and Diocletian, were whole building complexes, any part of which was huge in scale. Either covered more than 25 acres and was, in effect, a social center of male urban daytime life, a combined passive massage-parlor, sports palace, and coffee house.

**BATTEN**  A strip covering the joint between two vertical boards in house-scaled architecture. Common in "Carpenter Gothic", and wood Queen Anne houses. More a willful design detail than not, once tongue and groove had been invented as a weatherstop for two boards. Now it is a device to achieve the texture of shadows.

**BATTER**  The sloping face of a wall. Just as a concentric pile tends to a conical or pyramidal shape, a linear pile forms a steep berm: formal walls are "battered" to take account of such structural gravities.

**BAUHAUS**  Walter Gropius restructured the existing (1906–19) School of Arts and Crafts at Weimar (Henry van de Velde had run it) and renamed it Bauhaus (House of Building; 1919–24), first concerned with the crafts of the hand, then the crafts of the machine, and art machine-like in its qualities. He moved the school to Dessau (1925) to a new complex of his own design, a highly articulated functional group that expresses by each form and the treatment of surface (glazing and apertures within that form) the major and minor functions there housed. Bauhaus teaching tried to blend art and architecture with industrial techniques and modern programmatic needs, bringing the integration of the medieval building process back once more. Its greatest success was in giving opportunity to, and publicity for, artists and architects (architects: van de Velde, Gropius, Breuer, Meyer, Mies van der Rohe; artists: Moholy-Nagy, Kandinsky, Klee, Feininger). Almost the whole lot ended up in America when that amateur architect Hitler took over, replete with grandiose Neoclassical notions (see also *Speer, Albert*).

**BAY**  A structural set, composed of columns and beams or piers and vaults; it is one of a group of such sets. Each added unit makes *another* bay.

**BAY AREA**  San Francisco Bay, that is. Anti-paint architecture, shaggy, with blurred detail. The Bay is a basin, surrounded by suburban hills, in which flowered a low-keyed architecture of timber (fir) with redwood cladding, often dark-stained, shingled, unconcerned with eastern Establishment canons of proportion, taste, and meticulously pompous visual detail. This vernacular dominated the north, and, infrequently, was raised to lofty heights by architects of note: the great Northern California anti-Establishment guru Bernard Maybeck, and the more recent William W. Wurster, (Charles) Warren Callister, Ernest Kump, and John Carl Warnecke, a curious mélange of two calm leaders and two facile disciples. Wurster was the only pure one, usually creating ascetic brown boards of a New England Puritan in Northern California not-so-fancy dress.

**BAY WINDOW**  A glassed alcove projecting from a space and building, catching oblique views for its residents and serving as an important form in the building's architecture.

BAY WINDOW

29

B.B.P.R. *Torre Velasca, Milan*

**BAZAAR** A warm outdoor shopping street comprised of many solo merchants. The noise, sound, and smell in synthesis make a bazaar a symphony of merchandizing, rather than the compartmented, in-and-out, hot-and-cold stores of "temperate"-climated U.S. and Europe.

**B.B.P.R.** *Gian Luigi Bianfi (1910–1945), Ludovico Barbiano di Belgiojoso (1909–    ), Enrico Peressutti (1908–    ), and Ernesto Rogers (1909–1972) Italian Avant-gardists* Depressed under Mussolini, they blossomed in the post-World War II decade: the Monument to the Fallen (1948; particularly commemorating the first B., Bianfi, killed in the war in 1945), in Milan's cemetery; the Torre Velasca (1958, Milan), a multi-use, multistructured oddity in its time, fat higher floors bracketed over offices below, with romantically pitched roofs, of an almost conscious neo-historical silhouette. Peressutti, on loan to Princeton and M.I.T. in the fifties, gave New York its first sample of Italian commercial elegance at the Olivetti showroom (1955), Fifth Avenue, now unhappily demolished.

**BEAD** A slender finish molding, rounded.

**BEAM** A stiff, horizontal member bridging between its supports, and carrying the weight of floor or roof.

**BEAR** To transmit load from beam to column, beam to wall, column to footing, and so forth. A beam might "rest" on a column, but *bearing* implies the more descriptive transmission of load.

**BEAUDOUIN, EUGÈNE (1898–    )** *French Architect* Beaudouin and Lods designed the Open Air School (1932), at Suresnes, a Paris suburb, where walls roll back to relate children to surrounding nature. After World War II they produced many towers and slabs for high-density life, none of particular interest.

**BEAUFORT SCALE** A better measure of wind force than miles per hour, particularly for the windswept rural dweller. A gale (lusty word) is Force 9 (on the Beaufort Scale). Force 13 forbodes oblivion.

**BEAUX-ARTS** French: "fine arts." Loosely used as a term for the architecture of nineteenth-century France and its acolytes, proselytized through the École des Beaux-Arts (School of Fine Arts) in Paris, a national French architectural school supported by the government. The École was, in practice, more a scene for architectural development than a traditional teaching school. Sections called ateliers (literally: workshops) were led by prominent (sometimes flamboyant and/or egocentric) architects of the Establishment of the time who pursued a myth of palatial urbanism for the nation.

More importantly for architectural education, the Beaux-Arts concerned itself with large-scale problems of mass planning, crowds, major movements of people and vehicles: what architects call "circulation"—roads, boulevards, and streets, the arteries of the city's vascular system.

Beaux-Arts-trained architects dominated the profession in America from the 1880s to the First World War. Fortunately, however, their formalistic training in Paris was tempered by the exuberance, new materials, and technology of America (cf. Louis Sullivan).

**BED**   Plastic snuggling; as in a beam "bedded" in or on a wall with viscous concrete or mortar.

**BEDROOM**   Place of rest, love, nonaquatic ablutions, and just plain private retreat. The French *boudoir* gives it feminine propriety, and describes a quality of environment, rather than merely a geographical location of bed.

A bedroom can be a grand private apartment (in the general sense of the word, not the apartment-house sense), such as that of a king or Marie Antoinette; merely flamboyant and suggestive, as that of Jackie Gleason; or merely utilitarian, such as the sleeping decks and platforms of urban swingers that suggest the utility of love; while the monastic cell, which is in effect a private, apart bedroom, suggests frugal rest on an a-comfortable pallet, where love is that of the mind and heart, rather than the body.

A bed can be the most architectural of furnishings and even part of the architecture itself, a state perhaps maximized by the cupboard beds of Northern Europe. In canvas as a hammock, in wood as a pallet, in grass as a bower, it can also be a thing apart from buildings.

The proper, perhaps pretentious, apartment dwellers of New York's Fifth and Park avenues, Chicago's North Shore, and San Francisco's Nob Hill retired to "chambers," rather than bedrooms, or at least their architects so called them, believing in the twenties

31

BELLUSCHI *Equitable Building,*
*Portland, Oregon*

and thirties that beds were like undergarments, to be used but not mentioned.

**BEECH**   A dense domed tree (particularly the copper beech) that is an architectural object co-equal with the house it serves.

**BEHRENS, PETER (1868–1940)** *German Architect and Industrial Designer*   Behrens's industrial buildings, just before the First World War, inspired the (then) youthful Walter Gropius, Mies van der Rohe, and Le Corbusier. The A.E.G. works, an electrical turbine factory in Berlin, crossed engineering (clear, trussed span of workspace) with an engineering-like aesthetic: brick, steel, glass; the brick hard and wire-cut, as opposed to the soft molded brick of Northern European houses).

The Hoechst Dye Works (1920+) embraces a skylit brick Expressionist entry worthy of the most romantic German movie director's excesses.

**BEL GEDDES, NORMAN (1893–1958)** *American Industrial Designer*   Bel Geddes was a stylist of the new hardware and buildings of urban America; concerned with the visual meaning of movement and streamlining: the look, rather than the workings, of the machine idea, and the idea of speed. The 1939 World's Fair at New York displayed his special wares: the General Motors Building (Futurama) and the auto-generated streamlined dispersed cities it displayed.

**BELFRY**   Bellroom, usually at the top of a church's tower, below the spire, if there is one.

**BELL, ALEXANDER GRAHAM (1847–1922)** *Scottish American Inventor*   He not only "invented" the telephone (*invention* here does not mean conception, but rather its practical economic development) but was the structural precursor of Buckminster Fuller. Fascinated with a tetrahedron of struts as the most efficient structural form, he built early space-frames at his summer retreat, great lacy structures that promised to him light-boned aircraft and in fact found use in building hangars to contain them. (A tetrahedron has the greatest surface for the least volume, while a sphere has the least surface for the greatest volume.)

**BELLUSCHI, PIETRO (1899–    )** *Italian American Architect*
He blossomed in the Pacific Northwest, raising the handsome vernacular architecture native to that region to a state of formal virtue (and *not* virtuosity), at the Zion Lutheran Church (1945, Portland), a redwood barn of a building, center-steepled, as modern churches rarely are, a timber place sheathed with boards, speckled with tinted glass.

The Equitable Building (1950, Portland), pre-Lever House, is unmatched today for sophisticated sleek: flush, smooth, reflecting, it reputedly is within ⅜ of an inch of a true plane: a logical and creative architect's personal counterpoint (for a high-rise, fireproof, downtown building) to a suburban church (Zion).

Belluschi's later work, in association with others (St. Mary's Cathedral, San Francisco, with McSweeney, Ryan and Lee; Temple B'nai Jeshurun, Short Hills, New Jersey, with Gruzen and Partners), is, in the first case, based on structural virtuosity and visual gimmicry (four tilted hyperbolic paraboloids leave slots of light, bands that mark a linear glare from floor to peak), and, in the second, committee architecture, where single purpose falls victim to a compromising smorgasbord of too many people's too many ideas.

**BELT**   A strip of material or molding around a building, waistlike, as in a belt-course of brick or stone.

**BELVEDERE**   Fine seeing-place; a gazebo on top of a building, as in the glazed viewing rooms atop Victorian houses of General Grant's time.

**BEMA**   The place of the altar and its attendants in the Eastern (Greek or Russian Orthodox) Church, screened from the rabble by a grilled wall termed *iconostasis*, literally, the place for hanging icons, the sacred paintings that were thought to contain spiritual values.

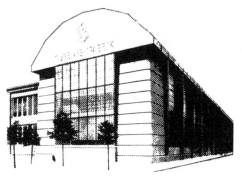

BEHRENS *Electrical Turbine Works, Berlin*

**BENEDETTO DA MAIANO (1442–1497)** *Italian Architect*   If one had a Florentine palace, one should have the best: not necessarily the most original, not the greatest in refinement of architectonic ideas and ideology, but a skillful end-*product*. Benedetto's Strozzi is huge, grand and terrifying, a visual social fortress centered around a grand courtyard (*cortile*) by Il Cronaca, who also completed the basic box according to Benedetto's designs. A corner site, a

33

pivot between street and small plaza, the Strozzi has all the ingredients of urban*e* form.

**BENJAMIN, ASHER (1771–1845)** *American Architect* First author of American "copybooks," those stylistic guides (with measured drawings and details) that allowed any carpenter to participate in good architecture (from *The Country Builder's Assistant* [1798] to *The Practice of Architecture* [1833]). The First Congregational Church (1806, Bennington, Vermont) is based on a plate in one of Benjamin's books. In his later years Benjamin actually built, as architect of record, the Olive Street Congregational Church, in Nashua, New Hampshire.

**BENT** A line of vertical and horizontal supports, parts of a series. Two columns and a beam, a single structural arch, or any similar assemblies in any material can be termed bents.

**BERG, MAX (1870–1947)** *German Architect* His Centenary Hall (1913, Breslau; structural engineer, Trauer) of ribbed dome concrete was the great-space alternate to traditional masonry (churchly) constructions.

**BERLAGE, HENDRIK PETRUS (1856–1934)** *Dutch Architect* The somber, almost churchlike brick volumes of the Amsterdam Stock Exchange (1897+) contain an exchanging space of light (natural) and delight: the edge of functionalism, restrained by traditional Dutch brickwork. Berlage is a protomodern commensurate with Eliel Saarinen, early Behrens, Auguste Perret, and Josef Hoffmann.

**BERM** A linear bump. Sloped earth (or other pilable material), double-sloped in its more pure form, creating a ridge. Berms might be one or a hundred feet tall. Smaller, they would be curbs; larger, artificial mountains.

**BERNINI, GIANLORENZO (1598–1680)** *Italian Sculptor and Architect* Master of the most grandiose Baroque architecture, sculpture, and urban design. His colonnade at St. Peter's Square in the Vatican embraces a plaza, upper arms straight, forearms curved, an enveloping architectural enclosure. In the basilica behind the *baldacchino* (1633) is a canopy of bronze, a static parachute. The twisted

BERG *Centenary Hall, Breslau, Germany*

columns (like licorice candy strips) cover an altar taller than the Farnese Palace. The Chair (Cathedra) of St. Peter, a glistening sunburst, dazzling the eye with light and form in an apse-positioned, but not-shaped, space, acts as center of a minichurch itself within the overall basilica.

The embracing colonnades of St. Peter's surround a gently undulating (for drainage) and sloping concave dish: Bernini made sure that all are aware of the size of the crowd present by the shape of the plane on which they stand, affording a sense of the whole to each standee.

Most beloved sculpture is the Fountain of the Four Rivers in the Piazza Navona (before the façade of S. Agnese, by his former student and competitor, Borromini).

**BILL, MAX (1908–    )** *German Painter, Sculptor, and Architect* In architecture, he was matter-of-fact, a remnant from his Bauhaus days: simplistic, direct, functional, and boring. He was director of the School of Art and Architecture at Ulm and architect of its new buildings (1953+).

**BIRCH** Light-colored and dense hardwood of northern climates used for furniture and plywood paneling. Birch was a code word and code material for an era of interior furnishings (1935–50), succeeded by teak (1950–56), and then an exotic wood anarchy (American walnut, zebrawood, etc.). Other wood is now frequently lacquered, or monolithically veneered with melamine plastic, or merely simulated plastically.

**BIRD'S-EYE** Before Wright (brothers, not Frank), Bleriot, and Icarus, the bird was the only thing privileged to soar over and see the earth's surface from an aerial view. Such views were synthetic, made as if man had a bird's wings and eyes. Consider the 1676 bird's-eye view of Rome by Nolli, an exquisite Baroque Italian draftsman. Hot-air balloons offered the possibility of first-hand experience in the eighteenth century, but the term "bird's" held and never became "balloon-eyed" or "-viewed."

**BLAKE, PETER (1920–    )** *German-English-American Architect, Writer, and Editor* Blake was editor of the (*Architectural*) *Forum* for years, then founded a new and ostensibly more independent magazine, *Architecture Plus,* which was, sadly, folded. He practices architec-

BENJAMIN *Olive Street Congregational Church, Nashua, New Hampshire* ture as well as preaching it, and has done well with a variety of partners. His books include *Marcel Breuer* and *The Master Builders.*

**BLIGHT**   The pathology of decay, where a vital organism, here inanimate, is passed into a state of slum and poverty by social fashion, flight, then fear. Blight is a state of community decay in downtown or dense urban areas, where panic sets in and those who love the place and care for its still solid bones flee, fearing property values in decline, and then physical attack: but the act of fleeing accelerates the very decline that they flee, and a panic not unlike that besetting the refugees of bombing sets in.

Urban renewal was the phrase for the stemming of blight, but its misuse gave it a bad name and bad press. The cure seemed more evil, or certainly less promising for the common man, than the blight itself. Self-help, self-renewal, and the regrouping of flagging spirits seem now more important than demolition and rebuilding, or even gross renovation.

**BLIND**   That which blinds vision, and the sun's rays, usually by covering windows from in- or out-sight. Eighteenth-century louvered blinds on the exterior of "Colonial" houses (usually Federal or Greek Revival) are revived today as vestigial decorations, often plastic, usually immovable, and insufficient in width to cover the opening they flank. Nineteenth-century blinds went indoors and were recessed internal louvered blinds, covering similar openings, but away from the weather.

**BLOCK**   A masonry module, as in block of granite or concrete block. Concrete blocks were invented not because they are intrinsically so cheap as a material (which they are) but because union regulations allow the placement (laying) of masonry units up to a certain weight by one man. The concrete block is that maximum unit and, hence, generates the lowest labor costs.

Concrete block has a variety of aggregates, colors, and textures, some quite exotic: striated or supersmooth.

BLOCK *Marseille Block by Le Corbusier*

**BLOCK**   A large building or set of buildings, more an English than an American term: but Le Corbusier's great stranded ocean liner at Marseille (housing, shopping, nursery schools, other entertainments all contained in a single hovering volume) is called the Marseille Block.

**BLOCKING** Backup structure for the built-in furnishings of a room. Blocking allows the placement of finish trim, cabinetry, and other special detail. It is the substructure to which we fasten that which is to be fastened.

**BLONDEL, JACQUES-FRANÇOIS (1705–1774)** *French Architect* Much re-admired architect-writer who honored in words and magnificent drawings the architecture of the Renaissance in France, particularly that of Mansart (François) 100 years before. Reprints (Gregg Press) have brought this and similar volumes firsthand to the students of the 1970s. Their concern with proportion and hierarchical design examples brings their attention to Blondel as an historical touchstone.

**BLUEPRINT** A print (copy) of an original tracing, usually a technical architectural or engineering drawing. At first such prints were made by exposure of photographic-like paper to the sun, which shined through the tracing paper "negative." Later both chemistry and mechanics advanced, with artifical light and machinery reproducing similar original drawings.

Nowadays it is likely that the prints will be black or blue lines on white backgrounds, by a process called Ozalid, but with the same intent and ultimate use as the blueprint. (No, Virginia, architects do not draw white lines on blue paper.)

**BOGARDUS, JAMES (1800–1874)** *American Inventor, Manufacturer, and Builder* His prefabricated cast-iron façades brought the technology of stick and beam cast-iron interiors of the 1840s to the exterior and light and view to occupants, but more importantly a new attenuated architectural elegance to the façade.

Cast iron gave the possibility of instant ornament in unlimited styles, producing more Ionic and Corinthian columns than Greece and Rome did in all history.

BOGARDUS *Cast-Iron Building, Washington Street, New York*

**BÖHM, DOMINIKUS (1880–1955)** *German Priest and Architect* The next step beyond Perret's church at Le Raincy was a totally "stained"-glass box. Böhm (and later Labatut) presented that neutral architecture (rich glass) at St. Maria Königen (1954, Cologne).

37

**BOILEAU, LOUIS AUGUSTE (1812–1896)** *French Architect*
His church, St. Eugène (Paris, 1854), is party to the great midcentury surge of French cast-iron engineering for architecture, joined by Baltard, Labrouste, and the polemics of Viollet-le-Duc.

**BOLLARD**  Bollards are chunky posts that, in a row, across a direction of traffic, forewarn of danger or permit traffic only of a certain size (people). Bollards along a waterfront frequently and formally indicate the paved edge of a sea wall and also serve as the anchoring point for hardware to which boats are tied. Sometimes chains are strung between bollards, which is one more level of security and warning. (It's always possible to step over and across the chain.)

  Modern architects have rediscovered bollards as a handsome device, sculptural as well as functional; in the Piazza S. Pietro, bollards surround the fountains by Bernini and others, preventing carriage traffic from striking the fountains but allowing people to go right up to the rim.

**BOLT**  Like Mutt needs Jeff, bolts need nuts to provide a fastening at both ends of a rod to hold something together.

**BOND**  The method of tying together and stacking a masonry wall so that all will work as a single structural unit. For example, a wall two bricks thick must be tied together; such brick ties are called headers, as their ends (heads), rather than their sides (stretchers), are exposed to view on the exterior of the wall. Bonding also became a decorative project: courses of common bond (headers continuously every seven or eight courses); English bond (alternate stretchers and headers); and Flemish bond (alternate headers and stretchers in each course).

**BOOTH**  A small structure in- or outdoors, where a service or goods are dispensed—a telephone booth or booth at a county fair, which implies a person-size space halfway in scale between a casket and a room.

**BORING**  The material taken from a hole bored in the ground by a hollow drill which, like a long, tubular cookie-cutter, removes samples from the earth and allows engineers and architects to analyze the subsoil and sub-rock present to aid or hinder the building at that point.

**BORROMINI, FRANCESCO (1599–1667)**   *Italian Architect*
Where Bernini produced grandiose extravaganzas in Baroque Italian architecture, Borromini cultivated a theatrical excitement from tiny spaces with extraordinary effect(s). S. Carlo alle Quattro Fontane, for the Order of Trinitarians, packs a church and two storied cloisters into a space scarcely larger than two common Bloomsbury or Greenwich Village Greek Revival houses. In the church, a lanterned dome lights a white-coffered self-underbelly, like a sail of bleached tripe. In one corner (outside) is built one of the four fountains for which the church is named.

At S. Ivo, a bizarre spiral ziggurat tops what is internally a complex ribbed geometry of dome, oddly similar to many appearing in Moorish-Spanish architecture. S. Ivo is part of a complex, of the Sapienza, a religious university and library; but the Borromini church became the tail that wagged the dog in its exuberant form/space/light, internally and externally.

Borromini also worked on the church of S. Agnese on the Piazza Navona, where his undulating plastic façade gives itself as backdrop to Bernini's Fountain of the Four Rivers, a just juxtaposition, particularly as Borromini had worked for Bernini and they had shared hard feelings about each other.

**BOSS**   The carved stone ornament absorbing structurally and visually the intersection of ribs articulating a Gothic vault (later all "carvings," including those of piers, capitals, ribs, and so forth, were *cast* in terra cotta; and, of course, so were bosses).

BOSS *On vaulting of St. Alban's Abbey Church, Hertfordshire*

**BOSWORTH, WELLES (1869–1966)** *American Architect*   Super Classic Revivalist, his American Telephone and Telegraph Building (lower Broadway, New York) superimposes eight tiers of Ionic "temples" (three office floors within each tier) of business on a strong Doric base, all crowned with a stepped pyramid and Evelyn Longworth's heroic Greek Spirit of Communications.

Bosworth went horizontal at M.I.T.—the Cambridge land is boggy—providing low-rise stripped Classical Revival, sprawling geometrically around a Pantheon-like dome.

39

**BOULLÉE, ÉTIENNE-LOUIS (1728–1799)** *French Architect* Can you imagine a 500-foot-in-diameter spherical monument to Isaac Newton? Boullée could, and drew it for our intellectual challenge and confrontation. His phantasmagorical mind dreamed of geometric spaces, only incidentally for human use.

**BOW WINDOW** A single curved membrane, rather than the bay window's box. Popular in Georgian architecture, the bow was made possible by the many small panes that could become polygonal segments of its curved surface. The larger sheet glass developed by later phases of the Victorian industrial revolution made single or few-sheeted panes possible for a squared niche that became the volume of a bay.

**BOX** An architectural container for something to be transported or stored. In more esoteric circles, a box is a hunting lodge: a shooting box.

**BOYLE, RICHARD, LORD BURLINGTON (1694–1753)** *English Patron and Architect* Palladian proselytizer through his commissions to others (Colen Campbell at Burlington House) and his own work, the Palladian Villa at Chiswick. He published Palladio's measured drawings of Roman Baths (*thermae*) and seemed, except for his villa at Chiswick (William Kent helped him), to be more interested in Rome as seen through Palladio's eyes than in Palladio himself.

BOYLE *Villa after Palladio, Chiswick, England*

**BRACE** A structural prop, stabilizing and/or reinforcing something that tends to buckle (or might, under some considerations). A brace is an extra structural part, or one for special service, as a wind brace in a high-rise steel-framed building, where it functions only under substantial wind to stabilize the frame, whereas the frame alone can normally survive.

**BRACKET** A structural support attached to a wall and bolted to or bearing thereon. Consoles and modillions are brackets in Classical architecture.

**BRAMANTE, DONATO (1444–1514)** *Italian Architect* The minitemple (the Tempietto at S. Pietro in Montorio, 1502) makes Bramante's most telling impact on the architecture of the Renaissance. This tiny object, scarcely a building, as the public cannot, even abnormally, go inside (one couldn't go inside a true Greek temple), is contained in a tight courtyard at S. Pietro, producing an impact far beyond its dimensions: a cylindrical colonnade with dome, bare and spartan.

Bramante's great Greek-crossed scheme for the new St. Peter's Church (1506+, in what is now known as the Vatican) was commissioned by Pope Julius II, who, unfortunately for Bramante, died when it had scarcely begun. It would have been concentric, nondirectional, and freestanding within a great plaza, each arm (nave or transept) domed with a lower dome, hierarchically reminiscent of Hagia Sophia and its Islamic reproductions, but visually very different: the Renaissance conception of domes being composite structures, their interior form unrelated to the exterior one; an inner visual skin suspended from an outer visual form. Bramante's Greek-crossed plan was inspired by the ideas and sketches of Leonardo da Vinci. Little trace of Bramante's beginnings remains in the St. Peter's we inherit today: greatest impacts are Michelangelo's dome, Maderna's Latin-crossed nave, and Bernini's plaza-embracing colonnade.

**BRASS** Copper and zinc, and sometimes lead (copper and tin generically are termed bronze). The two words (*brass* and *bronze*) have become overlapping in common usage, but both describe yellow-to-brown golden alloys that do not corrode but do tarnish (oxydize) and require polishing or maintenance to approximate a golden sheen. Alternately, a desired patina, from brown to green, can be allowed and maintained with little effort.

**BRAZIL** Latin exuberance, crossed with cultural immigration to a new land, produced architecture, modern and in quantity, that was the jealously watched idol of America and Western Europe in the late thirties and forties.

Brazilian architect Oscar Niemeyer, a son of expatriated Europe, and his planning associate, Lucio Costa, have had an impact many times that of their direct private practices (most recently and resoundingly at Brasília, Brazil's new capital in the central highlands, planned by Costa, and where the major public buildings are by Niemeyer).

Before these modern symbolists, the exaggerated Portuguese Baroque spread across Brazil, a late, perhaps vulgar, but vigorous architecture, designed to convert the savage natives to the civilized religion of the motherland.

**BREEZEWAY**   The roofed link between two portions of a house (or house and garage) that shelters from rain and sun but permits passage of air.

**BREUER, MARCEL (1902–   )** *Hungarian American Architect* As famous for his furniture as his architecture. At the Bauhaus in Dessau (Germany) in the 1920s, he developed tubular steel furniture, raising the material and its use to a new plateau of design.

Emigrating to England in 1935, he briefly practiced with F. R. S. Yorke. Then, in 1937, he went to Harvard to join Walter Gropius, his former director at the Bauhaus, who had preceded him at the invitation of Dean Joseph Hudnut. His American houses were, at first with Gropius, pristine, prismatic, white volumes, sympathetic to the white New England environment in which they grew; then, by himself, natural-wood boxed volumes of family life perched on stone pedestals, carefully, beautifully, and expensively detailed; finally, the public buildings he had drawn and modeled his whole life became, one by one, reality. Clients came almost as if to pick from his existing smorgasbord: the three-armed U.N.E.S.C.O. Building being one of his most symbolic, and repeated, prototypical examples.

Later, originality became a renewed need, and quality degenerated in such instances as the Armstrong Building at New Haven, the Nestlé and I.B.M. buildings in France—all ungainly and ill-proportioned.

The Whitney Museum (1966, New York), a tour-de-force, seems foreign to his development, a tricky, stepped-out building separated from Madison Avenue by a moat-space. It is a handsome warehouse of art within, festooned with external trappings that do it a bizarre harm, rather than serene justice.

BREUER *Whitney Museum, New York City*

**BRICK**   Cooked clay; the original, modular building block; the fudge of architecture, sometimes molded, sometimes cut from slabs. The size of brick varies, but it is always a function of a man's hand or hands, and how much he can place on, or in, a wall.

**BRIDGE**   The way to get from here to there across a void, supported at its ends and/or midpoints. A bridge can be small and made from joists, beams, or girders; or larger and of more exotic structure, such as trusses or suspended cables; or even more exotic, of tubular pre- or post-stressed concrete.

Most importantly, a bridge is a man-made object: it looms large in a natural landscape as a local stamp of man's passings and becomes, out of absolute functional necessity, a major architectural element, by design or default. The architecture of bridges has become a major concern of architects, although those bridges that are most successful didn't have them.

The George Washington Bridge was designed by engineers and architects together, the steel towers to be clad in stone (for a feeling of visual permanence and security, one supposes). Fortuitously, the client was persuaded to omit the stone when he saw the built bare, handsome towers.

The Brooklyn Bridge was created not only without aid of an architect but by a contractor who supplied design and construction services as part of his package: John Roebling and his son Washington, one who gave his life and the other his health to the construction. Cable manufacturers from Trenton, New Jersey, they brought that new technology to its highest structural and aesthetic peak. Now many critics believe it the greatest man-made structure ever built in New York (or half in, for Brooklyn became part of New York in 1898, 15 years after its completion, partly because of this new umbilical cord).

Other bridges for the thoughtful connoisseur include all those of Swiss concrete engineer Robert Maillart; all the others of the Roeblings (including that great one between Covington, Kentucky, and Cincinnati, Ohio); various Roman and Roman-derived bridges, mostly at Rome across the Tiber; those marvelous tensile structures now largely seen on the *Late Late Show* across tropical ravines, where "savages" pursue; and, at the opposite end of the scale, Japanese bridges within their contained garden complexes, as at the Katsura detached palace at Kyoto.

BREUER *Dolderthal flats, Zurich*

**BRIDLE IRON** A strap of steel hanging across both sides of a beam like the limp strap of a bridle. In the not-so-limp cradle of this bridle rests a beam, thereby picked up, supported, on the first one. By this device, openings in wood-joisted floors can be soundly structured to allow stairs through (particularly where the beams normally run in only one direction from side wall to side wall).

43

**BRINKMAN, JOHANNES (1902–1949)** *Dutch Architect* With van der Vlugt and van Tijen, he made one of the classic modern monuments, the Van Nelle Tobacco Factory (1928, near Rotterdam), a glassy high-rise place, spartan in the style of Gropius's Bauhaus.

**BRISE-SOLEIL** French: "broken sun." A sunshield on a building, more permanent than an awning but providing, largely, the same result: continued view and light without direct sun. The most famous are those of the Ministry of Education (1936+) in Rio di Janeiro, a building designed by Le Corbusier and executed by Oscar Niemeyer, Lucio Costa, and others. There, "Corb's" natural inclination for spare and planar light controls was fulfilled in a climate naturally needing them (unlike the relatively cool and temperate homeland of France).

BRODY *Joseph Ellicott Complex, University of Buffalo*

**BRODY, SAMUEL (1926–    )** *American Architect* See *Davis, Lewis,* for Davis, Brody and Associates.

**BRONZE** The first man-made and -used metal, significant enough to name a whole period of mankind: the Bronze Age. Copper and tin, blended, form an easily worked alloy of low melting point that can be poured, cast, molded, beaten, cut, and milled with relatively simple tools and resources.

Apogee of bronze are the Renaissance doors of the Cathedral Baptistery of Florence, a commission won in competition in 1401 by the sculptor-architect Lorenzo Ghiberti. (See also *Brass.*)

**BROWN, LANCELOT "CAPABILITY" (1716–1783)** *English Landscape Gardener* Nicknamed "Capability" because he said he was. The ultimate villain in respect to the American lawn: heath, copse, wood, formal garden all contributed their turf to his undulations, great grassy surfaces contained visually by lines of trees—not to limit the view but to imply the endlessness one could not see—and then punctuated with clumps picturesquely placed, a painter's landscape.

Blenheim Palace (Gardens; 1765+) is one of his works, prescient of America's Frederick Law Olmsted by 100 years.

He also built as an architect, but those, although large, are minor things.

**BROWNSTONE**  A town house, particularly one of those retrieved by the youthful middle class (from an oblivion of disinterest and rooming house futures). Town houses, as built in New York, Boston, Albany, and other waterfronted places, were faced with a soft red sandstone, brought by barge from the quarries at Portland, Connecticut, opposite Middletown, or up and down the Hackensack River.

Brownstone is the material; *a* or *the* brownstone is a place made therefrom.

**BRUNELLESCHI, FILIPPO (1377–1446)** *Italian Architect*  The great gutsy dome of the Cathedral of Florence (called Duomo in text and guide books) was the product of Brunelleschi and Ghiberti (the latter faded from the contract, occupied with other activities, including the doors of the cathedral's baptistery, for which he had won the competition in 1401). Almost 20 years and two further competitions later, he crowned the dome with a lantern and clad the drum with a multimarbled octagon of staggering monumentality (over Arnolfo di Cambio's nave and aisles).

In delicate counterpoint, and simultaneously (in design), Brunelleschi created the Hospital of the Innocents (Ospedale degli Innocenti; 1421+), a foundling hospital, sometimes called the first Renaissance building. In fact, all that historians (and tourists) look at are its elegant arcaded façade of slender columns and arches, and their spandrels (flat spaces above and between adjacent arches), embellished with round glazed blue and white terra-cotta plaques by the Della Robbias, depicting the innocents inside.

And, most sophisticated and complex is the Pazzi Chapel (1429+), in the cloistered garden of the church of S. Croce. A small building, it is both elegant in proportion and crude in its forceful massing, unusual, atypical, and truly Renaissance in its use of classic parts for remarkably original ends.

**BRUTALISM**  Vintage 1954 jargon, coined in reference to the powerful, crudely fabricated but elegantly designed concrete work of Le Corbusier's late years. The Smithsons, Alison and Peter (husband-and-wife team of English architects), applied it, although their own work cannot be so defined, even though it was and is vigorous.

More clearly "brutal" are the works of Maekawa in Japan, Doshi in India. Mere concrete with rough or crude formwork isn't brutal. The basic configuration of building and its plastic display (of its own

**BROWNSTONE** *Brownstone houses, Brooklyn*

guts: mechanical systems, plumbing, elevators, and so forth) are essential elements of a "Brutalist" building. Most classic example is the Istituto Marchiondi (1957, Milan) by Viganò.

**BRYGGMAN, ERIK (1891–1955)** *Finnish Architect* Bryggman's Cemetery Chapel (1941) at Turku encloses an interior of crisp arched and columned stucco, gathering and photographed with sun and plants: the latter qualities particularly important to the dark-dayed and -nighted Scandinavian.

**B.T.U.** British thermal unit. The awkward English equivalent of the metric calorie. Heating and air conditioning is measured in terms of B.T.U.s, a quantity of heat required to raise the temperature of a pound of water (about a pint) by one degree Fahrenheit.

Remember that heat is power or energy, cold is the lack of it; therefore, you can add or subtract heat to make a place or space hot or cold. Coldness is only the result. Heat removed from hot summer air will cause it to become cold-air conditioned.

**BUDGET** Allocation of resources to a particular, or several particular, needs or functions: one budgets time, money, or effort and makes it a measure against which the final reality can be evaluated.

**BUILDER** In current jargon, the broker who assembles the building processes (largely subcontractors) to consummate an architect's or engineer's wishes: documented through contract documents. The master builder was the medieval idea: he conceived, directed, and built the building in question; functions later separated and dispersed to architects, engineers, contractors, clerks of the works, subcontractors, and even clients.

**BUILT-UP ROOF** A roof made of built-up layers of felt and tar, laminated; a membrane that skins water away to its edges or to inset roof drains.

BULFINCH *Drawing of the State House, Boston*

**BULFINCH, CHARLES (1763–1844)** *American Architect* The State House on Beacon Hill crowns Boston, that still largely low-rise, high-density city, the most preserved urban collection of America's past. The gold-leafed dome (assembled by 1800) shimmers in sunlight over red brick and limestone, with later limestone wings by others. Bulfinch will always be remembered in official histories for *this* state house at the center of America's early beginnings.

He also had his turn at the Capitol in Washington, D.C. (1817–30). See also *Thornton, William* and *Walter, Thomas U.*

**BULKHEAD** A small structure penetrating the roof of a building, bringing a stair to its surface, sometimes containing elevator machinery, or merely allowing pedestrian access for emergency (and maintenance) purposes.

**BULNOSE** The fat rounded edge of a step or other architectural part.

**BUNGALOW** An Indian word (Bengali) for a single-storied house with veranda (another Indian word, meaning "generous porch"). It was adopted in the American twenties for small, unpretentious houses in wood, often shingled, with porches that formed a significant part of their architectural form. There was such consistency and strength that it became a style, with minor variants: stick-style bungalows, shingle-volumed bungalows, and so forth. No one has yet honored bunaglows with a treatise.

**BUNSHAFT, GORDON (1909–  )** *American Architect* Power combined with will and single-mindedness. For many years the chief design partner of Skidmore, Owings and Merrill (New York), Bunshaft gave us Lever House on Park Avenue, the Manufacturers Hanover Trust Company on Fifth Avenue, the Chase Manhattan Bank, the U.S. Steel Building; and, overseas, a whole string of American consulates in Germany, the Banque Lambert in Brussels.

In the liberated fifties he was criticized for his straight and narrow variations on the theme of Mies van der Rohe, prismatic, rectangular glass- and metal-skinned buildings reflecting the sky and the city surrounding. ("I'm going to keep doing boxes until I do a good one.") But he grew out of this self-straight jacket, and produced in the seventies a set of swooping forms: the Avon and Grace buildings, jazzy cartoons of zoning that care little for the city's urban design affairs.

**BURLE-MARX, ROBERTO (1909–  )** *Brazilian Landscape Architect* His sinuous gardens of contrasting textures paralleled the free-formalism of sculptors Arp, Noguchi, Nakashima, Moore, and

BUNSHAFT *Hirshhorn Museum, Washington, D.C.*

BURNHAM *Flatiron Building, New York*

Hepworth. Tropical and semitropical environmentalist, he embellished works of Niemeyer, Costa, and Villanueva, in particular.

**BURNHAM, DANIEL H. (1846–1912)** *American Architect*
Sometime partner of Burnham and Root (to 1891), and later grand planning consultant. The Monadnock Block (1891, Chicago), still standing, but threatened, is the last and largest wall-bearing office building in America (and, therefore, anywhere). With walls 6 feet thick at its base, it is a cartoon for explaining the need for a structural steel cage (which immediately appeared in the practice of the Chicago School's architecture). Walls began to occupy so much space that to build a building taller (and hence of even thicker walls) would be folly. The Monadnock is a handsome, smoothly spartan, undecorated plastic mass of masonry.

Later, Burnham (on his own, without Root) built New York's Flatiron Building (1902; embraced by the diverging paths of Broadway and Fifth Avenue at 23rd Street). Its triangular shape must have suggested a flatiron to many, although its height (the highest in New York at its date of completion) and proportions make the comparison seem far-fetched. Unlike the Monadnock Building, the Flatiron is richly ornamented Renaissance Revival, and a steel cage.

Between the two buildings his greatest influence was through direction and orchestration of the Chicago World's Fair of 1893 (World's Columbian Exposition), which redirected the main route of elite architecture from the recently virile and vigorous Chicago School (Richardson, Sullivan, Wright, Jenney, and Burnham's partner Root) to a Neoclassical city-sized advertisement for the École des Beaux-Arts. The strongly disciplined plan is again being admired, even by the most radical; but the architecture within that plan, immensely popular and widely copied, diverted America from true promise and possibility for forty years (popular because it was pre-Hollywood Hollywood, a stage-set for sometime life, a Disneyland of the nineties). Louis Sullivan's last great building at that exposition was his swan song; the fair killed most of his practice and left him in limbo till his death 31 years later (limbo, save for a few rural banks in the upper Midwest).

Lastly, Burnham was given the capital as a toy, and he projected completion of the grand neo-Baroque boulevard system for the District of Columbia that we see today. Originally planned by the French (volunteer in America) army officer Pierre L'Enfant, the District and its radial street system were spasmodically completed.

Burnham took the incomplete idea and infilled and extended it in the direction that L'Enfant had started. It is unlike most Baroque city planning, in that the streets are frequently too broad and ill-defined to be part of a visual axis system (like those of Pope Sixtus V in Rome, or of Haussmann's neo-Baroque post-Civil War Paris).

**BUSH-HAMMER**  Take a stiff brush (bush) and hammer it against the surface of any material and its inner life, form, grain will be exposed. The "bush" in question can be pneumatically powered to do substantial work.

**BUTT**  What they do, not what they are: two hinged halves of a hinge are called butts. One never speaks of *a* butt, but half a pair.

**BUTTERFIELD, WILLIAM (1814–1900)** *English Architect* Gothic Revivalist, a passionate bachelor whose pure personal force sold the church (of England) on an exuberant, perhaps brutal, poly-chromatic masonry Gothic, striped, banded, and decorated. A contemporary of John Ruskin, he gave form coincidentally to the words Ruskin orated in *The Seven Lamps of Architecture* (1849) and *The Stones of Venice* (1851–53).

**BUTTERFLY ROOF**  Those upraised planes (perversely opposite to the ridged gable) that suggest the outdoors, outlooking. A butterfly, on wing, is never photographed body-centered, wings down, but always wings up; hence the analogy.

**BUTTRESS**  Stolid masonry mass that props a building wall or vault by dint of its own weight. A *flying* buttress, however, is a composite affair: the masonry mass here becomes a tower propping an arched stone brace, which, in turn, holds the edge of a ribbed Gothic vault and prevents its demise.

   At New York's St. Patrick's Cathedral (1853+), architect James Renwick's careful neo-Gothic church, modern hollow tile allowed the vaults to be far lighter than those of stone in thirteenth-century France. The buttresses, erected there for academic correctitude, tended to thrust inward, collapsing the vaults in reverse. Sadly, they were removed, and the vaults float, held by their own configuration and the mere weight of the church's high (clerestory) walls.

BUTTRESS

49

**B.X.** The coiled armor of electric cable used in frame house construction; ostensibly for protection from rats. Newer technology has provided builders with plastic cable, resisted until recently by the conservatives who control the building codes of American cities.

**BYZANTINE** Byzantium, the ancient place-name, was renamed Constantinople after the Roman emperor Constantine moved his capital there in A.D. 330 (now, again renamed: Istanbul, in the chauvinistic continuum that demands an ethnic name for a place as new ethnic peoples occupy it). What is termed Byzantine should properly be called Constantine.

Our Byzantine legacies are twofold: the great murky spaces of Christian Byzantine churches and the Islamic mosques derived from them; and the two-dimensional designs associated therewith, in mosaic and incised stone surfaces and grillages.

Hagia Sophia (not Santa Sophia) is the proper name of Byzantium's greatest building: in translation, the Church of the Divine Wisdom. A swelling of domes from the ground to its crest, it soars with thin brick domical vaults over vast, vast internal space, punctuated by the spotlights of sun perforating the dome's tiny-windowed drum and walls. The minarets that flank it now are a later legacy from the time the church became a mosque.

There is much of Roman engineering in Hagia Sophia, crossbred with the centralized Christian planning of churches that, coincidentally, moved northward from the Middle East.

Byzantine as eclectic revival material has been a watery affair, relying on column capitals and decoration and simulated archaeology reminiscent of the pillage by Byzantium's own architects of "pagan," (i.e., Roman) temples for columns and parts they could incorporate as decor in their powerful volumetric architecture. The same building debris applied to 1930s sentimental archaeology equates with Piranesi wallpaper: cf. Bertram Goodhue's Christ Church, New York.

BYZANTINE *Capital and spring of arches, S. Vitale, Ravenna*

# C

**CABIN** A small, primitive, and isolated retreat, for solace in vacation or mere hermitage. Uncle Tom's was a white man's patronizing slave symbol. The *log* cabin, an imported Swedish accessory, is about as close to a natural residence as one could devise: one clears a homestead space, or, if no farming is in the cards, space sufficient for the cabin itself, stacking the logs, which are notched (to interlock at each corner: remember Lincoln Logs, invented by John Lloyd, son of Frank Lloyd Wright?). The uneven space between is stuffed, or caulked, with straw or mud or clay or all of them.

To crown it all, and keep one snug, a sod roof is most appropriate, again locally and naturally available, alive and self-maintaining (unless your aesthetics requires that you mow your roof) and, most important, an insulator at the point of maximum heat loss.

CABIN *Russian log cabin*

**CABINETWORK** The most elegant level of carpentry: rough carpentry frames houses; finish carpentry applies trim and details (termed *millwork* and made in a sawmill) to those houses; cabinetry comprises finish bookcases, kitchen cabinets, and the furnishings themselves.

**CAFÉ** Coffee, and hence, the place where it is sold. When the place remains, and fashions change, cafés dispense food, aperitifs, and more potent beverages.

The outdoor café is a modern architect's wishful tool for justifying much of the outdoor pedestrian space in shopping center, pedestrian street or plaza, and now, in its most sophisticated version, the glass-roofed courts of John Portman-designed hotel-motels (e.g., the Regency Hyatt House at O'Hare Field, Chicago).

**CAFETERIA** What happens in the Americanization of a café: a self-service restaurant, where the consumer picks up (and out) his own food and brings it to the place of consumption. The latter may range from an outdoor café to a dank hole.

**CAIRN** In lands where rocks seem to grow weedlike (say, New England and Scotland), their collection and disposal took on creative functions: in New England they became walls, both clearing and dividing the fields simultaneously. In Scotland they sometimes became cairns, landmarkers, points of sight and signal, and even refuge for small rodents; hence the invention of the cairn terrier to seek them out (the cairn is the ancestor of both Scottish terrier and the West Highland whites). The cairn was one of the earliest of bred companions for man, more "medieval" than Edinburgh's part mock, part real castle.

**CAISSON** A tethered boat, giving access to underwater construction and sometimes forming the foundation thereof. The caissons of the Brooklyn Bridge were (and still are) gigantic, ship-sized timber boxes, inverted in water, containing air for the workmen working within, and then forming the footings of the great stone towers that slowly pressed them into the muddy river bottom.

**CALIDARIUM** The Roman equivalent of a steam bath: a hot room, where one might bathe in hot water (within one of the great bath complexes, or *thermae,* as that of Caracalla or Diocletian).

**CALIFORNIA** Sometimes considered a state of mind, rather than a place or state of superpopulation. Schizophrenic, it embraces the cool, hilly, fog-swept, old Establishment understated architecture of the north (San Francisco, Marin County, Hillsborough) and the south's cacophony of heat, cars and their combustion, and the assorted jazz of commercial construction, dispersed, auto-fed, ephemeral.

Architects of the north include the late William Wurster, Joe Esherick, Owings' own branch of S.O.M. (Skidmore, Owings and Merrill); and the hero-historians Maybeck, Howard, Bartlett.

The south has heroes too: the Greene brothers, Irving Gill, Schindler; but it has lately lost the battle to the commercial cream: Luckman, Pereira, Becket, and, more importantly, the corporate giants, like Daniel, Mann, Mendenhall, and Johnson.

**CALLICRATES**  Ictinus and Callicrates, two of the earliest identifiable architects, designed the Parthenon (ca. 432 B.C.). Before came Imhotep, architect of Pharaoh Djoser's stepped pyramid at Sakkara in 2700 B.C.

**CALLISTER, CHARLES WARREN (1917–    )** *American Architect*  Callister (with Schindler, Henken, and the master's son Lloyd) was one of the most sophisticated of Wright's former student acolytes. His works embellish such romantic San Francisco suburbs as Sausalito and Tiburon (First Church of Christ Scientist, 1952) and reach, transcontinentally, to the elegant retirement development Heritage Village in Southbury, Connecticut.

**CAMBER**  The slight arching of a beam, when fabricated, to allow the dead weight supported by the beam to flatten it to a true horizontal when installed.

**CAMPANILE**  The freestanding bell tower of an Italian church, one third of a triad composition of church, tower, and baptistery. The Leaning Tower of Pisa is one, as is Giotto's tower of the Cathedral (Duomo) of Florence.

CAMPANILE *S. Giorgio al Velabro, Rome*

**CAMPBELL, COLEN (1673–1729)** *English Architect and Architectural Writer*  He published the *Vitruvius Britannicus* (1715), an ode to Palladianism so effective that Richard Boyle (Lord Burlington) became its first convert (and high priest). He went on to design in the Palladian idiom revived, including a smashing version of Palladio's Villa Rotondo at Mereworth Castle (now owned by the United Arab Emirates).

The *Vitruvius Britannicus* (now available in modern folio reprint) is a mine of line-engraved regal and sometimes royal fantasies converted to reality: drawn by the many draftsmen that Campbell employed, they suggest an implausibility, the dreams of grandeur of Walter Mitty. To speak of them as English country "houses" makes Yankee understatement seem like wild improvisation.

**CANAL** The artificially cut conductor of water that placates it for those shipping over falls (through locks) or along waterways that tend to silt. It is a permissive passage, where passage may be inconsistent or difficult.

Alternately, it is the urban street system of a city so tuned, where vast and heavy cargoes, brought long distances across the sea, can be delivered directly to warehousing without transhipping to trucks, trains, or carts; Venice and Amsterdam are two major cities so thoughtfully and handsomely served.

CANALETTO *Drawing of S. Simeone Piccolo, Grand Canal, Venice*

**CANALETTO, ANTONIO (1697–1768)** *Italian Painter* A great painter-draftsman who brought intense images of Venice (and Amsterdam) to the removed viewer. Water-based perspectives gave a hard-lined foreground to exactly rendered distant images. Nothing could have made Venice more lovely, or desirable, to those (almost all of us) who had or have never been there.

**CANDELA, FELIX (1910–    )** *Mexican Engineer* Slim ribbons of concrete are made to span great spaces and envelop, as man made sea shells, the space of public assembly and joy: the church of Our Lady of Miracles (usually published without its gross architectural finishes and detailing) is a sensuous set of concrete forms; and the restaurant at Xochimilco (that last remnant of Lake Texcoco, mostly filled for dry Mexico City modern) a tour de force of flower-petaled paraboloids.

Candela's problem parallels Nervi's: he is not an architect and must work with architects of lesser creativity than himself; he dominates, so that his bare bones and shells are magnificent but suffer when draped, festooned, and decorated with the superficial trappings of "architecture" that they could so happily do without.

**CANDLEPOWER** A somewhat whimsical measurement of light emission, in terms of candles, a term used more for nostalgia than reality. A candlepower is most certainly not the lightpower of one candle, but what a wishful candlemaker might hope for.

**CANOPY** Any covering over an event, usually temporary (canvas or wood) or bracketed from a building as an accessory, like an entrance canopy.

**CANT** The tilted edge (rising 2 to 6 inches) of a flat roof that prevents water spilling over, the roof in turn tilted away from its own edge back to drains within the building.

**CANTILEVER** A static lever, the arm of which supports a load or surface, or is the surface itself. Balconies are frequently cantilevered planes of concrete, particularly those toothy endeavors texturing the façades of downtown America's high-rise housing.

A fishing pole is a cantilever held in the socket of a fisherman's hands.

**CAPITAL** The head, and headlike crown, of a column, pier, or pilaster. Capitals, in the Classical architecture of Greece and Rome (Mycenae, Etruria, Byzantium, Egypt, Mesopotamia, and Assyria as well), matured as a code-symbol of the cultural group then dominant: hence Doric for the Dorians, Ionic for the Ionians, Corinthian for the Corinthians; to a certain degree apocryphal in that they were the products of central religious-political power and interest, terms lasting beyond their geography and time as does Georgian or mission style or Louis XIV. (See also *Orders.*)

CAPITAL *Ionic capital*

**CAPITOL** The buildings of government within its geographical capital. The Capitol of the U.S. is in the capital, Washington, D.C.; while the Capitoline Hill (bearing the Capitol) is at Rome, capital of Italy.

**CARACOL** Spanish for *snail,* a form glorified by a single seemingly astronomical structure at Chichén Itzá, Mayan-Toltec-Aztec remains in central Yucatán, Mexico.

**CARILLON** An assembly of tuned bells that can be played, as opposed to merely rung. Usually mounted in neo-Gothic towers, they sound the hymns of Protestantism across sin-filled Sunday streets.

CARLU *Palais de Chaillot, Paris*

**CARLU, JACQUES (1890–    )** *French Architect* Carlu was one of a great series of French Beaux-Arts proselytizers that American schools imported for their cultural rectification—Carlu at M.I.T., Cret at the University of Pennsylvania, Labatut at Princeton, and so forth. Their influence, long belittled, is only now being reappraised, and newly appreciated (as in the [New York] Museum of Modern

55

Art's retrospective of École des Beaux-Arts drawings, fall, 1975). Carlu was architect for the Palais de Chaillot in Paris, on axis with the Eiffel Tower and Champs de Mars (but on the other side of the Seine).

**CAROLINGIAN ARCHITECTURE** *Carol* = Charles + *Magne* = Leader = Charles the Leader. Charlemagne spent 46 years (768–814) as king, then as emperor of the Holy Roman Empire.

Aachen Cathedral (in the French-German no-man's land called Aix-la-Chapelle) is one of the great spartan-rich stone polygonal central spaces of all history, on a par with Rome's S. Stephano Rotondo and S. Costanza and S. Vitale at Ravenna.

**CARPORT** When modern architecture confronted the car, it at once considered it an appendage to the house: a mobile detachment, a portable piece, an exploratory vessel.

Its port (attachment) became a pass-through roofed area that allowed the car to dock against the house door, rather than be stored, in horse-barnlike fashion, in a garage.

**CARRARA** Italian mountain source of sheer, unfigured marble that provides the crisp white forms of classic and Classical architecture (with that of Pentelicus, the quarry of the Parthenon).

**CARREL** A monkish niche; later, a niche used by students for study within a library.

**CARRÈRE, JOHN (1858–1911)** *American Architect* The New York Public Library (1898+), by Carrère and Hastings, is full-blown Beaux-Arts facing Fifth Avenue, with sculpted guardian lions and formal terraces. Its rear, on Bryant Park, is a protofunctionalist expression of library stacks.

**CARTOON** A graphic idea, suggesting a three-dimensional product, as in the cartoon of a stained-glass window, drawn for the glassmaker's artisan-work. The cartoon is the design, or "artist's" product; the glass the artisan's result.

**CARTOUCHE** A scroll carved in stone on a building façade and inscribed with formal words remembering or honoring deeds: a cartouche cannot very well be humble.

CARRÈRE *New York Public Library*

**CARVAJAL, JAVIER** *Twentieth-Century Spanish Architect* The Spanish Pavilion at the New York World's Fair (1965) was an unexpected architectural delight. While democracy foundered in banality (cf. the U.S. Pavilion), the Falange of Spain provided an exciting building by Carvajal (Gruzen and Partners assisted): serene, rich, exciting, without the vulgar virtuosity so often symbolic of modern "fairs": stucco, tile, wood grills joined, incidentally providing that fair's only grand dining places (the Granada and Toledo restaurants). Good taste in food and architecture there joined.

**CARYATID** Minoan columns (as in the Palace at Knossos, Crete) were said to be imbued with spirit; the carved matter was believed to contain a holy being: a state sometimes called animism.

Caryatids, on the other hand, are columns in the form of erect women, supporting an architrave on crown-padded heads. Nothing could be more statuesque. These well-formed ladies had no claim to spirit or spirits. Those at the Erechtheum, near the Parthenon on Athen's Acropolis, are most notorious.

**CASEMENT** A window, door-like, that opens into or out of a space, usually a full aperture, as opposed to double-hung (upward sliding) or horizontal sliding units that can only be opened for a part of the glazed area.

**CASINO** A dancing place, a tennis place, a gambling place (Rococo garden architecture; the Newport Casino by Stanford White and Garnier's casino at Monte Carlo respectively).

**CAST-IN-PLACE** Concrete, poured, sluiced into forms to its permanent position and status, as opposed to precast or prefabricated concrete. Called *in situ* by the British.

**CAST IRON** Industry's revolution liberated manufacturing from the hands of man, increased his lot and his salary, and relieved him of the burden of handcrafts to a great extent. Carved stone and marble became too expensive; but the cause of this economic act, the revolution itself, provided the alternate cure: cast iron. Don't carve your columns, brackets, consoles, arches, cornices, and whatnots. Pour them. And pour them they did in endless handsome Palladian, Sanmichelian, Brunelleschian, pure Greek and Roman

CARYATID

57

façades that still line the streets of Manhattan's cast-iron district (inappropriately called SoHo these days).

More important, of course, than the façades were and are the guts of the buildings behind. There economics eventually decreed cast-iron columns instead of walls, to provide the flexibility of commercial layout, with wrought-iron beams to support each tier of floor superposed.

**CASTLE**   1. A large house protected and defended by walls, siting, moats, and ha-has, as well as people. 2. A royal fortified residence. 3. Where fairy, and sometimes real, princesses come from.

Buckingham Palace and the Louvre are palaces, as is Castle Howard. Neuschwanstein wished it were a castle, and its patron, Bavarian King Ludwig II, yearned for dragons and maidens but settled for Richard Wagner as houseguest. Hamlet had a castle, and whole Italian hill towns took a castle form (Volterra, dramatically). Castles in literature and architecture based on literature ( e.g., Neuschwanstein) are more an idea in the mind of an author and reader than an exactly specified building type.

CASTLE *Segovia, Spain*

**CAT**   A small horizontal stick of wood (say 2 × 4) that braces adjacent studs to each other and serves as a receiver of nails that fasten sheet material to the whole assembly (Sheetrock, paneling, or what have you).

**CATALANO, EDUARDO (1917–    )** *Argentine American Architect*   His own "hyperbolic paraboloid" house of 1954 at Raleigh, where he headed the department of architecture (University of North Carolina), focused attention on him. He later went to M.I.T., taught and built the monumental Student Center (1963), a large place that never learned the lessons of Beaux-Arts "circulation."

**CATARACT**   The cascades of a river, more precipitous than rapids, that are geological checkpoints, as the Nile's six cataracts between Cairo and Khartoum. On the Nile, the old (1902) and new (1972) Aswan dams are yet more impenetrable and impressive barriers.

**CATENARY**   The limp shape of a string, rope or cable, strung between two points under its own weight. Suspension bridges are almost-catenaries, equally weighted along their length by the weight of bridge surface (and travelers) below: the Brooklyn Bridge is the most famous and handsome product of catenary engineering.

**CATHEDRAL**   The church where a bishop is present and the site of his chair, or cathedra. Since bishops administer the church in large geographical areas, or where there is dense population, they traditionally are assigned to whole regions or cities: western Massachusetts, Chicago, Paris, Uganda are dioceses and have one cathedral each. *Cathedral* does not necessarily imply size, although pride and religious fervor caused their multiplication in areas such as the Île de France in the eleventh, twelfth, and thirteenth centuries: the cathedrals of Rheims, Chartres, Amiens, Rouen, Laôn, and Paris are all in an area the size of Connecticut and were almost simultaneously constructed, serving a total population of 500,000 zealots.

**CAULK**   The wattle and daub of modern architecture that fills crevice, slot, and aperture left after all is assembled. Usually an inert and semipermanent plastic material, it provides for, and corrects, natural mistakes.

**CAVETTO**   Later Italian word for earlier Egyptian-derived molding. Originally used to describe the profile of a house cornice plaited from straw and reeds that curved out from the face of a building. At a tinier scale, it became a molding of the same profile in Renaissance architecture.

**CAVITY WALL**   Two planes (called wythes) of masonry separated by an air space. They are braced to each other by metal ties. The assembly allows exposed masonry both in and outside a building, as the moisture that penetrates the outer wythe is drained off within the cavity.

**CEILING**   The top surface, or canopy, of an interior space: sometimes the underside of a roof, or floor, above; sometimes a separate and independent surface.

Under traditional pitched roofs, a ceiling is often the underside of an attic floor. In Renaissance architecture a hung (suspended) metal framework supports a complex configuration of plaster and wood domes, vaults, coffers, and other sinuous and geometric enrichments.

CATHEDRAL *Chartres Cathedral*

**CELLA**  The space within a Greek temple, a sanctuary of the god or goddess to whom the temple is erected. Not public in view or use, the space was incidental to the public's religious experience: a distant worship, where the building counted as an object, a role later inverted in the public, participatory, internal worship of Christianity.

**CELLAR**  Place of cells. Built space below ground (with, therefore, no built form). Frequently it is the storage and utility space of a modern house, rarely a functional necessity, as is a root or mushroom cellar or a cellar constructed for foundation reasons (to get down to solider ground or to make a building act as a boat in a soggy place).

**CEMENT**  The glue of architecture is Portland cement, a prepared natural (cooked) lime material that chemically solidifies when joined with aggregate, sand, and water and is shaped by a container (formwork) into which it is poured. It is, in one sense, artificial stone, except that with the aid of an armature of steel reinforcing bars it can serve as a beam or column, which stone cannot, except as a lintel (short beam) or stubby column; stone is brittle in the tension caused by either structural element's flexure.

Cement, generically, is any glue used to adhere one material to another: rubber cement, airplane cement, epoxy cement, asphaltic cement, and so forth.

CENOTAPH *Soldiers and Sailors Monument, New York*

**CEMETERY**  The cellar boxes of the dead, landmarked by simple stone (and, rarely, metal) slabs or grand memorial buildings. Their collective assembly, a kind of minisuburban garden city, devours the landscape for the sake of survivors' egos, an understandable but pernicious disease. Some ancient and rare cemeteries have preserved and even enhanced landscape (as Greenwood in Brooklyn), but most are dull, endless and antithetical to urban society.

If the annual death-mass (2%, or 80,000,000) were buried in cemeteries, it would occupy 80,000 acres (ten times the size of Rome) each year.

**CENOTAPH**  An abstract monument, as opposed to a memorial sculpture, to a person buried elsewhere. The Lincoln and Jefferson memorials are memorial buildings, but the Washington Monument and the Albert Memorial are cenotaphs.

**CENTERING**   The temporary scaffolding for an arch or vault, on which the masonry is temporarily supported until the keystone is placed and the mortar sets.

**CENTRAL HEATING**   A phrase invented by the English to describe what they don't have and consider, possibly, *nouveau riche* (i.e., American).

Central heating implies a furnace (with pipes or ducts), rather than a fireplace (or that other radical American invention, the Franklin stove. Yes, it was *Ben* Franklin).

**CESSPOOL**   Loose stone or grilled concrete forms a porous tank: where the waste of human life meets the ground (in most primitive style) and is leached (absorbed) therein.

**CHAIR**   A major piece of indoor sculpture, developed from those of Tutankhamen's tomb (through Louis XIV and myriad others) to Charles Eames or Le Corbusier. Chairs are like cars, personal ego items allowing license to their proprietors.

**CHAIR RAIL**   An over- or inlaid projecting piece of wood some 30 inches off the floor to deflect the impact of furniture.

**CHAMBERS, (SIR) WILLIAM (1723–1796)** *English Architect* A superbly Establishment architect, he tutored the Prince of Wales (later George IV) and served as George III's architect and surveyor-general (roughly equivalent to an autocratic director of public works) for England.

His Chinese Pagoda at Kew (Gardens) was a forerunner of the exotic rural monuments in England that produced ruins as products in themselves and Oriental garden structures *ad nauseum*. The prince became regent (1811) for his dotty father, and the Regency, as a style, drew much on Chambers's preliminary work.

**CHAMFER**   To dull an edge by skinning off its right angle to a 45-degree bevel.

**CHANCEL**   The stage of Christianity, where clergy serve the altar, and at whose edge the congregation kneels to take the blood and flesh of Christ (symbolically) at Communion. A physical place, the

CHAMBERS *Somerset House, London*

61

east (usually) end of a church, beyond the transepts or crossing (when they exist).

**CHANCERY** Building of an embassy, as in the American Embassy's chancery in Grosvenor Square, London, or the Papal Chancery (Cancelleria) in Rome.

**CHANDELIER** Holder of candles (*chandelles,* in French), and then, by custom, the suspended holder of candles. The word flowered, particularly in Baroque secularism, to embrace the polyglitter of any pendant sculptured light construction, first candled, then gassed, now electrified. Those at Lincoln Center's Metropolitan Opera rise and fall at the whim of electronically controlled motors.

**CHANNEL** Route for water, or traffic within a piece of water. Also a form of steel that, U-shaped, serves as a special structural member.

**CHAPEL** A personal religious place and space, where the one honored and worshipped is the cause or catalyst of construction (Lady Chapel at Westminster Abbey for the worship of the Virgin Mary); or, it is a private owner's place of worship of a generally accepted god, as the chapel (for Louis XIV by Hardouin-Mansart) at Versailles.

**CHAPTERHOUSE** The conference room of a monastic order, connected to its cloister (meditation), cells (dwelling), and refectory (dining). The large population attending meetings sometimes caused a major structural solution: Gothic vaulting to a central pier.

CHAPTERHOUSE *The Cloisters, New York*

**CHARRETTE** A cart (in French) that came to collect the architectural works (in drawing form) of a student in any atelier (professor's workshop) of the École des Beaux-Arts in Paris, mostly between 1860 and 1930.

The word came to mean the harried period in which a student's final drawings were, hopefully, completed. "On Charrette" was the period in which the designer literally finished his work on or in the cart on the way to judgment!

**CHASE** The space for conduits to pass (plumbing, electrical, etc.). One chases (cuts or allows space) through construction.

**CHÂTEAU**  Literally, "castle" in French. A country place, French-style, for the wealthy, if not the titled. Although identical in meaning, the château conjures up images of romance no English country house can: Chambord, Chaumont, or Vaux-le-Vicomte (châteaux) are grander thoughts than Grimsthorpe, Northwick Park, or Ebberston Lodge.

**CHERMAYEFF, SERGE (1900–    )** *Russian-English-American Architect*  One-time partner of Eric Mendelsohn (London, 1933–36). After winning the commission in competition, they created a classic modern monument, the de la Warr Pavilion at Bexhill (1934–35). Chermayeff taught at Brooklyn, the Institute of Design (Chicago), Harvard, and now Yale. His sons Peter and Ivan carry on the name as architect and graphic designer, respectively.

**CHEVET**  The whole set of chancel, ambulatory, and chapels in, particularly, a French Gothic church.

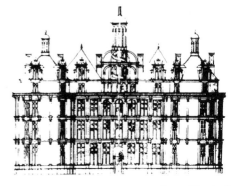

CHÂTEAU *Chambord*

**CHICAGO**  Steeped in the spirit of homesteading and the covered wagon, these pioneer urban outlanders embraced the new technology of structural steel and electric elevators. The skyscraper was born in Chicago, far from the oversophisticated architects of New York, where architecture was constipated by service to the very rich and constrained by its Beaux-Arts training, which considered the scale of a palace an appropriate urban form for everything. New York learned and exploited the Chicago lesson, but later and less well.

The Chicago School of architecture gave aesthetic stature to these high-rise grillage buildings. Saint of the movement was Louis Sullivan, whose Carson, Pirie Scott Store (1899) is a holy relic: a highly articulated steel cage, glazed with the Chicago window that filled each bay, and decorated with Sullivan's glorious decorative incisions (a kind of personal Art Nouveau).

More spartan and sticklike is the Reliance Building (1894, Burnham and Root). The "School" was concerned previously and simultaneously with an architecture of masonry and Romanesque arched bearing walls (Richardsonian Romanesque, as at H. H. Richardson's Marshall Field Warehouse) and started Frank Lloyd Wright on his ways, as he had worked for Sullivan, who in turn was a former Richardson employee.

**CHICAGO WINDOW** Horizontal window consuming a whole bay in steel-caged architecture; its unfortunate descendant is the picture window, a fixed central pane that had been flanked on both sides in the original by pivoted window sash.

**CHIMNEY** Even without need for heat or cooking, chimneys appeared to punctuate both romantic and formal compositions. Chambord, great palace of the Loire Valley, bears a roofscape of chimneys as decorated finials, equal to a peacock's plumage, to be seen and savored, crowning a formal Renaissance château.

Conversely, at the Casa Milá in Barcelona, by Antoni Gaudí, chimneys become exotic sculpture in a private roofscaped world, only partly and distantly visible from below.

The stone chimney has offered a compositional armature for a whole school of artsy-craftsy or just plain corny houses (except in the hands of Frank Lloyd Wright himself; at Taliesin, his Wisconsin summer home, they are at least camp).

CHIMNEYS *Chateau of Chambord, Loire Valley, France*

**CHOIR** The place in a church (often coincidental with the chancel) where choirs sing and sit, named after its sometime residents.

**CHROMIUM** That precious metal used sparingly to skin the less precious and both preserve and enrich it by a silverlike, nontarnishing reflectivity. In architecture it came from the automobile, where articulating parts adorn the basic painted metal shell. A symbol of modernity and industrialization, it reaches high style in the tubular furniture of Marcel Breuer and the flat steel bands of Mies van der Rohe. Evelyn Waugh dealt it a blow in *A Handful of Dust,* where the protagonist suggested (to bring the crumbling country house to modern high style) that he would chromium-plate the walls!

**CHURCH** A lord's house, but, particularly, the Lord's House for the public worship of Christ. Church architecture was born out of Roman precedents, modern in its time, and first adapted the basilica, or place of business, to house its liturgy. At the beginning of official Christianity (Constantine's edict of 312), consecrated basilicas became Early Christian churches, a style in their own right.

Samples of the style, if not the reuse of specific structures, include S. Lorenzo fuori le Mure (St. Lawrence Outside the Walls), at the east gate of Rome, and S. Apollinare Nuovo, near Ravenna.

**CHURCH, THOMAS D. (1902–    )** *American Landscape Architect*  Early professional in, in spite of Olmsted and Downing, a slow-growing profession until after World War II.

**CHURCHILL, HENRY (1893–1962)** *American Architect and Planner*  Churchill shared honors (in the 1930's) with Henry Wright and Clarence Stein as an early promoter designer of public housing. An attractive tile and glass store for Weyhe (art and architectural books) and New York's first suspended office building (floors hung from a central core) at 137 East 57th Street are his most noted commissions. He never received the critical praise he deserved.

**CHURRIGUERESQUE**  The exponentially multiplying decoration of the Late Renaissance and Baroque periods (seventeenth and eighteenth centuries) in Spain and Spanish colonies. To destroy a surface totally by carving created an excess of ornamentation that fits the analogy "you can't see the forest for the trees." José Churriguera (1665–1725) started it all.

**C.I.A.M. CONGRÈS INTERNATIONAL D'ARCHITECTURE MODERNE (1928–1960)**  The product of a patron (Hélène de Mandrot) and an occasion, the verbal birthings of Le Corbusier and Sigfried Giedion, C.I.A.M. tried proselytizing, but ended in doldrums, this new academy attempting to replace the remnants of the old (i.e., the École des Beaux-Arts). The arrogance of new libertarianism is often self-destroying; and the cure becomes the new disease. It faded like the old soldier (General Douglas MacArthur's farewell speech to a joint session of Congress, 1953: "Old soldiers never die, they just fade away").

**CIAMPI, MARIO (1907–    )** *American Architect*  Northern California's most sleek suburban maker of institutional forms: as in his corrugated doughnut (school) at Daly City (1959). He won (with acknowledged help of employees) the competition for the University Arts Center (1962, Berkeley), a facile solution to the problem stated, designed more for histrionic effect than use.

CIAMPI *School, Daly City, California*

**CIBORIUM**  Synonym for *Baldacchino.*

**CINDERBLOCK** Brick's bigger and coarser brother, formed and cast from Portland cement and an aggregate, this time of cinders. Various blends of aggregates and cement (which comes in shades ranging from white through gray to tan) create different colors and textures. The block size (usually 8 × 8 × 18 inches) is attractive economically, partly due to union regulations that allow a single man to lay it (it is at the maximum weight limit).

Block has achieved architectural distinction in recent years, at such buildings as Rudolph's New Haven housing for the elderly and those elegant houses of Joe and Mary Merz in Brooklyn rows. (See also *Block*.)

**CINQUEFOIL** Gothic tracery pattern, reminiscent of a five-leafed clover's silhouette.

**CIRCULATION** Analogy word, relating the movement of pedestrian or vehicle within a building, precinct, or city to the flow of blood in the body's circulatory system—both necessary for the life of their respective entities.

**CIRCUS** A building for view of athletic events by an audience: long, with rounded end(s), its geometry once accommodated chariot racing but also became the scene for many special and exotic events. The annual elephant and trapeze spectacle that we now enjoy (on behalf of children) in Europe, Africa, and America is named for its ancestor's assigned place and is, semantically, similar to calling a play a theater.

The Piazza Navona in Rome is the magnificently redecorated site of the Roman Circus of Domitian; its circus building has become the void that defines the space: four times as long as it is wide, with one rounded end.

**CISTERN** A tank for the storage of rain-gathered fresh water. The pump in rural and old-fashioned kitchen sinks drew from a well or cistern.

**CITADEL** 1. An internal city fortress (as opposed to its bastioned outer walls). The citadel is the concentric eye within the city heart that complements the ring of city walls. It is to a city as a keep is to a castle, the place to withdraw at last resort (cf. Quebec, Cairo, New Delhi).

2. An attached fort with its own identity, adjacent to a town, to draw and give fire, parallelogram to hexagon in plan. New York's Castle Clinton was, in origin, a semicitadel (impure, since it was round) on an island, connected by a bridge to the Battery, a defensive line of cannon protecting (in fashion similar to medieval fortified walls, but without the wall) lower Manhattan's tip.

**CITY BEAUTIFUL**   "Brand name" applied to the reuse of classical Renaissance forms in an ordered civic architecture, derived from the supersample of such ideology: the World's Columbian Exposition (Chicago World's Fair of 1893). The City Beautiful drew from the boulevards of Haussmann's Paris, linear gardenways, flanked with uniformly corniced housing, recalled in New York's Park Avenue (narrower, without the trees, and with taller buildings) and the diagonal avenues of Washington, D.C., as designed by Pierre L'Enfant, and re-birthed by Daniel Burnham, master planner of *the* Exposition.

CITY BEAUTIFUL *Columbian Exposition, 1893*

**CITYSCAPE**   Popword for the total and superficial visual arrangements of a city's buildings, streets, parks, planting, and street furniture (lampposts, light standards, hydrants, curbs, benches, fences, walls, bollards, manhole covers, paving). Cityscape borrows verbal intent from landscape. It is the major (and, paradoxically, most superficial) facet of what various concerned have termed from time to time civic design, city planning, and/or urban design.

**CIVIL ENGINEERING**   Engineering for the general public, as opposed to military engineering. Renaissance architects tended to specialize in the latter, often producing more fortifications than palazzi. When great public works became commissions (bridges, dams, water and sanitary systems, large-scale topographic arrangements and drainage) as part of the Industrial Revolution, civil engineering became a profession of and on its own.

**CLAPBOARD**   Long boards lapping (clapping) each other horizontally, like linear shingles, usually painted earth colors in the architecture of pre-1776 New England, later white (then expensive and a sign of wealth) in the affluent new technology of post-1800. The clapboard shields and drips the rain and dampness like a duck's feathers. It was the natural radial wafer split from a round log.

**CLASSIC** Of a superior taxpaying Roman class! (And hence desirable.) By analogy *classic* came to refer to the whole literature and physical environment of Rome, and, hence, by extension, Greece.

Now anything admired and superior of its kind is termed classic: classic cars, classic architecture, classic clothes.

**CLASSICAL** Classical architecture is classic, but, more specifically, architecture from fifth-century-B.C. Greece to second-century-A.D. Rome.

**CLASSICAL REVIVAL** The general term for Greek and Roman revivals, where literal use of Classical Greek and Roman building parts and assemblies contrasts with the concurrent revival of Renaissance architecture that used the same source materials to different ends. (See also *Greek Revival.*)

**CLASSICISM** A rerun of classic and Classical forms, as opposed to the Renaissance use of the decorative vocabulary of formal Classical parts arranged in new ways for new programs and a new aesthetic.

Classicism was concerned with the freestanding column and pediment, rather than their decorative or attached application, and even the simplification of the final idea into a geometry of cylinder, cube, and eventually sphere and pyramid. Classicism, therefore, embraced architects as diverse as Schinkel, Ledoux, Thomas Jefferson, and Lord Burlington.

**CLEAT** An extra piece of wood to which something may be fastened, as the cleat that supports your closet coat-rod.

**CLERESTORY** Clear story. Clear of the adjacent portions of the building below, usually windowed to allow light into the central space(s) of the building. A churchly dome is a kind of clerestory, but not normally so called. Most typical is the linear set of nave and aisles in a Gothic church, where the nave is higher, allowing clerestory walls over adjacent aisles and opportunity for stained glass to bathe the nave in diffuse and dim light.

Oldest extant clerestory is that of the Temple of Karnak at Luxor in Upper Egypt, now 3100 years old (Chartres is a mere 700).

**CLÉRISSEAU, CHARLES-LOUIS (1721–1820)** *French Architect*
Atelier teacher of Thomas Jefferson and the Adam brothers, as well
as Sir William Chambers. His own work was minimal in quantity and
quality, but that of his students far greater (and more international)
than any similarly ensconced patron of a Beaux-Arts atelier.

**CLERK OF THE WORKS** An imported term. Clerk is a somewhat more elegant function in England than its American understanding will allow; and *the works* is the English term for a
construction (building, bridge, highway). The clerk of the works is
the architect's full-time representative on a job to check that what
is being done is as intended.

**CLIENT** Party to the building process, a symbiosis as necessary
as that of a male and female being present at conception. Painters,
musicians, even sculptors create their end product unilaterally for
ultimate sale after the creative fact; architects' clients must employ
the architect *before* the creative fact (or act), and hence base their
choice on reputation and past history, not present product. Clients
have, therefore, much greater burdens in architecture. Those who
were great were blessed with foresight, rather than mere hindsight,
and often are due as much credit for their impact on the history of
architecture as the architect himself: Pope Julius II, Louis XIV, the
American Astors and Vanderbilts were setups as clients for aggran-
dizement of the church, the king, and the nouveau riche, in that
order. Modern clients are braver and, in that spirit, "put their
money where their mouth is." Great current clients include corporations and public (governmental) agencies. The General Motors
Technical Center and CBS Building, both by Eero Saarinen; the
Seagram Building, by Mies van der Rohe and Philip Johnson; the
Economist Buildings, by the Smithsons; much of the New York State
University system; the Sydney Opera House; Brazil's capital at Brasília: all are products of great government and corporate clients
taking a risk on the quality of a still-future environment.

**CLIFF DWELLING** Under a southwestern American cliff's brow,
and raised from the valley floor below, are tucked urban stone and
mudbrick clusters, dense, multistoried, civilizing retreats of the Indians who farmed the mesas above: Mesa Verde is most famous, in
southwestern Colorado.

CLIFF DWELLING *Montezuma's
Castle, Arizona*

69

**CLIMATE**  The weather of a place, suggesting a combination of temperature, dry- or wet-ness, and wind, and grossly called tropical, desert, temperate, rainforested, arctic, pleasant, or nice. Climate is the product of location on the surface of the globe and the by-products that go with it: sun radiation as the largest principal force of influence, wind, and the movement of moisture. Climate is the environmental state to which architecture is in part a foil, sheltering and shielding man, or harboring his conditioned environment.

**CLOISTER**  Originally the whole monastery or convent, but in modern usage the arcaded courtyard of medieval monastic life, a private open space between church and dwelling where monks might contemplate a manicured excerpt of nature and a framed sky. Cloisters contained herb and flower gardens.

*The* Cloisters is a collection of real French and Spanish monastic parts bought by Rockefeller money, disassembled, and re-created on northern Manhattan Island to form a super-Romanesque museum.

CLOISTER *The Cloisters, New York*

**CLOSE**  A private, closed place, giving access to houses; a private street and/or court. The rural English church (and/or cathedral) was closed by its close's courtyard walls.

**CLOSET**  A small room for self- or conferring privacy, later taken for description of private conferences of importance regardless of the premises ("the ambassador was closeted with the President"). In later, popular speech, the closet was reduced to nonhuman dimensions, as a storage compartment for clothing (pendant) and household supplies (shelved and hooked).

**COAT**  A skin-thick layer on any object or surface, most frequently paint or a paintlike material.

**COATES, WELLS (1895–1958)** *English Engineer, Journalist, and Architect*  From Ph.D. in diesel engines (London University) to disciple of C.I.A.M. Coates was an early modern English mass-houser. He helped Sir Frederick Gibberd win the competition for the Metropolitan Cathedral, Liverpool.

**COBBLE**  An almost round fieldstone, selected from those strewn about by nature's glaciers, collected in graded sizes (6 to 8 inches in diameter), and used for paving urban streets. Strictly speaking, most people's "cobblestones" are paving blocks, cut from hard stone, rather than naturally collected, for only the most venerable streets still retain the latter.

In northern New Jersey, houses are built of cobbles, giving them a kind of regular, round-rusticated, neo-Renaissance texture.

**CODE**　A set of legal rules that constrain the building process—building code, electrical code, plumbing code—most commonly based on need for safety, health, and the protection of neighborly interests.

**CODERCH DE SENTMENAT, JOSÉ ANTONIO (1917–　　)**
*Spanish Architect*　Simple, unselfconscious modernist, like his fellow countryman Carvajal or the Italian Gardella, his architecture is one of a low-keyed Cubism and spartan materials. Internal spaces are rich with natural materials, furnishings, and muted light. Witness his own house on the Costa Brava, where sliding shutters are the most strident architectural part on form that has the detail of vanilla ice cream: delicious. He also built an elegant modern town house in Barcelona for the painter Tapies.

**COFFER**　Deeply recessed ceiling or soffit ornamentations, square or polygonal, that suggest a highly gilt and polychromed tripe: sometimes added as a Baroque gesture on existing churches, as the cadaverous gilt extravaganza over S. Clemente or S. Maria in Aracoeli (both Rome); sometimes part of a whole new architecture, as at the Henry IV ballroom of Fontainebleau (Delorme) or the Pantheon at Rome.

**COFFERDAM**　Temporary dam to segregate workspace below water from the water surrounding; sometimes an open box, sometimes peninsular in relation to a structure or land mass to which it is attached. In common contemporary usage, sheet material is driven (like piling) into the ground, lapping with and interlocking its neighbor, a second membrane some feet away, and the intervening space filled with earth.

COLBERT *Phyllis Wheatley Elementary School, New Orleans*

**COLBERT, CHARLES (1921–　　)** *American Architect*　Colbert's Phyllis Wheatley Elementary School (1955, New Orleans) bears a structural steel frame as sophisticated and important to its architectural posture as that of Mies at Illinois Institute of Technology's Crown Hall (School of Architecture; 1956+) or the Smithsons' Hunstanton School (1954, Norfolk). It is a school *in* a truss hovering over open space below.

**COLLARBEAM**   The tie between two pitched rafters that limits their natural tendency to deflect or spread. Collars become the ceiling joists (supports for plaster or Sheetrock) in attic spaces.

**COLLATERAL**   Literally, at the side of. And, in finance, the presentation and commitment of objects or securities of value to guarantee a loan. Collateral must be portable and cannot, therefore, be real estate.

COLONIAL *New England house before 1776*

**COLONIAL**   The period of a place's architecture in its historical status as a colony, as in America or India or much of South America. Colonial America's history ended (according to Americans) in 1776, at the moment of the Declaration of Independence; according to Britain in 1783, the moment of the peace treaty.

*Colonial* (American), as a catchall, is applied popularly to almost anything before the Civil War: particularly houses and churches of white clapboard or brick, with many-paned, shuttered windows and gabled or gambreled shingle roofs.

In fact, only the simpler examples, those built prior to the Revolution, are properly cited. Most misnamed Colonial works are post-Revolutionary, the more sophisticated Federal and Greek Revival buildings that bulk grandly in Boston or Newport or Salem or scores of New England towns and villages.

More venerable are the earth-colored, small-windowed houses of the seventeenth century, as the Old Witch's House at Salem, and the rather grand brick architecture (artfully re-created with Rockefeller money) at Williamsburg, Virginia.

Spanish colonial architecture brought Baroque exuberance to many separate South American countries; the English colonial, in India, created late Renaissance pomp (Viceroy's House by Sir Edwin Lutyens).

**COLONNADE**   A row of columns supporting a beam or architrave or series of arches.

**COLUMBIAN EXPOSITION** *Chicago World's Fair of 1893*   See *Burnham, Daniel H.; Sullivan, Louis; City Beautiful.*

**COLUMN**  A vertical support; sticklike member of a structural system; usually slender. Wider supports include piers, pillars, and pilasters. Columns may be modern or ancient; steel, masonry, concrete, or cut stone; exposed to the eye or buried in a wall; incidental and practical supports or decorative and dominant (and even structurally unnecessary) architectural parts.

The Greeks used columns as the basic architectural element of their most important buildings: temples. The "orders" of architecture are those sets of parts, the most important element of which is the column (each set includes base, or stylobate, and entablature: architrave, frieze, and cornice, and are termed: Doric, Ionic, or Corinthian, each named after the place inhabited by a subgroup of ancient Greek culture).

Egyptians were concerned with the visual use of the column in internal religious space, to dominate and define that space: columns occupied almost as much area as the voids between them.

Minoans (very early Mediterraneans in Crete, ca. 2000–1200 B.C.) even worshipped columns (animism), placing them in the unlikely center of a small space as a sculptural-religious object imbued with life.

**COMMISSION**  The contract to create the design of a building or other object. It is a somewhat grander title than "order" or "employ" and implies a single, purposeful, prescribed product.

**COMMUNISM**  Liberal or radical politics do not by their nature support liberal or radical architecture, although after the Bolshevik victory in Russia there was a radical spin-off called Constructivism in the twenties. Short-lived, it was supplanted by Stalin's wishful wedding cakes, those towered, quasi-Renaissance structures he imagined might bring culture to the masses, or at least would be smoothly swallowed by them as the proletariat's just desserts taken from the late capitalist table. Art, even social art, requires leisure time to contemplate, unavailable in a proletarian society: buildings tend to be dumpy takeoffs of the architecture of the former masters.

Not surprisingly, in the late affluence of Soviet society leisure has become rampant, and architecture has revived its vigor, as in the many-splendored Miami along the resort strip on the Black Sea coast and the new Lincoln Center-like Hall of the People in the Kremlin, where the Supreme Soviet meets.

China's architecture is, naturally, at stage one, the nonleisured

COLUMN *Colonnade, Piazza S. Pietro, Rome*

frowse of the Soviet Union in the thirties. Time heals and changes, and the Chinese modern renaissance should flower by the end of the century.

**COMPETITION**   Competitions are devices to explore untapped architectural talent by requesting, formally, designs from anybody, or a specially selected group, and evaluating them one against the other before a pre-selected jury. Competitions have produced everything from the dome of the Cathedral (Duomo) of Florence to the exotic balloon sails of the Sydney Opera House. A competition can only be as good as its symbiotic contestants and jurors, and, unfortunately, many in recent years have been dominated by one or another juror to the detriment of the built product. The latter include the competitions at Sydney for the mentioned opera house and at Toronto for a city hall, both dominated by Eero Saarinen, a willful and arbitrary form-maker himself. The products are more sensational than substantial, rather extravagant attempts at virtuosity of form.

On the contrary, Florence's Duomo is a masterpiece, and McKim, Mead and White's Municipal Building (1914) a gem of urban placement. Most successful modern example is Kallmann, McKinnell and Knowles's Boston City Hall (1962).

**COMPOSITE ORDER**   When enough is not enough; late Hellenes and Romans crossed Ionic and Corinthian orders to produce this composite.

**COMPUTER**   An intellectual robot that, on orders of a human, performs functions laborious or even impossible (in the time available) to a human: an extension of his mind and intent. The computer is feared in architecture by the intuitive designer as a mechanistic alternative to his humanistic values, creativity, and foibles. The fear is based on a misunderstanding of the computer's true abilities; in fact, the only functions it replaces are rote and drudgery.

**CONCRETE**   Particularly Portland cement concrete: the man-made substitute for cast stone, chemically synthesized from cement, water, and aggregate. Later sophisticates understood its structural possibilities, in concert with reinforcing steel, and produced reinforced concrete (*béton armé*) that still competes with steel framing for the right to form the cage structures of American high-rise building.

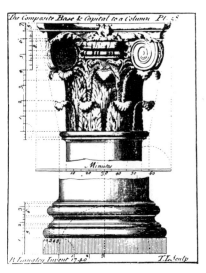

COMPOSITE ORDER *Column capital*

**CONDENSATION**   Water, dissolved in the air—as air (that fish breathe) is dissolved in water—comes out (condenses) when the temperature it touches is cold: hence condensation on a window pane, cooled by the air on the other side, causing the warm, wet air inside to dump its moisture on the pane. (The colder the air, the less its capacity to hold water.)

**CONDIT, CARL (1914–    )** *American Architectural Historian*
Serious historian of Chicago's nascent architecture and the whole technology of the Industrial Revolution. *The Chicago School of Architecture* (1964) and *American Building Art, Nineteenth and Twentieth Centuries* (1961) are classic textbooks in American schools of architecture.

**CONDOMINIUM**   A way of subowning an apartment house or other multiple dwelling so that each space is owned and mortgaged at whatever point it rests in space: on or off ground. The alternate is called *cooperative,* where joint ownership of a building is subdivided by assignment, one owning part of the whole, not his whole part.

**CONDUIT**   Linear void; a tube, shielded from damage, dirt, and moisture, laid into a building's construction at the start and available for the snaking of wires (electric, telephone, signal) at any later date.

**CONSERVATION**   The act of conserving buildings, cities, and environments for society; an act of economy of resource opposed to the relentless rebuilding of all cities and buildings that has been typical of, particularly, America.
  Preservation is an overt act in response to threat; conservation is the continuing love that forestalls the need for preservation.

**CONSOLES**   Brackets of (originally) stone that support projecting cornices, balconies, and other similar elements in Classical architecture. (See also *Modillion.*)

**CONTEMPORARY**   Of the moment. *Modern,* a more general term, describes a state of time and style contrasting with "antiquity." Antiquity to Rubens in his seventeenth-century book, *Palazzi Antichi di Genova* (1622), was the fifteenth century, while to us it seems before Christ. *Contemporary* is, however, a superficial and

CONSOLE *Bracket supporting an entablature, White House, Brooklyn*

ephemeral word, loosely attached to popular current architecture and design, rather than the more serious, long-lived modern movements. Pseudo-Danish furniture and stoned ranch houses might be contemporary for the record, while a Mies house or chair is modern suggesting the classic, as opposed to the expedient or timely.

**CONTOUR**   The shape or profile of anything, but particularly used for nongeometric natural form: contours of the human form, or land. The latter is described, in drawings, by contour lines that delimit the height (usually above sea level) of all points by connecting equal levels with a continuous line at fixed intervals (1-foot contours, 50-foot contours, and so forth). Thus, three-dimensional relief can be simulated with two dimensions, for breast, buttocks, hill, or mountain range.

**CONTRACT**   Any agreement to exchange goods or services for "consideration": something of equivalent value (in the eyes of the contractors), whether money or other goods and services. An architectural contract is the legal document supporting a commission.

**CONURBATION**   In urbanization, towns tend to bleed together, forming a continuous ultimate form. Sir Patrick Geddes coined and first used the word, in 1910, more a promise than a threat, now seemingly the ultimate fate of dense urban regions, such as the Washington-Boston "corridor," a string of cities tending to come together in a "linear" conurbation. (See also *Megalopolis*.)

CORBEL TABLE *Iffley, Oxfordshire*

**CONVECTION**   House heat is distributed typically by convectors, mis-termed *radiators,* warming air that passes by conduction (touch). The air becomes lighter, having expanded as it warms, and rises, causing it to wander about the room (convection).

**CONVENT**   A coming together, originally applied to a religious community of men or women; now, principally to women, as in a nunnery. The set of words describing such overlapping parallel buildings and communities includes *cloister, monastery, convent, nunnery, abbey.*

**COOPERATIVE**   Any venture of a group jointly owned and operated for their own benefit. A common use, however, is an apartment cooperative (co-op), where the total building is owned proportionately by shares of stock, and separate apartments are assigned by size and value in relation to that amount of stock. A condominium, on the other hand, allows each owner to own the physical space and form he inhabits, wherever located in space, and there is no necessary cooperative effort.

**COPING**   A linear cap that sheds water from the wall it shelters; commonly, in traditional architecture, stone copings shelter bricks (and the absorbent mortar joints between them).

**COPPER**   Elemental metal, corruption of *Cyprus,* the island known for its ancient mines. First of man's metals, it is crossed with tin to make harder and stronger bronze (the Bronze Age dates man's development parallel with knowledge of applied science); and with zinc to make brass.

Copper is the best commonly available conductor of electricity or heat and has a semiprecious beauty of its own. Like silver, it must be polished and, like silver, loses the depth of its finish when artificially coated and protected with plastic to prevent tarnish. As copper, it becomes wire in modern building; as bronze, window frames, hardware, and lavishly ornamented, carved or sculpted doors; as brass (copper and zinc), piping and so forth.

Copper was extensively used in primitive architecture to protect the end grain of wood from water and now relives that kind of experience as "flashing" (thin folded sheets to divert water within construction).

**COPTIC**   Ancient Egyptian Christians, apparently converted during the life of Christ's disciples. Their brand of "Early Christian" architecture used the concentric domed mud-brick of the Middle East, rather than the timbered Roman basilican form adopted by northern Mediterranean Christians.

**CORBEL**   A block or brick projecting from a wall's face and, in turn, supporting the weight of more masonry above or an applied load, as that of a wood, hammer-beamed roof truss. Corbeled masonry relies on the dead weight of more masonry above to counterbalance its short cantilever.

**CORBEL TABLE**   A series of corbels supports a series of arches, a common use of semistructural decorative brickwork in, most

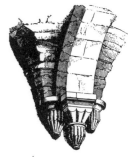

CORBEL *Corbel carrying arches*

CORBETT *Chase Manhattan Bank, Brooklyn*

particularly, northern Italian (Lombard) Romanesque architecture.

**CORBETT, HARVEY WILEY (1873–1954)** *American Architect* As head of the firm now transmogrified into Harrison and Abramovitz, he shares (with Reinhard, Hofmeister, Harrison, MacMurray, Hood, and Fouilhoux) the responsibility (and credit) for Rockefeller Center. Corbett was at the center of Art Deco and Art Moderne, thereby participant in an art form that took the stepbacked forms of New York's zoning and turned them to visual advantage.

**CORINTHIAN** The elegant and ornate "order" of architecture that was the principal vocabulary of major Hellenistic, and then Roman, architecture. Its capital, a carved assembly of acanthus leaves, crowns a slender, fluted, filleted column, often with an elaborated base (Pantheon, Rome; Supreme Court, Washington—the latter with cornstalks, instead of acanthus leaves).

As with Doric and Ionic, Corinthian was named for a geographic subarea of Greece.

**CORK** That useful tree's bark plugs wine bottles and also offers a warm, textured surface for cladding interior walls to which documents and drawings can be easily pinned. As floor tile it is handsome and soft, requiring substantial waxed maintenance to protect it from the penetrating dirt of wear.

**CORNERSTONE** The corners of a building, built first to anchor the exact plan dimensions, may memorialize its construction by a cornerstone, occasionally hollow to receive artifacts of the moment: a newspaper of the day and pieces of contemporary technology. A top hat, a silver trowel, pretty girls, a mayor were all part of the ceremonial trappings of laying it.

**CORNICE** The designed edge of a building against the sky: its hat or crown or capital, sometimes sorely needed by the designer, as in all Classical and Renaissance architecture, sometimes ignored, as in primitive or Cubist architecture. The cornice gives opportunity for enrichment, a bold line struck, a bold mass sculpted. Compare the cornice (or top element) of the Parthenon and that of any Florentine palace.

**CORRIDOR**   A run. A linear, tubular space, connecting the functional parts of a building, particularly where the tube is long and serves repetitive spaces (hotel or office building), as opposed to the hall of a private dwelling.

**CORRUGATED**   The sinuous (sine-waved), regularly undulating profile of sheet metal, asbestos, or plastic used for roofing and cladding of buildings. Corrugated paper, now available waterproofed and also used in building construction, is light and sturdy, its two sheets separated by a paper sine.

**CORTONA, PIETRO DA (1596–1669)** *Italian Painter and Sometime Architect*   He composed, at S. Maria della Pace, an urban set of events that made a church a physically interlocking part of its local neighborhood (a block off the Piazza Navona).

**COSMATI**   Decorative, inlaid marble with added stones, mosaiclike; ascribed to a prolific family named Cosma (Lorenzo, Jacopo, Cosimo, Luca, another Jacopo, and Giovanni) in the twelfth and thirteenth centuries. The façades of S. Miniato, S. Croce, and S. Maria Novella at Florence are Cosmati-esque, as are the floors of innumerable New York City Renaissance Revival banks from the 1920s.

**COSTA, LUCIO (1902–   )** *Brazilian Architect and Planner*   His buildings are more than competent (cf. the apartments at Parque Guinle; 1947+, Rio de Janeiro); but his fame blossoms from his master plan (1957) for the new high-landed capital city of Brazil, Brasília, born of the political-cultural symbiosis between Juscelino Kubitschek, President of Brazil, and Oscar Niemeyer, architect.

Costa's competition-winning plan is low-density, low-coverage, high-rise, with vast spaces articulating the individual monuments of the architects concerned: and there were many in addition to Niemeyer, who designed, principally, the great government buildings. Most descriptive document of the architectural distinction but urbanistic banality of Brasília is the French movie *That Man from Rio*, with Jean-Paul Belmondo, who traverses the spaces by foot (seemingly running for hours), by car (at high speeds), by aircraft (stunt biplane flying between great gravestoned slabs).

Costa cannot be faulted for the architecture; but he can be faulted for the sprawling, though geometric, plan, which gives an impression of order on paper, and even in long photographic perspective,

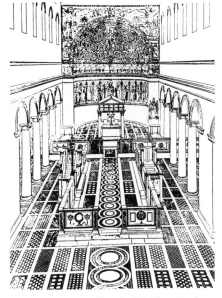

COSMATI *Church of S. Clemente, Rome*

but gives the individual human an ant's role, where he may find his ultimate scale only in the interior personal spaces assigned to him within a superblock.

**COUNTERSINK**  To let a fastener's head into a depression: the flush result is countersunk.

**COURSE**  A row or tier of masonry (brick, stone, or block). Coursing and bonding determine the structural system and the resulting skin pattern. (See also *Bond.*)

**COURT**  An outdoor room, a space contained by buildings and walls and open to the sky. A court*yard* implies a service function, merely concealed from others' view; a light court is usually a multi-storied wide shaft to allow light and air into the rear service areas of an apartment building; and a garden court, as in a Roman house (its atrium), is small in dimension, an intensely used outdoor private space.

**COVE**  A curved, concave molding, common as joint between floor and wall to allow easy cleaning.

**CRAM, RALPH ADAMS (1863–1942)** *American Architect and Writer*  Gothic Revivalist to the nation in the second round of the early twentieth century; as in the grand, great nave of New York's Cathedral (Episcopal) of St. John the Divine, and West Point's Chapel, or that at Princeton: correct, dry, and immensely popular with his wealthy clientele, who controlled and financed the vestries of America.

**CRANE**  A long-armed machine that is physically reminiscent of the long-necked bird after which it is named. The pivoted arm can swing from its pivoting base and raise and lower, over a tip pulley, the load concerned.

**CRAZE**  The erratic fracturing of a surface, particularly glazed pottery or tile, but sometimes other materials, such as plastic or even treated wood veneers.

**CREMATORY**  Alternate to cemetery. Cremation does not consume land, as do cemeteries. The act of cremation accelerates

CRAM *Cleveland Tower, Graduate College, Princeton*

"ashes to ashes, dust to dust" and relieves us of the cemeteries' quasi-architectural debris.

**CRENELATIONS** The crown of a medieval palace or fortification: those toothy ramparts shielding the shooter, while allowing space for his weaponry. Aficionados of Gary Cooper recall those propped bodies peering through the crenelated Foreign Legion outpost in *Beau Geste.* Crenelations were a Victorian code-symbol for castle, and many modest wood-frame and stucco houses sport crenelated ramparts (suitable in scale for 3-foot elves) to defend them, apparently from the lower classes.

**CREOSOTE** An oily (petroleum) brown staining preservative that colors wood and causes it to shed water, removing the probability of rot and/or insect attack.

**CREPIDOMA** The platform on which a Classical temple rests, three-stepped regardless of size and scale, whether the temple is 40 or 140 feet tall. Human scale is, therefore, not a concern, and the temple is a hierarchical formal form without scale.

**CRESCENT** A curved (half-round or half-elliptical) row of houses concave to a central space from which they are entered. The Royal Crescent at Bath, by John Wood the younger, is the handsome fulfillment of this approach: total form greater than the sum of its parts.

**CRET, PAUL (1876–1945)** *French American Architect and Teacher*
The Pan-American Union in Washington, D. C. (1908+), surrounds a tropical planted skylit patio: his usual French imports were of lesser delight. Cret taught at the University of Pennsylvania; his most famous student, and later employee, was Louis Kahn.

CRET *Pan American Union, Washington, D.C.*

**CRETAN** (and Mycenaean) What we now know as ancient "Greek" is mostly fifth- and fourth-century-B.C. Greek, the moment of consummation of Greek political and artistic civilization. However, *its* genesis was in Crete, most widely studied at and around the Palace of Knossos (also termed, by
spect, the Labyrinth). From perhaps 2000 to 1400 B.C., Crete was a center of civilization, paralleling Egypt's Thebes (modern Luxor)

81

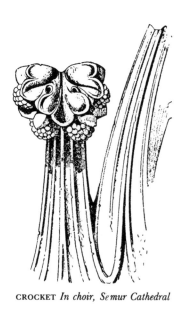

and Babylon. After 1400, mainland tribes (termed Mycenaean) dominated Crete and drew from its experience.

The Labyrinth of Knossos was a meandering, rambling, sprawling, disordered almost-maze: hence the common English word *labyrinth*, taken from it, and romantic novels concerned with finding and confronting the Minotaur (king and/or king-symbol) within it.

The Mycenaeans, on the other hand, found order and ordered their palaces on the Greek mainland around an axis, with a system that allowed for rational circulation. After 1200 B.C., southern Greek tribes took hold, and eventof course, Athenians led them all.

**CROCKET**   A teat, bump, or wart on the multipolygonal edges of a pyramidal ending (finial) of Gothic architecture.

**CROSSING**   The intersection of nave and transept, center point in a planned tic-tac-toe of space, sometimes crowned by a tower or dome (e.g., Ely and St. Paul's, London, respectively).

**CROSS SECTION**   A drawn record of a building, vertically sliced apart to show its inner structure and space. A plan is, literally, a similar horizontal slice.

**CRYPT**   The cellar of a religious space, widely touted in tourist guides and horror movies for vicarious horror, but, in fact, an indoor cemetery crossed with architecture.

**CUBAGE**   Quantity of volume within a building (in cubic feet or meters).

**CUBICLE**   Any tiny space larger than a closet, smaller than a normal room.

**CUL-DE-SAC**   A short, dead-ended place, one way in and out.

**CULVERT**   A minibridge, tubular conduit to carry weather (rain) under a new or man-made construction. Man's works displace (among other things) the natural flow of water.

**CUPBOARD**   A cup on a board; then a closet for cups, dishes, glasses; and, eventually, a small closet for storage of any kitchen equipment or food.

**CUPOLA**   A small dome and the shaft that supports it: the most phallic of architectural images.

**CURB**   An edge or constraint. For example, the curbed edge of a sidewalk, dropping to a gutter or street, constraining the water there rushing to a drain.

**CURTAIN WALL**   A building's skin, hanging from its bones (structure of columns and beams). Until the 1880s, buildings were (mostly) built with bearing walls, *bear*ing (i.e., supporting) wood or iron beams. Steel or concrete in effect demotes the function of walls to that of a skin shielding the occupants from weather, sound, and view.

**CYCLOPEAN MASONRY**   Cyclops was a myth, and so seemed the gigantic masonry of pedestals and retaining walls in the architecture of Crete and Mycenae to those who later viewed and named it. Huge, heavy, impossible (seemingly) engineering for mere men, it was placed with precision.

Similar, but not so named, is the ruin of Macchu Picchu in Peru.

**CYMA RECTA**   A Classical molding, concave in section above, convex below, like the back and bottom of humankind. Its converse, breasted above, sucked in below, is cyma reversa.

Cyma: something swollen, as pregnant with child.

**CYPRESS**   A wet-grown wood (swamp-bred) that survives, in later life, moisture from outside (as do redwood and cedar).

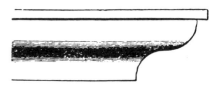

CYMA *Cyma recta (above)*
*Cyma reversa (below)*

# D

**DAILEY, GARDNER (1895–     )** *American Architect* His is a simple, direct, matter-of-fact modern architecture, ranging from the Owens House (1939, Sausalito, California), a box of posts, glass, and natural board and batten siding, to the Beachcomber Hotel (1951, Waikiki), a honeycomb of rooms made elegant by slightly bowed balconies of simple wrought-iron verticals.

**DAIS** Where subroyalty dined at the end of their medieval hall; raised, perhaps, not only for honor and over-sight, but to avoid the swill of the common cavorters eating on the main floor itself.
   Now it is what the honored guests at a formal dinner sit upon.

**DATUM** The reference place from which are taken measures of height and depth (i.e., "elevations"), thereby allowing measure of hill, valley, and building.

**DAUB** English term for mud used in building—as in daub and wattle construction.

**DAVIS, ALEXANDER JACKSON (1803–1892)** *American Architect* Versatile American architect (sometimes partnered with Ithiel Town) who ranged from Greek to Gothic Revival, all with consummate talent and taste: his Custom House, later Subtreasury Building, now Federal Hall National Memorial, graces Wall Street with a purist Doric Greek temple; Lyndhurst, a country-house castle on the Hudson at Tarrytown, sings of English Gothic Revivalism

DAVIS, ALEXANDER JACKSON *Colonnade Row, New York*

and romantic landscape design (the latter by similarly named and equally honored Andrew Jackson Downing). The Litchfield Villa in Prospect Park (Brooklyn) preceded the park, which grew around it after the fact; here, however, an Italian villa. And, as a piece of the hard-edged city, La Grange Terrace, sometimes called Colonnade Row, half of which still flanks Lafayette Street, once New York's most fashionable place.

Davis was one step beyond the copybooks that made individualistic architecture then possible (and he wrote some of his own for others). Like Sears Roebuck catalogs, illustrated books of building designs (assorted books with assorted styles for assorted building types) dominated the design process in pre-Civil War America and contributed to it long after. From them came much of the Federal, Greek, and Gothic revivals that carpenters and masons could translate directly for clients from catalog pages to reality. While most buildings came from English copybooks, Davis, Downing, Minard Lafever, and Samuel Sloan published their own and gave a special American flavor to the process.

**DAVIS, LEWIS (1925–    )** *American Architect*  With his inseparable partners Samuel Brody and Alan Schwartzman, Davis has raised social architecture (principally low- and middle-income housing) in New York to a state of civic embellishment and joy. No one even *tried* before them.

Their Riverbend Houses (1969), East Midtown Plaza (1971), and Waterside (1973) are, in importance, of a quality of urbanity unreached in New York since Williamsburg Houses (1930–37) or, before that, of non-multiple dwellinged Federal and Greek Revival town houses.

Brown-bricked, simplistic but not simple, incised with glass-eyed, brick-walled balconies, East Midtown Plaza is surrounded by land that is an orchestration of unselfconscious amenities for urban pedestrian life. Brick is honored and honorable; design is the servant of the user and resident, rather than an abstract and honored end in its own right.

One building away from their New York practice that must be remembered is the elliptical, earth-bermed, air-roofed U.S. Pavilion (1970) at Expo '70, in Osaka, Japan.

DAVIS, LEWIS *East Midtown Plaza, New York*

**DEAL**  English term for pine, as used in furniture.

**DECKING**   Pieces set in place to form a finished, or subfinished, surface on which one may walk.

**DECORATOR**   Maker and creator of the internal fancy dress of architecture: more elegantly, it may be interior architecture, as Le Brun as decorator complemented Le Vau and Hardouin-Mansart's Versailles.

To decorate is no put-down. Unfortunately, it is an easy province of the insecure *nouveau riche*, giving wives of no particular talent opportunity to bully their peers for a fee.

**DEED**   Record of ownership (contract and closing). A lawyer's description of real property.

**DE KLERK, MICHAEL (1884–1923)** *Dutch Architect*   Romantic founder of the School of Amsterdam. The Eigen Haard Apartments (1921, Amsterdam) are clean-cut Hansel and Gretel, plastic delights in natural Dutch brick for the workman in residence.

**DELORME, PHILIBERT (1512–1570)** *French Architect*   Rabelais admired him, and he responded with buildings in a spectrum from "outrage to vigor"! Chenonceaux, his romantic château-bridge, spans the Eure River (in the Loire Valley); a narrow, awkward structure for the user, it is analogous to living in a two-and-a-half-story covered bridge, in long, tubular spaces. From its gardens, seen along the river, it is a picturesque place of arches and piers supporting a mansarded château of simple form.

The Tuileries Palace, which closed the U-plan of the Louvre to make a rectangular O, was built for Catherine de Medici. It was burned (1871) under the commune that governed Paris after Napoleon III's ignominious defeat by Prussia.

The main façade of Fontainebleau is his, facing the Cour des Adieux (Court of Good-byes), where Napoleon I bade farewell to his court and troops on his exile to Elba in 1814. Napoleon chose Fontainebleau as his country court to evade overt comparisons with Louis XIV, whose ghostly image hovered over *his* Versailles. Just as the Louvre would be opened to the Place de la Concorde by the burning of the Tuileries and its subsequent demolition, Napoleon had the similar, fourth, street-fronted façade-building of Fontainebleau razed, exposing Delorme to first view.

DE KLERK *Eigen Haard Apartments, Amsterdam*

**DENSITY**  The number of anything per unit area: a sometimes meaningless term, since how many people are at a given point is not of particular significance, but rather how they are served by light, air, traffic, transit, and any city's total infrastructure. High density must be separated into the parallel, but grossly different, concepts of concentration and congestion.

**DENTIL**  The teeth of a cornice in Greek and Roman architecture; those small series of blocks that are reminiscent of wood joinery of the temple architecture from which the Doric order (in marble) was supposedly derived: the Etruscan megaron (in wood).

**DEPRECIATION**  The accounting of use (hence, wear) of capital "improvements" that reflects lessened value in each incremental time period. More important to the investor-developer is the fact that depreciation can be deducted from his income before taxes, with no passing of cash!

**DESIGN**  The act of creation: an architectural designer fulfills a client-program, creating space and form to house, shelter, and define that program. He is always constrained by the tenor of the times and, until recently, by a dominant style, the sum of pre-fixed attitudes common in the minds of a given culture or civilization.

A narrower view of design was that of Louis Kahn, who separated the basic form-idea from the design process and applied the term *design* to the final manipulation of established form.

**DE STIJL**  Group movement, "style," and magazine (born at Leiden, Holland, 1917). Fractured Cubism, as suggested by the early Wright (say, Robie House, 1909) and/or Cubist painting. Among the chosen were Oud, Rietveld, van t'Hoff, van Doesburg, Mondrian; and the most memorable holy place is Rietveld's Schröder House (1924, Utrecht)—and the holy object the Rietveld "chair."

**DEVELOPMENT**  A pejorative word, signifying building(s) en masse for profit as a first priority: housing developments, industrial developments, or what have you.

To "develop" suggests putting to use latent resources, as the developing of film articulates silver nitrate crystals exposed through a camera lens to light. And, in respect to land, the "improvement"

DELORME *Façade, Fontainebleau*

(i.e., "development") of it. Some open space and parkland, like a virgin nun, should survive "development" in perpetuity.

**DIMENSION**   The measure of a physical object in one direction or sense: length, width, height, radius, spacing.

**DIRECTOIRE**   Stylish politics, the period of France's "Directory," pre-Napoleonic Roman-aping period paralleling America's Federal and England's Georgian. Furniture seemed most important, although that attitude seems apocryphal in a period of revolution, violence, and bonfires.

**DOME**   A vault of rotation (inverted cup) that covers or shrouds a major concentric space in a whole building or major portion of it. The round forms of domes are transmitted and translated to the normal rectangular architecture that supports them by squinches and pendentives, exotic architectural parts that allow the cross-blending of two competing geometries.

Domes act like sea shells, their strength derived from their shape rather than their bulk strength. Made incrementally of parts (bricks, stone, tile), or monolithically from concrete, their resultant product is a membrane of structure.

Domes suggest the vault of the sky, and many historians say their symbolic meaning is one recalling that sky, and the heavens above it ("of celestial and divine significance," said dome historian E. Baldwin Smith).

**DONJON**   French word for *keep,* the inner, last-bastioned retreat of a castle, an island within the walled bailey, or open military grounds, surrounding it.

**DOOR**   A wall flap, allowing access; also a closure to travel, sound, light, and air. Honored in their ornamentation, doors and their "ways" become sculptural objects, great leaves to permit ceremonial entry and passage as well as control of the local environment. The architecture of many cultures has converted the door, hence doorway and entry, to a visual event with major form, sometimes in contrast to an austere and vernacular building surrounding it.

Compare: 1. A Churrigueresque door on an adobe Spanish church.

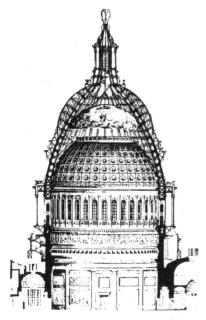

DOME. *The Capitol, Washington, D.C.*

2. The flamboyant porch (portal to a door) at Albi.

3. Any porched and pedimented façade.

Doors now fold or hinge or slide or roll up to be tucked out of the way of furnishings and other stored items.

**DORIC** The austere and lengthily refined system (order) of Greek columns and beams that gave "order" and hence an order to their first great architecture; from Paestum (a Greek colony in southern Italy near present Naples, ca. 535 B.C.) to the Hephaistaion (432 B.C.) was a hundred years of aesthetic refinement pursuing perfection of form.

Dorians were a Greek subculture, as were Ionians and Corinthians.

**DORMER WINDOW** A sleeper's window (from the French, *dormer*: "to sleep"); an eyebrowed aperture in a sloping roof. Most importantly it was used in the mansard roof, that bastard element that cheated the prefect of Paris, Baron Haussmann, from his law limiting buildings to six stories. This was possible because the seventh was not termed a floor, but attic or garret, and still was rentable (and cheap, for obvious reasons). Dormer windows alone lighted garrets, save for the special artists' skylights that replaced whole roof planes.

DORMER *Dormer window in a Gothic attic*

**DORMITORY** The spare housing of an institution, usually college or university, suggesting "place to sleep."

Modern dormitories contain living, smoking, dining, and bathing rooms, and even suites for groups of students or faculty. The sleeping aspect is, therefore, only one of their modern micro-city functions.

**DOSHI, C. V. (1926–     )** *Indian Architect* Careful student of Le Corbusier at Ahmadabad.

**DOUBLE HUNG** A window system where two sashes (framed sets of glass) are "hung" from counterweighted pulleys in overlapping vertical sliding tracks (or are compressed between spring-loaded tracks). It is a Dutch invention, as necessary to America as the balloon frame, because of its climatic appropriateness (i.e., weather-sealing): it is less apt than a casement window to bind as moistened wood expands.

**DOVETAILING**   Like clasped fingers, wedge-shaped members spline two boards together to form part of cabinetry, as in, say, a drawer's body.

**DOW, ALDEN (1904–    )** *American Architect* Dow's own house (1935+) at Midland, Michigan, owes much to his apprenticeship with Frank Lloyd Wright, much more to himself. Its sheltering roofs relate not only to earth but to water, and house and principal living space become part of their neighboring pond: view of air and water pressing half-and-half against the main room's glass wall.

**DOWEL**   A blind rod or peg used to align or fasten (with the aid of glue) adjacent parts of paneling or cabinetry.

**DOWNING, ANDREW JACKSON (1815–1852)** *American Architect and Landscape Gardener (Architect)*   Landscape architect, architect in imagination, he was a sometime partner of Calvert Vaux. They jointly embellished the architecture of Alexander Jackson Davis at Lyndhurst (see also *Davis, Alexander Jackson*). Downing's influence was more through publication (copybooks) than gardening or building per se.

**DOXIADIS, CONSTANTINE (1914–1975)** *Greek Architect, Planner, and Promoter*   A facile "lingo," persuasive charm, and public relations of great sophistication allowed Doxiadis to assume, briefly, a position of great international professional power. His magazine, *Ekistics,* purported to be expert in the science of planning. But the built products of his ideas are banal.

**DRAFTSMAN**   English=draughtsman. One who draws, and now, in American circles, the worker on the assembly line of "working drawings," those magical, mysterious lines on tracing paper that are reproduced as "blue"-prints.

The functionaries of an architect's office include draftsmen, designers, specification writers, construction supervisors, as well as those who fill the tawdry functions of accounting, management, sales, and ownership (proprietor or partners). One may embrace a variety (or even all) functions, but the roles in question are still there.

"Drafting" also implies free-hand drawing, a not-very-old usage describing anyone from Ingres to Canaletto to John Taylor Arms (the great architectural etcher) to Picasso.

**DRAKE, GORDON (1917–1952)** *American Architect* Architect of sequence, of experience more than object, Drake provided an American, Californian interpretation of domestic architecture, as inspired by the Japanese. The Berns House (1951, Malibu) is the only Drake house left in substantially original condition. Drake's career was cut short by a fatal skiing accident in 1952.

**DRAWING** Representation of something by lines marked on a flat surface, usually paper. A linear implement (pen, pencil) is implied. Drawings may indicate what something looks like (perspective, rendering, sketch, and, to a certain extent, axonometric) or how it is formed (presentation drawings of plan and section) or how it is built (working drawings).

**DRESS** To direct or align, hence trim to a true smooth surface and geometry, building materials such as stone.

**DRIP** An attractive route for water to leave a projecting building surface, so that it will clear the building face below and reach the ground. It is either a linear bump or reveal that causes the water to depart.

**DRUM** A tube that raises the skin of a dome high into space. The dome then visually clears the body of the church below, articulating its spherical form from a viewer's distance; at the same time, it makes both dominant and vertical the space it enshrouds: compare that of Brunelleschi at the Duomo of Florence.

**DRYWALL** Flat sheets of precast plaster (paper-covered) veneer partitions and make a wall dry; as plaster, spread in place, makes a similar wall wet.

**DU CERCEAU, JACQUES A. (1515–1590)** *French Architect and Engraver* Known for his books, grand historical records, rather than his buildings; cf. *The Best Buildings of France* (*Les plus excellents bastiments de France,* 1579). His grandson, Jean, built the Baroque "Horseshoe" staircase for Louis XIII at Fontainebleau.

*du Cerceau, Jacques A.*

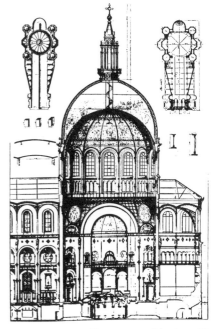

DRUM *Dome supported by drum, St. Augustin, Paris*

DUDOK *Vondelschool, Hilversum, Holland*

**DUDOK, WILLIAM M. (1884–    )** *Dutch Architect* A modern romantic in brick, he blossomed with the Town Hall (1930) of Hilversum, Holland, where a dynamic, romantic asymmetrical massing grew to a churchly tower, incised with horizontal slots to reveal ribbons of glass. Cubism (already flowered), the School of Amsterdam, and Frank Lloyd Wright's massing here merged. (Note that architects such as Mies followed similar routes on occasion: the Liebnecht-Luxemburg Monument; 1926, Berlin.)

The Vondelschool, of the same Hilversum tradition, is picturesque, sleek, and penetrated with a semiround vaulted entrance, reminiscent of H. H. Richardson, or Wright's later V. C. Morris Store. His brick is of the very bowels of Holland, his towers on both buildings a Scandinavian-Dutch oddity on secular buildings.

The Beehive Store (Bijenkorf; 1931), in part bombed, was willfully demolished in Rotterdam's rebuilding after World War II and replaced in function by a new Bijenkorf by Hungarian American architect Marcel Breuer (1957). Dudok's Beehive was a major modern building (erased from the literature of modern architecture with a kind of Bolshevik historical rewrite), of pale-yellow brick, ribboned glass, a bulky 2/3 cube, slashed with glazing and anchored with a slender, ever-present Dudokian tower.

The Dutch Pavilion at the Cité Universitaire, Paris, is white stuccoed Dudok, a formal diversion from his brick world.

**DUMP** The leftovers of civilization can be reduced, but not obliterated: they end in the dump, a kind of community dry sewage place that receives everything that no one can use or make disappear. Sophisticated dumps become sanitary landfills, where a useful topography for park use can recycle the experience for humankind once more; older dumps impinge on seashores and varying local natural ecologies, warping them, and destroying their possibilities for future natural development.

**DUNGEON** A cellar-prison, usually dank, dark, and medieval: where captives or those to be punished were sent. Rarely a place of distinction, except in the marvels of Piranesi's *carceri*, those drawn prisons that released imaginative form from current style and allowed him fantasies of quasi-real space.

# E

**EAMES, CHARLES (1907–    )** *American Designer*  An American neo-Renaissance man. He has provided leadership in architecture (his own steel house of 1949 at Santa Monica); furniture design ("Eames"chairs are now plural, not singular: the original, with Eero Saarinen, of bent plywood, in 1940; postwar, luxurious leather and bent rose-plywood on a chrome swivel pedestal in 1951); moviemaking (*Black Top,* 1950); the whole IBM space-theater experience at the New York World's Fair of 1965, with Eero Saarinen; and toys (most attractive of these are his houses of cards, slotted and playing-card-sized, that allow small hands to make great abstract constructions). And more and more. And more. And more.

**EARLY CHRISTIAN**  Between the first and fifth centuries A.D., the early Christians adapted Roman architecture to their own new liturgical needs, largely through the conversion of the basilica—or Roman place of law and business (not unlike the European Bourse) —to the assembly hall of Christianity. The ultimate stained glass of clerestoried medieval Christianity developed from the alabaster glazed clerestories of the basilicas of Constantine or Maxentius.

Early Christian basilicas include that original one of St. Peter (first pope and bishop of Rome), now replaced by the Maderna-Michelangelo-Bernini church, and the still-standing S. Agnese and S. Lorenzo, both "outside the walls" (of Rome). They not only simulated the plan and form of their commercial ancestors, but eventually were built of parts taken from Roman (i.e., pagan) temples.

EAMES *Interior of Eames house,*
*Santa Monica*

93

**EARLY ENGLISH** *Early English stained glass, Oundle, Northamptonshire*

**EARLY ENGLISH** The first major medieval style of England proper (England having been taken from the Angles and Saxons by the French Normans) is termed Norman, roughly equivalent to French Romanesque, lasting from the 1066 invasion to the late 1100s.

Early English is, therefore, a bald statement of the obvious: of the earliest English (Gothic) architecture, later to be followed by historian-termed Decorated and Perpendicular. It had a simplistic pointed arch, ribbed vaulting, with small windows punching through heavy walls, as opposed to the increasing glassiness and complex vaulting of Decorated; Perpendicular was even more so.

**EASEMENT** The easing (therefore easement) of access or right-of-way across the land of another: roads, utilities, water, and so forth pass by negotiated rights, without direct ownership.

**EAVES** A gutter is the lower lip of an eave, that sometimes detailed, sometimes hovering lower edge of a sloping roof that shields the wall below from rain and weather. Eaves were elevated to high status in Japanese wooden architecture and in early Northern California houses; they sheltered the former from rain and rot for over a dozen centuries and kept the latter from melting to slump (they were built of clay and would liquefy in rain, but remained sturdy if umbrellaed).

Frank Lloyd Wright adopted low overhanging eaves as a design device to accent the ground-hugging, pedestrian scale of his buildings.

**ECHINUS** The weight-holding form of a Doric capital: its refined form and refining development largely trace the 100 years of Doric evolution from the Basilica at Paestum (a Greek colony of the sixth century B.C. south of Naples) to the Parthenon (432 B.C.) in Athens.

**ECLECTIC** Like a child dressing from a trunk-filled attic, an eclectic architect assembles discriminate parts for his composed buildings from varied historic periods and geographical places. A decorator's attitude, where tasteful parts are, hopefully, assembled to form a tasteful whole. Classical columns, Gothic arches, and Byzantine domes might be intermingled picturesquely.

**ECOLOGY**   The balance between a life form and its environment: i.e., human ecology, plant ecology, bacterial ecology. In current slang it refers more to people and their use or misuse of the resources they have tapped to serve them; and to the effluents that they spill into the air, onto the land, and into the water to pollute (and, therefore, potentially destroy) the ecological balance between man, the air he breathes, the water he drinks, and the land where he grows his crops.

Urban ecology is concerned with the more limited balance between hard urban worlds of man-made streets and buildings, the arteries that serve and give life to them (i.e., streets, boulevards, and transit), and all the ways in whch man uses his self-made world.

**EFFLUENT**   Flowing gas or liquid leavings from natural or artificial processes; urine and/or the waste from a paper mill or sewage plant are effluents, but so are gas-borne soot from an electric generating plant and exhaled breath.

**EGG AND DART**   A linear-repetitive sculpture; decoration used as a complementary part of cornices at first (in Classical architecture), later as part of the plastered histrionics that covered everything with detail in nineteenth-century plaster revivals (Greek Revival, Classical Revival, Renaissance Revival). Alternate eggs and lance (dart) heads are in continuous bas-relief.

**EGYPT**   Where it all began for the urban architectural historian (nomads and scattered farmers excepted). Djoser's pyramid at Sakkara (25 miles from modern Cairo) is reputedly the first stone building in the world. Whether or not the role is exact, that stepped pyramid is a large formalistic object that anchors time at 2700 B.C. (4676 years ago, a careful point to remember when considering steel's 92-year life as a modern building material and reinforced concrete at, perhaps, 71).

Stone remained *the* material of major building (with a brick or two interspersed in alluvial cultures) until steel arrived: the stone Monadnock Block by Burnham and Root (1891, Chicago) was in the 4591st year of stone's 4676-year reign as maker of monuments; yet the builders of Sakkara had the technical ability to create the Monadnock (save for its elevators).

Egypt's lengthy Pharaonic history (3,000 years, or fifteen times America's 200) first raised an orchard of pyramids (716+) in the

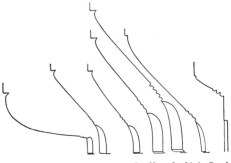

ECHINUS *Profiles of echini, Greek Doric capitals*

environs of Cairo at the time termed the Old Kingdom (from somewhat before 2700 B.C., to 2500 B.C.).

Then, at the modern town of Luxor (Greek Thebes, Egyptian Weset), the east and west banks of the river Nile supported an urban civilization of both the living and the dead. There, in the Middle Kingdom, the greatest temples were built: Karnak, Luxor, Medinet Habu; and the rock-cut tombs in the valleys of the kings, queens, and nobles still supporting the living today through tourism and archaeology.

Last chronologically is the New Kingdom (1600–300 B.C.). That "decline and fall" bore many gems, at Luxor (Hatshepsut's Temple), the great rock-cut temple of Ramses II at Abu Simbel (now on the border of Egypt and the Sudan), and the many gloried additions to the temples in and around Thebes by Ramses II, including what is immodestly termed today the Ramesseum.

The armies of Alexander relieved Egypt from status as a Persian province, founding Alexandria as the new capital. On his death, his general, Ptolemy, founded the Ptolemaic dynasty to and through Cleopatra, on whose death Egypt became a Roman province.

Many of the remaining temples in substantial form are Ptolemaic, and hence late, such as those at Abydos, Esna, and Edfu, and the lovely small temple complex on the island of Philae, sandwiched between the old, low Aswan Dam and the new, high one.

Sandstone and granite made it all, cut, dressed, carved, floated in the annual flood waters of the Nile to carry them to places otherwise inaccessible. Time, slavery, and brilliant engineering combined to make a gargantuan scale of god-like dimensions, where Pharaohs and their priests could meet, and then become, gods.

EIERMANN *German Embassy, Washington, D.C.*

**EIDLITZ, CYRUS L. W. (1853–1921)** *American Architect* The Times Tower in New York's Times Square, now severely altered, was Eidlitz's most prominent building. A slender and inefficient triangle in plan, it dominated the Square from 1904 to 1966, serving symbolically the newspaper that built it (the bulk of the paper's editorial and production facilities were in another huge structure a block away). Eidlitz's junior partner was McKenzie, who in turn was senior partner of a whole string of affluent architectural firms (McKenzie, Voorhees, Gmelin; Voorhees, Gmelin, Walker; Voorhees, Walker, Foley and Smith; Haines, Waehler and Lundberg). Eidlitz the fountainhead and later Ralph Walker were the most noted of the chain.

**EIDLITZ, LEOPOLD (1823–1906)** *Czech American Architect*
Eidlitz's professional fulfillment occurred with his joint appointment (with H. H. Richardson and Frederick Law Olmstead) as architect of New York State's new capitol at Albany, supplanting Thomas Fuller who had commenced it in 1871. The stylistic convolutions that resulted entertained politicians, the public, and architectural critics for a decade. Eidlitz and Richardson's design superimposed Romanesque Revival on top of Fuller's already-completed Renaissance Revival basement.

**EIERMANN, EGON (1909–1970)** *German Architect* An elegance of steel, floating in a grillage before the building proper, excepts Eiermann from the Miesian line which he normally would be ascribed to. The German Embassy at Washington (1963) is the logical outgrowth of his German Pavilion at the Brussels World Fair of 1958.

Less is more, with line more than mass (Mies's buildings are often massive and opaque, as are both Seagram's, where reflections in glass exaggerate its very solidity, and the Esplanade Apartments, where steel is so closely spaced, lusty and dominant, that it consumes the transparency of glass).

Eiermann is spare, attenuated, lithe, using the shadows of his own structure to liberate it from solidity.

**EIFFEL, GUSTAVE (1832–1923)** *French Engineer* Extraordinary engineer, whose basic ideas created the form of buildings: a quasi-architect. The Eiffel Tower became so dominant as to destroy the idea of the man himself. That shaft, built for the 1889 Paris Exhibition, remained the tallest man-made structure in the world until the 1930s, when New York's Chrysler, then Empire State buildings were crowned.

Eiffel was equally brilliant, but less renowned, for his Garabit Viaduct (1884) and, more important to Americans, for the Statue of Liberty, whose sculptured form was created by Bartholdi, and whose gargantuan reality was engineered by Eiffel.

**ELEVATION** Image of a building's face, like a pressing or rubbing. To elevate is to raise, and elevations are more in spirit with the *building* of a building than is a drawing that "describes" it. An elevation is not what someone sees, but rather describes what and

EIDLITZ State Capitol, Albany

97

how the building is, and how it is to be assembled (and, in a technical-visual sense, what it will look like).

**ELEVATOR**  A raiser, or lifter, that mechanically moves pedestrian and freight traffic *vertically* in a box called a cab. Some are lifted from above by cable, pulley, and motor; others, usually for shorter runs, are raised by hydraulic (oil) pressure, like the classic barber chair.

An elevator is vertical transit when it reaches the 110-floored scale of New York's World Trade Center: why not treat it in the same fashion fiscally, and for planners, as horizontal box travel by subway?

The elevator's invention, together with the development of the steel-framed building, gave opportunity for the skyscraper, Chicago's first great architectural contribution to America's architectural history. Need for concentrated commercial space and concurrent technology joined. (As with most inventions, need and fulfillment are almost simultaneous.)

**ELGIN MARBLES**  A rather dull tag for the sculptured remnants of the Parthenon, carted away to London and the British Museum by Lord Elgin (1803–12). Curiously and coincidentally, it preserved them from the ravages of Turkish gunfire when the Parthenon was shelled in 1821 (the Greeks were using it as a powder magazine). The remnants are the most glorious frieze and pediment sculpture in Greekdom, a classic Classical apogee of form, grace, and carved drapery.

**ELIZABETHAN**  The halting Renaissance of Elizabeth I's England (1558–1603). Hardwick Hall, Derbyshire, and Wollaton Hall, Notts, are surprisingly modern (to us), though of course they were even more so to Shakespeare and Co. Both were designed by Robert Smythson and John Thorpe and bear proto-Cubist massing glazed with large, large-paned windows that could have delighted an early Cubist. Humanism blossomed in art and science for man's benefit and ego, and what could grace that humanism better than a country house filled with light and a garden view?

**ELLWOOD, CRAIG (1921–    )** *American Architect* Elegant, simplified Mies for the affluent suburban Southern Californian.

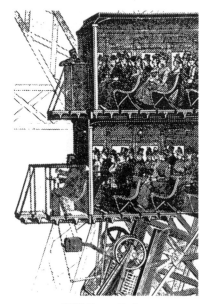

ELEVATOR *Eiffel Tower, Paris*

**EMPIRE** The colonial apogee that permitted Persia, Greece, Rome, and finally and most effectively, England, to spread their artifacts across the globe, bringing, they thought, culture to the barbarians, friendly environments away from home to the empire builders, and symbols of dominance to remind the restless locals of their subservience.

The side-effects give us extended architectural histories: England's Bath (after the Roman bath that graced it) displays buildings from A.D. 200 to the present, with distinction in all periods; certainly the baths themselves, and the Circus and Royal Crescent (town housing by John Wood the Elder and Younger; 1754+), spanning 1600 years between them, are a heady set.

Greece left Doric, then Ionic, then Hellenistic temples in Turkey, Syria, Libya, Italy, and Sicily. Romans (a practical lot) allowed urbanity to come to the whole Mediterranean with aqueducts, sewers, and baths, baths, baths.

But England's artifacts of powerful and sometimes pompous Renaissance parts mark Delhi, Rangoon, Cairo, Nigeria, and to a lesser extent Ottawa and Australia. This introduction to architecture gave understanding of choice to the locals, who promptly outdid their former masters (upon their "liberation") and built distinguished and appropriate modern architecture themselves or with the help of outside consultants (Le Corbusier in Chandigarh; Kahn in Dacca; assorted Londoners in Lagos; and so forth). A conscious imperial effort to educate colonial citizenry allowed that citizenry to acquire the knowledge and expertise so that they might further their own varieties of environmental change.

ELGIN MARBLES *Figure from Parthenon pediment*

**ENDELL, AUGUST (1871–1924)** *German Designer and Architect* His Art Nouveau stucco encrustation on the Elvira Photo Studio (1897+, Munich) is another much-remembered plate in the history of modern art and architecture.

**ENGINEERING** Applied science. Concerned with administering engines, the word's verbal aegis was expanded to include all of what America is (or was) most skillful at: applied science—the use of scientific knowledge to invent, develop, fabricate, and mass-produce life-style accessories (TVs, autos, gadgets, business machines) as well as man-made environmental structures: dams, highways, power systems, the cage, frames, and slabs of buildings.

Some of our greatest architecture is the product of engineers, and hence the semantics are blurred: the Brooklyn Bridge (John and Washington Roebling); or even Grace Church (James Renwick); and the soaring shells of Nervi, Torroja, and Candela. Though not trained as architects, they still gave graceful architectonic form to their client-programs.

ENTABLATURE *Parthenon*

**ENTABLATURE**   The whole crown of a Greek or Roman building. The entablature is the part of an "order" the column supports (architrave first, then frieze, then cornice—all subsections within the layered entablature).

**ENTASIS**   An optical correction: the designed swelling of a Classical column that corrects the eye's sense of concavity that would occur if the columns were straight. The eye sees light eating into darkness and hence the background sky devouring the bulk of a column's profile. Entasis compensates visually.

**ENTRANCE**   The pedestrian orifice to a building, allowing functional and symbolic entry. The entrance (see also *Door*) is a place for architectural articulation, where the very ceremony of entering may create a high order of architectural attention (leaving the balance of the building simplistic): cf. the Mount Vernon idea, where a porch and columns in simple, neo-Greek fashion suggest importance beyond that of the simple house behind; it was then copied *ad absurdum* by developers nationwide seeking similar pomp for their clientele.

**ENVELOPE**   The enclosure, or enclosing skin. A zoning envelope is that theoretical maximum volume that a zoning resolution (law) will permit on a given site. A building envelope is its horizontal and vertical maximum surface.

**ENVIRONMENT**   That which surrounds its living participant: ecology where there is a symbiosis; a hostile environment where there is not. Natural and man-made environments are similar and parallel to human and urban ecology.

**ERECT**   To stand up, as an obelisk, by direct action; as in the case of the erection of a penis. To build implies the assembly and stacking of component materials and parts. An erection is a more speedy,

100

simple, direct, and overt act. Erect a tent, a sign, a world's fair, but build a building, a palace, or a city.

**ERICKSON, ARTHUR (1924–    )** *Canadian Architect*  Erickson's grand opportunity came at Simon Fraser University (Vancouver, B.C.) where he created (with partner Geoffrey Massey) a great skylit galleria, an *indoor* plaza appropriate to that cool, wet climate. His earlier work suggested Yamasaki and Stone: happily he outgrew those beginnings.

**ERSKINE, RALPH (1914–    )** *English-Swedish Architect*  A romantic, and would-be Aalto, in timber and stone. His Sports Hotel (1955, Borgafall, Sweden) has been called "ground sculpture," its very roof the end of a ski slope.

**ESCALATOR**  Automatic scaling machine that, by endless collapsible and moving steps, raises and lowers population continuously, rather than the intermittent transport of an elevator. Department stores use them now almost to the exclusion of elevators, as the act of movement allows changing perspectives over the merchandise for sale, where the boxed elevator allows only the elbows and garlic of neighbors to pass the time in transit between floors.

**ESCROW**  A trusted person's or institution's place for care of money, deed, or legal document until a negotiation or act is fulfilled.

**ESCUTCHEON**  A hard, protective shield, concentric with an opening in soft material, to protect the material and align the passage of something that penetrates, as a key (and the escutcheoned keyhole) or a pipe escutcheon, where the carefully crude hole through a floor is trimmed and aligned by a sheet-metal doughnut.

**ESHERICK, JOSEPH (1914–    )** *American Architect*  Esherick's modest architectural statements are the antistylish products of his thoughtful solutions to client needs (in contrast to willful form- or monument-making). Esherick's works are mostly houses, but The Cannery, an industrial building, was reincarnated as an elegant shopping place.

ERICKSON *Simon Fraser University, Vancouver, British Columbia*

101

**ESPALIER**  Two dimensions from three, as a tree's volume becomes a flat plane. The training of a tree or bush against a south-facing wall or trellis, to capture maximum sun and the warm buildup from heat-retaining masonry, allowing early and maximum fruiting of the tree (and a handsome natural filigree).

**ESPLANADE**  Relaxed pedestrianism, where the sauntering of citizens usually interplays with a view or display, as in the esplanade along the Charles River in Boston (a linear walking park) or the Brooklyn Heights cantilevered deck overlooking New York harbor.

**ESQUISSE**  Sketch. And hence, being a word derived from École des Beaux-Arts usage, the late nineteenth- and early twentieth-century first designs toward a projected program, in Paris and America, that were the objects of criticism by the head of an atelier (architectural workshop).

An esquisse-esquisse (or sketch-sketch) was an especially simplistic quick sketch (sometimes called a sketch problem) that suggested talent or intellect and the direction of an effort.

EXPO'67 *West German Pavilion, Montreal*

**ESTATE**  State or standing of man: subverted to financial concerns in popular language, describing the estate of a person, summarizing his various wealth (or absence of it). *An* estate is later jargon for the land and buildings a person owns and lives on, which seem, to most, to dominate his state or standing, and hence, *are* his estate.

To describe anything of less than grandeur as *an* estate is tawdry malapropism.

**ETRUSCANS**  Those pre-Romans from Etruria, north and west of Rome, who started an architectural vocabulary with their articulated, one-room wood pedimented temples that were the antecedents of stone "ordered" architecture of the seventh century onward in what is now Greece and Italy.

**EXEDRA**  Classical alcove, semicircular or rectangular, originally to seat a group in a mini-amphitheatrical manner.

**EXPO '67**  Canada's 1967 World's Fair, newly dubbed "Expo" to differentiate it from the internationally unrecognized New York World's Fair of 1965. As with all fairs of this era, Expo was a smorgasbord of histrionic buildings, some, however, of distinguished but ephemeral architecture (Frei Otto's German supertent, American Bucky Fuller's 3/4 sphere).

**EXPO '70**   Japan's sequel to Canada, remote for almost everybody from the West, but noted to us for its remarkable American Pavilion (by Davis, Brody), an earth-bermed ellipse forming a people-filled reservoir canopied with an air-supported membrane, slightly bellied over the horizontal.

Many structures of distinction by Japan's Kenzo Tange filled the grounds.

# F

FAN VAULTING *Cloisters,
Gloucester Cathedral*

**FABRICATION**   The making or assembly of a whole out of parts, as with a car on an assembly line or a house in place. Most buildings are made from standardized components (most buildings are not *pre*fabricated). Their parts are the bricks and 2 × 4's available universally within our society—as opposed to prefabricated buildings, where assemblies of parts are *pre*fabricated in a factory and delivered as walls, floors, boxes, or whole buildings to the site.

**FAÇADE**   The face of a building, and its demeanor to the viewer, showing character. Rigid, it is likened to a mask; but masks are the false-fronted façades of humans, while a building's façade is its own natural face.

**FACING**   Human faces are the forms derived from genetics, worn and grown by experience, that give humankind character. Building facing is its skin, a thin and synthetic substitute for a face.

**FANLIGHT**   The radiating panes within a semicircular glazed opening, usually over an entrance, leaded, elegant; Georgian in England, Federal in America.

**FAN VAULTING**   The antistructural overelaboration contrived by late English Gothic (Perpendicular) architects, as at King's College Chapel (Cambridge, University and City). The form of the ribbed fingers that span such spaces suggests an unfolded fan: a tour-de-force, and an elegant, handsome one at that.

**FASCIA**  A linear face, involved with a structural system, or at least the idea of structure: as in the face of a Classical entablature, or in the top and projecting edge of a building joining the sky.

**FAULT**  In geology, a break or mistake in the substructure of the earth, faulting it for some uses: the infamous San Andreas fault in California is a natural line of relief for underground forces concerned with volcanic and/or earthquake action. Along that line repeated building constructions have failed; most serious was the San Francisco earthquake of 1906, cause of a new city plan, creator of a whole new architectural style through overt disaster.

**FEDERAL**  America's first style, named in honor of its newly federated republic of 1789. It parallels the Georgian (Renaissance) architecture of George III's England, using delicate Classical parts to articulate entrances and snug gambrel roofs with dormer windows that contained heat loss in cold and dank America (as opposed to medium and dank England).

**FEE**  Feudal lands, and now any land or lands. A fee is the ownership of the land under one's house or building (not the land itself, but the state of ownership).

Fees are also the prearranged payments to professionals (architects, doctors, lawyers, engineers) for the services that they provide: lump sums, as opposed to salaries, which are continuing payments to a continuous employee.

**FENCE**  The light metal or wood wall-substitute that separates here from there, and fends off real or symbolic enemies, coveters, robbers, or just plain rabble. The fence around the park of an English country house states the park's importance and grand limits. The backyard fence gives security and privacy; the barbed-wire fence divided the endless American western world into discrete parts that limited the range of the range.

**FENESTRATION**  A fancy word for windows and their arrangement in the façade of a building.

**FERRISS, HUGH** (1889–1962) *American Architect and Illustrator*
He served as renderer (professional illustrator) of the modern urban visions of Raymond Hood, Ralph Walker, and the whole

FERRISS *A fantasy study of urban forms*

105

FESTOON *Over fireplace, White House, Brooklyn*

Rockefeller Center team; more than draftsman, his own design input modified the thoughts of his clients.

His visionary drawings illustrated a New York of towers, intended to anticipate possibility, as did the visions of Sant'Elia or even the "prison" drawings (*carceri*) of Piranesi.

**FESTOON**   To ornament exuberantly with hanging or applied decorations: taken from the original *festoon,* a relaxed and hanging wreath much used in carved decoration. (See also *Swag.*)

**FIBERBOARD**   Compressed sheets made from the dust or grinding of wood, bound together to form both hard and soft boards (Masonite and particle board). They serve as underlayments for flooring or roofing, or, drilled with regular holes, are pinned to walls, allowing movable hooks to be applied for storage of tools or other devices.

**FIBERGLASS**   The fibrous spun glass that, in wool-like batts, is used to insulate buildings. Paper-covered and -contained, it is nailed and stapled between studs and rafters to minimize the flow of heat from inside to out.

Other fiberglass, woven into fabric and saturated with polyester plastic, is molded in limitless forms for chairs and other household objects: no one can avoid those endless metal-legged, pastel, shelled chairs in the bus stations and waiting rooms of America.

**FIELDSTONE**   The found stone of agriculture, common where glaciers passed by. Collected as walls—serving as both place of disposal and demarcation—and as a building material. Fieldstones in building are generally rough-rounded stones, in contrast to the rough, random, rectilinear shapes of ashlar (cut to shape). The same glacial stones form rocky beaches at the edge of glacial moraines, but there the stones have been smoothed to a near-eggshell finish by 10,000 years of post-glacial washing in the sea.

**FILL**   The stuff to infill void on or in land, or within a building process. Valleys or swales are filled, and fill is used to grade the final contours around a completed building: *fill* here means dirt, sand, gravel. And in modern commercial building construction, electrical conduits (pipes) are run in a filigree across a building floor to allow service at specified or random points: surrounding those conduits and forming a finished floor level is fill, light concrete that gives a flat surface for tile or carpet.

**FILLET**  The plane (a flat band) separating two adjacent flutes, particularly in an Ionic or Corinthian column: flutings of Doric columns meet in sharp edges called arrises.

**FINIAL**  The end of it all. Von Suppé, the Alsatian musical melodramatist, found it difficult to end his music, and his overtures (or beginnings) were his undoings, for to end them drained his total resources. Finials sympathize with him, for they, in aggregate, articulate the upward endings of a Gothic church, piercing the sky, conical and pyramidal pointers stopping the upward thrust of buttresses, bastions, and bulwarks.

**FINISH**  The final polish or rubbing or painting of a surface that finishes it; the last and ultimate act.

**FIR**  Soft evergreen cone-bearing tree (conifer) that ranges from the gigantic West Coast Douglas to the modest yellow. Fir is a straight-grained, high-strength wood, easily worked, sawn, planed for construction lumber, and the first choice of those who build with studs, joists, and rafters.

**FIREBRICK**  Brick made to resist the intense heat of fire, used in fireplaces and furnaces, usually smooth and light-tan or gray in color.

**FIRE ESCAPE**  The way out. In case of fire one escapes, but not on a stair for normal social transport. Wood-beamed brick buildings, particularly in New York (tenements, converted town houses, inexpensive early apartment buildings), bore fire escapes as a way out of an architectural style where only one stair was plausible. (The second would have devoured too much of the building's interior "economic" space.)

Steel balconies, bolted to a façade, allowed steep ladders to carry escapees to the street and permitted summer victims of the heat to lounge in relative pre-air-conditioned comfort on their grillages.

**FIREPLACE**  The core of life in a pre-centrally-heated northern climate. Heat and a place of cooking combined, it dominated early architecture, central to a dwelling. Its chimney crown served as a visual and structural anchor, and its bowels opened to serve, occasionally not only as room-dominator, but as a room in itself, a place for humans to enter and be in, not merely to face and/or cook (see also *Inglenook*).

**FIREPROOF**  More than incombustible: and therefore resistant to heat for a long period of time without structural failure or collapse. Steel is incombustible, but not fireproof, for it will soften and fail under continuing intense heat. Reinforced concrete, on the other hand, is fireproof, for the concrete is an insulator from the heat that might cause its contained reinforcing bars to fail.

In legal circles (building codes) "fireproof" is a relative state of affairs (four-hour fireproofing means survival of a material, conservatively, for four hours of maximum flame and heat).

**FIRESTOP**  Within a hollow wall something to stop passage of air and hence the flue-like spread of fire: a plug to the space in question, although the space may be thin and long (a firestop might be an inch by 10 feet).

**FISCHER VON ERLACH, JOHANN (1656–1723)** *Austrian Architect*  Baroque disciple (from afar) of Bernini, producing imposing and heavy-handed buildings. From Fischer to Neumann (30 years his junior) is to leap from a massive and endless parade with bands to a courtly minuet.

Note the Karlskirche (1716+, Vienna), a collection of Roman columns, porches, and pomp; a smashing and theatrical place.

**FIXTURE**  Attached and special component of a building's life, as an electric or gas fixture, or toilet fixture; imported prebuilt accessories of a specialized nature or use.

**FLAGG, ERNEST (1857–1947)** *American Architect*  New York's two Singer buildings and the U.S. Naval Academy are Flagg's best-known works. Perhaps more important over-all to history are the Scribner's bookstore (1913), on Fifth Avenue in New York, and Flagg's serious experiments in high-density housing alternatives to the dumbbell tenement. The Scribner's store is a grand "vaulted" commercial space of wrought iron and plaster, with terraces, mezzanines, and balconies for special book categories overlooking the

FLAGG *Engine Co. No. 33, New York*

best sellers below. The Cherokee Apartments (1900) are simple six-story courtyarded buildings, with barrel-vaulted tunnels to courts serving corner spiral stairs triple-hung, with windows giving access to narrow balconies that overlook New York's East River.

**FLAGSTONE**   A natural layer of stone, split from its strata, used largely for paving (split=schist/slate).

**FLAMBOYANT**   The flamelike tracery of Late French Gothic, sinuous, elaborate, sensuous. The word later was expanded to suggest general elaboration or ostentation, not only in buildings, but dress, style, and even manners. The north tower of Chartres Cathedral is Flamboyant in its literal sense, a later, and hence "modern" addition to a first, Romanesque south tower and a High Gothic body. It is an intricate and elaborated style that bears the flamelike detail of its name.

**FLANGE**   A turned-up or -down edge of an object, allowing attachment or providing strength, as in the flange of a steel beam. A flange is part of the original material bent or rolled to its flange function.

**FLÈCHE**   Arrow. The slim spire often found over the crossing of nave and transept in a church, usually a filigree of wood, stone, or even cast iron (cf. Sainte Chapelle, Paris).

**FLETCHER, (SIR) BANISTER (1866–1953)** *English Architect and Historian*   Banister Fletcher's *A History of Architecture on the Comparative Method,* first published in 1896, is a dry encyclopedic mass of erratically evaluated architectural resources: plans, sections, photographs, mostly of Europe, from Greece to a confused (in Fletcher's mind) present. Dismissed too frequently as the bible of the mere rote historian or student, its temperate use can supply source materials (particularly dimensions and scale) not easily available elsewhere.

**FLIGHT**   Those who climb stairs don't fly, but the stair itself flies from landing to landing, and is, therefore, a flight.

**FLITCH**   A splint; a plate of steel bolted to an insufficient wood beam to strengthen it.

FLAMBOYANT *Tracery, Salford, Warwickshire*

**FLOAT**   Used in smoothing newly poured concrete to form a flat floor or slab, a wooden pad that floats on the water rising from the curing material, finding its own level, and hence determining the level of the concrete.

**FLOOR**   The local bottom, where one stands, or onto which one falls. It may be an art form itself, in parquetry of inlaid wood or spread with woven rugs or marbled (plain, or inlaid). It is the platform from which we view experience and act out our life's events. Without walls, before an audience, it is called a stage.

**FLUE**   The conduit from fire to sky, allowing hot gases to rise naturally and be dispersed: one for each fire, furnace, or fireplace; clustered in composite chimneys.

**FLUORESCENT**   Light emitted from a chemical compound when excited (as by electricity): a fluorescent tube (lamp) emits light from its glass tubular interior-coated surface when excited by ultraviolet light that is, in turn, generated by mercury vapor captured within the tube, which is, in turn, excited by the 115 volts out of a local plug.

   Fluorescent lamps require much less power (wattage) and, hence, expense to operate them, but have a light less handsome and less directional than the point-sourced incandescent bulb. They are, however, almost the total light source of commerce for obvious reasons.

**FLUTING**   The semicylindrical valleys between edges (arrises and fillets) of Doric and Ionic columns (respectively). Or the general flutes of similar nature in any architectural detailing.

**FLYING BUTTRESS**   A *bridge* would be a more exact term; a stone member that braces a vault of a Gothic church by carrying the load over the intervening space (usually over the side aisle or aisles of the church) to a buttress.

**FOILS**   Tre-, quatre-, cinque-. The leaf-shaped voids that are the two-dimensional exedra of Gothic window tracery.

**FOLLY**   An extravagant building, often deliberately unfinished, that becomes the romance of succeeding generations; and, in En-

FLYING BUTTRESS

glish Regency architecture, the building of picturesque, exotic, and pseudo-historical structures as part of a romantic landscape that will bring folly to reason and, less often, reason to folly. Eccentrics supposedly built follies to reinforce their eccentricity; it is hard to believe that such needs required articulation. (See also *Wyatt, James*.)

**FONT**   The origin, our source, of ideas or ideals, as in the font of knowledge. Literally, an abbreviated fountain, in that it serves as basin for baptismal festivities (whereas a fountain is a jet or welling of water that has an outside source and replenishes itself, usually with vigorous display).

**FONTAINE, PIERRE F. L. (1762–1853)** *French Architect* Napoleon gave him, as favorite, the opportunity to create a style, now called Empire (after Napoleon's apocryphal one). With his partner, Percier, he wrote, proselytized, restored and built buildings.
1. Wrote *Palais, maisons, églises à Rome* (1798).
2. Restored much of the Palais Royal, Fontainebleau, Versailles, Compiègne, and Saint-Cloud.
3. Built the rue de Rivoli and the Arc de Triomphe du Carrousel.
Most important monument of all is the rue de Rivoli, where street, building, and sidewalk work in concert to produce a happy separation of traffic and an architecture to complement it: it faces the north wing of the Louvre, which Fontaine and Percier also completed, thus creating, for a moment, both sides of the street. (Lefuel, with Richard Morris Hunt's help, veneered their façade later with the face that remains today.)

**FONTANA, DOMENICO (1543–1607)** *Italian Architect* Architect to Pope Sixtus V, whose concern and vision for the larger idea of Rome was translated into the completion of vistas that interconnected the major religious monuments of the city (punctuated by obelisks that he erected at visual intersections).

Fontana designed the Lateran Palace (that complement to the Vatican attached to the Pope's diocesan church, S. Giovanni in Laterano), eventually abandoned as a papal seat in Rome proper when a compact with Mussolini defined the Vatican city-state and the popes withdrew there to their minimal estate (in papal landownership's history).

FONT

FOUNTAIN *Aqua Felice, Rome*

**FOOT** The bottom of a place, where there is a top, as a mountain, cliff, or hill (but even hills *are* feet: foothills). A foot has no place in a plain, except as the foot-ing of a building or structure.

**FOOTING** The feet of a building's legs. The meeting of ground and structure, where columns and beams press, through the footings (now almost always pads of concrete), their weight against the ground (earth, sand, rock). Usually buried from sight underground.

**FORMICA** A brand name for melamine plastic, skinning veneer of counter tops and walls, resistant to normal kitchen liquids, juices, and chemicals; versatile in color and pattern (endless); savior of American womanhood from the wear and maintenance of oilcloth and natural and painted woods.

**FORMWORK** The mold in which concrete is formed into building; often of wood, now more often of steel, each section is plastic-coated to slip from the firm-set finished product without chip or crack.

In the 1950s it was fashionable to "express" the texture of the formwork in finished concrete, showing the crude grain of wood used and the joinery between the boards or sheets of plywood. Even the metal blocks, called inserts, holding the ties (which braced the formwork through liquid concrete in tension) became a decorative game. Rather than the nature of the materials, it was the nature of the formwork that was expressed.

Forms are frequently not only demountable, but re-assemblable, making concrete more economic and, therefore, more competitive with steel framing (which must be sprayed with fireproofing to protect it from possible collapse under fire and heat: required by every building code).

In England, forms are called shuttering.

**FORUM** The public meeting space of a Roman city, where people and issues, gods and civic life, confronted each other. In our present-day watery language, the word confers honor on any group of speakers forwarding or dissecting an issue, an outlet for public life and interchange more frequently electronically displayed on television than in the handsome physical urban spaces for which the events were named.

*The* (Roman) Forum is a place of temples and civic affairs behind the Capitoline Hill, nestled against the Palatine Hill. The Capitoline Hill contains Michelangelo's conversion of the Senate and two other buildings into an exquisite urban space and complex (the Capitol of ancient Rome); and the Palatine Hill bears the ruins of palaces (word-named for the place where they were invented), particularly those of Nero and Augustus, that were the secular monarchs' place for overview of the Forum below.

**FOUILHOUX, J. ANDRÉ (1879–1945)** *French American Architect* The Rockefeller Apartments, with Wallace K. Harrison, are elegant bay-windowed luxury units that penetrate a New York City block and bring light and a garden to interior rooms and the lobby. Fouilhoux was also present at the birth of Rockefeller Center.

**FOUNDATION** The whole set or system of support between a principal structure (or building) and the ground beneath. Mostly below, but sometimes partially above grade and visually exposed.

A foundation is the joint and/or transition between man-made geometry and natural topography, taking into account natural strength and bearing capacities of the land on which it rests.

**FOUNTAIN** Aquatic urban decoration and symbol of urban life-blood: pure water. Water in Rome made the city possible when it had been sapped by disease bred in the malarial marshes abounding about it. Arrival of pure water by aqueducts was celebrated by fountains, largely a Baroque art, as water was largely the product of Baroque engineering: the Aqua Felice of Pope Sixtus V complemented his urban street system and brought Rome's finest water to the Moses Fountain, still used and celebrating today.

A later and more grandiose fountain is the Trevi, an overtoured stopping point more remembered for its Hollywood movie role than for any real historical events.

**FOYER** A social airlock that decompresses the act of meeting at the moat (or front door) and allows time and ceremony for one to enter the social fray of the living room or great hall.

**FRANKLIN STOVE** Ben again. Franklin devised this cast-iron practicality to heat those unable to afford a fireplace. In effect, an industrialized (and more intelligent) way of pre-central heating,

FOUILHOUX *Rockefeller Apartments, New York*

113

now still widely and happily used by many sometime cold-weather users of weekend ski houses or beach retreats.

**FRANZEN, ULRICH (1921–    )** *German American Architect* An early exponent of the hovering roof, divorced from walls below by a glass infill (cf. Beattie House, 1958, Rye, New York). He has, in his design maturity, produced great, cadaverous brick forts, one of the smallest and most handsome of which is the new building for the Jehovah's Witnesses in Brooklyn Heights (1970).

**FREEMAN, FRANK (1861–1949)** *American Architect* Unsung, unlisted, unknown until recently, this versatile eclectician of the 1890s is Brooklyn's greatest architect (America hasn't claimed him yet).

The Jay Street Fire House (1892), a Romanesque Revival château, is on a par with anything by H. H. Richardson (but without the technical-aesthetic innovation of Sullivan). And the Hotel Margaret bridges that gap (or lack) with a bayed façade (which looks over New York's upper bay) of riveted copper on a brick body (unhappily now all painted battleship gray).

Freeman's work embraced Renaissance and Romanesque revivals (best example of the former is the Crescent Athletic Club, now St. Ann's School; of the latter, the Jay Street Fire House) and Chicago School experimentation (Hotel Margaret and the Bushwick Democratic Club); never shy and seldom polite, his works are adrenalin among the serene Federal-Georgian and Brooklyn brownstones.

FRANZEN *Beattie House*

**FRENCH BALCONY** The narrow perch to view the air and city common to all Latin cultures, where the private man wants view and feel of the public world at the edge of his own private one. Anglo-Saxons and other Northerners tend to exclude personal involvement in the city from their privacy, save for the ill-used postage-stamp balconies of modern housing or the occasional barbecue-oriented terrace. The French balcony offers opportunity for venting passions to the neighborhood, as well as relating to the changing climate around one, without the cost or complexity of a room-sized balcony-terrace.

**FRENCH DOORS** The paired glass casement windows, door-length, to step through onto a French balcony.

**FRESCO**  An integral illustration absorbed into the very plaster (wet) of a wall, as opposed to being applied to its surface.

Leonardo da Vinci's *Last Supper* (on the wall of S. Maria della Grazie, Milan) isn't a fresco, although it should have been, as the oil peeled from the plaster surface after moisture penetrated from the outside: had it been a fresco, it would have survived, more or less intact, although occasionally it might have been soft and damp.

**FRET**  Endless Greek geometric figure that forms the basis for banded patterning, painted, inlaid, or in relief.

**FREYSSINET, EUGÈNE (1879–1962)** *French Engineer*  French structural concrete engineer, in a pantheon with Torroja, Eiffel, Maillart, Candela, and Nervi: all of whom have been creators of structures of folded and molded concrete sheets, powerful membranes and ribs spanning great spaces handsomely with minimal material. Freyssinet built bridges as elegant and spare as those of Maillart, such as that at Elörn (1926); his hangars at Orly, bombed and destroyed in the Second World War, were his greatest buildings.

FREYSSINET  *Dirigible Hanger, Orly*

**FRIEDBERG, M. PAUL (1933–     )** *American Landscape Architect*  Proselytizer (with Lawrence Halprin) of urban landscape Italian-style for America: hard-paved, plaza-contained, treed, fountained, and anti-grass. His Riis Houses Plaza (1966, New York) is still his best, unequaled by others.

**FRIEZE**  The formal enriched and sculpted band within a Classical cornice between the architrave, or visual "structure," and the cornice (top or roof edge). The frieze is a filler that rests between two hard-worked parts and allows the formal storytelling of a culture to illustrate, cartoonlike, a record of great deeds and public events. (See also *Zoophorus* and *Parthenon.*)

**FRONT**  Like *face* or *façade,* it implies direction, a side of importance, made up cosmetically to the approaching viewer. But in much of architecture, as in Palladio's Villa Rotonda at Vicenza (suburban Venice), there are multiple fronts; and in any architecture that is freestanding within a natural environment, there is frequently more than one approach of equal merit and attention (cf. Philip Johnson's

115

glass house in New Canaan, or even the White House—street front and garden front; Versailles, Monticello, and so forth).

**FRONTON**   The handball court of Mexico (and of the Indians from whom the Spaniards learned it). In Mexico's waves of romantic neoprimitive (but modern) architecture, the form of the fronton became a handsome freestanding object, as at the National University: stone truncated pyramids embracing the concrete courts themselves.

**FRY, E. MAXWELL (1899–    )** *English Architect*  Fry's fame rests largely on his historic partnership with Walter Gropius (1934–36): the occasion of introducing the ideas of the Bauhaus to England. A simple Cubism combined to produce suburban houses and a public school (Impington College, 1936).

Impington is a series of articulated forms, "expressing" on the exterior classrooms, entrance, auditorium, and office block. This, in no wise, makes the internal workings of the building "function" in a more smooth or superior fashion. It was said, however, to be "honest" and expressive of the true nature of the building. And, in fact, glassy Impington provided copious natural light and direct access from classroom to adjacent nature at a time when interplay between child and a natural world at his own level grasped the minds of architects internationally; Beaudouin and Lods were almost simultaneously producing their Open Air School at Surésnes (north of Paris). Impington was a reaction to the crowded dark Victorian "city," seeking to bring sun and nature to the sun- and nature-starved child.

Fry and his wife, Jane Drew, assisted Le Corbusier in the planning of Chandigarh.

**FULLER, RICHARD BUCKMINSTER (1895–    )** *American Innovator, Inventor, and de facto Architect*  "Bucky" to all, Fuller's concern with resources and their use to bring the greatest good to the greatest number of people brought him to exotic technologies as early as the 1920s. His structural geometries created the geodesic dome and inspired a whole series of variable "space-frames"—in effect, two-way trusses that work as close to isotropically as any structure of sticks and bones can (isotropic means that the structure is equally effective in *any* direction, as opposed to normal beam and

FULLER *Space Frame*

116

truss construction that spans from here to there on a rectilinear grid).

Not only domes and trusses but cars (the Dymaxion Car of the thirties, a tear-dropped three-wheeled portable living room); houses (the Beech Aircraft House, 1949); geography (the *Life* magazine-published polyhedral globe of 1954); and the whole issue of energy resources, conservation, and getting the most for the most people with the least effort occupy his fertile mind.

It is difficult to read his words or listen to them, for they are many and confusing: look at the deeds and you will rejoice.

**FUNCTIONALISM** A word embraced by those who, like all believers, believe themselves the true ones, bringing to architecture the virtues of reason and reasons for virtue: as in spare construction through prudent use of technology, with maximum logic in planning a program's three-dimensional needs; where the program (the building's requirements translated into an architectural recipe) becomes the product (the building). All this—rather than any formal design attitude, where a building's visual design allows necessary space as a secondary priority (i.e., the whole Renaissance).

Source of functionalism was the Bauhaus and those who made and used it—illogically, in many instances, since the virtue was often used in name only to create a new visual ideal. Certainly most of those who promoted functionalism as virtue believed in their own success. And equally certainly, it was frequently wishful thinking disguising a new aesthetic.

Compare Mies van der Rohe's spartan buildings, where the very bones (of steel) seem exposed. The true bones are encased in concrete for reasons of fireproofing, while the visible grid on the exterior is a decorative appliqué, analogous to a Halloween skeleton suit. But *nolo contendere:* the buildings are in fact both elegant and usable, and should not be burdened with a merely "functional" appellation.

**FUNK, JOHN (1908–    )** *American Architect* He rejected the Bay Area's shaggy textures and stained wood and made buildings both crisp and painted, as at his house on Russian Hill's Chestnut Street (1948, San Francisco).

FUNK *House, San Francisco*

**FURNACE** A fiery place and space that makes heat for a building by combustion and then transmits it through air, water, or steam via

FURNESS *Pennsylvania Academy of Fine Arts, Philadelphia*

pipes and ducts to the rooms or spaces in need. Furnaces also heat ores to create pure metal, or to form or temper it.

**FURNESS, FRANK (1839–1912)** *American Architect* Ultimate Victorian, employer of that great American chain's first link, H. H. Richardson, who in turn hired Louis Sullivan, who in turn was Frank Lloyd Wright's self-named *lieber Meister* ("dear master"). Furness exuberantly combined the bizarre Classical–Gothic vocabulary of the late nineteenth century with its technology of iron, as in the Pennsylvania Academy of Fine Arts.

Long ignored, if not forgotten, he was given renewed recognition in the 1950s in *Architectural Review;* he has since been the subject of a major exhibition at the Philadelphia Museum of Fine Arts (1973) and a handsome and extensive accompanying catalogue of the same date.

**FURNITURE** The fulfillment of architecture by portable equipment for human activities: sitting, lying, lounging, eating, reading, meeting: the unattached fixtures that have, traditionally, been the easy variables in stylistic change. Furniture anticipates architectural futures, experimenting at minimal cost and effort with form and space.

**FURRING** The falsework that coats or clads a wall or ceiling, aligning its surface for the finish material, and allows air to circulate behind.

**FUSE** The purposely weak link in an electric circuit that will fail (melt) if the circuit is overloaded. If no fuse were present, the whole system would overheat and possibly start a fire. The fuse both stops the action and signals it.

Garden City sub-urbs, straddling the country-city line. Most of those who followed did not understand (or resisted "planning" as a Socialist plot), and suburban America is the generally unplanned and amorphous product.

**GARGOYLE** Waterspout honored by, or honoring, sculpture, most impressive in Gothic detail as the gargoyles of the Cathedral of Paris (Notre Dame). Griffins, chimerae, monkeys, and monsters seemingly scare off the evil spirits, whose existence the church denied (except in a mind's-eye vision of Hell).

**GARNIER, CHARLES (1829–1898)** *French Architect* No building could be more important to the public grandeur and posture of Baron Haussmann's newly boulevarded Paris than the Opéra, terminus of a major new boulevard (de l'Opéra) from the Louvre. Garnier won its commission in competition in 1861 and completed it in 1875 under the early days of the Third Republic. The Opéra of the time was a contemporary experience of composer-audience symbiosis (Wagner and Verdi were in full swing), where the social event of opera attendance was as important as the music-theater performance itself. The public spaces at Paris are grandiose in size and ornament, many times the size of the auditorium they nominally serve, allowing vast hordes to descend staircases gowned and tiaraed like the royalty of romantic fiction they cared to ape.

Garnier's ultimate (and logical) next commission was the Casino at Monte Carlo (1878), fodder for untold musical comedies and foundation of the principality now ruled by a prince and his movie-star consort.

GARNIER, CHARLES *Opéra, Paris*

**GARNIER, TONY (1869–1948)** *French Architect* One set of elegant prescient drawings deservedly brings honor to this talented son of the Paris Opéra's architect: the Cité Industrielle (1904) illustrates pictorially a planned city (town) of limited size (35,000), with articulated functional parts (neighborhoods of residence, industry, and private affairs). Most startling architecturally is the aesthetic of simplistic (Cubistic) concrete, perhaps inspired by the contemporary work of Auguste Perret (particularly his still extant apartment house at 25 bis rue Franklin, 1903). Garnier went on to be the city architect of Lyon (a living eventually must be the compromise of all).

GARNIER, TONY *Cité Industrielle, Paris*

121

**GAU, FRANZ CHRISTIAN (1790–1853)** *German-French Architect* German-born, Italian-trained, Paris-practicing architect whose great neo-Gothic church Ste. Clothilde (1846+) reincarnated thirteenth-century Île de France cathedral architecture in the heart of Paris. Its iron-trussed roof was an early engineering feat in this center of iron architectural innovation (cf. Labrouste's Bibliothèque Ste. Geneviève, 1843; Baltard's Les Halles, 1854; Duquesney's Gare de l'Est, 1847).

**GAUDÍ, ANTONI (1852–1926)** *Spanish Architect* Not involved in any renaissance or movement, he turned the silk purse of Count Güell into the handsome, elegant, and extraordinary sow's ears of the Palacio Güell, Parque Güell, and Chapel of Sta. Coloma de Cervelló.

Most important, and non-Güell, is the crypt (basement church) and façade of the Sagrada Familia (Church of the Holy Family) at Barcelona, on which he began work in 1884 and continued for 42 years until his death. The Casa Milá (apartment house, 1905) shared his talents with the affluent. The plastic façade, fluid detail, and sculptured parts shocked and startled Barcelona and still baffle first viewers. Gaudí's has become, largely through the efforts of fellow architect-Spaniard José Luis Sert, a new-found architecture in the last 20 years, accepted and honored, whereas it had been considered merely bizarre.

**GAZEBO** Point of view, where garden perspectives may be observed in a garden pavilion; an object of distant view and perspective (admiration) in its own right.

**GEDDES, (SIR) PATRICK (1854–1932)** *Scottish Biologist and Planner* The first to relate the problems and science of biology to the sociology of city life, rather than arranging a city for military, symbolic, autocratic, hierarchical, or accidental purposes. Ebenezer Howard was his contemporary.

His works include *City Development* (1904). He was professor at Dundee, 1889–1918, then, in reprise after "retirement," at the then colonial Bombay, 1920–23.

**GELLER, ABRAHAM (1912–    )** *American Architect* Gathering and nurturing of young design talent has made him a great postgraduate educator (in the real world of professional practice).

GAUDÍ *Church of the Sagrada Familia, Barcelona*

He is also known as an architect of diverse, distinguished buildings. Geller's Upper Queens Medical Center (1957), prize-winning Franklin D. Roosevelt Memorial competition scheme (1960), and Aaron Davis Center for the Performing Arts at New York's City College (under construction, to open in 1977) show his constant and dramatic design development.

**GEORGIAN**   The German-bred English kings of the eighteenth and early nineteenth centuries, and the tastefully constrained architecture that is their namesake. London's Bloomsbury, a development of the Dukes of Bedford on their suburban estates, allowed the flowering of Georgian mass-housing with discrete beginning and ending sets of buildings and squares, proportioned from stone and brick with restrained Classical-Renaissance parts, certainly mannered—but definitely with manners, for those who cared about such a society.

**GESSO**   The strong, glue-filled plaster of the Renaissance that allowed a surface or object to be bulked out (as in a picture frame). It could be carved and gilded and was a Baroque and Rococo essential for the ornate enrichments that adorn such architecture.

**GHETTO**   The section of a city where Jews lived, or were forced to live, segregated from the general mainstream. Their self-imposed strictures established their Casbah-like containment and allowed territory to be identified with Judaism.

The word, loosely applied, speaks of minority populations—black, Hispanic, Indian, etc.—and their neighborhoods.

**GHIBERTI, LORENZO (1378–1455)** *Italian Sculptor and Architect*   Sometime partner with Brunelleschi in the construction of the dome of the Cathedral (Duomo) of Florence, Ghiberti is better known and more clearly honored for his competition-winning bronze doors of the same cathedral's baptistery (1401). They mark, in the opinion of many historians, the beginnings of Renaissance sculpture, bringing humanistic (real, as opposed to stylized) representation to biblical scenes.

**GIBBERD, (SIR) FREDERICK (1908–    )** *English Architect*   Harlow New Town (1947+) was Britain's first post-World War II attempt at neo-Newtownism, planned by Gibberd at a point in his-

GIBBERD *Metropolitan Cathedral, Liverpool*

tory blurred by that six-year war's break in experience and tradition, a tradition started by the original classic new towns, Hampstead and Letchworth, recorded successes of Ebenezer Howard-inspired, Unwin-directed architecture-planning.

Harlow was the victim of the bland modern-materials-arrangement architecture of that period in Britain. Its town center is a catalogue of various masonries and other accessories applied to quasi-medieval planning. Gibberd won the competition (with Wells Coates) for the new Liverpool Cathedral, a jazzy cone, lit from a grilled cylinder above.

**GIBBS, JAMES (1682–1754)** *Scottish Architect*  St. Martins-in-the-Fields (1722), across from the National Gallery at Trafalgar Square, is an image turned to a rubber stamp in America: Roman temple façade, steeple à la Wren, and balconied Classical interior, reincarnated at St. Paul's Chapel (1766, New York); St. Michael's, Charleston, South Carolina; King's Chapel (1749, Boston); and so forth.

His Italian remembrances (1703–9) resurfaced in a variety of later buildings, neo-Baroque, neo-Mannerist. His *Book of Architecture* (1728) contained a plate converted into Washington's White House by Irish American immigrant architect James Hoban.

**GIEDION, SIGFRIED (1893–1968)** *Swiss American Architectural Historian*  Court chronicler of the Bauhaus who fancied Baroque and Rococo spaces with his left hand, while proselytizing for Gropius, Mies, and their allies with the right. The "constituent facts" of all history suggested common purpose in all historic periods, equally usable, in his mind, if separated from stylistic posturing and boiled down to an essential purpose. (Cf. the original bible: *Space, Time, and Architecture,* 1941.)

Giedion was also an important patron, commissioning the Dolderthal Flats in Zurich (1934; Marcel Breuer, Alfred and Emil Roth, architects).

**GILBERT, CASS (1859–1934)** *American Architect*  The Woolworth (5 and 10) Building (1913, New York) was for 17 years the tallest building in the world. So speak the guidebooks. More eloquently described, it raises its sheer and total height from the sidewalk building line, no setbacks marring a pure and overwhelming

GILBERT *Woolworth Building, New York*

form: Gothic terra-cotta details incidental to a consciously vertical expressionism.

Gilbert's gilt pyramidal-towered U.S. Courthouse (New York) and Supreme Court building (Washington) are less radical (or modern) but are careful artifice at the least. The Supreme Court building, a superphony Roman temple, bears a pediment (complete with sculpture, long-destroyed on most Classical remnants) ornate with representations of friends and family, but most importantly Gilbert himself. The Americanization of the Corinthian order is here done (as A. J. Davis did it in Brooklyn's Litchfield Villa) with cornstalks replacing the acanthus.

**GILL, IRVING (1870–1936)** *American Architect* Remembered for his period of cut, sliced, pure-white stuccoed concrete block form: early simplistic, superficially related to the concurrent north European Cubism (cf. Adolf Loos). In fact, Gill's work in the semitropical watered desert of Los Angeles was romantic, a foil to verdant nature, and unrelated to any significant plan-space ideas: in effect, a decorative idea not to have decoration: ergo, the Dodge House (1916). He first worked (before L.A.) for Adler and Sullivan in Chicago.

**GIOTTO (ca. 1266–1337)** *Italian Painter, Sculptor, Architect, and Mason* At Florence, Arnolfo di Cambio's nave (of the Duomo), altered and fulfilled by Talenti, crowned by Brunelleschi's dome and detail, faced by the Ghiberti-doored baptistery, has Giotto's campanile (tower) as its foil, a painter's object and space-place.

**GIRDER** The spine that supports a building's ribs (beams): a major member in the hierarchy of floor and roof supports, it springs from column to column and, in turn, carries beams or purlins or joists.

**GIULIANO DA MAIANO (1432–1490)** *Italian Woodcarver and Architect* Continuer of Brunelleschi's work at the Cathedral (Duomo) of Florence, proselytizer of Michelozzo: one by-product of his great success is the Palazzo Spannocchi (1473, Siena), sand-colored rustication on a minipiazza.

**GIULIO ROMANO (1492–1546)** *Italian Painter and Architect* The pleasure garden/palace, Palazzo del Te (1526, Mantua)—a

GIOTTO *Campanile, Cathedral of Florence*

daytime pleasure place (tea palace), not a dwelling—is a surprising one-story super-courtyarded building prescient of seventeenth-century French palace-garden design (Vaux-le-Vicomte, Versailles).

He was concerned more with effect on the viewer than with the abstract purity of the object, and continued these efforts at the cathedral (Mantua) and his own house.

**GIURGOLA, ROMALDO (1920–    )** *Italian American Architect*
Two near misses in competitive architecture promised buildings of grand and urbane qualities: his second-prize design for the Boston City Hall competition (1962) promised a building whose contained plaza (self-embraced) interlocked its space (like clasping hands) with the larger Civic Center plaza surrounding: a simple architecture with complex urbanity, as opposed to the winning Kallmann, McKinnell and Knowles scheme that is complex architecture with simple urbanity.

His winning design for the National A.I.A. (American Institute of Architects) Headquarters in Washington was watered down, then dumped, by the forceful personality of fine arts commissioner Gordon Bunshaft (who then proceeded to fulfill without constraint his own neo-Classic ambitions on the Mall: the white, cylindrical Hirschorn Gallery). He practices in New York and Philadelphia.

**GIZEH** That Cairo super-suburb, across the Nile, where more than a million Cairenes now dwell in semi-urban multiple dwellings akin to New York's Forest Hills. Bisected by a boulevard that leads to the pyramids (Cheops, Chephren, and Mycerinos), its gridded streets fill the void between the Nile and the desert, the flood plain of ancient times that led to the desert edge and allowed transport by water of the heavy limestone and granite veneer of which the pyramids are built. The quiescent, nonflooding, many-dammed river now lies quietly between narrow banks; and upon the vacated plain to the west is Gizeh.

**GLASS** The original transparent membrane, sealing and separating environmental conditions. Vision and light remain; sound, air, the environment (and, to a lesser extent, burglars) are skinned out. Now, Plexiglas, Lexan, styrene, and, on occasion, even Saranwrap have joined the cause. Largely made from silica sand, glass is one of the few inexhaustible materials.

GOFF *Bavinger House, Norman, Oklahoma*

In the eighteenth century glass became a symbol of wealth: costly, apparent and transparent, it allowed the tax collector, by counting windows, to easily impose one kind of graduated-wealth tax.

Glass gave America, in particular, its most opaque (and literally shallow) architecture, in the guise of transparency. Lever House (1951) brought the glass building to sophisticated architectural distinction and financial success, all on Park Avenue: its very reflectivity reads as an opaque form.

**GLASS BLOCK**   A building block of cast glass, hollow, assembled from two square bowl-shaped pieces, that allows light but not direct view through a wall without the hardware (or ventilating possibilities) of a window.

Glass blocks were a major element in the new fashions of Cubist architecture: they could be part of the sleek-cut Cubism of white plaster planes, flush, detail-less, and allowing a simultaneous interplay of interior light.

**GLULAM**   Glued and laminated wood members, mostly for use as girders and beams. Their built-up, composite construction allows creation of structural parts of any size (far greater than that allowed by a single tree) and a uniformity of quality (knotless and checkless) that permits more slender beams than those of monolithic tree-cut members. Glulam can be formed in curved shapes on assembly, allowing arches that can parabolically or semicircularly span auditoriums and sports arenas.

**GOFF, BRUCE (1904–     )** *American Architect*   Wild man of architecture, his bizarre and wonderful buildings made Frank Lloyd Wright seem an Establishment banker. His Beavinger House (Norman, Oklahoma) is a stone shell interlaced with cables, light, reached by bridges, festooned with bracketed subnests. It is wonderful, strange, anti-Establishment, of a time when anti-Establishmentism was unacceptable.

**GOLDBERG, BERTRAND (1913–     )** *American Architect*   Smooth talk occasionally leads to smooth and even distinguished architecture. Thus was created Marina City (1963, Chicago), a sixty-five-story fluted column of apartments on the banks of the Chicago River. Vertigo and wind were problems with its petaled balconies. Goldberg went on to other and more arbitrary architectural geometries.

GOLDBERG *Marina City, Chicago*

127

GOODWIN *Original Museum of Modern Art, New York*

**GONDOUIN, JACQUES (1737–1818)** *French Architect* Neo-classical architect. His Paris Medical School (1769+) was designed as a temple to Aesculapius, the Roman god of medicine. More obvious is his neo-Roman column in the Place Vendôme (1810), similar to Trajan's at Rome.

**GOODHUE, BERTRAM GROSVENOR (1869–1924)** *American Architect* Eighteen sixty-nine was a vintage year for the birth of architects: Frank Lloyd Wright, Edwin Lutyens, and Charles Rennie Mackintosh, as well as Goodhue; although Goodhue was a romantic archaeologist, while the others were romantic modernists. Goodhue's St. Bartholomew's Church (1919+, New York) is a free collection of Romanesque and Byzantine parts, a charming urban place, its parts pre-aged (the architects of Byzantium, and the Romanesque in turn, had pirated Roman temple parts and materials), with brick and stone intermixed to simulate the patchwork of maintenance. It is a charming folly.

**GOODWIN, PHILIP (1885–1958)** *American Architect* Co-architect with Edward Stone of the original Museum of Modern Art building (1939, New York) and later catalytic author of *Brazil Builds* (1943), which, with G. E. Kidder Smith's photographs, was a bomb that shocked the world with the vigor of Brazilian architecture (both old and avant-garde).

**GOTHIC** Of the Ostrogoths and Visigoths, who overran the weak and declining Classical world. They bear the name of namesaked Gothic—that apparently non-intellectually derived manner of building, sometimes blamed (or praised) for or honored by, the pointed arch.

Aside from superficial detail and mannerisms (the pointed arch, ribs, bosses, finials, and so forth), Gothic is a structuralist's dream, and field for the eternal argument: are the great piered and ribbed Gothic vaults the visual by-product of engineering or the engineering by-product of vision, or some of both? Whatever the true answer (and its discussion will employ a legion of architectural historians for generations), Gothic is a monolithic architecture of stone that, like a great crustacean, embraces vast space for religious service and fervor, lit through its bony orifices with the dappled light of stained glass, which tells (for the illiterate peasant), the cartooned story of Christ. Gothic's slow development allowed stylistic and urban change that crossbred the romance of change with the basic body: within one church, as at Chartres, the main towers are of totally different periods and styles (north fifteenth-century Flamboyant; south eleventh-century Romanesque); and the meandering spaces of Gothic buildings, streets, alleys, and courtyards were the by-product of time, not device or design.

Gothic is a national, group architecture, of master masons and their guilds, and commanded a vast share of the national product of its times. Cathedrals in the Île de France absorbed more of the economy than the total U.S. budget now consumes of ours, as if for every $100 billion spent for national defense, we were to spend $200 billion for public works to the glory of God.

**GOTHIC REVIVAL**   The forms mostly of medieval France and England, revived there and in the United States (in its remembered Englishness). John Ruskin's several books (*The Stones of Venice*, 1851–53, for example) claimed that Gothic was a moral question, having been created by the Good (i.e., religious), and therefore could, conversely, create good among the present wicked. The posture gained many acolytes, and Gothic became the style not only in its healthy revival for English country churches, but for the decorated appliqué of otherwise neo- or Late Renaissance buildings: e.g., the London Houses of Parliament (see also *Barry, Sir Charles*).

**GRADE**   The level of ground at a given point and, particularly, in relation to a building. The grade of a lawn is "graded" around a completed structure's foundations.

**GRADIENT**   Slope of the ground.

**GRAFFITI**   The real pop art: naïve but sometimes artful scribblings, casual or careful, of the public on the walls, floors, and furnishings of public places, ranging from the carved hearts of lovers in a park to the spray paint murals that have almost obliterated the form of New York's subway cars.

**GRAIN**   The directional structure of a natural material related to the way it grew or was made. Wood grain is the code of growth, each concentric ring of annual growth a sign of the moment of pause, or hibernation, in a tree's annual life. All wood grain is made of linear tubes that carry sap throughout a tree.

GOODHUE *Panama-California Exposition, San Diego*

129

Grains in stone are the compressed striations of geological chemistry and pressure.

**GRASS** When loosely used, refers to lawns: a live and lively rug that is nature-tamed to the extreme: golf, croquet, and old-fashioned tennis are bred from and dependent upon grass. English romantic landscape gardening stretched square miles of undulating grass topography over not only England (and Great Britain) but English-speaking and Anglophile lands, in areas so large that they are referred to as parks, not lawns.

Grass, and its formal context, the lawn, has covered most of suburban America, elevating its care and feeding, if not to an art form, to a national obsession.

**GRÉBER, JACQUES (1879–1962)** *French Architect* Imported purveyor of École des Beaux-Arts attitudes; as critic with Paul Cret at the University of Pennsylvania, he peddled those attitudes to an eager American audience: bankers, businessmen, the idle rich; architects of tradition all flocked to his tasteful thoughts.

In the end his important contribution was Benjamin Franklin Parkway in Philadelphia, a grand boulevard that connects visually the city hall and art museum, flanked by a set copied by Paul Cret from the Place de la Concorde (Free Library and Court House, rather than the original's Hôtel Crillon and Ministry of the Marine).

**GREEK REVIVAL** The Greeks were revived as much for their political virtues (real or imagined) as for the slim architectural parts borrowed for the enrichment of town and country houses. A Greek Revival house of 1820–40 has certain bolder proportions than its Federal predecessor. The orders (here a flattened Doric or Tuscan) are presented as a portal to the front door: pilasters at each side, perhaps a shallow pediment supported over, originally festooned with antefixes, vestigial ornaments like the Mercedes-Benz radiator cap. The house plans were sensible, light, airy, and in New York brought with them indoor plumbing: "closets," bays without windows, projecting into the rear yard, attached privies relying on gravity only. The closets were promoted to *water*closets (w.c.'s) about 1830, delivering their effluent to a cesspool (drainage pit) in the backyard.

The "noble" and "simple" Greeks inspired statuary in the Greek manner. Buildings simulating Doric temples became banks, and the

GREEK REVIVAL

orders, or sets of columns and their related parts, were revived, but for vastly different purposes and in wildly assorted materials. The marble of Pentelicus became limestone, granite, wood, stucco and, finally, cast iron. The material seemed unimportant, the illusion overwhelming.

Greek Revival embraces places ranging from Wall Street's Federal Hall National Memorial (formerly the Subtreasury Building and almost an archaeological Greek Doric temple from the outside) to a simple row house of the 1830s, brick, and with only a doorway ornamented with pilasters or columns torn from the literal Greek fabric.

**GREEKS** From 600–300 B.C. they pursued a search for eternal and absolute perfection, the ideal against which all might be measured. These were the criteria: the true, the good, the beautiful= ethical, moral, handsome=honest, serviceable, and gorgeous.

We look at the Greeks as if they had colonized the earth from outer space. They gave us measures of art, mind, and life. Greek architecture was one of sculpture, of the freestanding building-object, specially sited and placed for public homage and power. Little remains to record the private life of their cities, their houses, shopping and ordinary places of commerce: the mass-secular existence. All attention is focused on the few permanent remnants of their time—the temple, the theater, the stoa, the agora: the public place and object.

**GREENBELT** A land- or city-planning idea, calling for the containment of a city to a fixed physical size (area), belted by a green circumferential band of public lands and farming before suburbs can again appear to eat the wilderness. Cities thereby can become articulate and discrete places, as they were when contained by defensive walls in medieval times, and as they are not in the megalopolitan sprawl of Los Angeles or Tokyo.

**GREENE, CHARLES SUMNER (1868–1957), and GREENE, HENRY MATHER (1870–1954)** *American Architects* The saving graces of Los Angeles, admittedly not contemporary, but without reservation modern. The greatest "stick" architects ever, their braced, pegged, interlocked fir-timbered buildings (Gamble House, Pasadena) would bear the respect of a classic Japanese carpenter, but were party to form- and space-making much more complex—

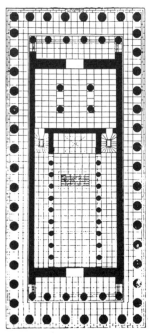

GREEKS *Plan of the Parthenon, Athens*

GREENE & GREENE *Gamble House, Pasadena*

131

great pilings of wide-roofed volumes, complex meandering wood cages, sometimes infilled, sometimes open for porches, porticoes, and balconies.

**GREENE, HERBERT (1929– )** *American Architect* He inhabits the Oklahoma of Bruce Goff and was his disciple. He embraced organic attitudes so vehemently that his buildings seem more organs than organic: the Greene House is a shingled shell, inside and out, the kidney of Paul Bunyan, the shingle style (as reported by Vincent Scully) taken to its furthest reaches.

**GREENHOUSE** *Green* for its contents: sun-grown plants in a winter atmosphere contained by glass (no ultraviolet here). The greenhouse reached an apogee in Victorian times, aided by the technology of cast iron and operating cast-metal hardware. Great urban parks carried vaulted, domed, and cupolaed envelopes of flower and jungle, scaled and spirited as secular cathedrals (cf. Bronx Botanical Gardens, San Francisco's Grant Park).

But for one score of glorious years greenhouses transcended plants and became great halls of public assembly and exhibition, samples of the highest architecture of their time: the Crystal Palace of London's 1851 exhibition, built by greenhouse-gardener-builder Joseph Paxton, honored by the namesake herself, Victoria (promoted by her husband, Prince Albert): crystalline and palatial.

GRIFFIN *Newman College, University of Melbourne*

**GREENOUGH, HORATIO (1805–1852)** *American Sculptor and Writer* Sometimes classified as Greek Revivalist, he studied with the Danish sculptor Thorvaldsen. Our best memories of him are in his writings that anticipate (architectural) functionalism: "I contend for the Greek principle, not Greek things. If a flat sail goes nearest wind, a bellying sail, though picturesque, must be given up. The men who have reduced locomotion to its simplest elements, in the trotting wagon and the yacht *America,* are nearer to Athens at this moment than they who would bend the Greek Temple to every use" (see *Memorial of Horatio Greenough,* by H. T. Tuckerman, 1852).

His gargantuan torso of Washington seated, nude to the waist, and draped as a Roman emperor, with hand raised in gladiatorial salute, so shocked Victorian America that it was removed to an obscure niche in the old Smithsonian Institution (from the Rotunda of the Capitol).

**GRIFFIN, WALTER BURLEY (1876–1937)** *American Architect*
Former worker for Frank Lloyd Wright (and later husband of
Wright's principal draftsman, Marion Mahony). In 1912 he won the
competition for the new capital of Australia, Canberra, and was lost
to American architecture thereafter; he left the Melson House, in
Mason City, Iowa, that same year.

**GROIN** The sharp curved edge formed by the juncture of two
cylindrical surfaces (vaults: as in Roman basilicas and baths and
Romanesque churches). A rib along the same line forms the rib cage
of a similar geometry visually: one of the principal engineering
advances that lightened the dead weight of Romanesque to create
Gothic and allowed its attenuated elegance.

**GROPIUS, WALTER (1883–1969)** *German American Architect*
His students affectionately called him "Grope." His life of building,
writing, and teaching was a search for truth for twentieth-century
architecture, directed at the social ills of urban society, using its
technology both practically and aesthetically. Low-keyed and low-
voiced in a frantic society and among oververbal professionals, he
had the arrogance of an egoist who knows he's right and can't deny
that virtue to the world.

GROPIUS *Graduate Center,
Harvard University*

The Fagus Shoe Factory (1911; Alfeld, Germany) and the model
office-factory of the 1914 Deutsche Werkbund (German workers')
Exhibition were the beginnings of his private practice (after working
for Peter Behrens). The Werkbund offices—glassy-sheathed space
with a stylish composition of brick base and entry, floating (Wright-
inspired) penthouse roofs, and transparent, semicylindrical, glass
stair volumes—seem out of his carefully detailed simplistic mainstream: the Fagus factory, Siemenstadt Housing (1929), and the
Bauhaus, greatest individual work and vehicle for his teaching. In
1925 the Bauhaus was moved to Dessau from Weimar, where
Gropius had been enlisted as its director in 1919. He had renamed
the school to signify his concern that the many white- and blue-
collar trades of building must once again join together as in the
master builder/guild symbiosis of the great medieval cathedrals.
Others who joined him there at varying times included Mies van der
Rohe (director, 1930–33), Marcel Breuer, and László Moholy-Nagy.
Gropius's final American involvement as principal design teacher
at Harvard fleshed out a whole generation of younger American

133

architects (ranging, however, from the Gropius-like asceticism of Richard Stein to the romantic expressionism of Paul Rudolph). He practiced in medieval-like semi-anonymity with a flock of younger partners (Fletcher, MacMillans, Thompson, et al.) as The Architects' Collaborative (T.A.C.): the Federal Building in Boston's new Civic Center (1968); a major scheme for the University of Baghdad (1963); the U.S. Embassy at Athens (1961); and the Harvard Graduate Center (1949). Of them the Center is, perhaps, closest to Gropius's ideals: the later buildings catch the germs of stylishness from T.A.C.'s peers.

**GROTTO**  An artificial cave, part of a romantic landscape design, as by Kent, Chambers, et al. In an era (eighteenth century) where ruins were constructed from scratch as scenic improvements, an artificial, naturalistic cave-grotto seems hardly unusual.

**GROUND COVER**  Low dense plants that carpet the ground, as does grass, with a rougher texture, requiring no cutting or other fanatic maintenance. Most common in America are ivy (English or Boston), pachysandra, and myrtle (also called *Vinca minor*).

**GROUNDS**  The usable land incidental to and around a building (there are *grounds* keepers to keep and maintain it); usually applied to an institution (college, hospital, etc.) or great estate.

GRUEN *Plan for Fort Worth, Texas*

**GROUT**  Tucked between tiles after they are laid, to fill the voids between. It may be cement or plastic or lime, any wet substance that will chemically harden in place.

**GRUEN, VICTOR (1903–    )** *Austrian American Architect* Northland Shopping Center (Detroit, Michigan) brought the architecture of America's greatest auto-fed shopping centers to its apogee: a spiral urban complex of buildings of substantial materials and design quality, an urban pedestrian island in a sea of cars. Much credit is due to him for persuading a client (Hudson's department store) to make the shopping center artistically respectable.

**GRUZEN, BARNETT SUMNER (1903–1974)** *Latvian American Architect* Barney Gruzen's talent was his ability to make the new and unusual, even experimental, into real buildings in the rough world of public architecture in and for New York City. He yearned for design prominence, seeking staff designers who might lead Kelly and Gruzen (later Gruzen and Partners) to glory, and through his own tough political savvy turned his fantasies into reality: the American Express Pavilion at the New York World's Fair (1965); Chatham Green and Chatham Towers Housing. Later, with partners, the firm went on to the New York City Police Headquarters, Schomburg Plaza, and other works of remarkable quality in New York's urban landscape.

**GUARINI, GUARINO (1624–1683)** *Italian Mathematician and Architect*  His architecture is of Turin, a north Italian crossbreeding of his own post-Euclidian mathematics with admiration for Borromini (25 years his senior).

Structures of domes, lanterned and ribbed, were his specialty. And their lying-on-the-back-looking-up-at-the-ceiling illustration seems to be his photographed fate. Has Guarini ever been recorded from a normal eye's place in space?

S. Lorenzo (1668) and S. Sindone are his most remarkable dome-lanterns suggesting a larger potential architectural geometry of vaults and arches (now all destroyed, and unrecorded except in words).

GRUZEN *Chatham Green, New York*

**GUASTAVINO**  That Spanish-family vaulting brought from Barcelona to America. Tiles, laminated in layers, could, under the Guastavinos, span great spaces without scaffolding. Easiest viewed example is New York's Grand Central Station Oyster Bar. It was also the structure, secretly and privately (great engineering remained disguised for two generations behind Beaux-Arts neo-Renaissance pomp), of the Metropolitan Museum galleries and old Pennsylvania Station (both by McKim, Mead and White).

**GUIMARD, HECTOR (1867–1942)** *French Architect*  Six years younger than Horta, and inspired by him, he created a plastic architecture best illustrated by his own house on the avenue Mozart, Paris. The best of his talents were in metalwork design, such as the entrance gates at 16 rue de la Fontaine, or 142 avenue de Versailles, and those bronze, glass, and enamel lighted Metro entrances that make Paris so memorable.

135

GWATHMEY *Robert Gwathmey House, Amagansett, New York*

**GUTTAE**   The peg's-head ornaments carved in marble under the cornice edge of a Classical Greek Doric entablature, supposedly reminiscent of the wood-pegged architecture from which it was derived.

**GUTTER**   A half-round, half-square, or other-shaped open-water conduit at a building's edge, pitched from the horizontal to carry rain away to dry wells or storm sewers.

**GWATHMEY,   CHARLES (1938–    )** *American   Architect* Gwathmey has been prematurely bundled into a set to produce the "New York 5" or the "Whites" (with Peter Eisenman, Michael Graves, John Hejduk, and Richard Meier). This glib subclassification is inaccurate in that his best work is neither white (i.e., of neo-Cubistic stucco) nor overintellectualized. The house for his father, painter Robert Gwathmey, was an excellent first: smooth flush boards creating prismatic form.

**GYPSUM**   A plaster base, glue and body, as portland cement is the glue and body of concrete. Gypsum is coarser, but fireproof, as compared to lime plaster (lime is $CaCO_3$, gypsum is $CaSO_4$).

# H

**HABITABLE**   Place or space where one can live with sufficient light, air, sanitation. A cave or the bare woods can be habitable, under the circumstance of primitive life standards, or in camping in the wilds. Definitive standards lie within the balance of a culture's wants and needs: a monk's cell is against the law in New York; and a cave might seem a palace to a cold nomad.

**HABITAT**   The environment of a living creature is its habitat, and its ecology is the balance between creature and habitat in all senses: location, climate, food supplies, other life. "Habitat," more flippantly, is a place to live; that of Expo '67 at Montreal (Habitat, by Moshe Safdie) is a grand piece of architecture, unhappily unrelated to the North American building process, which is saddled with archaic codes, and the equally archaic procedures of construction dictated by union contracts. Ergo, it was, and duplicates still portend to be, wildly expensive.

**HACIENDA**   A Spanish (and reasonably grand) ranch house.

**HADFIELD, GEORGE (1764–1826)** *Italian-born English American Architect*   He was one of a long line of superintendents of the Capitol's construction; replaced in 1798, he was "liberated" to work for the city's needs (Washington, D.C.). The city hall and Arlington House (1803+) are memorable Greeks, in a city that later embraced mostly Roman wallpaper.

HADFIELD *Proposed Treasury Building, Washington, D.C.*

137

**HA-HA**   Very English term for a negative fence, a ditch to contain the ramblings of domestic animals. Useful for zoos as well, in a deeper and even less traversable form.

**HALFPENNY, WILLIAM M. H. (1687–1755)** *English Architect and Writer*  Copybook writer for the gentleman builder, and builder for gentlemen. He produced at least 20 volumes of sometimes Palladian illustrations: plans and elevations (compare the contemporary books of Batty Langley, Samuel Sloane).

**HALF TIMBERING**   The timbers are not halved, but half of the architectural display is in the timber frame, analogous to modern steel or concrete framing, infilled with brick, or mud and straw (wattle and daub). Half timbering provides the engineering of basic nonmonumental English and French medieval houses, housing, inns, and minor public buildings.

**HALL**   Space between specialized rooms to give access to them and to allow for social interchange; perhaps tantamount to an internal plaza. But also used for any passage, however mean or short, in residential architecture.
   Medieval houses and castles often had a *great* hall, the assembly place of the family or court, fire-lit and warmed, with small cubicles adjacent.

**HALPRIN, LAWRENCE (1916–   )** *American Landscape Architect*  Designer of contained, planted, pebbled and watered experiences, in the spirit, at times, of the Japanese or the Moors. Halprin's McIntyre Watergardens (1961, Hillsborough, Calif.) are worthy of the Alhambra, royal palace of the Moors in fourteenth-century Spain. He shares modern urban landscape design honors with M. Paul Friedberg and Robert Zion.

**HAMILTON, THOMAS (1784–1858)** *Scottish Architect*  Greek Revivalist in Edinburgh (along with Playfair).

**HAMLET**   Diminutive term for a separate community of very few houses and people and of modest wealth.

**HAMMER BEAM**   A structural set of timber for roofing a medieval English hall (as a refectory). Each piece leans on the set below

HALPRIN *Auditorium Forecourt Fountain, Portland, Oregon*

(compare corbeled masonry), a sequential idea, additive in thinking and action (as opposed to a truss, which acts as a monolithic whole).

**HAND**   The technical term for the way a door swings: to the left and away is said to be with the left *hand,* and to the right similarly.

**HANDRAIL**   The top member of a railing or balustrade, to guide one's hand and give security from tripping.

**HANGAR**   A word for a shelter, assumed by the aviation industry to describe an airplane's garage, a natural, immense open place in the later generation of commercial planes: a 747 is as large as St. Peter's; the DC-3 would fit in a high-school gym. The hangar has given pure engineering one of its most magnificent architectural vehicles: as those of Freyssinet at Orly, or Nervi at Fiumicino.

**HARDBOARD**   A hard, smooth board pressed from wood granules (as opposed to the softer particle boards made from coarser sawdust). The fine grain and binder, when heat-treated (under pressure and temperature), gives a fine sanded and sandable finish for modest furniture and, when drilled, pegboard.

**HARDENBERGH, HENRY J. (1847–1918)** *American Architect*
The Plaza Hotel (1907), Dakota Apartments (1884), and the Art Students' League (1892)—all in New York—are elegant environments for civilized or civilizing life, ornate and richly spatial places of an eclectic Late Renaissance Revival set of architecture. Their elaborately detailed delights have preserved them from destruction, in spite of the greater profit developers foresaw from their replacement. In the case of the Dakota, its residents bought the building, converting it to a cooperative.

**HARDOUIN-MANSART, JULES (1646–1708)** *French Architect*
The first organization architect, whose vast practice was supported by a staff of designers and superintendents. He took the elegant beginnings of Louis XIV's Versailles by Le Vau and stretched them to the monumental scaled façade that confronts Le Nôtre's gardens today in mannered limestone.

The Invalides Chapel (of the military hospital, The Invalids) is French Baroque at its apogee; appreciated by Napoleon, it was

HARDOUIN-MANSART *North wing of palace, Versailles*

139

co-opted for his tomb: a high domical composition (cf. the Val-de-Grace).

Most important to the city-dweller, however, is the Place Vendôme (1698+)—originally the Place Louis le Grand (XIV)—where a major urban space was excised from the medieval city. A uniform façade shields myriad functions (Hôtel Continental, stores, houses, offices). Originally Hardouin-Mansart had hoped for great public uses, but, by default, it became a grand space serving lively but ordinary city requirements.

At Versailles two special delights of Hardouin-Mansart are his Grand Trianon, a kind of on-campus luxurious retreat for the king and in itself an elaborate country palace (Camp David on the grounds of the White House); and secondly, the chapel, a sober Baroque, with the physical dimensions of a major church.

**HARDWICK, PHILIP (1792–1870)** *English Architect* Memorable for his Euston Station portal, a Greek Revival propylaea (formal gate) destroyed, seemingly willfully and viciously, by the British government railway philistines: a moving moment in the then mushrooming worldwide sensitization to landmarks preservation.

Hardwick was architect to Thomas Telford's engineering-dominant work at the St. Katherine's Docks.

HARRIS *Weston Havens House, Berkeley*

**HARDWOOD** Slow-growing deciduous trees produce hardwood, as opposed to fast-growing evergreens, which are soft. The former include oak, maple, ash, birch—all common in finish flooring, paneling, furniture, and cabinetry; the latter include fir, pine, hemlock, spruce—most now used for structural members (studs, joists, columns, and beams of a building), where hardness is the secondary, flexed strength the primary, consideration.

**HARRIS, HARWELL HAMILTON (1903–   )** *American Architect* His tiny house in Fellowship Park (1935, Los Angeles) is a dream, a Japanese floating pavilion in a moss- and fern-encrusted ravine. Later, his houses were more spectacular, as that inverted trussed hill-hanger on Panoramic Way (1941, Berkeley), and the slotted wood "fort" below (same year). He went to the University of Texas to teach, then North Carolina, still pursuing a minor practice, but leaving his major artifacts behind.

140

**HARRISON, PETER (1716–1775)** *English American Architect*
Rhode Island's greatest architect, immigrant from England who educated himself for his later and magnificent accomplishments. Gibbs's books were handy and gave Harrison his source material for King's Chapel (1749, Boston) and the Touro Synagogue (1759+, Newport), America's oldest extant Jewish building. Most telling remnant is the Brick Market (1761+), a formal, almost Palladian, arcaded and pilastered brick box, elegant among the banal shopping center buildings that now surround it.

**HARRISON, WALLACE K. (1895– )** *American Architect*
The Benign Compromiser, whose curiously valuable talents include architectural design arbitration: of the United Nations complex and Lincoln Center, both in New York and both wargrounds of competing egos. In more unilateral action, his firm held responsibility for design of Nelson Rockefeller's Hollywoodian boondoggle at Albany: the South Mall, a modern acropolis surmounted by stylish, high-density, but scarcely urbane, objects.

The United Nations buildings, form-child of Le Corbusier, was officially the product of an international committee (Le Corbusier, France; Oscar Niemeyer, Brazil; Harrison for the U.S.; and others). Unlike Lincoln Center, where the committee could divide the spoils, each member retaining a building as his share, the U.N. was a joint product, molded under the dominant prestige and will present: Le Corbusier. But whereas philosophy and form came from that font, agreement required executive direction (by Harrison), who caused the chosen product to be officially disgorged. Secondly, the committee needed one or ones to execute reality: and Harrison and Abramovitz became the architects of record, to translate the concept into contract documents and construction. It is a bold concept for New York, a sample of a Le Corbusier "towers in a park," but both economics and urbane taste will prevent its repetition.

Harrison left one very personal mark: the First Presbyterian Church (1956) of Stamford, Connecticut.

**HAUNCH** The masonry that supports the "spring" of an arch: its diving board across the space spanned.

**HAUSSMANN, (BARON) GEORGES-EUGÈNE (1809–1891)** *French Alsation Lawyer and Administrator* From 1853 to 1870 Haussmann was effectively Napoleon III's sub-dictator for Paris,

HARRISON *Presbyterian Church, Stamford, Connecticut*

HAUSSMANN *Boulevard de l'Opéra, Paris*

concerned with its total administrative and operational problems. He is remembered in architectural histories for the great boulevard system he *completed* (the Champs Élysées, among others, was already there). Equally important were his public transit (omnibuses, horse-drawn), aqueducts, sewers (now even tourist attractions), and parks (Bois de Boulogne), and the great, now destroyed, cast-iron markets, Les Halles.

The boulevard system related, visually, the principal monuments of the city and expedited traffic; but, more importantly, it produced a neo-Baroque visual order commensurate with that Pope Sixtus V and his architect, Domenico Fontana, had imposed on Rome 200 years earlier.

**HAVILAND, JOHN (1792–1852)** *American Architect*  The Egyptian-pyloned "Tombs" (1836), now destroyed, were prison and court combined for New York, and now largely a detective-story allusion ("Take him to the Tombs").

The Eastern Penitentiary (1829) near Philadelphia was a crenelated fortress, one of America's first design exports to Europe. His book, *The Builder's Assistant* (1818), described the Classical orders to American artisans.

**HAWKSMOOR, NICHOLAS (1661–1736)**    *English Architect*  In a simplistic (in detail) geometrician's Baroque, Hawksmoor's solid (perhaps stolid) churches pick up where Wren's pretty ones leave off (he was draftsman to both Wren and Vanbrugh). St. George in the East (1715) and St. Mary Woolnoth (1716) are towered with forms anticipating Sir John Soane's Regency 100 years later. Solemn, austere, vigorous, lusty, a virile architecture in counterpoint to Wren's and Gibbs's delicate virtuosity.

Wren built fifty-two churches for London after the Great Fire of 1666, Hawksmoor but five (after 1711).Virtuosity reigned in Hawksmoor's  Gothic West Towers of Westminster Abbey flanking Henry Yevele's nave.

**HEAD**    The top of a door or window; hence, where a man's head must clear.

**HEADER**    A brick whose end (head) is exposed in the face of a wall, usually serving as a tie to bond a double-brick thick wall together. The pattern of headers frequently becomes a decorative idea. (See also *Bond*.)

**HEARTH**   The floor of a fireplace, over which a fire burns, and over which food was traditionally cooked (hearth and home suggest personal bed and board to the traveler). The front hearth projects a brick, stone, or tile apron into a wood-framed floor to prevent the combustion of its home.

**HEAT**   Energy of one form (as is electricity or a waterfall or fission or fusion) that flows to any place with less of it. Heat flows to cold (absence of heat) unless constrained by insulation or isolation, and hence from furnace to house as necessary to replace that which escapes outdoors (or, conversely, air-cooled conditioning combats the heat that infiltrates and radiates into the cooled internal space from without). In modern office buildings the excess heat of people and lights needs air-cooling to temper it, even in the dead of winter.

**HEDGE**   An interlocking shaped and trimmed set of shrubbery designed to fence or demarcate property and bar vision or entry. Hedges, being discouraging, but not impenetrable, suggest hedging, the financial act of protecting an absolute by an alternate investment.

**HELLENISTIC**   Pertaining to the new Greek (and therefore Hellene) colonies gathered by Alexander's conquests between 356 and 323 B.C.: North Africa, the Middle East (Syria today), Egypt, Asia Minor (Turkey today). Greek art became sophisticated and self-conscious in its exportation en masse. The scale inflated to one grandiose; ornament ranged from ornate to overt encrustation, and buildings often served more secular (humanistic) purposes.

(In Hellenistic Egypt the Ptolemys—progeny of Alexander's general who made himself Pharaoh after Alexander's death—took the vocabulary of the New Kingdom and left us several of the most perfectly preserved temples at Philae, Esna, Edfu, and Dendera.)

The most emulated Hellenistic monuments are the Choragic Monument of Lysicrates (Lysicrates won the choral competition and honored his own success in 323 B.C.); the tomb of King Mausoleus at Halicarnassus; and the Temple of Artemis at Ephesus. (Compare, in modern dress, a Wren church's spire; Grant's Tomb; and the U.S. Supreme court.)

HAWKSMOOR *Christ Church, Spitalfields, London*

143

**HENKEN, DAVID (1915–    )** *American Architect and Builder*
Henken was an early Wright apprentice, whose faith did more for his master than that of myriad acolytes in search of their own identities: Neutra, Soleri, Tafel, et al. Henken built Usonia, the community of Wright-inspired buildings north of the Kensico Reservoir, at New Castle, New York. The place is dominated by the Wright-designed Friedman House. Henken's own designs were modest attempts at humanism.

**HENNEBIQUE, FRANÇOIS (1842–1921)** *French Architect* *Béton armée*, they called it (reinforced concrete), and Hennebique was one of its first users: bridges, factories, and other structures society considered a-visual or unimportant were built in this then-considered crass and radical material. (For aesthetic developments in concrete, see both *Perret, Auguste*, and *Garnier, Tony*.

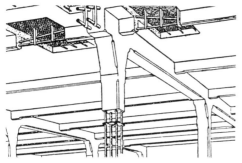

HENNEBIQUE *Drawing of a reinforced concrete construction*

**HERSHEY, PENNSYLVANIA** A planned paternalistic, Victorian company town, source of the bar of the same name. Civilizations and cultures pass, but chocolate and liquor last through eternity.

**HEXASTYLE** With six columns: *hex-* is Greek for *six*, and *-style* is *column*.

**HINGE** The movable, leaved pivot on which a door hangs.

**HIP** The straight-edged external meeting of two ascending roof slopes (as opposed to the internal one that forms to a valley). A hip roof is one with no gables, with eaves at one height all around.

**HIPPODAMUS OF MILETUS (542?–468? B.C.)** *Greek Colonial Architect* Colonial Greek who came to Athens and, in effect, founded town planning through abstract and ideal propositions: a rectilinear grid, segregated classes (of people), and functional differentiation of a city's parts were new and forward-looking ideas in a society of random growth (except for an occasional agora or acropolis). His fame was established by Aristotle, who wrote about him.

**HIPPODROME** A place for horseplay.

**HOBAN, JAMES (1762 ? –1831)** *Irish American Architect* The White House is a product of his Dublin memories of Leinster House, catalyzed by James Gibbs's (1728) *Book of Architecture* (1728). After it was burned in the War of 1812, Hoban supervised its restoration to a state that survived until 1948, when Harry Truman vacated it for temporary residence in Blair House (a substantial guest mansion, Greek-Revived, across the street). The body was removed, the clothes starched and propped, new structural guts (of steel and concrete) installed; old ornaments and paneling (and furniture) replaced; and it was better than new, but it became the hard ghost of its original self (the floors don't creak).

Harry added a balcony within the south semicircular porticoed colonnade, much to some purists' despair.

**HOFFMANN, JOSEF (1870–1956)** *Austrian Architect, Book Illustrator, and Furniture Designer* A proto-Cubist architect usually lumped with his contemporary Joseph Olbrich; his teacher, Otto Wagner; and his art-historical soulmate, the Scot, Charles Rennie Mackintosh.

His works include the Convalescent Home (1903, Purkersdorf), Palais Stoclet (1905, Brussels), and those elegant bentwood chairs that are still widely used by the most radical modernists (they are exquisitely comfortable, a state of grace rare in modern furniture).

**HOIST** A top-lifter; a cable suspended from crane or scaffold.

**HOLABIRD, WILLIAM (1854–1923)** *American Architect* Holabird and Roche were both present at the birth of the Chicago School and among its principal generators. Holabird's Tacoma Building (1886) brought architectural distinction to steel-cage architecture, first employed by William Le Baron Jenney (for whom he had worked as a design engineer) at the Home Insurance Building (1883+). In effect, the Tacoma was the Chicago School's *aesthetic* birthing, starting the track of articulated cage architecture that ran for only seven vigorous years to its denouement: the World's Columbian Exposition (Chicago World's Fair of 1893), which blessed an American neo-renaissance.

HOLABIRD *The Republic Building, Chicago*

**HOLFORD, (SIR) WILLIAM (1907–    )** *South African-English Town Planner* The blitz erased the old City surrounding St. Paul's, but, almost in a miracle (in the age of disbelief in the efficacy of God

145

HOOD *Former McGraw-Hill Building, New York*

and religion), St. Paul's itself was spared. Holford seized this equally miraculous architectural opportunity and replanned the area (1955+). It suffers from the *Architectural Review* disease: i.e., the drawings show a promise of urbanity (mostly in small things—textures, paving, street furnishings, lighting) which just isn't there in the final product. Quaint and romantic building relationships (as so well described by Camillo Sitte) don't work at the scale of building necessary for modern business and residential functions.

**HOLLAND, HENRY (1745–1806)** *English Architect*  Son-in-law of Capability Brown. He was the elegant architect of Brooks's Club (1776). Also of interest are Southill (1795) and Berrington Hall (1778), country houses.

**HOMESTEAD**  The (U.S.) Homestead Act of 1867 specified that ¼ square mile (160 acres) was yours if you would permanently dwell there and till it. It was an inducement to population movement westward, and it worked.

**HOOD, RAYMOND (1881–1934)** *American Architect*  New York's late-blooming response to the Chicago School, Hood either directly designed or indirectly catalyzed New York's greatest buildings: the McGraw-Hill Building (1931) is a towered cage clad in glazed brick and glass, a blue-green outlander standing lone and lonely on West 42nd Street (now occupied by Group Health Insurance, Inc., since McGraw-Hill removed to Establishment Row on the Avenue of the Americas, a street of buildings nominally part of the inflated, but debased, Rockefeller Center complex).

The Daily News Building, on East 42nd Street, is a bridge in design development between McGraw-Hill and Rockefeller Center: vertical slots of windows and stacks of handsomely patterned brickwork separated by plain brick pilasters. Hood was present at the creation (but not fulfillment) of Rockefeller Center, accompanied by his intellectual progeny (Corbett, Harrison & MacMurray; Reinhard and Hofmeister; Fouilhoux). He died 2 years after its development (1932–40) began.

**HORIZON**  The ultimate horizontal, sky's meeting with earth (in fact the silhouette of the earth against dust-reflected sunlight). Those who have never been to, or at, sea cannot appreciate the absolute of a horizon—in a black night, far from sound, light, and distractions (sunset on a placid-dead Indian Ocean off Ceylon, knife-edge of black on black).

**HORSEPOWER**  A wistful machine-age allusion to the animal- and human-powered world. A million horses couldn't supply a million horsepower; no one could harness and organize even a fraction of that number. The measure is a word romance, based on 33,000 foot-pounds of work each minute defining a horsepower (lift 1,000 pounds 33 feet in a minute and *1* horsepower will be expended).

**HORTA, (BARON) VICTOR (1861–1947)** *Belgian Architect* Art Nouveau's inner circle seems (in retrospect) to include (among others) van de Velde, Guimard, Munch, Tiffany, and Horta. Historians' minds respond like Pavlov's dogs and register Art Nouveau when Horta's name is spoken: an unfortunate limitation that prevents his larger architectural ideas from bearing their own weight. The Maison du Peuple (House of the People; 1896) in Brussels is a steel and glass romance, steel sinuous, glass accommodating; certainly Art Nouveau, but much more: the structure is the decoration, the space magnificent.

**HÔTEL**  The French town-palace, traditionally with walled forecourt, that joins the hard urban street with, at its best, a garden-park behind (in capsule, a mini-Versailles).

Hôtel de la Vrillière (1635, Paris), by François Mansart, is a classic hôtel. Hôtels were also any big urban public buildings, as a *hôtel de ville* (town hall).

**HOUSE**  The shell of life, and container for single and family activities, that with human use becomes a "home." A hermit crab makes a house, if not a home, of a shell it finds and picks up in passing. An unoccupied house is not a home.

**HOUSING**  Dwellings en masse when discussed as a commodity or resource, as opposed to merely a set of apartments or houses. Housing is a political (and hence, planning) phrase, suggesting urban affairs, design, and the pressures of supply and demand reminiscent of "welfare," "education," and "national defense." Unfortunately, those concerned are less influential than those who created agricultural subsidies or bombed Cambodia.

HORTA *Maison du Peuple, Brussels*

**HOWARD, (SIR) EBENEZER (1850–1928)** *English Stenographer and Practicing Utopian* Clerk, dreamer, realist, and Utopian, his fertile and independent imagination took hold of Edward Bellamy's *Looking Backward* and generated a whole concept of the detached (satellite) city, bearing virtues of both city and country (hence, the *"Garden" City*), self-contained with work, play, residence, and culture (See also *Garden City.*)

**HOWARD, JOHN GALEN (1864–1931)** *American Architect and Planner* Fourth-placed competitor selected to complete the winning scheme of Emile Bénard in the 1899 competition for a master plan for the University of California at Berkeley. Phoebe Appleton Hearst financed the competition, with Bernard Maybeck as its professional adviser and manager. Howard was already on campus as architect of the Mining building, built in memory of Mrs. Hearst's husband (a building with a ponderous Classical-Spanish exterior and spectacular, lacy glass-roofed interior).

Howard is lovingly remembered by generations of Berkeley architecture students for the "Ark" (1906), a shingled shell that housed the School of Architecture until recently.

**HOWE, GEORGE (1886–1955)** *American Architect* With the bright young Swiss, William Lescaze, Howe designed the P.S.F.S. (Philadelphia Savings Fund Society) Building in the sad but vintage modern year of 1932. Apocrypha would have Lescaze's brilliance complementing Howe's native W.A.S.P. business acumen and salesmanship. Counter-apocrypha claim a pox on both houses, with Lescaze an opportunist manager of talented employees. And recent investigators claim a basic Howe talent, as exemplifed later and on his own at the Thomas House (1939; Mount Desert Island, Maine).

**HOYT, BURNHAM (1887–    )** *American Architect* He designed that Gothic reinforced-concrete office building-church, Riverside (1932; John D. Rockefeller's Baptist Church and money) for Pelton, Allen and Collins.

More refreshing is his Red Rocks Amphitheater (1941) near Denver, a natural terraced bowl for concerts, serving 9,000 people.

**HUE** What most call "color": modified by chroma (intensity or brilliance) and value (lightness or darkness). A light (value) bright

HYPERBOLIC PARABOLOID *Massena, New York, Country Club*

(chroma) yellow (hue) vs. a dark (value) medium (chroma) (red (hue), for example.

**HUMAN SCALE**   Related to humankind, as a basic module or measurement, and subject to differing interpretations in different times and cultures. (See also *Modulor.*)

**HUNT, RICHARD MORRIS (1827–1895)** *American Architect* Professional organizer, Establishment talent, link between the first formalists educated at the Paris École des Beaux-Arts and the emerging American "profession." He was first president of the A.I.A. (American Institute of Architects); designer of the north wing of the Louvre (in the office of Lefuel, who veneered Percier and Fontaine's rue de Rivoli façade with his own newer and fancier dress); and architect of the inverse-snobbery-named "cottages" at Newport for Vanderbilts (the Breakers and Marble House), the main body of New York's Metropolitan Museum of Art, and the monumental pedestal for the Statue of Liberty.

HUNT *Marble House, Newport*

**HUT**   A very small house; minimal place to live.

**HUXTABLE, ADA LOUISE (1921–   )** *American Architectural Critic*   In the renaissance of American architectural criticism, Ada Louise Huxtable is the solid, thorough, thoughtful conscience of the Northeast: in *The New York Times* (and occasional books such as *Classic New York* [1964] and *Will They Ever Finish Bruckner Boulevard?* [1970]) she shreds the villains, furthers the preservation of landmarks, and honors real and grace-filled urban virtues (as opposed to the flashy, the flamboyant, the theoretical hopefuls). Somehow the true, the good, and the beautiful surface joyfully again. Not since the pedantic Russell Sturgis and the acid Montgomery Schuyler has popular attention been turned critically to architectural events by the daily press in this way (Lewis Mumford's measured words in the *New Yorker* in the late forties and fifties were to a narrower, though national, audience, and were less topical).

**HYPERBOLIC PARABOLOID**   A skin placed and defined in space (a sinuous rigid tent) by mathematical logic. Stretched plastic, wood, concrete, or even steel can be the sheeting of a hyperbolic paraboloid. Examples include Felix Candela's Church of Our Lady of Miracles in Mexico City, and Victor Prus and Norval White's Massena Country Club at Massena, New York.

**HYPOCAUST**  The raised, air-heated floor of a Roman bath, warming it radiantly through its hot surface.

**HYPOSTYLE**  In ancient Egyptian temple architecture, a hall of columns, many and big, more important than the space they intercept. Most grand is the hypostyle hall of the Temple at Karnak (in modern Luxor, ancient Thebes). A walled complex the size of a large town, Karnak's greatest moment is its hypostyle, as large as Notre Dame, two thirds as tall. Carved with ceremonial bas-reliefs and hieroglyphics, the columns reveal narrow views in a person's travel, opaque stone to eyes off axis.

HYPOSTYLE *Parthenon, Athens*

# I

**ICONOGRAPHY**   A word borrowed to describe the symbolism of a person, place, or religion. An icon is the almost animistic symbol of the Eastern (formerly Roman) Church, split from its mother as the Roman empire expanded. Icons (paintings) were given symbolic value greater than their painted images.

Iconography is the study of icons, or use thereof; but an intelligent dilettante, I(saac) N(ewton) Phelps Stokes, published between 1915 and 1929 a six-volume *Iconography of Manhattan Island*, verbally and visually recording everything of merit that modeled its topography, incised its landscape, or festooned its man-made environment —from the naked, tree-filled Indian isle to the stone-concrete-steel crust that it is today. Faint footprints remain, tracks of a softer past, and all these, in time sequentially, are recorded by Stokes.

**ICONOSTASIS**   Place of icons, symbolic paintings of the Eastern Orthodox Church (split from Rome to form Greek and Russian orthodoxies). The screen wall that separates the standing congregation from the three-compartmented ceremonial east end of the church, it contains spaces equivalent to the Roman church's chancel and chapels.

**ICTINUS**   In partnership with Callicrates, he produced in nine years the most admired, copied, and emulated building of all history: the Parthenon, dominant element of the Acropolis of Athens, completed in 432 B.C. Later their ultimately refined Doric "orders" were revived in myriad points of the globe, by myriad architect-builders, in myriad materials (wood, stone, cast iron, plaster) in a "Greek Revival." At times, even direct copies of the Parthenon (1896, Nashville) were attempted; mostly the revival borrows parts for a portico or porch, or merely the emphasis of a doorway or the interior ornamentation of plaster rooms.

IGLOO

**IGLOO**  A pure form from the ultimate raw material, water—here admittedly solid, and hence temporarily termed *ice*. It is inexhaustible, and serves not only as sophisticated building block, but insulates its internal residents (regardless of the cold outside an igloo is a minimum of 32 degrees Fahrenheit, the fixed cold of ice insulating one from the greater cold outside). The only problem might be the internal melting of the domed hemisphere (from body heat, fires, etc.). Of course, if one then sloshed water on the exterior, one would have an igloo of indefinitely increasing volume and thickness (an engineering possibility not yet faced by those formally trained).

**IL CRONACA (SIMONE POLLAIUOLO) (1454–1508)** *Italian Architect and Writer*  He completed Benedetto da Maiano's Strozzi Palace in Florence, that beautiful, bumpy, courtyarded box, unexcelled in the Renaissance. The court is his alone.

**IMHOTEP (ca. 2760–2690 B.C.)** *Egyptian Architect, Physician, and God*  Prime minister of Egypt under Pharaoh Djoser, he was also architect of Djoser's funerary complex, a mini-city for afterlife surrounding a great ceremonial courtyard and serving as the first burial pyramid of Old Kingdom kings (at Sakkara, 25 miles southwest of modern Cairo). The stepped stone monolith is, in some minds, the oldest remaining stone building in the world, similar from this historical distance to the ziggurats in mud-brick of Mesopotamia; but those were stepped, spiraled routes to religious ceremonies at their peak, while Sakkara is the static place of afterlife, priests serving the mini-city at its pyramid's foot.

Imhotep's pyramid was the first of more than 700 that still, complete or in ruins, dot the plains of the desert west of the flood plain of the Nile—located at the river's flood edge so that limestone and granite could be brought to the site by water.

**IMPLUVIUM**  Catch-basin in the central courtyard of a Roman house, where surrounding roofs slope inward, gathering and directing the water to it: a natural water-supply system still used in water-barren places with high rainfall, like Bermuda. The space of the courtyard is the atrium, which contains and surrounds the impluvium.

**IMPOST** A corbeled or bracketed piece of masonry projecting from a wall and supporting an arch or part of a similar roofing structure, such as a hammer beam (see also *corbel*).

**INCANDESCENT** The hot light of electrically excited metal wire protected from combustion by an envelope of glass, drained of air, called a bulb (by the public) or a lamp (by the technicians). Inefficient in energy consumption (compared to fluorescent or metal halide or sodium vapor or mercury vapor), it is a warm and happy light for people at a one-to-one scale. In office buildings, it is extinct —except for drama in a lobby, elevator, restaurant, or cocktail lounge.

**INCH** 2.54 centimeters, a twelfth of a foot; the measure that has driven English-systemed (and -speaking) architects mad by its complex addition.

**INCINERATOR** The burning furnace for unwanted combustibles: usually paper waste and garbage (the one for people is called a crematorium). Modern problems for incinerators are the new awareness of their secondary waste (gas, smoke, solids flecking the sky) and the need to control that pollution as much as that of the solids put in the front end. Technologically possible, pollution-free incineration is wildly expensive, more so than any alternative (including exporting the garbage to Kamchatka and paying X million dollars to the Soviet government for the right).

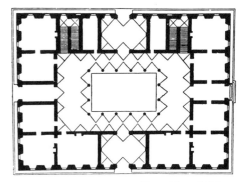

IL CRONACA *Plan of Strozzi Palace, courtyard by Il Cronaca*

**INCISED** Cut into, as lettering on a gravestone or façade, or the sunken relief of Egyptian sculpture and hieroglyphics, especially those of Akhenaten that were at Tell el Amarna.

**INDIA** The territory of British India was so large and articulate in form as to be termed a *sub*-continent, now, in turn, subdivided into Pakistan, India, and Bangladesh. The architecture of temples —Hindu, Buddhist, Moslem—is the largest block of built history in all three countries.

Modern architecture, designed by both native and imported talent, has built distinguished major buildings for politics on the subcontinent. Chandigarh, the capital of the Indian half of the split state of the Punjab (split in the partition of India), is from master plans of, first, the late Polish American architect Matthew Nowicki, with English architect-planners Maxwell Fry and Jane Drew; later Le Corbusier took charge (with his cousin Pierre Jeanneret) and built the major political monuments while myriad English, French, and local architects built the infill of bulk housing and services.

Chandigarh's Secretariat (office building), Governor's Palace, and High Court are giant, carefully placed functional concrete sculpture, amid vast landscape—photogenic and, happily, first-rate symbolism around which to rally the populace.

Similarly, at Dacca, now the capital of Bangladesh, Louis Kahn created from the native brick of that alluvial country a grand Capitol of simple materials and modern thinking that equals Chandigarh in visual symbolism, but with a lower-keyed posture. Great brick arches, vaults, and bearing walls bring the overwhelming dignity of understatement to the new country.

At Ahmadabad, Le Corbusier built a number of buildings, houses, and the Mill Owners' Headquarters. Perhaps more importantly, it is the seat of one of India's two major architects, C. V. Doshi (Charles Correa is the other), whose Corbusiesque buildings are personal statements based on Le Corbusier, but as the foundation of his own further development.

INDIA *National Assembly Building, Dacca, Bangladesh*

**INDUSTRIALIZATION**   Building components have always been made at a distance from the site where they are composed into buildings, as brick in Mesopotamia or obelisks in Old Kingdom Egypt. The former, because it is in quantity, must be produced by an organized system and implies industry (the latter is custom work in a quarry).

Industry is the organized, continuing fabrication of something someone wants, with or without mechanization. The Industrial Revolution was based on the tapping of energy to produce power-based industry, the revolution being one of economy, possibility, quantity, and speed, hence a revolution of degree. A hundred million bricks could be made with the resources formerly assigned to a hundred thousand.

In the late twentieth century, in architecture, the word suggests not only degrees of efficiency and value but a scale of larger and larger parts or sections of the building in question: whole bathrooms, wall panels, room-boxes, systems of structure, mechanical equipment, assembled and/or fabricated in silent assembly-lined perfection. The promise is more real than the accomplishments.

**INGLENOOK**   Fireroom space. A sitting nook within a fireplace volume.

**INLAY**   To lay into an incised design another material, usually a different-valued and -hued wood. But marble and other fine-grained stones may be inlaid as well.

**INSOLATION**   The screening of a building or place from the sun's rays to minimize the sun's radiated heat and glare. A summer umbrella is insolation: e.g., the parasol.

**INSULATION**   A material (or assembly) that will cut the loss of heat or passage of sound from one built place to another, or from the inside out.

**INTERNATIONAL STYLE**   The academic blessing of the real world's avant-garde by act of exhibition at New York's Museum of Modern Art (1932; Henry Russell Hitchcock and Philip Johnson). Their chosen architectural spectrum was white Cubism, laced with glass and steel windows: as that of Adolf Loos, Walter Gropius, Le Corbusier, Mallet-Stevens, Oud.
The phrase stuck and has been loosely applied to a larger body of world-renowned architecture, but its pure meaning is lost, and its application sloppy.

**INTRADOS**   The armpit of an arch.

**INWOOD, HENRY W. (1794–1843)** *English Architect*   St. Pancras Church in London by Inwood and his father used parts or wholes of all the monuments in Greece in one building, a staggering challenge, a kind of composite retrospective of another, unwilling civilization.

**IONIC**   The Ionians are blamed for or blessed with this classy, elegant order of architectural parts, capitals analogous to rams' horns, a more effete and (visually) less sturdy column system than Doric, used almost simultaneously on the Acropolis for the Erech-

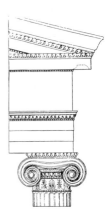

IONIC *Entablature*

theum, Propylaea, and the tiny elegance of the Temple of Nike Apteros.

Ionic was exported in quantity (and in inflated sizes), as Doric was not, creating the great Hellenistic (the late Greek architecture after Alexander) temples of Artemis at Ephesus, of Baalbek, of Palmyra. The later Corinthian was embraced, packaged, sold, and used by the Romans.

**IRELAND**  Peatbogs, potatoes, and poverty, a groundgrown and stewed ecology, spare of hard resources, generating buildings of stone, turf, thatch, and straw. Irish monumental architecture was imported to Ireland by the British proprietors of Irish land, who created a Georgian Dublin greater in its quantity and quality than London itself, and country houses to match the homeland: largely in a class war based on subtle ethnic differences, or, who had it first?

**IRON**  The element that named an age and whose discovered use allowed change in the ways of civilization, its techniques and possibilities: the nature of its warfare, building, and accoutrements.

Iron is the body of steel; smelted from iron ore, it by nature retains carbon, the residue of combustion. The carbon present determines structural characteristics of hardness, softness, malleability, and whether or not the iron has been elevated to the status of steel (by carbon reduction).

**ISIDORUS OF MILETUS**  A thousand years after Ictinus's Parthenon, Isidorus (and partner-uncle, Anthemius of Tralles) designed the Church of the Divine Wisdom (Hagia Sophia) at Constantinople, Emperor Constantine's Eastern Christian capital. This prototype of ballooning domed and semi-domed vaults became the later model for a whole history of Moslem architecture (Hagia Sophia itself, now a museum, was first converted to a mosque with added minarets).

ISIDORUS OF MILETUS *Hagia Sophia, Istanbul*

**ISLAMIC**  Islam describes the many races of the Moslem or Mohammedan or Muslim, practitioners of the medieval religion founded at Mecca by *the* prophet.

**ISOMETRIC**  A geometric drawing technique that illustrates a building or structure with verticals of true length or dimension, but with horizontals (plan dimensions) distorted.

# J

**JACK** A portable device for lifting heavy weights—cars, houses, or more—from below by alternate principles of physics: the screw, hydraulic pressure, and/or leverage. Jacks are, almost unfailingly, cast-iron and steel constructions.

**JACOBEAN** The architecture coincidental with the reign of James I.

**JACOBS, JANE (1916–    )** *Canadian American Writer* Jane Jacobs brought the community to the Planning Commission (and process) of New York, a noble democratic act to some; to others, a Pandora's box that has never quieted. Her successful blocking of Robert Moses's usually relentless process of demolition, here proposed for the west part of Greenwich Village, has made her an architectural folk-hero. She beat the Establishment and recorded that and other fights and thoughts in *The Death and Life of Great American Cities* (1961) and the *Economy of Cities* (1969).

**JACOBSEN, ARNE (1902–1971)** *Danish Architect and Furniture Designer* Unmannered buildings, and furniture with great manners. His town houses at Söholm (1949), staggered, clerestoried, multi-leveled spaces, provide the peak of Danish possibility: elegance, style, without ego or self-consciousness. As with much success, it is frequently subverted by too many quick demands: his was exploited at the S.A.S. (Hotel) building in Copenhagen (1960), a

JACOBSEN *Rowhouses, Soholm, Denmark*

157

rather tired rerun of Bunshaft's Lever House—glass prism on glass prism.

**JAIL**   The English gaol, originally conceived as a fort to keep the enemy in, rather than out (or a dungeon, to keep them down), became the American jail with the same basic Anglophile concepts: great stone fortified, bastioned, walled cities not seen since Carcassonne or Volterra. Two marvelous examples are H. H. Richardson's Allegheny Courthouse and Jail at Pittsburgh, and John Haviland's bastions and battlements at Philadelphia (1829).

Jails evolved from containers for those to be constrained—and, in fact, punished for their misdeeds by such confinement to rehabilitation campuses. The new architectural product is reminiscent of a modern college with discipline, rather than an ancient fort with license.

**JAMB**   The vertical flanking cheek of a door or window.

**JAPAN**   Island cultures breed similar stamina, high motivation, and, possessing few resources, create processing industries as their unique specialty. England, in effect, invented the Industrial Revolution; Japan, in a reprise, has re-invented it. The cast-ironed and textile world of the English 1850s has given way to the automobile, TV and computer world of the Japanese 1970s.

England imported its major architecture from France—Norman (the French Romanesque that came with the Norman conquest); Japan imported its very writing (ideographs) and original building types from China, its mainland French counterpart. Timber was a major element in both cultures, but the English relied more on stone bearing walls with timbered floor and roof framing. The Japanese developed the *whole*-timbered building, with an elaboration of interlocking timbered joints. Because of the small horizontal dimensions available in their hilly, mini-landscaped country, their complementary gardens are small, but intensely developed, to offer a variety of controlled and sequential visual experiences within short distance and time. (Cf. gardens and buildings at the Katsura detached palace, Kyoto.) Japanese residential architecture retained a classic and simplistic style, unassuming, but highly refined, an architectural (as opposed to an unconscious and primitive) vernacular. Its planning again rested on interlocking experiences with surrounding gardens and garden views.

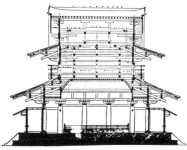

JAPAN   *Kondo, Horiuji, Nara*

158

Modern Japanese architecture is both vigorous and intensely antitraditional. Compare particularly the work of Kunio Maekawa and Kenzo Tange. Tange is the more famous, or perhaps notorious, since his highly publicized competition-winning Memorial to the Dead at Hiroshima. His Tokyo City Hall, a stylish office building, and his great arena for Expo '70, of spectacular concrete shelled roofs, are enough in themselves to remember his whole professional contribution.

Maekawa, a much older and less assuming man, was a student in the rue de Sèvres office of Le Corbusier in his youth. In Japan he created a block of apartments (Harumi Flats) that challenges the master's own (Le Corbusier's Marseille Block).

**JEANNERET, CHARLES-ÉDOUARD** See *Le Corbusier;* his pseudonym for architecture.

**JEANNERET, PIERRE (1896–1968)** *Swiss-French Architect* Cousin of Le Corbusier, and partner in projects such as the mass housing at Chandigarh (Punjab, India).

**JEFFERSON, THOMAS (1743–1826)** *Architect, Legislator, and U.S. President* Perhaps the last "renaissance" man, author of the Declaration of Independence, admirer and connoisseur of Greek and Roman civilization, "democracy," and archaeology; architect by self-education (with the advice of Clérisseau)—but that more so, and more professionally, than his contemporaries; inventor; multiple elitist, ruralist, and antiurbanist; man, father, country gentleman.

Monticello (1769+), his Virginia house-mansion near Charlottesville, is most known. Domed like a minuscule Pantheon (that great Roman pagan temple now a church), brick, the red and white of Georgian ever-present, it is a personal, personally created house for self, himself.

JEFFERSON *Monticello*

The University of Virginia (1817+), in Charlottesville, is a formalistic (but informal in use) Renaissance palace with outbuildings, suborned to the function of a college. At the time of its construction it was part of the master-slave system and society that ordered its functioning parts. (Benjamin Latrobe helped Jefferson with the design, but the extent of such aid is moot.)

The Virginia State Capitol (1796) was designed while he was in Europe and based (with the help of Clérisseau) on the Maison

Carrée, a perfectly preserved Roman provincial temple in what is now Nîmes, France. The Capitol is an inflated and en-windowed version of the original, an extrapolation analogous to the act of making a Gothic church tower into an office building (cf. Riverside Church Tower, New York).

**JENNEY, WILLIAM LE BARON (1832–1907)** *American Engineer and Architect* First examples of reality always bear a kind of notoriety, in spite of their qualities, or lack thereof. Jenney's Home Insurance Building (1885, Chicago) is the first recorded iron-and-steel-caged high-rise building, the first pulse of technology that was to become, at a much higher level of technologically inspired visual design, the Chicago School: Sullivan, Holabird, Root, Burnham, Roche et al.

**JERRY-BUILT** Slang for shoddy and flimsy construction.

**JESSOR, HERMAN (1893– )** *American Architect* Jessor is America's most prolific architect of housing, mostly for his client, the union consortium United Housing Foundation, archetypal nonprofit New York houser: Co-Op City, Rochedale Village, Hillman Houses, and others—homes for 150,000! Robert Venturi has perversely honored Co-Op City for its "ordinariness," its "banality," its service to populist art and needs. And, in fact, its services are legion—both in its excellent apartment plans and facilities and its unusually modest purchase and maintenance costs.

**JIG** A device to guide the work of a tool, as a frame to align work to be drilled would be a jig for a drill press.

**JIGSAW** A slim-bladed saw held on a tensed frame to cut intricate shapes out of flat stock (wood, metal). A whole architectural style became possible simulating Gothic stone intricacies with jig-sawn flat boards as decorative enrichment of the American balloon frame.

**JOG** An arhythmic bump in a building (in or out, projection or recession).

**JOHANSEN, JOHN McL. (1916– )** *American Architect* Early New Canaanite, his first efforts were a formalist, symmetrical pavilion architecture analogous to the then current neighboring work of

JOHANSEN *Oklahoma Theatre Center, Oklahoma City*

Philip Johnson, and near Marcel Breuer's shaggy stone and vertical cypress boxes. Johansen is a modern eclectic, drawing value from many directions of modern architecture: his product ranging from the Warner House (New Canaan, 1958), through the neo-Celtic United States Embassy in Dublin (1964), to the Mummers' Theatre in Oklahoma City, an extravaganza of boxed spaces umbilically related to each other, articulating parts as if the liver's presence were unknown and had to be slung from the body so the world would know it was rare. It is existentialist in Johansen's mind, a kind of antidote to the formal compositions of most modern work. Whatever he has tried has been, however, either spectacular or elegant.

**JOHNSON, PHILIP (1906–    )** *American Architect* Midwesterner (Cleveland), he stormed New York (at age 26) with an exhibition and book touting an "International Style" (1932; with Henry Russell Hitchcock).

Concern with, and criticism of, architecture, led him to become one. At 43 he built one of the great touchstones to which historians relate: his own glass-pavilioned house in New Canaan, Connecticut, based on his admiration for Mies van der Rohe. Some of his later stylistic adventures are located on the surrounding land: first, his own private bedroom pavilion, a circular-windowed retreat with John Soane plaster-vaulting; then an island-isolated neo-Regency "folly," a miniature Lincoln Center, an arched gazebo on a lake below his promontoried house; and lastly an underground art museum for his private collection, bulging the landscape with its pregnant, skylit form.

An elegant bachelor, a social lion, and one of the most spontaneous and verbally articulate architects of the century, Johnson is a wonderful anachronism of grace, manners, and versatility, a dilettante who has equaled the best efforts of almost all others in each one of his dabbles.

JOHNSON *Folly, New Canaan, Connecticut*

**JOINER**   The machine that makes two parts compatible, trimming them equally to a precision that will fit their edges or ends without a joint of space—and, ideally, with the joinery shown only by the varied color and texture of the two parts.

**JOINT**   The meeting of any two materials—brick to brick, wood to wood, stone to steel. All are joints to be considered by an architect for problems of strength, penetration of moisture, and loss of heat.

The architect's solution of "joinery" is the act of "detailing" a building.

**JOIST** A small beam, usually of wood, sometimes steel, aluminum, or concrete; joists are the ribs of a building, and a girder is its spine.

JONES *Whitehall Banqueting House, London*

**JONES, INIGO (1573–1652)** *English Architect* By his own distinguished products he did for England what Brunelleschi and company had done for Florence. An Italophile, in his maturity he savored Palladio.

After 15 years as a stylish Baroque stage designer, he went to Italy and, on his return to London, became Surveyor of the Royal Works (a title roughly combining royal architect and director of the nation's public works). In that role he built the Queen's House (1616–35) at Greenwich (an eastern London suburb) and, more strikingly, the Banqueting House on Whitehall (1619), a Palladian transport of staggering beauty and grandeur originally part of the Palace of Whitehall, once the sovereign's residence, but by Jones's time fallen from favor (St. James', Westminster, and, later, Buckingham palaces replaced Whitehall).

Equally important, and parallel to his royal duties, he designed on raw land owned by the Russells (dukes of Bedford), Covent Garden, England's first park-like square, complemented by his own surrounding urban residential architecture. The church at Covent Garden, St. Paul's, remains, a Roman-Tuscan throwback, with a roof structure of wood of an almost Etruscan archaeology (precursor of the marble detailing of fifth- and sixth-century Greece). First a residential precinct, it later became a market (and site of the Covent Garden Opera House). Now, in turn, deserted by the market, it is in process of conversion to renewal uses (tear down, obliterate, build anew).

**JUVARRA, FILIPPO (1678–1736)** *Italian Architect* Southern Italian who migrated to Turin and prolifically embellished that city with palaces, churches, and housing.

The Superga (1727) near Turin and the Stupinigi Palace for the King of Savoy are his most renowned works. His Italian training was grafted with the many qualities of Austrian and south German Baroque, a facile amalgam that caused magnificent, but not necessarily original, design.

One could only wish that there were more like him, who selected well from what had been done well before, and did not always insist upon originality for its own sake.

# K

KAHN, ELY JACQUES *Municipal Asphalt Plant, New York*

**KAHN, ALBERT (1869–1942)** *German American Architect* First among modern American industrial architects, whose most remembered crystal palace is the Dodge Half-ton Pickup Plant's Export Building (1938, Detroit).

**KAHN, ELY JACQUES (1884–1972)** *American Architect* With Robert Jacobs, he built a modern monument, New York's thin-concrete-shelled Municipal Asphalt Plant (1944), in the spirit of Swiss engineer Robert Maillart. He never again soared to such heights.

**KAHN, LOUIS I. (1901–1974)** *American Architect* Kahn's middle-aged self-renaissance searched anew for the reasons for architecture's forms, challenging basic programs that had been issued as standard dicta to architects as casually as the "order of the day" to docile military troops. He sought the basic meaning of education, re-search, and attempted to fulfill those needs with new sets of forms. His success is mixed, his intentions magnificent, and, on occasion, he may have created the greatest buildings of the 1960s and 1970s, as in the new Capitol of Bangladesh at Dacca (formerly East Pakistan) and the Salk Institute at La Jolla, California. Each uses the absolute technologies of its local environment: the former, the baked mud-brick of alluvial Dacca, arched and vaulted, maximizing the potentials of local resource; the latter, a serene and lusty set of post-stressed concrete serving a laboratory at its most advanced state.

He was a bear of a presence, a muddled talker with a clear mind, whose product transcended his talk. Kahn was trained in the Beaux-Arts at the University of Pennsylvania, worked with the formalist Paul Cret, was partner of Oskar Stonorov and others in early bare architecture of the Philadelphia region. But he was a sleeper of modest competence until 1951—then burst on the public scene of magazines with the adulation of students, as if in a reincarnation.

Mill Creek Housing, in west Philadelphia, was his one excursion into social architecture, pleasant but not very important; Richards Medical Center at the University of Pennsylvania (Philadelphia) is a hyperarticulated set of research forms, more important intellectually than in practice. (They are very limited laboratories for practical medical research.)

He may be remembered as the greatest American architect after Frank Lloyd Wright.

**KALLMANN, GERHARD (1915–    )** *German American Architect and Teacher*   Teacher of architecture (Cooper Union, Columbia), he joined with Michael McKinnell and Edward Knowles to win the Boston City Hall Competition (1962). Academics and theorists, their first application of reality has been a resounding critical and popular success. It suffers in plagiarized copies by lesser architects in lesser places, who borrow its mannerisms (the multi-tiered windowed cornice) as exterior decoration. It is closest of any American effort to English Brutalism.

Kallmann-McKinnell also has given the Boston Five Cent Savings Bank and parkers at the Boston Civic Center buildings of great architectural distinction.

**KEEP**   The central retreat of a medieval castle, in both the benign and defensive senses. One retreats in battle to the (inner) keep and is there kept. One retreats from worldly affairs in less militant times. The keep is the core of the apple-castle.

**KENT, WILLIAM (1685–1748)** *English Architect, Painter, Landscape Architect, and Furniture Designer*   The man who invented what the French call the English Garden, a consciously natural and informal landscape design, later culminating in the work of Capability Brown. Kent saw the possibilities of natural landscape; Brown groomed it like a *coiffeur*, outdoing nature in his use and contrast of "natural" textures.

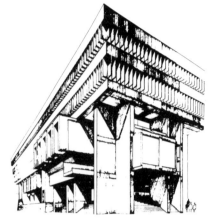

KALLMANN, MC KINNELL & KNOWLES
*Boston City Hall*

165

He was a protégé, as well, of Richard Boyle, Lord Burlington, sometime architect and partner.

**KEYSTONE** Stone arches are made of wedge-shaped stones (voussoirs), radiating from that point in space around which the arch rotates. The center stone (keystone), fixing the structure at its peak or apex, is the key and final element, which locks the assembly together to act as a monolith.

**KIESLER, FREDERICK (1896–1965)** *German American Architect* In practice with Armand Bartos, as Kiesler and Bartos, he built little. Most pragmatic product was his movie theater in Greenwich Village (Eighth Street Playhouse; 1929, New York).

Kiesler's Endless House, an amorphous cavelike volume and form (for the Museum of Modern Art, 1959; a theoretical object never built), released him into willful anthropomorphic spaces of arbitrary size, shape, and scale. The Sanctuary for the Dead Sea Scrolls (1959, Jerusalem) was his most notorious public monument. but, perhaps, his least successful act of real architecture.

**KIESLER** *Model for Endless House*

**KILN** The nonfiery but very hot furnace in which natural materials are heated to harden, to merely dry, to burn and change in chemical composition, to fire (hard-glaze) with a surface coating, or to induce any of many other states of change.

Clay is hardened to pottery; wood is dried from green; cement is burned; pottery is glazed—all variations on a process in the same basic superheated oven for nonfood.

**KILOWATT** A thousand watts, measure of power named for the Scot James Watt, who, in his native canny way devised a penurious measure, only 1/746 of the English horsepower (a fatter measure of the same power). Kilowatts are the normal totings of electrical usage, and the electrical company's charges are attached.

**KING POST** Central vertical member of a simple truss.

**KIOSK** Turkish pavilion, as for viewing the Bosporus from one's summer garden. Now adapted to any pavilion, open and for casual activities in garden or town square; and, more recently, any small structure in a city for selling and dispensing newspapers, tickets, or information.

**KIRK** The Scot's church. Brought to mind is John Knox, that terrifying tormentor of Mary, Queen of Scots, in the abbey kirk of Holyroodhouse, Edinburgh.

**KIRK, PAUL HAYDEN (1914–    )** *American Architect* Kirk brought excellence to the simple stained-wood architecture of the Pacific Northwest. Avoiding the corny new-found idiom of "shaggy" wood shingles (shakes) and "cathedral ceilings," he designed such buildings as his brother's house in Seattle (Blair Kirk House, 1951) with elegant and precise details (but still in wood).

**KITCHEN** Cooking place, mechanized in modern America, but originally another fireplaced room assigned to preparation of food. The modern electrified, gassed, ventilated, and exhausted kitchen approaches the refinement of an environmentally controlled job-lot factory, limiting the effort of its mistress (occasionally master) in time and muscle while expanding choice. Quality of cuisine is not, however, a necessary product; and the very mechanization has allowed prepared foods of dubious taste and nourishment to supplant the excellent simplicity that is the mark of superb American, French, Italian, Chinese, Japanese, and even Eskimo cookery.

The mechanized kitchen is obviously a terminal of plumbing, both water-supply and drainage, of ventilation and exhaust ductwork, of electricity and gas-fired energy. As communications center of a mother-organized family, it is the heart of the house, communicating with street, car, deliveries, child play areas, dining and living spaces; and, as ultimately expressed in the architecture of Frank Lloyd Wright (cf. the Hanna House, Palo Alto), it is the physical skylit center of a pinwheel of surrounding activities.

**KNOB** An organized bump for holding, grasping, wielding; elevated to elegance as a *door*knob, that belabored piece of metal that allows us privacy and access at our will—or, with aid of a lock, security. Its decoration is a major architectural entertainment: with design attitudes as diverse as the smooth spherical chromium plate of the Bauhaus or the wonderful detail of an ornate nineteenth-century French lever.

**KNOLL, HANS (1914–1955) and FLORENCE (1917–    )** *Furniture Entrepreneurs* In the infancy of modern American architecture, it was quicker and cheaper and more plausible to set the stage

KIOSK

167

of style with furniture and lighting than with architecture. Knoll helped fill the voids, with a catalogue of furniture by Eero Saarinen, George Nelson, Richard Stein, and many others. The Womb Chair and its mates became modern status symbols. To buy from Knoll was a kind of taste insurance, an approved modern.

Modern architecture has changed in 30 years to a richer, more eclectic and self-assured, less-disciplined affair, and its furnishings with it. Now it is common for antiques, Le Corbusier-revival, and genuinely new design to be mixed in the house of all but the most insecure, and Knoll's expensive tastemongering has been replaced by myriad suppliers. Knoll now is appropriately a subsidiary of an office furniture corporation, selling safe and substantial taste by the acre.

**KOCH, CARL (1912–    )** *American Architect* Fascinated with the idea of industrial housemaking, he developed the Techbuilt House, now a substantial business distributing through dealer-erectors simple handsome boxes, functional, and of bland good taste if not elegance: safe for the middle-class dabbler in modernity. His custom work is a blend of the New England tradition with the tight spartan style inspired by the Harvard Graduate School of Design in the late thirties and early forties. Acceptable constipation.

**KREMLIN** *Citadel* in Russian. *The* Kremlin is, of course, the citadel of Moscow, the fortified container of all the special religious and political architecture and its contained treasures that the tsars kept from covetous neighbors. The Kremlin became, therefore, the nickname for those in power there resident, as is the White House or Buckingham Palace.

**KUMP, ERNEST (1911–    )** *American Architect* Kump is one of the more versatile and facile West Coast architects, switching from a mid-1930s European (and antiseptic) Fresno City Hall (1941; with Charles Franklin) to shaggy and verdant homeliness: Foothills College (1965).

# L

**LABATUT, JEAN (1899–    )** *French American Architect and Teacher*  Labatut was brought to Princeton in 1928 at the peak of École des Beaux-Arts (Paris) influence on American architectural education. His training in grand public scale was reflected in his creation of landscapes and monuments: gardens for the Duke of Alba in Spain; illuminated fountains for the great lagoon of the New York World's Fair of 1939; and the monument to José Martí at Havana (a pre-World War II competition, built after the war). More permanent has been his influence on two generations of Princeton students, including Charles Moore, Robert Venturi, and the some-time heads of schools of architecture at Oregon, Berkeley, Rice, M.I.T., City College, Auburn, University of Virginia, V.P.I., and others.

LABROUSTE *Bibliothèque Nationale, Paris*

**LABORATORY**  A place where scientific work is performed. A laboratory is, like a kitchen, a utility terminal, served by water, gasses, electricity, and other special forms of energy. It is, therefore, a relatively fixed place in any arrangement. To relieve it of such strait jackets, Louis Kahn pursued the ultimate flexible lab at the Salk Institute in La Jolla, California. There alternate floors contain the service spaces (pipes, wires, tubes, and ducts) for the laboratory rooms interleaved.

**LABROUSTE, HENRI (1801–1875)** *French Architect*  The first architect to elevate iron (here cast) to a role in great architecture, at the Bibliothèque Ste. Geneviève (1843–50, Paris). An architecture of guts rather than a formal or public style, it arranged a delicately articulated volume of elegant reading room spaces within a "Florentine palace" fancy dress surrounding it, but a fancy dress remarkably unfancy in its austerity, a proper eclectic shell for the radical innards. (Cf. the same attitude of modern insides and a neo-Renaissance shell at Pennsylvania Station; 1910; McKim, Mead and White.)

Later he designed the reading room of the Bibliothèque Nationale, with an equally and differently delightful inside.

**LABYRINTH**  The Palace at Knossos, Crete, Minoan headquarters earlier than 1600 B.C., a complex, rambling maze of rooms and spaces, public and private. Ancient Greek legend a thousand years later (those Greeks of 600 B.C. and later—descendants of Minos and Mycenae) considered Knossos the place of confined residence of the mythical Minotaur, whose annual tribute of seven youths and seven maidens sent by Athens was mitigated by Theseus, who slew him (or it). Theseus' confounding problem was, of course, if one could find the way in, how could one get out again? (A very long string was the answer.)

**LADY CHAPEL**  Mary's Immaculate Conception placed her in a paradox: object of secondary worship in a monotheistic religion. Old habits are hard to shake, and the worship of saints was analogous to the worship of random subsidiary gods in Egyptian, Greek, Roman, or Hittite pantheons.

The construction of a Lady Chapel for the Cathedral of St. Patrick in New York was more an architectural than a theological reminiscence.

**LAFEVER, MINARD (1798–1854)** *American Architect* Gothic Revivalist and copybook author: *The Beauties of Modern Architecture* (1835), *The Complete Architectural Instructor* (1857), *The Modern Builder's Guide,* and *The Young Builder's General Instructor.*

The Old Merchants' House at 29 East 4th Street in New York is apparently a collection of plates from Lafever's books, made real. His more substantial works include the Gothic Revival Church of the Saviour (1844, Brooklyn) and Holy Trinity Church (1844, Brooklyn), both English country churches set in a foreign city. Federal (Old Merchants') and Gothic Revival weren't enough of a chal-

LAFEVER *Church of the Savior, Brooklyn*

lenge for him: he produced a neo-Egyptian (pyloned) church at Sag Harbor, Long Island.

**LAG**  A kind of superscrew, bolt-headed for wrench action. Used for attachment of hardware to timber or timber to timber, where through-bolting is impractical, impracticable, or too much trouble.

**LALLY**  The "patent" cement-filled iron pipe-column that allows fireproofing *in*side rather than out. Most steel is fireproofed by coating it with an insulating and fire-resistant concrete shell, and sometimes with a sprayed veneer of asbestos fibers. But with basic physics behind it, the Lally, with concrete on the inside, can remove and store the applied heat of fire, rather than just fend it off. (In more exotic, later structures, steel columns have been filled with water to remove fire-borne heat and avoid the necessity of any other fireproofing.)

**LAMELLA**  A cagelike configuration of small timbers arranged to make a vaulted roof structure; precursor of Fuller's geodesic geometries, yet more pragmatic, and of a lower-rise, nonspherical form more adaptable to current economics. It was popular during the steel shortages of the Second World War.

**LAMA, ALFRED A. (1900–     )** *American Architect and Politician*
Political architects are common in America, but the architect-politician is rare. Lama, as a New York State assemblyman, co-wrote the law publicly assisting the finance of "middle-income housing," a device to make multiple dwellings of substance in the city to retain the fleeing middle class.

He designed projects under his own law, but they are of lesser interest.

**LAMANTIA, JAMES (1923–  )** *American Architect and Painter*
Some of the greatest architectural adventures have been in the creation of elegant shops for elegant wares and clients: l'Art Nouveau, Paris (after which that movement was named); Wright's V. C. Morris Store, San Francisco; Purcell and Elmslie's Edison Shop, Chicago; B.B.P.R.'s Olivetti Showroom, New York; Warner-Leed's Bonnier's shop, New York. Lamantia's Twentieth Century (New Orleans, 1956) is the peer of all these, with a powerful timber

171

baffled façade that brings unusual architectural power to a commercial streetfront. He has since turned to painting.

**LAMINATED**   Layered and fused to form a monolithic whole, as plywood, or melamine (trade-named most frequently Formica) on a kitchen counter.

**LANCET**   A tall, squeezed Gothic arch, as in the tip of a lance, vertically elongated.

**LAND**   A minute vertical dimension, in relation to the size of the earth, separates "land" from water. Except for geological texturing (mostly the work of glaciers, earthquakery, and cooling), a smooth billiard ball of earth would be skinned with water, landless—yet, paradoxically, largely composed of "land," the stuff of earth from core to skin.

Dimpled into depressions, pimpled into mounds, positive and negative topography make a space for water to subside and land to rise, or we would be (if we were at all) nomadic sailors riding rafts woven from the rushes of the sea (all salt, since land's separating containers and sluices that retain rain and conserve it from salt would be absent).

Land is what one owns or returns to or comes from—the piece of our habitat that gives reference, place, and power to all of us. A piece of land is not like a piece of cheese: it cannot be destroyed but merely abused, deluged, scorched, scarred, or exploited. Unlike cheese and life, it is eternal (in our short counting of earthly affairs), never diminishes in value (both dollar and social), gives little income or produce on occasion, but is relentlessly returned to the rolls again and again for a new round of farming or industry or war.

**LANDING**   A place for pause, a platform of transition where one sets foot, as on a stair leading from one run of steps to another, or from a boat or stagecoach to where the traveling stops.

**LANDMARK**   One can mark a land's boundaries, but, more importantly, one can give it status by marking it with a structure that gives both land and marker greater importance than the sum of their separate contributions. Landmarks, loosely, have come to include even those in the densest city, where the land is obliterated

LANCET *Lancet window*

by the marker resting on it, as a brownstone in Brooklyn, or the Strozzi Palace in Florence: a significant object that then overrides the importance of its location—a building or structure important for its own sake.

Landmark laws are those designed to protect buildings and other man-made artifacts (parks) from exploitation or demolition. Common in Europe, they reached America in the sixties and seventies to protect the waning stock of old or great or rare architecture and neighborhoods from oblivion.

**LANDSCAPE**  A pictorial (and hence perspective) concept of one's on-land surrounds, as opposed to an abstract design idea. Renaissance humanism in the late fourteenth century allowed for personal rather than formal or symbolic postures and positions, and hence the idea of the pictorial or picturesque: one person in one spot perceived one image arranged by the chance of his position— a special experience for an individual human that came to be another humanistic idea.

Later came the conscious manipulation of landscape by designers: hence landscape architects from Capability Brown to Lawrence Halprin.

**LAND USE**  The planners' term for what activity can go where for the best functioning of a place (city, state, region): housing, industry, commerce, transport, parks, greenbelts, education are some of the broad uses articulated on plans by colored zones of possibility. Modern planners are, however, concerned with the interlocking of activities, sometimes vertically stacking complementary functions. Simplistically, cities have built apartments over schools and transportation integrally with offices, implying a three-dimensional interplay of possibility, rather than a mere parceling of horizontal land or zones.

**LANGLEY, BATTY (1696–1751)** *English Architect and Writer*
*The Builder's Compleat Assistant* (1738) was enough to memorialize this articulate gardener's son: his copied talent decorated England, Scotland, Ireland, America, and God knows where in the era of copybookism, when architecture was the sophisticated product of good literature (visual) transported by good craftsmen to reality.

THE
BUILDER's JEWEL:
OR THE
YOUTH's INSTRUCTOR,
AND
WORKMAN's REMEMBRANCER.
EXPLAINING
SHORT and EASY RULES,
Made familiar to the meanest Capacity,
For DRAWING and WORKING,
I. The FIVE ORDERS of Columns entire; or any Part of
an Order, without Regard to the Module or Diameter.
And to enrich them
With their Rusticks, Flutings, Cablings, Dentules, Modillions, &c.
Also to proportion
Their Doors, Windows, Intercolumnations, Portico's, and Arcades.
TOGETHER WITH
Fourteen Varieties of Raking, Circular, Scrolled, Compound, and Contracted
Pediments; and the true Formation and Accidenting of their Raking and Returned
Cornices; and Mouldings for Capping their Dentules and Modillions.
II. Block and Cantaliver Cornices, Rustick Quoins, Cornices proportioned
to Rooms, Angle Brackets, Mouldings for Tabernacle Frame, Pannelling,
and Centering for Groins, Truffed Partitions, Girders, Roofs and Domes.
With a Section of the Dome of St. Paul's, LONDON.
The Whole illustrated by upwards of 200 Examples, engraved on 100 Copper-Plates.
By B. and T. LANGLEY.
LONDON,
Printed for R. WARE, at the *Bible and Sun*, on *Ludgate-Hill*. M,DCC,LVII.

LANGLEY *Title page of* Builder's Jewel

173

**LANTERN** A small tower over a church's nave, crossing, or dome, bringing natural light to the building's central gloom, as in that of Brunelleschi over the dome of the Cathedral (Duomo) of Florence: a finial to the distant dome, a substantial temple to the adjacent human, a light source to the vast spaces below.

**LAP** Where two neighboring pieces not only touch but over*lap.*

**LAPIDUS, MORRIS (1902–    )** *American Architect* The very image of Miami Beach is one wrought, promoted, and ingrained in our memory-banks by Lapidus, whose Fontainebleau (1954), Americana (1956), and Eden Roc (1955) hotels are, in the words of Oscar Hammerstein, "about as far as they can go."

His architecture is scenic design, a stage-set for the sublimating middle class of, particularly, northeastern urban America, whose desires want fulfillment like those of a spoiled princeling, turned on and off at will: fairy wonderlands, *their* style; extravagant entertainment; strawberry cream cheesecake, in and out of bed.

Lapidus is excellent at it all. His later work is simpler and more pragmatic.

**LASDUN, DENYS (1914–    )** *English Architect* Student of the quietly avant-garde Wells Coates; partner of the Tecton group (remember the London Penguin Pool and the Highpoint Flats?). Lasdun came into more than his publicly acknowledged own with the luxurious St. James Flats (1960). His apogee was his public housing at Bethnal Green (1959), where he crossed a highly articulated concrete Brutalism with neighborhood revival (preserving old row housing), never before or since matched by him or others.

Lasdun's star was tarnished by competition when James Stirling blasted the English and other friendly viewers in the early sixties by creating his ebullient crystalline Engineering Center at Leicester (University). Stirling is smashing. Lasdun is elegant, thoughtful, and, perhaps, more permanent for people (as opposed to ideology), as is the Georgian of Bloomsbury.

LASDUN *Housing, Bethnal Green, London*

**LATCH** A catch to hold a door or window closed, not locked. "On the latch" refers to lockable doors, where a pushpin or knob can, conversely, leave them unlocked, or "on the latch."

**LATH**  Thin wooden sticks (and, later, their technological substitutes) that form the armature for plaster, as reinforcing steel does for concrete. The forming in space of lathing allowed the architecture of the seventeenth and eighteenth centuries' adventures in convoluted vaults, apses, exedrae, and what not, which brought cheap space modulation to the architecture of, particularly, southern Germany, Austria, and northern Italy (Neumann, the Asam brothers, and Zimmermann, who was a plasterer/stuccoist first, architect second).

**LATROBE, BENJAMIN (1764–1820)** *English American Architect and Engineer*  At the age of 31 he assisted Thomas Jefferson in the exterior detailing and completion of the Capitol at Richmond, Virginia. Later, and on his own, he did the Waterworks of Philadelphia (Greek Revival for the Greek-revived city-name), a Tuscan-columned complex atop a stone bastion controlling the edge of shallow falls on the Schuylkill River.

Most memorable is his participation in the design and construction of *the* Capitol at Washington, completed before the War of 1812, rebuilt after the fire damage of that war.

Baltimore Cathedral is his too, a histrionic example of the Classic Revival, facile in that Latrobe had an equal (and submitted) proposal in the Gothic alternative.

**LATTICE**  Made of lath; the woven product therefrom makes a garden-simulating decor, suggesting the climbing possibilities of ivy or grape, without the need of the real and growing thing. Diagonal latticework painted green decorates the imaginary garden worlds of indoor tennis courts and cabañas, at little expense, and with maximum illusion.

**LAURANA, LUCIANO (ca. 1420–1479)** *Italian Architect and Painter*  The Duke's Palace at Urbino is a landmark of Italian Renaissance architecture. Laurana not only "decorated" it with fireplaces, window sash, and other not so superficial detail, but created its magnificent courtyard (*cortile*), much remembered in the drawn and photographed literature of the Renaissance.

**LAVATORY**  The washing place of society, small-roomed space of basined water and waste, usually with water closet attached. The lavatory is described euphemistically as a "powder room."

LANTERN *Gothic Tower*

**LAWN** Grass's ambition and fulfillment, honored and extolled by Capability Brown (and his teacher, William Kent). A lawn is the miniature field of domestic grain and grasses, tamed for the green walking, but mostly looking, of the owner's life-style.

**LEADER** The tube that conducts water away from a gutter, leading it to safe ground or sewers. Leaders are the pipes that hug the side of America's houses, draining the eaves troughs.

**LE CORBUSIER (1887–1965)** *Self-trade name of Charles-Édouard Jeanneret Swiss-French Architect* He was creator and catalyst, causing buildings of unique distinction to rise symbolically pan-geographically.

The government buildings at Chandigarh (capital of the partitioned Indian section of the Punjab) are vigorous concrete plastic honeycombs, with great ramps and parasol roofs.

Housing blocks, first at Marseille (1952) and Nantes (1955), and then Berlin (1957), are in themselves urban subsystems (three-dimensional multifacility neighborhoods) functionally reminiscent of landlocked ocean liners (in concrete).

In the U.S. his mark is the basic form of the U.N. buildings, watered down by a committee of which he was only a member and executed by a local firm (Harrison and Abramovitz) that clad his bold form with slick, chic "wallpaper" curtains. But at the Carpenter Center for the Visual Arts at Harvard, his intentions broke through (with the guidance of Spanish American architect José Luis Sert, dean at Harvard and former Le Corbusier acolyte).

Bold, "brutal," usually of concrete, his work brought primitive forms through modern technology to the new needs and building types of modern urbanism. Poetic, inconsistent with his own dogma, his output was small but of a quality that at first seems facile, and with continued life and use, eternal. Cf. Notre Dame du Haut (1955, Ronchamp) and Le Couvent Ste. Marie de la Tourette (1960, Éveux-sur-L'Arbresle).

**LECTERN** A prop for a reader's notes or elbows; formal furnishing of a church or lecture hall.

**LEDOUX, CLAUDE-NICOLAS (1736–1806)** *French Architect* Mathematical and geometric in his formal designs, his most impressive work is his Saltwork City at Arc-et-Senans, amazing in that its

LEDOUX *Forge aux Canons, a proposed cannon factory*

supreme formalism was built at all: a vast geometrical complex for the processing of salt, with all the dwellings, offices, and physical support facilities necessary.

**LEFRAK, SAMUEL (1918– )** *American Builder* Lefrak City (New York) is a uniquely American product: a developer's solution (for profit, with no governmental subsidies) to the mass housing needs of dense urban areas; practical, economical, serving a vast need without the support of any architectural ideology. ("House" architect of record was Jack Brown.) Lefrak's products are comparable to the works of the United Housing Foundation (architect, Jessor), America's most prolific houser, without the latter's nonprofit mantle. Lefrak has toyed with greatness (as at the 300-acre Sunnyside Yards in New York) and proposed there a whole sub-city vaster than any private dream before or since (Gruzen and Partners, Architects). His impact as the largest private housing owner and taxpayer in New York is staggering, economical, and public-serving, in quantity; populist, banal, or just plain dull, in quality: a quandary.

LE CORBUSIER *Pilgrimage Chapel, Ronchamp*

**LEMERCIER, JACQUES (1585–1654)** *French Architect* Architect of the Pavillon de l'Horloge of the Louvre; the Palais Royal for Cardinal Richelieu; and the domical church of the Sorbonne.

A good guy, skipped by most histories as a dull or just competent architect (in a world where competence is rare). The Sorbonne is one of the great domes of the Renaissance. He also finished the dome of the Val-de-Grâce, started by François Mansart, a later and more elaborated version of the Sorbonne.

**L'ENFANT, PIERRE (1754–1825)** *French Architect and Soldier* Expatriate major in the American Revolutionary army, he remodeled New York's first city hall into the Federal Hall, the nation's first capitol, on the porch of which Washington took his oath of office in 1789. That elegant Federal building (equivalent to English Georgian) later gave its functions (as capitol) to Philadelphia, then Washington, and its site to the Custom House, later Subtreasury Building of 1842, a still extant Doric Greek temple by Ithiel Town and Alexander Jackson Davis.

Later, and more memorably, he surveyed and literally laid out the great boulevard system of Washington, siting the Capitol and Mall and many of the radial boulevards, plazas, and roundabouts. The present layout is the result of the completion and extrapolation of

L'Enfant's plan by Daniel Burnham, who, as hero of the great Chicago World's Fair master plan of 1893, was commissioned to finish and extend the work that L'Enfant had begun.

**LE NÔTRE, ANDRÉ (1613–1700)** *French Landscape Architect* His gardens for Vaux-le-Vicomte, the château of the failing finance minister Fouquet, are the empirical study for those at Versailles from which he was co-opted by Louis XIV. Versailles would have taken most men of normal energies several lifetimes, but Le Nôtre managed it with dispatch (28 years), as an encyclopedia of the possibilities of plant life and the formal spatial organization of landscape (formally formal and formally informal, as at the romantic "hamlet" for Marie Antoinette). Le Nôtre did equally handsome but simpler gardens for the Royal Palace at Fontainebleau and various other amusing resorts of Louis.

**LEONARDO DA VINCI (1452–1519)** *Italian Painter, Inventor, and Architect* Leonardo's *Last Supper* has become a tourist screen masking his extraordinary Renaissance virtuosity and invention, a creative cornucopia of humanism. Most remarkable in retrospect (our hindsight, his foresight) are his schemes for multitiered city traffic, separating pedestrian from wagon, storage access and facilities from the life of the streets above: street, arcade, and subway (beneath) interplay the articulated functions of city life.

Drawings for centralized (Greek-crossed) churches apparently influenced the real plans of Bramante for St. Peter's, and Leonardo's fascination with the hardware and sites of military action left some of the most handsome and remarkable sets of bastioned drawings ever.

**LE QUEU, JEAN-JACQUES (1757–1826)** *French Architectural Fantasist* Crazy-mad symbolist architect whose ideas vacillated between the super-udder and the super-penis: he wished to build a dairy in the form of a cow, her genitals the entrance portal.

**LESCAZE, WILLIAM (1896–1969)** *Swiss American Architect* Early agent of Cubism in the U.S. (Norman House; 1941, New York), he joined with George Howe to create the P.S.F.S. (Philadelphia Savings Fund Society) Building (1932), an avant-garde affair (office tower), floors cantilevered at their ends, the windows like industrial sash. Lescaze didn't move much further and in his last

LESCAZE *Philadelphia Savings Fund Society*

buildings regressed to the fat set of picture frames known as One New York Plaza. His one moment of glory (P.S.F.S.) is enough for a whole life.

**LESCOT, PIERRE (1500–1578)** *French Architect*  Part of the east (and venerable) courtyard of the Louvre (Palace) called the Cour Carrée, or Square Court, is his—the oldest piece of a continuing architectural extravaganza, which ended with Lefuel in 1878, 332 years after Lescot began.

**LE VAU, LOUIS (1612–1670)** *French Architect*  Creator of the basic body of Versailles, later expanded and altered by Hardouin-Mansart and others. Le Vau's services were drafted by Louis XIV after Finance Minister Fouquet (Le Vau's patron) was exposed for embezzlement. (Or was it jealousy when the king saw Fouquet's château, Vaux-le-Vicomte, Le Vau's greatest single building, decorated by Lebrun, landscaped by Le Nôtre?)

**LEVEL**  Flat and/or horizontal. Level is a state of gravity, all points on its plane surface equidistant from the center of the earth. We check that state by *a* level, or rod, containing an alcohol-suspended bubble that indicates how level the subject is in any linear direction. Horizontal is a visual idea, relating to the horizon, an arced edge of the earth (in silhouette against the lighter sky), but so large in radius that it is apparently flat and, for a human's practical purposes, level.

**LEVITT**  William the father, but, more importantly, William and Alfred the sons, gave their name to a special sort of suburbia, much maligned for its sheer size, nerve, and impact just after World War II. In retrospect, they were amateur and de facto planners, who tempered their sprawl of single-family dwellings with meandering roads and access and more 3-D planting material than Olmsted would have dared, making a tour through their precincts a soft and blurred experience, unlike the endless phalanxes of a Daly City (San Francisco Peninsula's endless row housing, visible all at once, as well as its essential bulk). Levittowns now garnish New York's bedroom communities in both Nassau and Suffolk counties; near Trenton, New Jersey; and even Paris. The pejorative word they were accused of giving our language has turned from caterpillar to butterfly, and, except with the most hardnosed theoreticians, what the

LE VAU *Chateau of Vaux le Vicomte*

Levitts have built tends to be the best of bulk speculative suburbia to date (new towns, such as Columbia and Reston, aren't counted, as they aren't populist, but upper middle class).

**LIBRARY** Place of books, whether the collection itself or the building that houses it. The displayed bound edges of books form a rich and textured mosaic that is one of the great natural raw materials of traditional architecture. The visual qualities are so admired that the bindings without the contents are not infrequently made the false wall texturing of a pseudo-library, suggesting the life and interest of an occupant who, perhaps, has not the time for books but needs their implied intellectual contents as a stage-set.

Public, or just centralized, libraries are one of the great public acts of architecture, suggesting both the grandeur of knowledge and its universal availability.

The Bibliothèque Ste. Geneviève (Paris) by Labrouste is a landmark in the technology and aesthetic delights of cast iron. The Laurentian Library allowed Michelangelo to experiment in the most abstruse ways of Mannerism. The New York Public Library by Carrère and Hastings gives a viewer grandeur for reference that is equal in architectural import to that of a major cathedral. The Morgan Library by Stanford White is the ultimate urban luxury for one intellectually aspiring cultural hobbyist who said, in reference to yachts (an equally telling comment on White's architecture): "If you need to know how much it costs, you can't afford it."

**LIEN** Legal attachment of an asset, limiting its use or enjoyment until a debt is paid.

**LIFT** The equally expressive English term for the American elevator.

A lift is also a pile or stratum, as in a garbage dump, where a layer, limited in thickness, is applied each day: a layer cake of garbage, laminated with the icings of sanitary earth between.

**LIGHT** Light is the visible by-product of dissipating energy (sun, bulbs, lamps, fire), so intrinsic to our own evolution that we can't imagine our life form and style without it. Many creatures nevertheless exist without light, or reject it by choosing night as their context.

Light, canned, joining with air-"conditioning" systems that allow

**LIBRARY** *Morgan Library, New York*

us tempered air to breathe, made possible the endless interior commercial spaces we use today. Removed from natural light and air, man survives, but at a great expense of energy, and largely (except in the case of defensive caves and vaults) to exalt the exploitation of urban land: the fattest, deepest, most artifically conditioned environment will be the most profitable (cf. any shopping center, any factory, and a thousand office buildings in America where the space rented is divorced from the world outside).

Also, a pane of glass that admits light and is, hence, *a* light within a multipaned frame.

**LIGHTHOUSE**   The architectural beacon that signals danger or gives navigational direction to sea travelers. The design of lighthouses traces the technology of tall structures and that of light-making over two thousand years. The Pharos (lighthouse) at Alexandria was one of the Seven Wonders of the World. Brick cylinders or polygons, tapered concrete towers, even balloon-framed houses have held high-mounted lights of kerosene and whale oil lensed with elegance and precision; now flashing electronic lights, on spare metal frames, without buildings or personnel, supplant the handsome architecture that begat them. Sorry for us, happy for the security of sailors.

**LIME MORTAR**   Mortar, that shim and glue of masonry, made from sand, lime, and water, a soft and plastic affair that allowed thin and elegant jointing in Georgian architecture. The crude stuff of today, cement mortar, results in fat joints.

**LIMESTONE**   The compressed crustaceans from a million years of pressure on the sea bottom; the sandy ice cream of building construction, which with a bit more heat and torture produces marble, its senior partner and elder brother. Limestone is an ancient building material, for it was easily workable: sawn rather than hacked or chipped, as was granite. Egypt first used limestone and sandstone (even softer) for its bulk architecture 5,000 years ago. Today it is usually the unworked wallpaper of pretentious building, a thin skin intended to give a sense of permanence and élan to cheesy commercial construction.

**LINOLEUM**   The original resilient floor, of linseed oil and cork dust on a canvas backing.

In sheets it has unrolled across the kitchens and bathrooms and even living rooms of America. Now the elderly relative shoved to the back room by asphalt, vinyl, and vinyl asbestos—which are monolithic castings in squares and rolls.

**LINTEL** What keeps an opening open; a beam supporting masonry (brick, block, or cut stone) over the relatively small widths of window and/or door. Originally lintels were cut stone, a visible architectural part; now they are concealed steel, and the brick seems to float across an opening like wallpaper.

**LIVING ROOM** A dubious phrase in transition between parlor (or salon) and family room. One lives, hopefully, everywhere; but a "living room" implies the catchall activities of a family not involved in the kitchen or dining room or bath or bedroom or hobby-filled cellar or garage. A living room is frequently the very underutilized airlock between residents and visitor, seldom entered otherwise. More fascinating is the possibility that a studio apartment (one room) is a bedroom for incidental living, rather than a living room for incidental bedding.

LOOS *Steiner House, Vienna*

**LOBBY** The staging area for a great hall or meeting place or apartment or office building or event: as in the lobby of a theater; or that of the United States Congress, where lobbies are paid people (lurking in the actual lobbies of Congress), the agents of vested interests.

**LOEWY, RAYMOND (1893–    )** *French American Industrial Designer and Stylist* Loewy's imprint on American culture has been largely in expendables: from cigarettes (where, in 1942, "Lucky Strike green went to war," making the stylish whitening of that cigarette's package a patriotic event); through his sleek Parker 51 pen; to automobiles, where the 1947 Studebaker, with wrap-around rear windows, was considered the most avant-garde event in Detroit since the 1936 Airstream Chrysler.

Loewy's adventures in architecture (mostly with architect partner William Snaith) are less happy, and unfortunately his stylish buildings—mostly department stores and specialty shops—are more permanent fixtures in our lives than cigarettes and fountain pens. His view of himself is perhaps best expressed by the title of his 1951 book: *Never Leave Well Enough Alone.*

**LOFT**  Floored space above; and lofty. Lofts are the empty or simple attic spaces of architecture that allow happenings by default: a hayloft is the happy extra benefit of a timbered, pitch-roofed barn —the cows below, the hay weather-protected in the pitch-roofed attic above. An urban loft, named by analogy, is the high, open-spaced, many-floored place of storage, industry, art, and dwelling —untailored, raw, and usable, in theory, for anything.

**LOGARITHM**  In high-powered mathematics, one adds the powers (squares and cubes, for example) to multiply the numbers concerned. Refined use of such addition is logarithms, and the tables there derived allow multiplication by addition, a subterfuge that should bring more volunteers out of the fear-filled mathematical woodwork.

**LOGGIA**  More pretentious phrase for porch or even freestanding open place or structure, where one waits (or consorts) in relation to attached or nearby buildings. The Loggia dei Lanzi in Florence is an arcaded gallery filled now with sculpture of monumental scale that relates to and serves the Piazza della Signoria.

**LONGHENA, BALDASSARE (1598–1682)** *Italian Architect* S. Maria del Salute, across from the Piazza S. Marco in Venice, is this Venetian's greatest contribution. A cold Baroque place, it is large, largely detailed, and extravagant of theory; a concentric hall, bland inside, its user must be entertained by added decor, such as the purple cloths and canopies that constrict its entrance and apses on occasion.

As a vistaed object viewed from the piazzetta across the Grand Canal, it is a sculptured success, a handsome artifact to be looked at but not visited. Longhena built palazzi and churches here and there in the neighborhood of Venice (island and mainland) and is noted in gondola trafficking for the Palazzo Pesaro, also on the Grand Canal.

**LOOS, ADOLF (1870–1933)** *Czech-Austrian Architect* Loos's Steiner House (1910, Vienna), in a score of architectural and art histories, is our memory of his historical role—spartan, bare, and

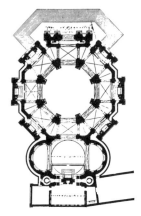

LONGHENA *Santa Maria della Salute, Venice*

Cubistic before Cubism was a formal movement (he wrote an article called "Ornament and Crime" in 1908).

Loos (pronounced Lohse), like Irving Gill, arrived at his spare and unornamented form by himself, far distant from the emerging Mies/Le Corbusier power structure, perhaps more as a negative decoration-destroying idea than any positive philosophy.

**LOUVER** One of a series of slats of wood or fins of bent metal to allow passage of light and air, but not vision.

**LOUVRE** The royal palace of France in Paris, started in the sixteenth century by Lescot, last remodeled by Lefuel in the nineteenth. Now the National (Art) Gallery of France.

**LOVETT, WENDELL (1922– )** *American Architect* His experiments with light steel framing (his own house, Bellevue, Washington, 1951) combined that elegantly used material with timber, corrugated metal deck, and cement asbestos board.

**LUBETKIN, BERTHOLD (1901– )** *English Architect* Organizer of the Tecton group, which opened English eyes to the possibilities of modern architecture at the London Zoo (cf. the Penguin Pool, 1933). Their success in building the avant-garde might rest on the plausible theory that architecture, as well as disease and the medication to cure it, should be tried on dumb animals first.

The Highpoint Flats (1934) are the people's reward from these researches: an early elegant luxury apartment group.

**LUCKMAN, CHARLES (1909– )** *American Architect and Salesman* Architect turned salesman, re-turned to architecture in his middle years (1950), Luckman's very name is prophetic. The Depression inflicted its worst on those concerned with capital expenses for society—architects and builders—driving Luckman, along with others, into unrelated professions. Happily for him, his greatest strength is as a salesman: he rose through the ranks of Colgate-Palmolive-Peet and then the Pepsodent Company to become its president; then President of Lever Brothers, Pepsodent's parent corporation, at 37. One of his first acts was to move the headquarters building from Cambridge, Massachusetts, to Park

LUCKMAN *Madison Square Garden Center, New York*

Avenue, to be near the advertising agencies with which a soap and suds manufacturer would be most concerned.

Apogee of his crossbred career was as client of Gordon Bunshaft of Skidmore, Owings and Merrill, designer of that modern monument, Lever House (1951), first and most elegant curtain wall of glass in America and first stilted building for New York (a curious adaptation of Le Corbusier's "pilotis").

In conflict with his board of directors, and heady with his success as a patron of architects, he left Lever Brothers and returned to practice in his trained profession, first as a partner of former classmate William Pereira, in Southern California, then alone as a supernational firm, Charles Luckman and Associates.

The "new" Madison Square Garden Center (1968) is his prime New York work; also, the Prudential Center (1965+) in Boston and myriad office complexes across the country. Financially successful, often sleek, they are precisely what the client wanted (or believes he wanted)—photogenic from certain angles, with new materials and details of the almost latest styles; new, but leavened with the experience of others for a few months' or years' exposure in the architectural press.

**LUG**  Grasper for attachment with or to anything with glue, cement, or what have you. A lug cast into the backform of a tile is a peg into the soft world of mastic that affixes it to a wall or floor.

**LUMBER**  The collective mortuary of trees: prepared, sawn produce that is the raw material of carpentry, whether light-framed or timbered.

**LUMEN**  A measure of light's quantity produced by any source, but based on a candle, a measure as happily anachronistic and misleading as horsepower.

**LUNDY, VICTOR (1923–    )** *American Architect*  Sinuous bender of glue-laminated timber. His early churches in Florida are simple and delightful wood tents; his later and more monumental buildings, such as his Intermediate School 53 (1972; Far Rockaway, New York), are clever, elegant ideas, products of a virtuoso.

**LUNETTE**  Little moon. Strictly, it is the half-circular wall under a vault, often penetrated by a window (i.e., the little moon).

LUNDY *St. Paul's Lutheran Church, Sarasota, Florida*

185

## LUTYENS, (SIR) EDWIN L. (1869–1944) *English Architect*

Born the same year as Frank Lloyd Wright, Lutyens shared some of his genius and much of his originality, but lacked the clean break with historic form and forms. Tudor remnants recurred in Wright too (the Moore House in Oak Park, Illinois), but Lutyens leaned on and exploited them (in an originality of use, function, and arrangements) rather than basic space and form.

In effect, Lutyens clad traditional space and functional arrangements in a fancy dress of originality and delight, while Wright juggled a set of forms and spaces in consonance to create an external image commensurate with his interior dramatics.

Lutyens built many a modest (15- or 20-room!) country house (cf. Tigbourne Court, 1899) and a few monsters. His most famous remnant is the smashing and pompous grandiosity of the Viceroy's House at New Delhi (1913).

## LUXOR

Modern Nile city 400 miles south of Cairo, near and overlapping the Greek-named Thebes, where the major monuments of Middle and New Kingdom Pharaonic temples and tombs still remain, straddling both sides of the river (City of the Dead on the west, City of the Living on the east).

Gizeh and Sakkara, near Cairo, harbor the 712 Old Kingdom pyramids of Egypt; Luxor conserves the temples of Luxor and Karnak, the Valley of the Kings, and myriad other major monuments. Aswan's dam holds back new Lake Nasser, at whose southern end, almost on the Sudan border, is Abu Simbel, temple of New Kingdom Ramses II. That quartet of cities is the viewer's key to what remains of 3,000 years' civilized work: but more than half the treasure is at Luxor alone.

LUTYENS *House*

# M

**MACADAM**  An engineered way of roadbuilding, with crushed stone laid over graded earth, veneered with the rolled asphalt that is itself often incorrectly termed macadam. Named after John McAdam, Scottish engineer (1756–1836).

**MACHICOLATION**  In the overhang of a castle's crenelations (the wide-spaced teeth between which Gary Cooper shoots at the Riffs), stone or brick steps out (i.e., is corbeled), with arches to allow space between: an architectural device that allows boiling oil to be poured on the enemy. Rocks, bullets, and other weapons are optional alternates.

MACHICOLATIONS

**MACHINE**  A set of parts made and assembled to assist man's work—to manufacture, till, transport, lift, lower, pump, inflate— and ease or quicken life's apparent needs. Egyptians succeeded in creating our most monumental architecture without the wheel. Their machines were the body's frame, a natural machine of tensile muscle, the leverage of limbs.

**MACKINTOSH, CHARLES RENNIE (1868–1928)** *Scottish Architect*  His life was almost coincidental with Wright's, although only two-thirds as long. Mackintosh has not the notoriety of Wright, but without question equaled his talent in the little-toured city of Glasgow, particularly at the Glasgow School of Art (as designer in the firm of Honeyman and Keppie): a prismatic, lusty, highly articulated stone and glass studio building, romantic in form and

187

MAILLART *Bridge near Berne, Switzerland*

siting, pragmatic in plan and use. Mackintosh was fascinated with Art Nouveau, that sinuous decoration drawn or wrought in metal, and continued to use it at the school and elsewhere in counterpoint to his hard rectangular buildings and furniture forms.

A chain of tearooms (the Scottish Victorian equivalent of the coffee shop) for a Mrs. Cranston decorated many blocks of Glasgow with interior wood, natural and stained, that speaks from Morris (William) and in concert with Wright. As with many talented men, Mackintosh was self-destructive and lost his practice of architecture after age 45, turning to painting and moodery.

**MACKMURDO, ARTHUR H. (1851–1942)** *English Artist, Furniture Designer, and Architect* His drawings were the basis of Art Nouveau, and he was a source and inspiration for Mackintosh. He was a bulwark of the English Arts and Crafts movement.

**MADERNA, CARLO (1556–1629)** *Italian Architect* He converted St. Peter's (Rome) from the Greek cross of Bramante and Michelangelo into a Latin cross by his nave that became the tail of the body and a monumental façade that greets us today across Bernini's embracing plaza. Maderno's S. Susanna and the dome for S. Andrea della Valle are better architecture, but less overwhelming in scale; and certainly less notorious.

**MAEKAWA, KUNIO (1905–    )** *Japanese Architect* Student and draftsman for Le Corbusier at his rue de Sèvres, Paris office, he brought back Le Corbusier's thoughts and his own intellectual vigor to Tokyo. The Harumi Flats are a symbolically berthed ocean liner, a landlocked micro-city of life floating in a grassed sea. And the Setagaya Community Center is a socio-cultural megacenter: Lincoln Center and the South Mall combined in distinguished dress. Maekawa's architecture is "brutal," studied, and plastic, but nevertheless restrained and discreet (in comparison to Tange and/or the more histrionic Japanese Metabolism Group).

**MAGAZINE** A storehouse of military goods (or bads), usually a fortlike building concerned with containing any unfortunate explosion from within.

**MAILLART, ROBERT (1872–1940)** *Swiss Engineer* Slim sheets of concrete, curved in ribboned planes, span deep Swiss mountain gorges; prismatic forms in contrast to raw and precipitous nature. Avant-garde in his time, he practiced architecture by default, as did the Roeblings: the result, unconscious and beautiful.

Swiss bureaucrats, doubting his slender, non-Classical ideas, exiled his products to the deepest mountains and wildest gorges, away from population centers. As with the exotic structures of Nervi or Torroja or Candela, they were accepted in the name of economics, not art, being the *cheapest* solution to the problem at hand (while the bureaucrats yearned for Neoclassical splendor).

**MAIN**   The trunk served by branches (as a main street or electrical main), sending branched traffic or circuitry or piping to the ultimate local and small-scale dweller, user, or potty.

**MALLET-STEVENS, ROBERT (1886–1945)** *French Architect* His own house on the rue Mallet-Stevens in Paris is second-echelon Cubism. (Will the street name survive the house and his memory?)

**MANHOLE**   Access diaphragm to the innards of a city's arteries of water supply, waste, communication, and power (gas and electricity). Their covers of cast iron are an art form of some distinction.

**MANOR**   The grand term for tenant farm: the *manor* describing the land, a manor *house* housing its proprietor. Logically such housing was imposing, particularly in the southern United States, under a plantation/slave economy that evolved into a tenant/manored economy: Greek pillars were white and elegant trappings to the work, which was mostly the growing of bulk produce in the soil, as cotton or tobacco.

MANSARD *Delamar Mansion, New York*

**MANSARD**   The bastardization of *Mansart,* whose steep attic urban roofs allowed an added story on a building, an idea co-opted by Parisian builders after Baron Haussmann decreed in 1852 that the new boulevarded houses of Paris might have only six stories (a seventh, the Puccini-romanticized garret, came from the "non-floor" of a mansarded attic).

**MANSART, FRANÇOIS (1598–1666)** *French Architect* Arrogant French Classicist, he was architect for the *nouveau riche,* a rising class of the French Renaissance. Maisons Lafitte (1642) is an elegant country house for de Longueil, a monolithic limestone mass

189

MANSART *Ste. Marie de la Visitation*

inside and out, monochromatic, understated, elegant. At Blois, the last face of the courtyarded sequence of château building is that unit built by Mansart for Gaston d'Orléans (with the proto-"mansarded" roof), similar in spirit to Lafitte. And in Paris, the extravagant church of Val-de-Grâce, finished by Lemercier.

**MANSION**   Old-fashioned term for pretentious dwelling, gaining its importance by contrast rather than any absolute status. *Mansion* is an American term more concerned with social-climbing than architecture: e.g., a material goal to house the insecure (whereas the secure and wealthy disparaged their fifty-room marble châteaux, as at Newport, as "cottages").

**MANTELPIECE**   Originally the hoodlike masonry structure (i.e., mantle) that supported a chimney's fireplace. In later usage a mantel has been either the whole framework around a fireplace or its overhanging shelf for centralized display of photographs and knickknacks. The mantel has, on occasion, even supplanted the fireplace, with the latter simulated.

**MAP**   The Latin *mappa,* or napkin, seems singularly appropriate for *map,* or diagram that tells how to get from here to there and where there is! A map is an abstract diagram (plan) of the relative position of anything, an immense site plan of city, precinct, or world. Its lines on paper simulate natural and man-made places and landmarks. To abstract further or simplify it into diagrammatic form is self-defeating (as is the New York City subway map), for the diagram of a diagram is comprehensible to neither realists nor idealists. (To draw on a napkin or tablecloth is the ultimate privilege of the executive lunch: diagrams, statistics, and the way to one's suburban house for a party—hence, a minimap.)

**MARBLE**   Hardpressed limestone, veined with the relief lines of geological pressure and therefore figured with handsome detail when cut and polished. Marble is the sliced and decorative stone wallpaper of modern commercial building, but was originally the essential and hard-wearing structural stone of austere Classical architecture (Carrara and Pentelicus were its mountain sources in Rome and Greece). Misuse and overuse have diminished its Classical virtues and reduced it to the level of expensive Formica and Permastone.

**MARKELIUS, SVEN (1889–    )** *Swedish Architect* The Economic and Social Council Chamber of the United Nations Building (New York) was the design province of Markelius—an early bare-boned and bare-ducted display of environmental systems (air-conditioning ducts and plumbing pipery), laced together visually with a grillage of Swedish wood. Handsome furniture, dramatic lighting, and good taste (always *taste*). Markelius's greatest moments were at Vallingby (1953–59), that Stockholm suburbanization that brings urbanity to the commuter in a way unequaled elsewhere: with plazas, elegant paving, and street furniture, it contains possibility for events and action that may never materialize; the stage is there, but hardly the mood, and rarely the actors.

**MARTIN, (SIR) LESLIE (1908–    )** *English Architect* Sometime architect of the London County Council, he sought out and allowed the injection of British variations on Le Corbusier into the new public housing of his time: at Roehampton (1956+) through the London County Council's architectural staff under Martin.

With his partner in private practice, Colin St. John Wilson, he has produced much in the same spirit at Oxford, Cambridge, and Leicester universities.

MARTIN *Apartment Houses, Roehampton*

**MASON** A stone- or brick-builder assembling the precut or precast or extruded parts of a masonry building.

**MASTABA** The mud-bricked (and later stone-walled) tomb of an Egyptian noble of the Old Kingdom, coincidental in time with Pharaonic pyramid building. Mastabas are flat-roofed rectangular volumes, with sloping (battered) walls for structural stability and a maze of rooms for the afterlife of the deceased. They are scattered about the sites of the 712 pyramids west and southwest of Cairo, stretching from Gizeh at the north along the edge of the western desert.

**MASTER BUILDER** Ex post facto title for the designer-craftsman-foreman of a medieval structure in particular. The language of the time did not allow for an architect as a separate identity, and, as a composer might score and conduct his own music, the master builder orchestrated the total building process. Drawing, therefore, was an incidental activity, for drawing is modern communication between architect and builder, who, if coincidental in the same

191

person, can go from idea to three-dimensional reality by full-scale layout on the site. (Perhaps a romantic idea in a world of plumbing and dense household equipment, but plausible when the product is a monolithic stone cage, as were Gothic churches. In effect, a modern needs drawings at a minimum to coordinate the various "trades" of a basic building—plumbing, heating, and electrical services—so that their separate craftsmen can interlace them in time and space.)

**MASTIC**   A skin of thick adhesive that levels and adheres a finish material, such as Formica or resilient tile or even preset parquetry of wood; all the functions of glue with the added capacity to align or level.

**MATISSE, HENRI (1869–1954)** *French Painter and Illustrator* His personal architectural space is the Chapel of the Dominican Nuns at Vence, where his painted tiles, vestments, and liturgical trappings are housed in a simple white stucco box with blue-tiled roof on a Mediterranean hillside. His painter's image of housed Mediterranean life was less self-conscious.

**MAYAN**   Chichén Itzá displays a masonry architecture, abstract but with a rationalism for its forms that architects can only trump up today. The stepped pyramid of El Castillo, the bold and bare handball court, the observatory called the Caracol: these are elemental forms for specific purposes that our contemporaries yearn to equal.

MAYAN *Pyramid, Uxmal*

**MAYBECK, BERNARD (1862–1957)** *American Architect* His fertile and unpublicized practice left landmarks of virtuosity ranging from sheer technology (his own house clad in cement-dipped burlap bags) to bizarre use of Classical parts (Bay Area Queen Anne), to handsome new space(s). The First Church of Christ Scientist (1910, Berkeley), clad in asbestos sheeting(!), is a timbered, Classical- and Gothic-parted redwood structure, happily interlocking with gardens, gated like a Japanese temple; a lovely place, an extraordinary set of architecture.

Equally offbeat is the setting for the Pan-Pacific Exposition of 1914, a wire-lath and plaster Beaux-Arts extravaganza, complete with exedra, island, temple, dome, reflecting pool—now replaced (not restored) by a concrete copy. Does fantasy need reality?

**MC COMB, JOHN (1763–1853)** *American Architect* Partner of Joseph François Mangin for New York's elegant city hall (1812), a crossbreeding of Mangin's memories of Louis XVI with Mc Comb's Federal talents. The latter can be separately enjoyed in handsome row houses now moved and restored on New York City's Greenwich Street (at Harrison) and drawn recollections of the demolished St. John's Church (at St. John's Square), a Gibbsian design equal to the earlier St. Paul's Chapel (1766; still standing). He also designed the now restored Castle Clinton (fort for the War of 1812).

**MC KINNELL, NOEL MICHAEL (1935–     )** *English American Architect* See *Kallmann, Gerhard.*

**MC KIM, CHARLES FOLLEN (1847–1909)** *American Architect and Civic Designer* McKim and Stanford White were the two "design" partners of McKim, Mead and White, anchored to reality and organized by their common business associate Mead. It is always difficult to separate authority and responsibility in a multiheaded practice, but McKim is, without question, the designer of the greatest Roman bath away from home, old Pennsylvania Station, a good copy, improved, of the *tepidarium* (warm bath section) of the baths (*thermae*) of the emperor Caracalla, at Rome, 1,700 years later. The station's space was used for a pedestrian concourse, an antechamber to an even grander place, a crystal palace (steel- and glass-roofed train shed) entrance to the trains themselves. Later, when electricity allowed their confinement, the trains were decked over to expand the walking area above, and much of the grandeur of arrival was lost. The shed was disguised from the street by Roman architecture that enveloped the concourse and train shed as one, to satisfy those who considered mere glass and steel an engineer's tool, and unworthy of architectural display.

The Boston Public Library (now expanded by Philip Johnson) is an austere Renaissance palace, dour in the way that Boston has always unconsciously aped Florence, but also suggested to McKim by Labrouste's Bibliothèque Ste. Geneviève, which is, as in the spirit of Florence, an almost conscious understatement of the internal opulence it masks.

**MEANDER** The Menderes River in Turkey was so tortuous in its flat wanderings that it gave name to any wanderings of anything. And to a form of mazelike geometric decoration.

MC COMB *City Hall, New York*

**MEDIEVAL**   Of the Middle Ages, a murky period from the fall of Rome (Gibbon's term melodramatically describing Rome's collapse and the diffusion of power), around A.D. 400, to the Renaissance (of art and humanism) in the fourteenth century. Some precise art historians like to pin the birth of the latter on the competition for the bronze doors of the baptistery of the Cathedral in Florence: 1401.

Early Christian architecture borrowed the timber-spanned basilican forms of Roman commerce—S. Lorenzo fuori le Mure (A.D. 432, Rome); S. Apollinare in Classe (A.D. 534, Ravenna)—quarried Roman ("pagan") temples for columns and other instant architectural parts, and built with the foreknowledge of an existing tradition, both in engineering and form, by artisans switching clients but not intrinsic architectural attitudes. (The Roman basilica became the Christian basilica.)

MEIER *Smith House, Darien, Connecticut*

The Romanesque blossomed when the gathered intellectual wits of, particularly, French builders and religious leaders, reflecting on their own Roman history, took up again the Roman vault and arch and translated the squat, wide, timber architecture of early Christianity into a lofty, if not soaring, set of stone tiers, spanned by stone vaults. One engineering step beyond Rome, they designed ribs to be infilled with stone membranes for vaulting, rather than constructing self-supporting vaults that incidentally created groins (the line that a rib follows). (The Abbaye aux Hommes, left in passing by William the Conqueror in Caen, in, not surprisingly, the year 1066, and England's Durham Cathedral, are Romanesque gems.) English Romanesque was termed Norman, brought by the French Norman conquerors; the same architecture left behind by the same people in Normandy is called Romanesque.

Gothic is the sinuous, thin-shelled apogee on the arc of development Romanesque began: now soaring, transparent, with plain and colored glass, delicate, refined engineering and architecture in concert. Its ultimate set of accomplishments is the ring of cathedral churches that surrounds Paris in what is called the Île de France: Chartres, Amiens, Rheims, Laon, Rouen—middle-class monuments to Christ from the agricultural wealth of the Île.

**MEETING HOUSE**   The religious house of the Society of Friends (Quakers), austere boxes that spurned the grandeur and ornamentation of even the simplest Federal church, made from plain white clapboard or brick; prismatic volumes now admired in retrospect.

**MEGALOPOLIS** Jean Gutman's superword (and book) jumps the metropolis in scale to continuous clusters of major cities—as the line from Boston to Washington he describes—each metropolis reaching for the next, their edges potentially blending into a continuum: the megalopolis.

**MEGARON** The main room of a very ancient Greek (i.e., Mycenaean) house; that is, the living room.

**MEGASTRUCTURE** A supercity part, larger than a building or even a group: often a structural system into which the components of urban life can fit, as at Habitat, that great multicellular construction at Expo '67 in Montreal (see also *Safdie, Moshe*).

**MEIER, RICHARD (1934–    )** *American Architect* Meier's mature work is in large measure concerned with a pristine revival of Cubist architecture of the twenties, particularly that of Le Corbusier, although the revival is one of basic tenets—attitudes toward space, form, color, and texture—rather than any literal reproduction. (His peers, Peter Eisenman, Michael Graves, and John Hejduk, have been more concerned with the ideology, while Meier and Charles Gwathmey have produced the end product. The group is neatly termed the New York 5.) Meier's Smith House, on a point of land at Darien, Connecticut, is a rich sample of interlocking vertical spaces, all packaged in crisp white.

**MENDELSOHN, ERIC (1887–1953)** *German Israeli-American Architect* Early science fiction consumed Mendelsohn's attention until his forties, a combination of interest in the drawing of visions, if not visionary architecture, and formal ideas akin to, at their best, the nonbuilt architecture of Sant'Elia, at their worst the *Late Late Show.* The Einstein Tower (1919, Potsdam) expresses the latter type well, a crusty molded confection that would have served Hansel and Gretel's witch.

But the ugly dwarf grew into a handsome fellow, and the Schocken Department Store (1926, Stuttgart), in contrast, is a sleek, practical, elegant place, anticipating Skidmore's best by more than a generation. As with Gropius, Hitler, in effect, drove Mendelsohn to London, where he practiced with Serge Chermayeff (the de la Warr Pavilion at Bexhill is a standard textbook illustration); from there he wandered to Israel and left behind the Hadassah University

MENDELSOHN *Schocken Department Store, Stuttgart*

195

Medical Center (1936+) on Mount Scopus; and finally to the U.S.

Maimonides Hospital (1946+, San Francisco) and a series of midwestern synagogues were his final works, plastic inventive ideas on their way to a fulfillment never quite reached. (The elegant Maimonides Hospital appears like the center part of a long and unrealized sausage.)

Mendelsohn's problem seemed to be the challenge or demand for originality within himself: when he submitted·to it he was at his worst; when he suppressed it and carried a simpler idea to a more thorough conclusion, he was magnificent; e.g., Schocken.

**METOPE**  In a Doric temple's order, the staccato set of spaces between vertically slotted triglyphs, sometimes sculpted like a mini-frieze.

**METRIC**  The system of measure generated by the First (French) Republic, used throughout the non-English-speaking world, and to some extent within it; decimal, rational, saving of time and money. We stubborn Americans mutter over sixteenths of inches, feet, yards, and acres while our more reasonable Latin contemporaries work with decimals and multiples of meters.

**METROPOLIS**  Mother City (cf. Athens), which came to mean the mother and its brood huddling close by Mom's loins: a set of interlocking civic entities that need to work as one in function but have myriad political heads. Metropolitan government is the joint venture of the brood to act as one at least in certain affairs (such as New York's Metropolitan Transit Authority, Boston's Metropolitan District Commission, or the Greater London Council).

**MEWS**  The back-alley buildings of townhousing, for stables and the dwelling of servants, now elevated to middle-classed (residential) charm, born of nostalgia and bohemian economics. Originally, mews were the places and cages of molting hawks. The English king's stables were built on one royal site, co-opting the word as well as the place. In turn it has been co-opted once more for modern romance.

MEXICO *Fronton Courts, National University, Mexico City*

**MEXICO**  A relaxed Latin society that embraced modern architecture before the uptight gringo, to give it a panoramic history of building unequaled in the Americas, ranging from the stone religious complex at Teotihuacán (now a suburb of modern Mexico City) through Olmec, Mayan, Toltec, Aztec, Baroque Spanish, Artful Foklorico, Sleek Modern, and the maturity of the present day.

The House of the Magician at Uxmal in Yucatán is a pyramid of "life" (admittedly for the extinction of life through sacrifice, not its continuing sustenance) in contrast to those of Egypt, security tombs for the dead. Any of myriad Baroque churches (say the one at Coyoacan) are rich and ornate trappings for the poverty and repression of the seventeenth-century peasant's life. And the clear color, rich mosaics, and glazed diagrammatic office cages of modern Mexico City are ingenuous and naïve, lovely and in unpretentious contrast to the rigid formalism and pretension of much of Protestant and Jewish North America. (Compare the University City, Mexico City; the now dated Hotel Bamer from the forties; and the houses of the upper middle economic class in the lava-bed gardens called Pedregal, a "garden" suburb.)

Mexico has its own multicultured semimelting pot of Indians (assorted descendants of Aztec and Maya), Spaniards, and gringos, immigrant as businessmen. Climates of the tropics, semitropics, high savanna, mountain, and seashore provide a range of programmatic architecture that spans as much in site and climatic demands as it has in the richness of history.

**MEZZANINE** A middle place, the half-floor between the floor and ceiling of a principal floor, as in a store or theater.

**MICHELANGELO BUONARROTI (1475–1564)** *Italian Everyman, Architect, Painter, Sculptor, and Poet* No one had a more potent influence on the art of the Renaissance; yet he built little, most of which was finished, if ever, long after his death. The Medici Chapel in the Church of S. Lorenzo in Florence and the vestibule of the library (Laurentian Library), part of its monastery, are small rooms of great architecture and, in the case of the first, with sculpture equal to its setting.

In Rome, the Capitol, that set of three ancient Roman buildings (center of political administration), was remodeled to contain a plaza with the happily preserved bronze equestrian statue of Marcus Aurelius, perhaps the only Roman bronze of note not melted down for its metal value. The brute façades bear pilasters of two stories —superorders that were much copied later—and arcades that shelter the stroller from an August sun.

MICHELANGELO *Dome of St. Peter's Basilica, Rome*

197

But last and most important is the building torso of St. Peter's: nave, dome, and body started by Bramante. Michelangelo expanded the plan, fattening its piers for the heavier dome anticipated, planned and started that dome, and left that dominant object to be completed by della Porta and Fontana, with a Latin nave (unanticipated) by Maderno and a colonnaded plaza by Bernini.

Michelangelo was a grump, and a messy one at that, littering his personal life with debris, behavior so suited to the modern image of an artist that he became its prototype.

**MICHELOZZO DI BARTOLOMMEO (1396–1472)** *Italian Architect and Sculptor* Sometime partner of Donatello in both architecture and sculpture, he succeeded, on Brunelleschi's death, as master of the Florence Cathedral's (Duomo's) construction. But his own work, the Palazzo Medici (later bought and occupied by the Riccardi family and sometimes termed the Palazzo Medici-Riccardi), is the genesis of a whole family of architecture serving in our times banks of the 1920s and clubs of the turn of the century (New York's University Club by Stanford White).

Michelozzo remained as architect for the various residential and business interests of the Medici family, building not only in Florence but in Milan.

MIES VAN DER ROHE *Crown Hall, Illinois Institute of Technology, Chicago*

**MIES VAN DER ROHE, LUDWIG (1886–1969)** *German American Architect* A classic rather than Classical architect, whose goal was perfection, rather than originality.

One of a modern pantheon in architectural literature, with Le Corbusier and Wright, he countered the former's concrete plasticity and the latter's spatial extravaganzas with a serene set of boxes, at their most dramatic modulated by staggered planes of exquisite materials—e.g., the Barcelona Pavilion (1929), which gave him a vehicle for furniture in concert with his luxuriously constrained architecture: the Barcelona Chair, still coveted luxury object of the Modern Art aspiring rich.

More recently, after his appointment as professor of architecture at the Illinois Institute of Technology, he designed (1939–60) a whole campus of prismatic volumes of steel, glass, and brick—intellectually determined from a gridded site plan; a spare, industrial but refined aesthetic throwback to his work with Peter Behrens in Berlin.

The Seagram Building (unpopularly called 375 Park Avenue by

its prudish and anti-liquor tenancies) is a bronze and bronzed-glass classic lesson in office building construction that has been revived for many clients in many cities, but always less successfully (Charles Center, Baltimore; U.S. Building, Chicago; Nun Island, Montreal; and others).

Mies was like the stone of stonemasonry, his father's trade, in which he was first apprenticed: a superficially dour man of few words, relentless in his single-minded attitudes, a perfectionist. But with the humor of many great architects, he lived in an ornate Victorian house, painted white for purity, but exotic in detail.

**MIHRAB** A niche in a mosque's wall containing the Koran and indicating the direction of Mecca; not dissimilar to the Ark of Judaism containing the Ten Commandments, or Ark of the Convenant. Both religious furnishings are directed to words, rather than the crucifix of the Roman Catholic Church or the symbolic cross of Protestantism.

**MILL** The early machinery and buildings of agricultural produce, grinding wheat to flour or sawing trees into lumber. Later and more loosely it described many basic industrial plants: the raw-material processing of the steel mill, cotton mill, and so forth.

Early mills tapped simple-sourced natural power: water at a fall, wind on a plain—the former common in hilly New England, the latter the basic machinery of flat, alluvial Holland. The windmill's simple-formed architecture, lusty-timbered, strong-shaped, delights most of humanity, and many are reclaimed as charming houses or tea-rooms or shops for the "sticky bun" trade.

**MILLS, ROBERT (1781–1855)** *American Architect* The Washington Monument (1836–84), super-obelisk that would have made Imhotep slaver with jealousy, is his apogee, as much in sheer height (555 feet) as architectural importance. A hollow, square, and tapered tube, it is a cenotaph (as opposed to the sculpture-centered Jefferson and Lincoln memorials) and not a tomb.

Mills built the quite magnificent U.S. Treasury (1839) in a Roman and Renaissance Revival. Architect-President Jefferson discovered Mills and urged him on his architectural ways and way.

**MINARET** A tower attached to a mosque from which the crier (Arabic: muezzin) calls the faithful to prayer in and at their day's work. Modern muezzins have been supplanted by tape recorders and loudspeakers that blare from, say, the Mosque of Gamel Abdel Nasser at Aswan with a vigor a mob couldn't sustain.

Minarets are frequently slender and elegant annexes to a mosque, as at the Blue Mosque of Istanbul, where four pencil-thin towers, hatted and balconied, allow multiple muezzins. But in the boondocks of Egypt, a minaret may be squat, mud-bricked, with sticked balconies, serviceable for the neighborhood, and primitively handsome.

**MINOAN**   See *Cretan.*

**MINSTER**   A monastery's church, in England, or the church with which there used to be a monastery; or just any big church. Westminster is a classic word-fulfiller, nevertheless, since it was a monastery and is thought of as a church without one (although contrariwise it is called Westminster Abbey, a somewhat redundant saying).

**MIQUE, RICHARD (1728–1794)** *French Architect* Latter-day architect at Versailles under Louis XVI (who blew it all on the same premises) and Marie Antoinette. His works seem so outrageously lavish that they might start a French Revolution on their own: Marie Antoinette's own luxurious apartments in the palace, a theater in the Petit Trianon, the Temple of Love, the Belvédère, and the Hamlet, where Marie playacted at being a shepherdess, her closest move to the commoners to whom she recommended cake.

Rhymes with pique.

**MISSION**   A religious sending to save and/or convert the heathen: in American experience only those Spanish satellites that dotted the California coast, handsome remnants of stuccoed compounds ornately entranced; husbanded today, the fond remnants of a culture American California has been hard put to equal.

Missions *from* America have littered the Orient, Africa, and other lands, proselytizing the savages with an arrogance (backed by money and architecture) that history has deflated. In any case, our missions elsewhere haven't started any architectural movements.

**MITER**   The cornered intersection of two materials (wood, marble, steel, whatever) cut at a 45-degree angle to meet each other: a corner that presents only knife-edges to the world, no thickness.

**MIZNER, ADDISON (1872–1933)** *American Architect and Socialite* Mizner brought an appropriate stage-set for the rich to Palm Beach (Florida): an amateur scenic designer, concerned with the exterior image, streetscape, and situation more than with the internal workings of his buildings—although the latter were frequently grand, charming, and of appropriate Spanish Revival materials. Everything inside and out was of stucco, tile, and wrought iron, a serene understated form of architecture, phony to the historian but a happy relief from un-phony virtuosity (cf. particularly the Via Mizner, adjacent to his own house, with shops and a pedestrian way; transplanted Spanish vernacular urbanity).

**MOAT** A body of water surrounding and isolating those who wish to be alone; man-made. Usually moats are slender bands around large fortified buildings. Therefore, the lake around a castle-island is not a moat.

Dig a ditch around the family stronghold, fill with water (alligators optional), bridge with a drawbridge, and add, for final effect, a portcullis.

**MOBILE HOME** The portable wheeled prefabricated housing unit that evolved from the trailer industry, but mobile only in the way it is moved from shop to semipermanent place. Bucky Fuller's visionary units of the thirties considered the helicopter as a possible but extravagant delivery system for similarly made industrial housing units.

**MODERN** The *new* style (although *contemporary* may surpass it as a statement of the moment's time, without benefit of style). Modern is always *now*, as was Brunelleschi in 1440, Bernini in 1660, Sullivan in 1880, and anything on the front burner at the prescribed time; modern transcends newness—a particularly difficult affair in this present lush, nouveau riche world of anything goes.

**MODILLION** A carved scroll of a bracket, horizontal in placement (as opposed to a console, which is similar in form but vertical). Both are Hellenistic and/or Roman in source, parts of an elaborated temple architecture.

MODILLION *On ceiling cornice, White House, Brooklyn*

**MODULE**   A unit to be used as a measure but, more importantly, a prebuilt part of a building. A brick is a module, but in modern affairs modules are precast walls, rooms, or larger parts of a multifamily, multiuse building. Modular means a system or building composed of modules—the unit of any size repeated to make a house, neighborhood, or city—factory-made and delivered to the site, as in a forest of stacked mobile homes (cf. the stacked apartment modules of Habitat).

**MODULOR**   Le Corbusier's system of proportioning based on the male human body, a handsome set of values that keeps the unwary from straying to awkwardness. Systems are like splints, not crutches, allowing the author facility to proportion his buildings consistently with grace; a crutch would be a self-conscious display of system. The Golden Section was a Renaissance and simpler proportion—a whole is so divided that the smaller part is to the larger as the larger is to the whole.

Of course the Modulor allows not only the aesthetic arrangement of parts in a proportioned system, but also the proportions of space as they relate to man's use: travel, passage, walking, sitting, standing, and sleeping. In that they are functional economies of space as well as its aesthetic maximizers.

**MOHOLY-NAGY, LÁZSLÓ (1895–1946) and SYBIL (1903–1971)** *Hungarian American Designer and Teacher; His Wife, Critic and Teacher*   One of the Bauhaus, he came to the U.S. after Hitler's rise to power, as did his fellow teachers Gropius, Mies, and Breuer. A designer concerned with issues common to painting, sculpture, and architecture, he taught at Harvard and wrote: most important works are *The Language of Vision* and *Vision in Motion.*

After his death his wife achieved minor fame in her own right, teaching architectural history at Pratt Institute, writing *Native Genius and Anonymous Architecture* and a volume on the works of the modern Venezuelan architect Carlos Raúl Villanueva.

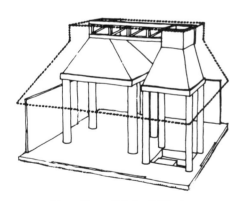

MOORE *Moore House, Orinda, California*

**MOLDING**   The shaped band of wood (or other material) that covers and enriches a joint, profiled in section, as if squeezed out like toothpaste, but normally "milled" of wood, precast of plaster, or "laid on" in wet plaster by a scribing tool.

**MOMENT**   The force within a bending lever, prying a counterweight; or the force of any stiff stick—wood, steel, or what have you—flexed at both ends or spanning between wall and wall, stick and stick, and deflected by weight. The power to resist within the stick is expressed mathematically by "moment."

**MONASTERY**   See *Abbey*.

**MONITOR**   A raised portion of a roof; a clerestory to allow entry of light along its sides, particularly in continuing bands over factory work areas.

**MONOLITH**   Of one piece, as a cliff; or the individual stones of Stonehenge. Something appearing to be or called monolithic may only seem to be of one piece, as a church all of limestone inside and out, although piled of separate jointed stones.

**MONUMENT**   Remembrance of things or persons past; a marker, sculpture, building of any size, but of special design to give importance, large or not.

The Choragic Monument of Lysicrates remembers his Chorus, just as the Football Hall of Fame remembers the persons and events of football. A tomb, a mausoleum, a memorial (as in Grant, King Mausolus, and Lincoln respectively) are monuments; and, by analogy, buildings can become consciously, subconsciously, or by default monuments to their patrons, architects, or donors—Palazzo Medici, Michelangelo's dome of St. Peter's, and the Elmer Bobst Hall (library) at New York University respectively.

**MONUMENTAL**   Having the force of, or serving as, a monument. A building or object more important and impressive than its size; a mere pilgrimage church can be monumental (Notre Dame du Haut, Ronchamp, by Le Corbusier), while a cathedral can just be big (Liverpool).

**MOORE, CHARLES W. (1925–    )** *American Architect*   Acting as a funhouse mirror, Moore has taken the ideas of the enriched modern architecture of the fifties, sixties, and seventies and changed their wave length by subtle distortions that have consciously crossed history with his own work (his own house in Mill

MONUMENT *Prison Ship Martyr's Monument, Brooklyn*

203

Valley, California, used retired Tuscan columns for radical modern work).

He has brought the Pop vernacular to elegant intellectual sophistication through a cutout, paint-on game for a neo-Baroque ego; and he has rehonored the shingle-style vernacular of the eastern 1890s with a western seacoast town (Sea Ranch) of rambling shingled plasticity (in the 1960s).

**MORGAN, JULIA (1872–1957)** *American Architect* Notorious for her false castle for William Randolph Hearst at San Simeon, California (but no more false than Ludwig II's Neuschwanstein), she contributed to the Bay Area's early modern thoughts in houses and house-scaled buildings, as at the Women's Club (1918, Sausalito), a simple western shingle-style building, or St. John's Presbyterian Church (1910), a simple shingle takeoff on her former employer Bernard Maybeck's First Church of Christ Scientist.

**MORRIS, BENJAMIN WISTAR (1870–1944)** *American Architect* The Great Hall of the Cunard Building (1921, New York) ranks as one of the great commercial architectural spaces of all time: a vaulted place of cathedral proportions, built for the accounting of Cunard freight operations. Later (1928) Morris built J. P. Morgan's library annex, a lavish repository of books and Renaissance art.

**MORRIS, WILLIAM (1834–1896)** *English Architectural Patron, Furnisher, and Philosopher* Morris's act of building a house in suburban London (the Red House on Bexley Heath, designed by Philip Webb) inspired him to design, produce, and sell furnishings (Morris, Marshall and Faulkner): sinuous two-dimensional design and naturalism, suppressed to graphic abstraction, became his vocabulary for wallpaper, fabrics, carpets, and stained glass.

He believed in (and lectured on) a "people's art," a blend of socialism and hand-of-the-people's craft. Unfortunately the cost of his handsome handcrafts was out of reach of all but the rich, an analogous problem to that of the Bauhaus, which demanded "artifacts" industrialized and made by machine: in the end they were handmade to look as if they had been made by machine!

He also invented our grandfathers' favorite Morris chairs.

**MORTAR** The stuff for bedding masonry, stone or brick, allowing a state of level: lime mortar from lime, water, and sand; cement mortar the same, substituting cement for lime. Lime allowed elegant and thin joinery in Georgian architecture; cement tends to make a coarse course.

**MORTGAGE**   A bank's loan toward a building's cost and/or that of its renovation. Usually a large percentage (50–75%) of its value, it is returned to the bank as amortization (installment payback of the principal) over a period of years, together with interest: a diminishing loan, grossly in concert with the diminishing value of a depreciating (worn and torn) property.

**MORTISE**   The interlocking wood fingers of two adjacent cabinet planes: sides of drawers or the boxed case of a cabinet proper. Mortise and tenon are male fingers into female pockets, joinery connecting one slab-side to another.

**MOSAIC**   Decoration or images of many hard parts, an assembly of tesserae, the small pieces of marble, stone, glass, wood, or anything that are the dots—like a printed halftone—that assemble an image at a larger scale. The Romans used mosaic marble for floors, illustrating and remembering events of importance in the life of occupants of the building they floored: as in a Pompeiian house, illustrating family members; but, more often, merely abstract geometric and floral decorations.

**MOSER, KARL (1860–1936)** *Swiss Architect*   The Church of St. Anthony (1926+, Basel) is a concrete cage, grilled to receive stained glass (compare the similar work of Perret at Le Raincy, a Paris suburb, in 1923). Moser was the first President of C.I.A.M. (Congrès International d'Architecture Moderne).

**MOSLEM**   Follower of the faith of the prophet Mohammed and, hence, a member of Islam (the collective body of Moslems—Muslims in Arabic—and their nations). Moslems are also variously referred to as Mohammedans or Musselmans (Turkish).

Moslems embrace populations of all Arab lands, plus Turkey, Iran, Pakistan, Indonesia, parts of East Africa, parts of Russia, with minor minorities in many places.

Moslem architecture is, therefore, one of analogous climate and topography and of the common religion embraced by Islam, and can range from the sandstone medieval mosques of Cairo (cf. Ibn

MOSER *St. Anthony, Basel*

205

Tulun) to the wooden churchlike mosques of rural Turkey and Russia, and the wet-wood alluvial bamboo cages of Karachi and Singapore.

**MOSQUE** The temple of Mohammed, assembly room for prayer toward Mecca, holy place-object of Islam in modern Saudi Arabia, and banned to all but true believers (i.e., Moslems).

**MOSQUITO** The maximum altitude of these aerial pests might influence the height of dwellings, for mosquitoes don't ever reach 50 feet. Urban man is more elevated than the insect flyers, and, hence, urban dwellings need have no screens above the fourth floor.

**MOTEL** In purest form, cars are tethered at a motel room's door, as a cowboy's horse was at the saloon. For those American nomads without trailer or camper, the motel allowed a happy symbiosis of car and resting place without tippable bellboys and baggage travel. But we can't leave well enough alone. Like a dog worrying a toy, we fuss with our best products and design, changing for its own sake. The motel (cf. Disneyworld's forest of them) is now a twenty-one-storied, bellboy-encrusted, tip-mazed Las Vegas export, with all the disadvantages of a hotel and none of the advantages of real elegance and good food.

**MOTIF** The theme upon which design is a variation, as an acanthus leaf is the motif of a Corinthian capital, or a lily becomes the crocket of a Gothic finial.

**MULLETT, ALFRED B. (1862–1935)** *American Architect* Mullett was Architect of the Treasury in the days when that division of the U.S. government included such diverse subsidiaries as the U.S. Coast Guard and public works. His Second Empire Victoriana sprouted everywhere. Happily, new-found concerns with the delights of grand Victorian space arose at the time many of his buildings were endangered. Most prominent is the old State, War, Navy Building (1871+; now the Executive Office Building) next to the White House, a dour granite wedding cake decorated with 900 Doric columns and a mansarded roof of heroic proportions (Mansart's at Blois would be dwarfed). Another close shave for Mullett was the old St. Louis Post Office in the same idiom (it was almost reduced to a parking lot).

**MULLION**   The major support member between adjacent panels of glass, or doors, or window sash, as in the aluminum posts separating glass sheet in a store's front or the stone ribs separating lead-glazed areas in a Perpendicular Gothic English church.

**MUMFORD, LEWIS (1895–   )** *American Writer and Philosopher*   Mumford was an early critic of modern architecture in and for America (*The Brown Decades,* 1931; *Sticks and Stones,* 1924). His dispassionate honesty aimed at toppling Establishment idols, meanwhile offering kind words for the Davids of the time: Wright, Sullivan, Richardson—men who confronted but did not dispel the Grand Beaux-Arts myth (the white World's Columbian Exposition of 1893 vs. the brown works of the Davids).

Mumford's *The Culture of Cities,* 1938 (later rewritten as *The City in History,* 1961), is a classic text on city development and part of his larger series concerning the entwinement of civilizations and their technologies.

**MUNTIN**   The small bar separating small glass within a sash (that assembly of glass, muntins, and frames that is an operable piece or set, as a double-hung window or door).

**MURAL**   Painted (or frescoed) wall surface decorating the architecture and honoring the use of a space. As in the *Last Supper* by Leonardo da Vinci at S. Maria della Grazie (Milan) or the social activist wall paintings of Thomas Hart Benton (Capitol; Jefferson City, Missouri) or the Mexicans Orozco, Siqueiros, and O'Gorman.

**MUSEUM**   Place of the Muses, some of whom are more equal than others, in accordance with the fashions of the day. Museums are the warehouses of art, with iceberg-like display spaces, where the trafficked surface occupies only 50% of the volume, and displays 25% of the resources of the whole affair.

Museums are a Victorian concept (you never saw a museum *in* antiquity, only *of* it), and they display the hard-won artifacts of one culture's combat with another.

Trophies of war, objects of admiration (and/or jealousy), and conserved parts of nature (butterflies, whole whales) are the musings of museums. Lord Elgin's marbles (the frieze and pediment sculpture of the Parthenon) in the British Museum and the sculptured, potted, bas-reliefed treasures of endless tombs of Egypt

MULLETT *Executive Office Building, Washington, D.C.*

207

(Metropolitan, Brooklyn, British, Berlin museums) are prominent instances of pillage removed for the edification of white Anglo-Saxon Protestants (who perhaps need it).

**MYCENAEAN** Mycenae, in pre-Classical Greece, was the architectural historian's intermediate cultural step on the Mediterranean's north shore (in cultural concert with Egypt on the Mediterranean's south) after Crete and before Athens. Its architecture (the traces are very limited) was the ancient architecture of what we now term Classical Greece: as at the Treasury of Atreus, a beehive-domed underground vault (1200 B.C.).

**MYSTIC** Mystic, Connecticut, is one of the set of seaports that exploited the sea's riches when they were the most accessible of any to a primitive, pre-industrial society. Boats and harpoons, hooks and nets were ancient tools that allowed a small coastal town with harbored river to become a Colonial urban landmark. Now Mystic's building remnants, left aside in the rush of commerce elsewhere, have been conserved, with added buildings and ships, a scenic set that as a result entertains scrambling mobs of family America with discreet commercialism. Federal, Greek Revival, and Jigsaw Gothic America occupy land; whalers, schooners, and yawls are harbored next door.

# N

**NAIL** The cheap nail and the sawmill made for mushrooming America the sticks and fastenings of its greatest independent architectural contribution: the balloon frame. Each depended on the other for success: the finally cheapened industrially produced nail needing something to fasten; the sawn sticks and ribs of housing (studs, joists, rafters) needing fastening.

Nails are now myriad in variety, specialized for use as fasteners of shingles or Sheetrock or timber or flooring; for delicate and concealed finishing, for spiking and holding great timbered weights and stresses.

NASH *Regent Street, London*

**NAOS** The inner place of the gods in Classical Greek and Roman architecture (and therefore the principal inner room of the temple, equivalent to the Christian's participatory nave).

**NARTHEX** The open porch of a church; later, any kind of vestibule, transition between the open world and the world of churchly ritual and ceremony.

**NASH, JOHN (1752–1835)** *English Architect and Urban Designer*
Creator of urban stage-sets that give a uniform and grand scale to central London, quite out of style with its accretion of town-housed urban villages (Bloomsbury to Chelsea). His Regent Street, sinuous and picturesque, seemingly the product of change, time, and multiple architects, gives the passerby an operatic view of London from Regent's Park to Trafalgar Square, as if London were front-staging

its country cousins with urban grandeur (while they might miss the delights of Covent Garden or Bloomsbury).

Nash is also notorious for the exotic quasi-oriental Royal Pavilion at Brighton (1815+) and was known to have created such diverse products as a neo-thatched cottage, Gothic castles, Italian farmhouses—all with grace and facility.

**NAVE** The people's place, as the chancel is the place of God's symbols and his priests, and the transepts (or cross arms of the church) the place of monks and brothers. The nave rises above the aisles of a Gothic church and brings stained light in. Its ribbed structure's shell reminded its namers of a ship, *navis*: an inside-out, upside-down, religious ship bottomed to the sky and heavens.

**NECK** The circled joint between column and capital that articulates their separate identities; or a flat banding, sometimes molded (hence, a molding).

**NECROPOLIS** Even the dead have their polis (city). *Acro*-polis is highest city, or part thereof; *metro*-polis is mother city, and hence the collection of sub-cities so mothered; *megalo*-polis is extended city or cities, and hence collections of those that overlap each other; *necro*-polis is city of the dead, or super and symbolic cemetery. At Thebes (modern Luxor) the Middle and New Kingdom royal dead were buried in the valleys of the kings, queens, and nobles—a west bank necropolis opposite the living city on the east bank.

**NEIGHBORHOOD** The collection of life surrounding a place or person, which gives color and quality to it or him or her and is the mini-civilization of which he, she, or it is a part. A neighborhood is largely an urban idea, where things and people are so densely related that they interrelate, inevitably and inexorably.

**NELSON, GEORGE (1908–    )** *American Designer and Architect* The Sherman Fairchild Town House (1940) was an early venture (with William Hamby) into new and plastic use of tight urban space. Nelson is known more for his furniture and exhibit design, as at the American Exhibit in Moscow, 1962.

**NELSON, PAUL (1895–    )** *American French Architect* Expatriate American whose early experiments in structure and equip-

NELSON *Swagged leg chair*

ment put forth the theoretical Suspended House (1939) and the mast-supported museum (Palace of Scientific Discovery; 1938). He is a soul-mate of Alexander Graham Bell, Buckminster Fuller, Jean Prouvé, and Robert Le Ricollais: concern with maximum technological product for minimal resources identifies all.

Nelson's hospital at Saint Lô is particularly remembered for its carapace of an operating room: lights, air conditioning, and subservient equipment all part of a hovering concrete enclosure: the oyster shell containing the pearl of an operating table.

**NEOCLASSICISM** The more academic version of Classical (Greek and Roman) revivals, which seemed more concerned with the parts of Classical buildings than their whole nature. Neoclassicism, if not co-opting whole buildings, co-opted whole sections of them, with a verve for purity and austerity that chose Doric more often than Ionic, the monolithic more than the assembly of multiple materials.

**NEON** An excitable gas (electrically) that is inert (chemically). An element, and therefore indivisible by normal chemistry, it participates in glowing linear signs, orange-red (within a tube of glass, bent to letter shapes, electrodes at each end). Other similar gases produce other colors and mixture blends, but all are generically called neon and make neon signs, America's greatest contribution to Pop Art and camp culture.

**NERVI, PIER LUIGI (1891–    )** *Italian Engineer and Contractor*
Penultimate creator of great concrete-shelled spaces for sport, exhibitions, aircraft hangaring. Sometimes termed architect, but in fact his purely engineered spaces transcend architecture, and do better without it. Compare the exhibition hall (Palazzo delle Esposizioni; 1948, Turin)—soaring, translucent, elegant (corrugated, prefabricated) membrane against the sky—with the snuggled dumpy architecture at its edges (toilets and ticket rooms).

The Palazzo and Palazzetto dello Sport for the 1960 Olympics were domed stadia for mass-sheltered view. Later, in Turin again, an exhibition pavilion, high-walled with exterior glass to display innards (impossible with domed and vaulted forms), gave a sixteen-"treed" umbrella to the Palazzo del Lavoro (1960).

Orthodox multicelled buildings were done with prominent ar-

NERVI *Hangar, Fiumicino Airport, Rome*

NEWSOM *Carson House, Eureka, California*

chitects: the U.N.E.S.C.O. Building (1956, Paris) with Marcel Breuer; the Pirelli Building (1960, Milan) with Gio Ponti.

Faith in the efficacy of Nervi transcends reason. Lesser or less confident architects have hoped his engineering injected into their veins might create great and bold form. Hopefully, his best products are those bare spartan engineering remnants that can live alone, the product of the unselfconscious engineer-contractor who gains commissions because of his *economies,* and incidentally leaves behind space both monumental and beautiful.

**NEUMANN, JOHANN BALTHASAR (1687–1753)** *German Rococo Architect* The pilgrimage church of Vierzehnheiligen (Church of the Fourteen Saints) is the greatest reality and cartoon of the Rococo; appropriately Bavarian, a synthesis of space, structure, and decoration: Bach's sound translated into intellectual space-form design.

Neumann's staircases are almost as important as Vierzehnheiligen. Those in the Bishop's Palace (1735, Würzburg), with ceilings by Tiepolo; Bruchsal (1732); and Brühl Castle (1748, Cologne).

**NEUTRA, RICHARD (1892–1970)** *Austrian American Architect* Neutra, an eastern European ego transplanted to the ego-land of Southern California, presented the classic, romantic image of architect to his clients: accented (Viennese and exotic); hirsute before hair was suggested as high style; eccentric, willful, high-handed, a great person-presence, and a towering talent.

His works are separately compartmented in the histories of architecture, outside the neat categories of Sullivan, Wright, Le Corbusier, Cubism, Mies, de Stijl, and so forth. But Neutra's residential work combined advanced industrial and structural techniques as early as anybody. Health House (a children's home; 1927, Los Angeles) is an early and radical use of a light steel cage and provides sunlight, fresh air, glass, views, and the tinkle of children's dancing voices!

The Von Sternberg House (1936) was later purchased by *Fountainhead* author Ayn Rand (speaking of egos!). Then there were the John Nicholas Brown House (1936; Fisher's Island); the Kahn House (1940; Telegraph Hill, San Francisco); the Holiday House Motel (1948, Malibu Beach). All are residentially scaled cages (steel, concrete, and/or wood), highly articulated structures, with lush foils of planted landscape. His garden apartments and row housing also retain a scale of private identity, of articulation of the place of living.

Neutra is dismissed with too much dispatch by many single-minded or single-tracked purists. His personality (and writings) put them off, too seemingly arrogant, too floridly verbal; but the hard reality of his talent is his buildings of vigorous white-planed Cubism, equal to most later European products, and his later, lusher developments in concrete and wood.

**NEWEL** The pillar and post of a stair, from which springs the very beam (stringer) that supports the stair, and to which are attached balustrade and handrail. It is structurally a mast anchored to the floor (or through it). Newels are at the base of a stair, and at each change in its direction.

**NEWSOM, SAMUEL and JOSEPH** *Twentieth-Century American Architects* The house at Eureka, California, for lumber magnate Eugene Carson is polychromatic, jigsaw, latticed, mansarded; an encrustation of such superb efflorescence that it is the norm against which extravagant excess in American stick and shingle architecture is measured. The Newsoms were prolific and built many wood eclecticisms, but none quite matched the Carson House.

**NEWTOWN(S)** A blurry word these days, gathering to its bosom such diverse experiments as those inspired by Sir Ebenezer Howard, Sir Patrick Geddes, and the Garden City movement before and between the two world wars: Letchworth (1903+); Hampstead (1907+); Harlow Newtown (1947+); and Cumbernauld; Tapiola; Vallingby; Reston; Columbia.

To some they are urban constructions of modest controlled size in a satellite position to a central city; to others they are balanced scattered urbanizations, self-sufficient, interrelated, but where the residents stay at home and don't commute. To others they are opportunities for controlled display of architectural virtuosity and social discipline.

NIEMEYER *Niemeyer House, Brazil*

**NICHE** A small carved (or omitted) void in a wall, where something for display or honor may be placed, as a sculpture.

**NIEMEYER, OSCAR (1907–   )** *Brazilian Architect* His architecture is cartoonlike, diagrams imposed regally (and hence like largesse) upon the populace. His fame grew from his participation on the Brazilian team producing the magnificent (Le Corbusier-designed) Ministry of Education (1937) in Rio de Janeiro. But his own work is devoid of the rich functional sculpture of Le Corbusier, composed of concrete shell and slab forms, and free forms—as in his own house (1953, near Rio) and the complex at Pampulha (1943, near Belo Horizonte): clubhouse, casino, and church (a neatly combined Latin program).

Most monumental are his buildings at Brasília, where a long friendship with Juscelino Kubitschek, first mayor of Belo Horizonte (and client of Niemeyer), then president of Brazil, brought him to the vortex of development. Niemeyer built the President's Palace, a rather sophisticated diagram crossed with fanciful colonnades unhappily reminiscent of Lincoln Center. Later the Cathedral and Square of the Three Powers (buildings of two branches of the legislature, plus the Secretariat).

Brasília is a sea of space, accented with freestanding buildings, terminals of auto-age travel—all rather detail-less, bland, and with not many redeeming features. That he did it at all seems more important historically than what he did, unlike the new city of Chandigarh, where the central buildings by Le Corbusier are splendid and rich documents.

The best view of Brasília for those who will never have the chance to go is the movie *That Man From Rio,* with Jean-Paul Belmondo: he travels through the "town" by car, is chased across great barrenness between buildings on foot, and flys in a borrowed airplane among major monuments. A smashing indictment of this megalomaniacal and boring folly.

NOWICKI *Livestock Judging Pavilion, Raleigh*

**NILE** The Nile. Linear water-highway, irrigator, and urbanizing line of Egypt from Alexandria to Aswan's high dam (the first cataract). The Nile's annual spring flooding became a great engineering tool, allowing transport of heavy stone to a site removed from the edge of the river (and hence to the edge of the desert): obelisks, limestone, and granite for pyramids floated as much as 600 miles from quarries to building sites.

**NOISE** The other need for insulation, which keeps heat in in winter (and out in summer) and, hopefully, can prevent or limit transmission of noise. The best cure for noise is to stop making it but, failing that, sheer weight of isolating walls is the best cure (and, as second best, double walls—each independent of the other structurally—with insulation).

**NOOK** A corner attractive for use or storage (nooks and crannies). An inglenook is a corner within a fireplace's mass to sit and warm; a breakfast nook borrows the cosy thought for a small place, contained on three sides, to break one's fast.

**NORMAN** The Normans took over from the Anglo-Saxons in 1066 and brought with them French Romanesque architecture, the first great English building style since Roman London and the baths of Bath. William the Conqueror had built at Caen, his point of departure, two great Romanesque churches, Abbaye aux Dames and Abbaye aux Hommes; their progeny are the Romanesque churches of England, termed Norman: the naves of Durham, Norwich, Ely, and Peterborough cathedrals, for example.

**NOSING** The overhanging edge of a stair's tread, frequently rounded or molded, sometimes square. Some modern architects have avoided nosings completely (as fussy and impure) by sloping the riser back to the tread below to allow toe space (the original point of nosings).

**NOVELTY SIDING** Tongue and groove boards, molded to give a shadow line at the joint; when used outside, the joint leaves an open slot to provide a shadow to simulate clapboard, yet with a flush-boarded surface.

NOYES *IBM Selectric II typewriter*

**NOWICKI, MATTHEW (1910–1949)** *Polish American Architect* Commissioned to design Chandigarh (with Mayer and Whittesey), he died at the beginnings of that work, so gloriously completed by Le Corbusier. Nowicki's great building is the Livestock Judging Pavilion (1950; Raleigh, North Carolina), a tensile steel roof slung between two great concrete arches, cross-legged and tilted in opposition to each other.

**NOYES, ELLIOT (1910–    )** *American Architect and Designer* I.B.M.'s many buildings and typewriters are by Noyes, as well as the general supervision of their design program (Saarinen, Lundy, and so forth).

**NYMPHAEUM** Temple of the nymphs (minor mountain goddesses, represented as lovely girls). By allusion, and with minimal imagination, the word came to mean a place of pleasure, hopefully with nymphlike maidens in attendance and decorated with fountains and statues. In our own time its architectural state has been degraded to that of movie palaces of the 1920s or lobbies of Miami Beach hotels of the 1950s.

# O

**OAK** Venerable hardwood of damp and temperate climates as in Old and New England. In the former's case they seem to go on forever, great vaulted leaf-domes over the grassy parks of Tom Jones.

Oak's tight grain, strength, and impermeability have made it a classic material for substantial (and sometimes carved and massive) furniture (of the climates where it grows), while pine (English = deal) is the soft wood of common or simple furniture.

**OBELISK** Land finial, freestanding Egyptian temple memorial; a slightly tapered, square shaft, crowned by drastic beveling to form a pyramid tip. Carved with hieroglyphics, obelisks punctuated the ground plane of temples and, paired, marked the entrance pylon's gates. Some were more than 100 feet tall, monolithic granite, floated on site across the Nile's flood—or rolled on site across undulating topography (Manhattan) using cannon balls!

**OBSERVATORY** Place for observations, usually of astronomical affairs: planets, stars, meteors, comets. Largely the house of a telescope and shelter for its viewer, it takes some of the most extremely functional forms, most common of which is the rotating dome, slotted for the telescope's projection. In more radical instances, it assumes a shape seemingly more akin to a rocket launcher, as that at the University of California (Berkeley) by Skidmore, Owings and Merrill.

**OBSERVATORY** *University of California at Berkeley*

217

**OCTASTYLE**   Having eight columns on its façade, a temple term in the ordered architecture of Greece and Rome.

**OCULUS**   Eye or eyelike; a round window.

**OFFICE**   Office buildings are the cellular cages within which offices are disposed for single and multiple tenants, the largest and lushest commercial speculations of urban life. Their full possibility was first realized in Chicago, with the almost simultaneous development of the commercial elevator and the steel-frame cage (1880+).

Sheer height was at one point the symbolic goal of New York offices: the Flatiron Building, the Woolworth Building, the Chrysler and Empire State buildings. Their finial forms made the old skyline of New York—much romanticized and now crushed by the giant prisms of the World Trade Center.

London and Paris are slowly and unhappily following this megalomania, unnecessary economically, but the adrenalin needed, apparently, by a highly competitive speculative builder or corporation president.

Office buildings are the America's greatest architectural contribution, skyscrapers giving the cityform an image like Mont St. Michel, a clustered group-pyramid rising from flat land or water surrounds.

**OFFSET**   A break in a building's form for a purpose, frequently from legal constraint, like New York's skyscrapers that, from 1916–61, had setbacks that were offset from the floor below to provide light to the city's streets. In England offsets describe the detailed setback of a Gothic wall or buttress, occasion for a molding to cover the joint's transition.

**OGEE**   The double curve of a superpointed arch (the ogee arch) that appears in both Moorish and Flamboyant (French) Gothic architecture.

**OGIVE**   French word for a pointed arch, and the Gothic architecture that used it.

**O'GORMAN, JUAN (1905–    )** *Mexican Architect and Painter*
The National University library is both architectural product (with partners) and opportunity for display of lava-tesseraed murals by

O'GORMAN *Lava mural, University Library, Mexico City*

O'Gorman, obsessed with the history of Mexico expressed in these natural-colored stones from his own land. The Secretariat (office building) of the Department of Public Works is a pictorial cartoon of history, much more extensive and lavish (architecture by others). More exotic is his own bizarre grottoed house, a crusty bit of bricks and pottery, a seeming ruin (no *conscious* ruin implied, as it was with the Regency British).

**OLBRICH, JOSEPH MARIA (1867–1908)** *Austrian Architect* Radical architectural pioneer and member of the Sezession, the society that seceded from the reaction they knew surrounded them. The Sezession promoted Jugendstil (Youthstyle, taken from *Jugend,* a polemical magazine), the Germanic equivalent of Art Nouveau.

The Sezession building is spartan, almost Cubist, moderately molded, with a filigreed hemisphere of a dome, its metalwork in spirit with the sinuous metalwork of the Sezession artists.

His Hochzeitsturm (1907, Darmstadt) reminds many of Mackintosh, a brick Cubistic break with the canons of the more sinuous Art Nouveau, but without its total rejection: its towered form ends with what has been compared to organ pipes.

**OLMSTED, FREDERICK LAW (1822–1903)** *American Engineer and Landscape Architect* Andrew Jackson Downing and Olmsted are the great landscape architects of all American history. None came before. Most since are makers of large gardens or urban arrangements (not unimportant services, but scarcely the molding of land at any serious scale).

Olmsted's break came when he was hired as the superintendent of newly mapped Central Park, in the then northern wilderness of New York's Manhattan Island. With Calvert Vaux as architect, he entered the competition for the park's final design, and won it with his plan called Greensward in 1858.

Other major works were Prospect Park (plan, 1867; Brooklyn); Fort Greene Park (1868, Brooklyn); Riverside Suburban Plan (1868; Riverside, Illinois); Tompkins Park (1871, Brooklyn); Morningside Park (1873, Manhattan); Mount Royal Park (1877, Montreal); U.S. Capitol West Terraces and Grounds (1875–78); Eastern Parkway (1868, Brooklyn); Arnold Arboretum, (1879, Boston); Back Bay (The Fenway; 1879, Boston); and Lawrenceville School, Groton School, Stanford University, Harlem River Drive, and so forth and so forth.

OLBRICH *Sezession Clubhouse, Vienna*

219

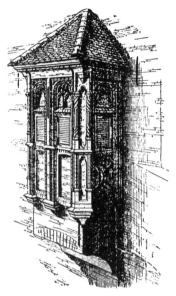

Prospect Park was his apogee, a constructed topography (as was Central Park) composed in a manner that would have pleased Capability Brown: great sweeps of mown lawn surrounded by planted deciduous forests, worthy of a castle, yet a park of the people, with artificial lakes, temples, bridges, carriageways, sculpture, and fountains—a stage-set for nature-lovers bonded to the city, and seeking an accessible nature more super-natural than the sparse plain woods of scrubby Long Island.

**ORANGERIE**   An orange-house (or green and orange house!) for growing oranges in northern climates, usually an orthodox walled and roofed building, glazed to the south. Oranges were once of such repute and expense that their growing was a proper kingly enterprise, as at Versailles, with the orangerie by Hardouin-Mansart for Louis XIV—a negative place, its roof the main terrace overlooking the main gardens, its face below looking upon a depressed paved plaza, where some of the 3,000 trees might be trundled out in the warmth of summer.

**ORATORY**   A private chapel, but its private nature may be privacy of a special interest. St. Joseph's Oratory in Montreal is a pilgrimage place where, reputedly, the lame and infirm regain normal health through prayer.

**ORDER**   Those kits of parts that formed the ancient Classical vocabulary of architecture, and then, in modified form, that of Renaissance, Georgian, Federal, Greek Revival, Renaissance Revival, Queen Anne, and what have you architecture.

Orders include column, base, capital, entablature (that topping of a building comprising architrave, frieze, and cornice; or their equivalents—beam-image, decorative banding, and roof edging). Doric, Ionic, Corinthian, Tuscan, and Composite are the hierarchy, in descending order of importance (and increasing order of use). Cass Gilbert's capitals on the Supreme Court in Washington, while appearing Corinthian, use cornstalks instead of acanthus leaves (perhaps they should be called Iowanian).

**ORIEL**   A bay window up high, usually in medieval architecture; of masonry and propped by a projecting corbeled stone from below: a place to catch a special view.

**ORIENT**   East (the rising sun and those whose cultures surround it, as viewed from the West, or Establishment, viewpoint).

Because conscious placement of religious buildings relates to the East, they are oriented. The loosened word describes the placement, and hence "orientation," of a building in any prescribed direction.

**ORNATE**   The state of decoration that exceeds the architecture it adorns: as do the decorations and uniforms of central European operatic royalty (and the later blooming Latin American dictators aping them). Churrigueresque is a particularly ornate architectural style.

**ORTHOGONAL**   Something right-angled (the right or straight or orthodox, or even simply understood and constructed angle). Most of our built environment is right-angled (hence orthogonal).

**ORTHOGRAPHIC DRAWING**   The drawn record of orthogonal building—termed plans, elevations, and sections; technical drawings with exact information for construction or recording.

**ÖSTBERG,   RAGNAR (1866–1945)** *Swedish   Architect*   The Stockholm City Hall is a modern romance—modern in its new use of form and materials, romantic in its obvious eclectic analogies with the past (cf. the Doge's Palace, Venice; the quasi-religious towered bell; and so forth).

OSTBERG *City Hall, Stockholm*

**OTTO, FREI (1925–    )** *German Engineer*   Tentmaker to the nation and international places, as at the luminous German Pavilion at Expo '67, Montreal. Mast, cables, and fabrics interlock to shelter and enclose great spaces like the multiple sails of a many-rigged ship.

**OUD, J. J. P. (1890–1963)** *Dutch Architect*   Early white purist Cubist concerned with houses and housing, in opposition to the School of Amsterdam of de Klerk and company. He slipped in middle life and produced a bastard and facile modern style that belies his earlier self-discipline.

**OWINGS, NATHANIEL A. (1903–     )** *American Architect*
Supersalesman, bon vivant, he sold both administration and Congress on his services (Skidmore, Owings and Merrill) for the new Air Force Academy at Boulder, Colorado, conceived as a modern acropolis for cadets, so bare and prismatic in design as to appear a full-sized model in its mountain surrounds, a sketch to be consummated later (Walter Netsch of S.O.M.'s Chicago office designed it). His own spirit is in California's Big Sur at his own romantic wood house, far from this act of business, but also is expressed through the lusty work of his home office (San Francisco).

Owings is still senior partner of it all (S.O.M.'s branches in San Francisco, Portland, Chicago, and New York).

# P

**PAGODA** Multi-tiered temple; a thick tower giving advertisement and presence to Buddha in the landscape (China and India mostly, but occasionally Japan, Burma, Cambodia, and elsewhere).

**PALACE** The Palatine Hill in Rome bore the house of the emperor Augustus, which was, therefore, termed Palatium, source-word of *palace,* a term by allusion describing residences of emperors, kings, bishops, and princes.

**PALAZZO** Italian palace; and place of grandeur downtown anywhere in Italy, whether occupied by a prince or the *nouveau riche.* An Italian palace is an architectural, rather than a social or political, term.

**PALE** A stake; member of a cheek-by-jowl series that comprises a fence or paling. Modern variations include some picket fences, closely slatted, and the "French" picket fence of peeled and pointed sticks.

In very Old England, *the* pale described a fence defining a piece of territory; hence, the area around Dublin controlled by the English invaders of Ireland. The expression "beyond the pale" meant unsafe, unprotected, beyond the limits of legal, rightful, and/or religious power.

**PALISADE** Pales for defense, sometimes as a vertical fence, often in primitive earthworks a horizontal set of more hefty wood lances

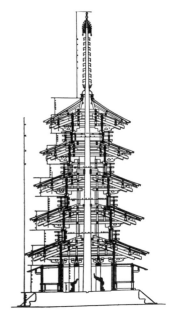

PAGODA *Cross section of pagoda, Horiuji, Nara, Japan*

223

PALLADIO *Palazzo Thiene, Vicenza*

set into the sloped sides of a defensive berm, a nasty obstacle for foot or horse soldier to surmount under fire (the fort at Prescott, Ontario, for example).

**PALLADIAN** Like Palladio, not of him. Inigo Jones, Colen Campbell, Lord Burlington, and Thomas Jefferson were suppers at the table of Palladio, while Vincenzo Scamozzi was his disciple and proselytizer.

Palladianism covered a number of manners and parts, including the columned-arched set started at the Basilica, and the formalistic multi-porched villas such as Rotondo.

**PALLADIO, ANDREA (1508–1580)** *Italian Architect* Nicknamed Palladio after Pallas Athena, Goddess of Wisdom, by his mentor, Giangiorgio Trissino, poet and mathematician who gained a place in architecture vicariously through his intellectual ward (Andrea's Venetian father was named Piero dalla Gondola, a Marxbrotherian name from which his son happily escaped).

His first and boldest work was the Basilica at Vicenza (inland summer resort of the Venetian wealthy), an alteration of the very early Renaissance Palazzo della Ragione, enclosed with loggiaed arcades that became the classic motif of Palladianism: arches flanked with columns—cadaverous, deep-shadowed.

His many palaces are far more complex in proportions, plan, and the hierarchy of their parts, but none matches the Basilica in lusty vigor. The Palazzo Chiericati (Vicenza, a town palace), with a light and airy two-storied colonnade, was started next. Then the Palazzi Thiene and Valmarana, more opaque, masculine masses of rusticated and pilastered stone. The Teatro Olimpico took the newly won science of perspective and created a stage simulating an urban street scene, tilted up and constricted inward to suggest depth, distance, vista.

His churches, S. Giorgio Maggiore and Il Redentore, on sub-Venetian islands, are grand Corinthian-columned and -pilastered temples, domed and bright-lit but with less fascination than the intricate interplays of his palaces and villas.

His villas, particularly the one called Rotondo (sometimes Capra) near Vicenza, gave opportunity for freestanding form in the landscape. Rotondo, domed, with four symmetrical temple porches, is an ultimate formalism, a symmetrical plan with rooms at four corners without great planning logic, and a central dome-lit space.

Much admired, it was copied by English architects Burlington at Chiswick and Campbell at Mereworth Castle.

Palladio as author and self-advertiser published *Four Books of Architecture* (*Quattro libri dell'architettura,* 1570) and, earlier, what became a standard text- and drawn-book record of Rome, *Le antichità di Roma* (1554). Books led his admirers to his buildings and into the cult of Palladianism: sometimes aping him, sometimes building ancient Rome as seen through his eyes and drawings.

**PANAMA CANAL**   Man's biggest cutting of land connects Pacific and Atlantic oceans through a series of locks that raise and lower boats from the salty Atlantic to a series of central fresh-water lakes, then down to the salty Pacific (and vice versa). To confuse the issue, the canal goes east from the Atlantic to the Pacific due to the meandering of the Isthmus it intersects.

**PANE**   A subdivided part of a window sash, common in the architecture of early glass, when large sheets were difficult and expensive to make. English Gothic architecture (secular) is an architecture of leaded panes in wood frames; while American Colonial, then Federal and Greek Revival are architectures of increasing pane size, set in wood. The cognoscenti (word for "knower" to confuse the unknower) describe houses with phrases like "six over six" (six panes in each half of a double-hung window sash).

**PANEL**   An area or plane of material within a frame or structure, as a panel within a framed door or the paneling of a room within framed containing members. Flat boards lining a space do not create paneling. They are flat boards.

**PANI, MARIO (1911–    )** *Mexican Architect*   Prolific houser, his Alémán Project (1949) and Juarez Project (1952) provide low-cost multi-bedroomed housing for the families of government employees in stylish surroundings (Multifamiliares Presidente Alémán; Multifamiliares Presidente Juarez). Duplex apartments are served by open-access corridors on alternate floors in concrete-framed, brick-infilled buildings, enriched with painted bas-reliefs by Carlos Mérida.

**PANTHEON**   A building to all the gods. The Pantheon at Rome (A.D. 120–202) gives example in one place of the extraordinary

PANI *Multifamiliares Presidente Juarez, Mexico City*

225

concrete engineering of Rome that served an architecture of varied Imperial programs and purposes (aqueducts, baths, temples, housing, the varied fulfillments of multifaceted urban needs).

**PANTILE**   An S-curved tile for roofing, the S-laps allowing cover from weather for adjoining joints.

**PANTRY**   Place of bread (*pain*). A pantry is, usually, a space between kitchen and dining room, the staging area of formal dining.

**PAPIER-MÂCHÉ**   Chewed paper, or papier-mâché (never *paper* mâché). Paper, wet and mixed with glue, is molded into shapes of sculpture that can be glazed similar to pottery: a common Spanish tool for festivals and ephemeral events, as the piñata (often of clay, but now more frequently of papier-mâché for economic Latin Americans), the animal-shaped container of Christmas goodies, struck open with sticks by children in Spanish countries on Christmas day.

**PARAPET**   Breast guard, hence breastwork, the upturned edge of a building that protects those behind it. Seldom used for its literal source-meaning (as is battlement) but rather for preventing those *on* from falling *off*.

PANTHEON *The Pantheon, Rome*

**PARGING**   The mortar coating of masonry which makes it more impervious to moisture (where old and soft or below grade). Stucco is an end in itself, parging is an expedient.

**PARISH HOUSE**   The membership of a church is its parish; a parish house is the place for nonliturgical meeting of its members.

**PARK**   A piece of land preserved in its natural state (or landscaped artificially) for the enjoyment of people. Parks are opportunities for dense civilizations to enjoy samples of the wilderness they have obliterated; or view animals that no longer can be wild; or just gain relief from the hard, man-made environment that surrounds them. Olmsted, for example, made many of the last (Central, Prospect, and Mount Royal parks) and suggested some of the first (Yosemite Park).

An English park is often the private grounds of an estate, walled, and kept by keepers for planting and game.

**PARKING**   The open storage place of automobiles, a land-eating activity that has consumed (and for profit) much center city land, as citizens demand private mobility. The piazzas of Italy, the *places* of France, the market squares of Great Britain, and the demolished landmark buildings of America have given way to seas of cars, even where only a minority of the population uses them to get to the place in question.

**PARQUET**   Hardwood, thin and in small pieces that form a patterned floor veneer of the same- or many-colored woods. Highly polished they form a surface of elegance (Henry IV Ballroom at Fontainebleau by de Carpi, whose complex floor echoes the wood and gilt grand coffered ceiling overhead).

**PARSONAGE**   A Protestant rectory; the parson's house, as opposed to the house of the parish.

**PARTITION**   A separator, and, in building, a wall that defines a room and subdivides the body of a building into parts, as opposed to a structural or bearing wall, necessary for the building's support but which may yet, in addition, partition a building.

**PARTY WALL**   Common wall between two row houses that supports the beams of both and separates the space, light, air, and (one hopes) sound of each from the other.

**PASSAGE**   The act or place of moving from here to there; in building an enclosed linear space, a tube of movement between rooms, apartments, offices.

**PATINA**   The weather-coating of brass, bronze, and copper, acquired through age (and the chemical oxidization of the metal). It is considered handsome, although the aesthetic vagaries of two eras may require one to polish brass, the other to allow a patina of verdigris (green oxidization). *Patina* is loosely applied to any mellowing and aging of building materials: stone, clay, brick, metal, and so forth.

**PATIO**   Paved courtyard of a Spanish house, usually surrounded by the house itself or by walls, to make it a central open space, comparable to a Roman atrium. Modern exploiters have borrowed

PARQUET *Parquet floor, Henry IV Ballroom, Fontainebleau*

227

the term for a postage stamp of concrete adjacent to a basement suburban playroom, or any outdoor passive play area for people.

**PAVILION**   First a tent, then any light garden structure; later, the parts of a hospital big enough to have parts—an odd and heavy fate for a word of lightness and air.

**PAXTON, (SIR) JOSEPH (1801–1865)** *English Gardener and Greenhouse Builder*   Paxton translated a career in gardening into one in the design and engineering of greenhouses, first as friend of the Duke of Devonshire, for whom he created great glass and metal ones at Chatsworth. Later, and more famously, he proposed his Crystal Palace for the Great Exhibition of 1851, an uninvited but wild success, a supergreenhouse for display, prefabricated of cast iron and more than a third of a mile long. He was to the architecture of his time what Nervi is to ours.

The progeny of the Crystal Palace invaded many places, including New York, where one occupied the space of what is now Bryant Park until it burned, as did its proxy parent (the original was dismantled and re-erected, a staggering feat, before it burned).

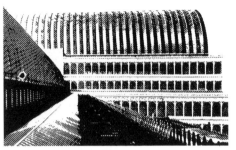

PAXTON *Crystal Palace, London*

**PEDESTAL**   Foot of the place: in its Classical origins, the base that supports a column (which, with true Greek humanism, had a foot). Later, a pedestal was the supporting base of statues or anything that needed "to be placed on a pedestal."

**PEDIMENT**   The triangular gabled end of a temple roof-front, which the basic colonnade supports and in which, usually, is a panel of attached but nearly full-rounded (semi-freestanding) sculpture.

Pediments became decorative parts for Renaissance architecture, crowning windows, tombs, and sculptural compositions. Later their form, with Baroque showmanship, was fractured, broken open.

**PEI, IEOH MING (I. M.) (1917–    )** *Chinese American Architect*   (Pronounced Pay) Classic formalist, his exquisite detailing has made commercial projects of great elegance: Mile High Center (1955, Denver) or the John Hancock Building (1973, Boston; with partner Harry Cobb).

**PENDANT**   Hanging; and in architecture, the stalactite boss in Late Gothic elaborated vaulting.

**PENDENTIVE** Triangular piece of a sphere that fills the space between a round dome and a square supporting structure, as in a Byzantine church (e.g., Hagia Sophia). The geometry is complex to speak of, let alone build, and was a major breakthrough in domed engineering in the fifth and sixth centuries A.D.

**PENTHOUSE** Originally an appendage attached to a building at grade, a lean-to or shed. Later an appendage above its main roof for storage, equipment (as that raising an elevator), and/or machinery. Lastly it described latter-day dwellings on apartment house rooftops for elegant terrace living. In the 1920s the top floors of buildings were for servants, and were set back of lighter, cheaper, and less ornate materials and construction. When the fashions dictated the delights of roof-type elegance, the same spaces were usurped and ornamented for their new occupants, but not renamed.

**PERCIER, CHARLES (1764–1838)** *French Architect* Partner for twenty years of Pierre Fontaine, favorite of Napoleon. See also *Fontaine, Pierre.*

**PEREIRA, WILLIAM (1909–    )** *American Architect* Sometime partner of Charles Luckman. At 29 he built the Lake County Tuberculosis Sanitorium (1939; Waukegan, Illinois), an avant-garde, Aalto-like, low-rise gardened refuge for the chronically ill.

Lately a superbusinessman, he works the Far West and West Coast, most grandiosely on the "urbanization" of the Irvine Ranch near Los Angeles.

**PERGOLA** A formal arbor covering a walk, with columns supporting light beams (joists) that may be entwined with vines, pendant with grapes or flowers, or just an architectural breaking of the sun.

**PERIPTERAL** Columns all around, as at the Parthenon. The word qualified the building, not the participating columns.

**PERISTYLE** The columns and colonnade of a peripteral building; or, inside out, the similar columns and colonnade of a courtyard.

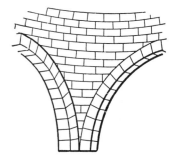

PENDENTIVE *Drawing of a spherical pendentive*

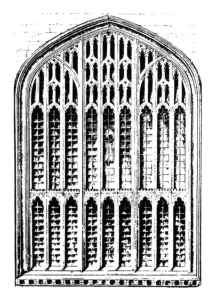

**PERPENDICULAR** *Tracery, Kings College Chapel, Cambridge*

**PERKINS, DWIGHT (1867–1941)** *American Architect* A contemporary of Frank Lloyd Wright, he once shared offices with him. His Carl Schurz High School (1909) is of articulated brick surmounted by deeply pitched roofs: a vigorous architecture paralleling Wright's, but less renowned. Both his son and grandson carry on his architectural traditions.

**PERPENDICULAR** The last version of English Gothic architecture, where glassy boxes were lit with vast stained glass (churches) or clear glass (country and city houses), separated by slender soaring muntins and mullions; high flat vaults (among them the complex elaboration of lierne, then fan vaulting) gave open-halled spaces of grandeur (King's College Chapel; 1515, Cambridge).

**PERRAULT, CLAUDE (1613–1688)** *French Physician and Architect* The east front of the Louvre, designed in 1667 for Louis XIV, was his amateur and avant-garde composition (with the advice of Le Vau and Lebrun). The freestanding sets of paired columns were a radical break with the applied and attached orders of the rest of the Louvre (and all France to that time). Bernini submitted a competitive design, and some of it was usurped here.

**PERRET, AUGUSTE (1874–1954)** *French Architect* Concrete aesthetician and, happily, contractor by inheritance: he could build what he believed in. As a result, his apartment house at 25 bis rue Franklin (1905) still stands, as the first foray into the potential of concrete as an architecturally expressive material.

Notre Dame (at Le Raincy, a Paris suburb) is a grilled cage church, towered in concrete geometry. And the Museum of Public Works carries a ribboned concrete helix of a stair floating through another grilled, naturally lighted space.

His last works, at Le Havre (1945), the miniskyscraper at Amiens (1947), and the housing blocks at Marseilles (1954), are formalistic, the dregs of his talent (inflated and pompous; and, hopefully, they will be stricken from the balance sheet).

**PERSPECTIVE** The simulation of the eye's view, where distant objects diminish in size, and objects within that view taper to a vanishing point on the horizon. Discovery of perspective (or its simulation) was one of the great toys and wonders of, first, Renaissance painters, and then Baroque scenic designers (cf. the Teatro

Olimpico at Vicenza by Palladio or the Scala Regia to the Vatican by Bernini). To toy with perspective in the real environment, exaggerating, and deceiving the eye, became an end in itself.

**PERUZZI, BALDASSARE (1481–1536)** *Italian Architect* His Villa Farnesina (Rome) is an elegant in-town garden villa of the high Renaissance. He was one of the almost never-ending contributors to St. Peter's (as Bramante's assistant). Partnered with Antonio da Sangallo the younger, he started Italy's Pentagon, the grand Villa Farnese (1530, Caprarola; later finished by Vignola, and now the official summer residence of Italian presidents).

**PETERS, WILLIAM WESLEY (1912–   )** *American Engineer and Architect* One-time son-in-law of Frank Lloyd Wright (he married Svetlana Wright), he served as engineer at the elbow of the master. On Wright's death he became director of the Taliesin Associated Architects, who seem to keep alive Wright's most decorative excesses without any real understanding of his great form and space.

**PEVSNER, (SIR) NIKOLAUS (1902–   )** *German-English Architectural Historian* Sometime editor of the *Architectural Review*; teacher and/or professor successively at Leipzig, Munich, Berlin, Frankfurt, Cambridge, and London. Editor of the *Pelican History of Art,* a monumental country-by-country voluminous record of Western art and architecture; author, particularly of *Pioneers of Modern Design* (1936) and *An Outline of European Architecture.* Few have contributed more knowledge of, and thought to, the history of architecture as we know it.

**PEW** Fixed bench of a church, sometimes doored and compartmented; originally proprietary, owned by someone who gave or rented it.

**PIANO NOBILE** Principal and important, but not ground (or American first) floor of a house, as in an Italian palazzo. The piano nobile is equivalent to the brownstone or town house "parlor." Its literal translation is "noble floor," implying that the space contained and expressed is for noble architectural purposes (no social nobility implied).

PERRET *Apartment house, Paris*

231

**PIAZZA**  The English plaza and French *place* are literal translations of word and potential experience, but both lack the cultural vitality and intense architectural experience a piazza offers: the Piazza S. Marco and the Campo of Siena are symbiotic affairs of buildings and places for people; not parades self-consciously made to induce the citizenry to enjoy an otherwise unenjoyable city, but inevitable settings for the pursuit of a vigorous social life in the mild outdoor Italian climate. A gregarious people can fulfill itself, its social intercourse, mental stimulations, sex life, hunger, and thirst in and through the life circumferential to and centered in a piazza. We pasty white northerners come to sip and sup at its edges, to infuse vicariously its potential influences; but as Katharine Hepburn knew (in the movie *Sumertime*), the caterpillar of one species cannot become the butterfly of another.

In nineteenth-century America (and still in New England) a veranda was called a piazza.

**PICTURESQUE**  Meriting a picture, composed as if a picture, and/or the self-conscious ordering of a composition to be a composition, balanced by its several asymmetrical parts. The Hudson River School of landscape painting (although it also painted elsewhere, not merely the Hudson River) was consumed with the extravagances of nature: mountain, river, valley, chasm, waterfall, sunset, pinnacle (Frederick Church, Biemayer, and so forth). Renwick and Dudok and Alexander Jackson Davis were three of the picturesque architects of their respective ages.

**PIER**  Fatter than a column, shorter than a wall; that mass of masonry that supports arch, lintel or beam, necessarily of a scale suggesting bulk (a Gothic pier vs. a Greek column; or the piers of a stone bridge).

**PILASTER**  Attached and rectangular column, with all of the parts and perquisites; in high relief from the wall it serves and decorates. It is a foil to, and/or participating part of, a freestanding colonnade or porch working in concert with it.

**PILE**  An underground column, braced by the earth it penetrates, that supports the foundation of a building in soft ground. Short of a pile (or piles), a foundation would be held up by a footing, a flat spread pad that distributes weight to the soil or rock below.

PIER *Pier supporting arches, Malmsbury Abbey*

**PILLAR**   A loose word for a vertical supporting member somewhere between column and pier. Used colloquially. Avoid it.

**PILOTI**   The elegant French term for columns that raise a building off the ground, allowing air and traffic below; appropriated by Le Corbusier, first and most famously for the Swiss Pavilion (dormitory) at the Cité Universitaire (residential area) of the University of Paris.

**PINE**   Softwood, evergreen, conifer wood of the common man, easily worked with hand tools for furniture and household trim. The English call the wood of pine "deal."

**PINNACLE**   The small spire, ending in a finial, that tops a Gothic buttress.

**PIPE**   Hollow (usually round) tube for transmission of liquids or gasses or use as a structural stick (pipe or Lally column). May be of steel, cast iron, concrete, brass, copper, plastic: to bring water, remove sewage, supply gas, support a building.

**PIRANESI, GIOVANNI BATTISTA (1720–1778)** *Italian Draftsman*   Visionary viewer and recorder of Roman remnants and their potential for Baroque space. *Della magnificenza ed architettura dei Romani* (1761) contained the plates now separated and framed everywhere. His *carceri* ("prisons") were fantasies of dank Baroque space, extrapolated from sunlit Roman engineering.

**PISANO, GIOVANNI (1245–1315)** *Italian Sculptor and Architect*   Architect by dint of his role as master mason of the Cathedral of Siena, inlayer of its façade of marbles (cf. Orvieto, S. Miniato at Florence).

**PITCH**   The amount of slope of a roof in terms of angle or other numerical measure: one unit of horizontal rise for three units of horizontal shelter—expressed as 1 in 3.

**PLAN**   A map of a building drawn as if sliced through its construction at window-height, showing arrangements of spaces, thicknesses of walls, size and placement of windows and doors; in effect, the key drawing that instructs the user how to navigate or the builder what

PINNACLE *Peterboro Cathedral, Peterboro, England*

and how to build. Theseus must have had a plan of the Labyrinth at Knossos to find the Minotaur, for string didn't come that long.

**PLANK**   A thick board for decking or cladding, which might be called timber if used as a beam or girder—as pirates did with the structure cantilevered over the sea: to walk the plank. Their consulting semanticists must have advised them that since their plank was portable, not fixed, one did not have to call it a timber.

**PLANNING**   A word of chameleon-like usage that assumes the coloration of its user and is, therefore, almost useless in a general interprofessional conversation. For example, city planning, urban planning, master planning are all commonly used to describe professionals at work. But city planning, to one group, describes only the allocation of a city's financial resources to assorted capital expenditures; while to others it is a super-architectural scheme of things. A city's master plan could, therefore, be anything from a financial statement to a vision.

To plan, of course, is to prepare a schedule of events, plans, ingredients, and tasks. The fact that architectural arrangements are *a* plan, and the act of making one might be termed "planning," confuses pure meanings any separate usage might have.

PLATT *131–135 East 65th Street, New York City*

**PLASTER**   A slurry of lime or gypsum, sand, and water that can be applied to walls (or a grillage of lath to form a wall) and hardens in its final coat to a hard, smooth, white surface if properly leveled and troweled.

Plaster is applied in coats, or layers, the first over a metal mesh (wood lath or slats, in the old days) or a perforated precast plasterboard. All of these armatures are called lath: wire lath, wood lath, and rock lath respectively.

**PLASTERBOARD**   The precast, paper-veneered sheet material used in place of wet plaster and called, therefore, drywall. A common trade name is Sheetrock.

**PLASTICS**   *Plastic* means moldable, pliant; and hence plastics are the family or nation of synthetic organic materials from a variety of sources that can be shaped in any form cheaply and accurately to form a product, from hard and brittle to mushy and strong. Plastics comprise furniture, kitchenware, toys, parts of cars, and in architecture everything from a kitchen counter (melamine) to flashing (vinyl), that sheet material that ducts water out of a building's joints at eave or window head.

**PLAT**  A plan of a site for a building, town, or development; an engineered legal drawing.

**PLATE GLASS**  Flat glass (plate = flat), in contrast to the relatively wavier and rippled drawn glass, made by rolling, squeezing, or pulling like taffy. Plate glass is cast, and its surface can therefore be flat as a windless sea. Most large sheets are plate.

**PLATERESQUE**  The low-reliefed and highly carved Spanish decoration that encrusted architecture with its frostings in the sixteenth century. The word's literal translation is "like a silversmith," a disturbing notion when translated to an architectural scale.

**PLATT, CHARLES A. (1861–1933)** *American Architect*  He designed, prolifically and for the very wealthy, great Greek and Georgian Revival country houses at a palace scale: Sylvannia, Faulkner Farm, Gwinn, Villasera, and so forth in the wealthy precincts of Long Island's North Shore and Philadelphia's Main Line, in particular. Most importantly, however, he contributed to the advance of urban apartment housing design at Lexington Avenue and 66th Street in New York, again for the wealthy, but duplex units of brilliance and grace, exemplary for urban manipulation at any scale and price range.

**PLAYFAIR, WILLIAM HENRY (1789–1857)** *Scottish Architect*  Playfair's name is as simplistic, seemingly, as the architecture he represented: the pure and puritan Greek Revival of the Royal Scottish Academy (1822) on Princes Street, Edinburgh, and the later National Gallery of Scotland (1850) next door. Doric and dour.

PLAYFAIR *The Royal Institution, Edinburgh*

**PLAZA**  The English version of piazza or *place* (Piazza S. Marco, Place Vendôme), rarely the paved outdoor room of its Italian counterpart, but sometimes a cool Italophile (Inigo Jones at Covent Garden) slips one into the stream of urbanization. The squares of Bloomsbury are, in fact, miniparks surrounded by streets and buildings. The market squares of the English boondocks may be more like the hard-surfaced places of Italy, filled with the stalls of vendors.

**PLENUM**   The dumping ground (or sump) of air where it is collected to return to air-conditioning machinery, as above the suspended ceiling of an office, through which ducts supply warmed, cooled, conditioned air. The surrounding plenum (literally, a "full" place; and hence a closed space) gathers the leftovers and returns them to the source.

**PLINTH**   The very bottom support, as of a column, or the base of a pedestal (composed of multiple Classical parts).

**PLOT**   A small piece of land, sufficient for the user's use, as for a small house. Also, environmental change is subject to plots, those carefully contrived anarchistic or revolutionary events that eliminate buildings, places, and people. Most famous is that of Guy Fawkes to blow up the Houses of Parliament (1606)—not Barry's and Pugin's, which remains today, but the predecessor.

**PLUMB**   The state of being vertical. A plumb bob, or weight, on a string pointed to a target is, in effect, a radius of the earth, and hence a perfect vertical. *Plumb* means *lead* in Latin, so we can assume lead made the original bobs, now mostly stainless steel.

**PLUMBER**   "Worker in lead"; still one of the activities plumbers pursue. Pipes at one time were lead; now merely the joinery between cast-iron sections (drains) is filled with lead and packed with oakum (short hemp fibers).

**PLYWOOD**   Thin wood sheets laminated with glue into sandwiches of three to many layers, the grain alternately crossed. They are peeled like paper from a log into a continuous spiral sheet, chopped into 4-by-8-foot rectangles, and sent into the world to sheath buildings, make furniture, provide the underlayment of floors. They are made, therefore, in widely differing qualities, with hardwood facings, plain smooth fir, or, where all is concealed, even with knots.

**PODIUM**   The architectural plateau on which a building rests: in Greek architecture called a crepidoma, of which the top step, and hence platform proper, is the stylobate. But podium is that service for any building of any time, and can also support the conductor of an orchestra or the orations of a demagogue.

**POELZIG, HANS (1869–1936)** *German Architect* Early symbol-creator of modern architecture: his Water Tower (1910, Poznan), a steel cage infilled with brick, is eternally printed in all substantial references to the term *modern.*

Later, Expressionism grasped him. Many fantasies, unbuilt, were fulfilled by the built fantasy of the Grosses Schauspielhaus (1919, Berlin), where plastic Expressionism reached an ultimate fulfillment of stalactite-encrusted vaults.

**POINTBLOCK** English term for a single tower raised in contrast to surrounding lower buildings, and hence a pointed accent to the local urbanization (of housing).

**POINTING** The removal and restoration of mortar at the weather face of a building after time has had a hand in its wear. Mortar is excised, new mortar packed in place. If done by hand, it can be done with delicacy; if by sandblasting, the face of brick or stone is blasted away with the mortar, causing fat joints and a change in scale—a particularly unhappy experience in the delicate joinery of Federal and Greek Revival houses. What was a pencil line becomes that of a blunt crayon.

**POLK, WILLIS (1867–1924)** *American Architect* Polk's Hallidie Building (1918, San Francisco) is the original glass curtain wall.

**POLLUTION** The corruption of part of the environment by man's wastes: solid, liquid, or gaseous; or, more specifically, garbage, sewage, and air pollution respectively. Wastes are "treated" sometimes, but their treatment is a palliative not all-consuming—for the scientific incineration of garbage, for example, leaves ashes remaining, and that of sewage and polluted air is, at most, 90% effective, and that at staggering cost. The best solution for pollution is not to make it.

Garbage has been piled into mountains, pressed into building blocks, burned at high temperatures (pyrolisis), and/or just thrown by the wayside. Nothing except landfill (mountain-making) has yet been economical. Unhappily the frugal Europeans who enjoy industrialization as elegant as ours, and have managed to avoid much of the paper and plastic debris in which we wrap ourselves, are being subverted to our ways. Perhaps the Alps can be complemented with the Galps (Garbagefrau and Matterwaste).

**POLK** *Hallidie Building, San Francisco*

PONTI *Pirelli Building, Milan*

Water pollution from sewage is a lesser problem, for it can be "handled" if we want to finance such processing. Surprisingly, the major problem everywhere except such gross places as New York is aquatic life, not disease or even the anti-aesthetics of the stuff itself. Waste in water devours oxygen in its process of decomposition, stealing it from the fish life dependent upon it. If fish don't concern you, the problem is largely aesthetic.

Air pollution from automobiles is minor compared to the effluents of coal and oil burners. As a result, a tropical society should be relatively unpolluted. But by the magic of circumstance tropical societies tend to have the oldest cars and cheapest gas, which make up for their deficiency in pollution from heating. Cairo is so smoggy that to see the Pyramids across the Nile would require X-ray technology.

Our profligate lives could well be disciplined to reduce all these problems drastically. Shock treatment may be necessary to precipitate such a move.

**PONTI, GIO (1891–     )** *Italian Architect and Designer* Stylist of buildings and furniture, his best and most classic endeavors were the rush-seated chair of 1946, distributed by the millions, and the Pirelli Building (1960, Milan), a tapered concrete and glass prism pictorially, if not picturesquely, modeled on a concrete-cored armature by Pier Luigi Nervi (one of the latter's few engineering works with and for architects).

His style is at best stylish, and quickly dull as its novelty wears, an anticlassic state, whereas the B.B.P.R. group who built the neighboring Torre Velasca, although creators of novel buildings, avoid novelty for its own sake and, perhaps, are antistylish creators of handsome and useful buildings.

**POPE, JOHN RUSSELL (1874–1937)** *American Architect* The Jefferson Memorial and the National (Mellon) Gallery were consummated by Pope's professional heirs: Otto Eggers and Daniel Higgins (superb draftsman and consummate businessman respectively).

**PÖPPELMANN, MATTHAEUS DANIEL (1662–1736)** *German Architect* Architect of the Zwinger (1711–20, Dresden), an extravagant Rococo pleasure palace.

**PORCH**   The sheltered entranceway to a building that serves equally in some architectures as the outdoor lounge for a family's summer (remember gliders on the front porch?). Porches are important to American architecture, and often provided the richest detail of columns, brackets, jigsaw Gothic scrollwork—equal as an event to the ordered colonnades of a Greek or Roman temple: *they* were porches too.

**PORTA, GIACOMO DELLA (1537–1602)** *Italian Architect* Mannerist and facile, he had the ability to finish what others had started: Michelangelo's Capitol and the Dome of St. Peter's; Vignola's Il Gesù. The dome for St. Peter's (above the drum) recalls, in an elaborated version, that of Brunelleschi at the Cathedral (Duomo) in Florence.

**PORTAL**   A literal or symbolic gate, entrance of ceremony, not merely to be viewed, but used.

**PORTE COCHÈRE**   The American carport's ancestor: a carriage or horse port for sheltered arrival at a house. It implies, of course, a substantial (if not grand) house, since who else would be catering to the needs of carriages.

The French original was a vehicular entry (opening) to a courtyard.

**PORTCULLIS**   The guillotine of doors that slams down to close the castle's gate, as the drawbridge draws, and Douglas Fairbanks, enhorsed, leaps across the widening space to rescue a medium-fair damsel.

Portcullises are iron or wood, with sharpened lances at their bottom edge to impale one who almost made it.

**PORTICO**   An *entrance* porch.

**PORTLAND CEMENT**   Cement simulating the elegant limestone of the island of Portland, off England. Limestone dregs, left from the neat block-sawing of building limestone, are crushed, burned with clay, and converted into builder's cement from which mortar to lay the blocks in and on was made—and concrete for more elaborate engineering.

Portland cement is to building as salt and sugar are to cooking,

PORTE COCHÈRE *From a 19th-century Paris townhouse*

239

a basic ingredient without which whole civilizations would change. Before its wide use, starting in the nineteenth century (which was also before the use of steel-cage framing), brick and stone were set and jointed with lime mortar that produced an elegant thin joint (see Federal houses) but required brick and bricklayers of great precision, and with plenty of time. Modern economics can't allow for such graceful and time-consuming craftsmen. Portland cement mortar allows speed, and the error-absorbing device of fat joints.

**PORTLAND STONE**   British building stone, originally white fine limestone from the island of Portland; later, any such limestone, and other soft stones, white, gray, or brown.

**PORTMAN, JOHN C., JR. (1924–     )** *American Architect*   Portman shocked the conservative American profession by not only designing but building and owning his architectural products. He first boomed at the Peachtree Center in Atlanta, most spectacular building of which is a giant atriumed hotel: an extraordinary private central space surrounded by access balconies to rooms overlooking it. In various (and increasingly sophisticated) versions, he has contributed this instant urban object (self-object in that it doesn't participate in the rest of the city but is narcissistic unto itself) to San Francisco and Chicago (O'Hare Field) and soon will open on Broadway.

**POST, GEORGE B. (1837–1913)** *American Architect*   The first New York Times Building (1889), one of New York's early skyscrapers, was Post's, but without the sense of verticality or caginess or glassiness that distinguished the burgeoning Chicago School of the time. The Produce Exchange (1878) on Bowling Green and the Long Island Historical Society (1876, Brooklyn Heights) were two Italian Romanesque Revivals, terra-cotta and bricked monoliths of great elegance (the former is demolished, the latter in full glory). No one had combined these elements before—i.e., Italian Romanesque and terra cotta—in any monolith (and so Post here invented his own eclectic game).

The Great Hall of the Metropolitan Museum was designed by Post as a draftsman in the office of Richard Howland Hunt, son of Richard Morris Hunt, the museum's principal architect.

He is also said to have helped invent the "room and bath" package of modern hotel design, first expressed at the Buffalo Statler.

POST *Long Island Historical Society, Brooklyn*

240

**POST AND LINTEL**   Less than column and beam, which can be a continuous beam over a number of columns or a continuous column rising between a series of beams. Post and lintel implies short column (post) and a beam sufficient to span a window, as if the two were equivalent to a man's height and armspread respectively (cf. the Modulor of Le Corbusier).

**POSTERN**   The way out. A door for assignations or escape at the concealed tail of a building, castle, or town.

**PRANDTAUER, JAKOB (1660–1726)** *Austrian Architect* The Monastery at Melk, crowning a bluff, overwhelming the Danube; an elegant hulk of church and monks' dwelling embracing a courtyard that captures a west vista through its west-facing un-building wall: a giant Palladian arch. White stone, white stucco, gray-brown bulbed towers, domes, lanterns, and finials; a Baroque body, infilled later and internally by others.

**PRECAST**   Usually concrete poured into molds or forms at the plant or staging area, and transported to the site of use after set and rigid. Old-fashioned garden ornaments were precast, and so are whole walls, beams, and floors. When the pre-pouring gets serious, it is termed modular, or prefabricated, or industrialized, but those words indicate more a state of mind than a change in technique.

PORTMAN *Proposed hotel for Times Square, New York*

**PREFABRICATION**   The making of much, most, or all of a building in factory or off the final site, to be transported later and assembled. (See also *Industrialization.*) Prefabrication is a word of mystery and romance: mystery because so much is said of it and so little done; romance because it is a convenient evasion of reality by those who want to discuss that which is not possible, on the theory that an idea is an ideal, but reality is automatically compromised by its very state.

**PRESTRESSED**   The steel bars that give concrete its sinews (concrete is excellent compressed, but fragile when tensed; the steel provides the tensile portion of strength), and are stretched in advance by tightening their threaded ends with nuts. The concrete is thus given a boost in its ability to act as a beam.

241

**PRICE, BRUCE (1845–1903)** *American Architect* A shingle-style architect: original, willful, exuberant, prolific: the (William) Kent and Chandler houses (1885; Tuxedo Park, New York) are small but refined versions of his earlier wild West End Hotel and "The Craigs'" (1879; Mount Desert Island, Maine).

Price's more commercial ventures included the Château Frontenac (Quebec City), the Hotchkiss School (Lakeville, Connecticut), and 100 Broadway (New York City).

**PRICE, (SIR) UVEDALE (1747–1829)** *English Writer on Landscape* Sir Uvedale considered that landscape might look like painting rather than vice versa, a not unlikely thought in the era when painters were the avant-garde conceivers of the Baroque as applied to nature. He wrote a voluminous *Essay on the Picturesque* (1794), establishing that state as an honorable one with a stylistic virtue of its own.

**PRIMATICCIO, FRANCESCO (1505–1570)** *Italian Architect, Painter, and Sculptor* The theater wing of the Palace of Fontainebleau, built as the Wing of the Handsome Chimney (Aile de la Belle Cheminée), is by Primaticcio, without question Fontainebleau's most powerful formal design (excepting the minor forms of the Horseshoe Staircase and the Gate of the Dauphin at the palace). The twin raked stairs are Cubist compositions, leading past a rich and niched façade (originally filled with Roman bronzes) to a theater installed by Louis XV (in Primaticcio's body, which had been built under Charles IX). The wing ( and space of the former theater) now serves as a studio for the summer American School at Fontainebleau.

PRICE *American Surety Company, New York*

**PRIMING** The first act in painting: the preparation of a surface to cut its absorbency and prepare it for the even and fast adherence of paint.

**PROFILE** The contour of an object or person; in the latter case most frequently called silhouette. A silhouette is a one-way idea, a blackened foreground delineating mass against a light background —an impossible condition for most building parts; hence the profile is simulated as a section.

**PROGRESSIVE ARCHITECTURE** (Initialled *P/A*) An unfortunate name, conceived in a philistine's mind when confronted with the need for liberal progress. Architecture is architecture, whether historic or modern, and to be progressive is to be self-conscious. But in spite of this verbal millstone (and that, of course, is why they condensed their image to initials), *P./A.* is a good magazine, one of two regular monthlies in America today (*The Architectural Record* is the other).

Thomas Creighton, Jan Rowan, Forrest Wilson, and John Dixon have been the editors of the past 25 years.

**PRONAOS** The open vestibule of a Greek or Roman temple (in front of the naos, or holy place itself).

**PROPYLAEUM** In front of the gate, and hence a monumental structure within which the act of entering is contained: on *the* Acropolis of Athens is *the* Propylaeum.

**PROSCENIUM** In front of the scene (or scenery). The arch that frames a stage's action and the apron over which curtain calls burst forth from behind the curtain. It is the lap of the stage, the display place for extra and special events.

**PROUVÉ, JEAN (1901–    )** *French Passionist and Metalworker* Prouvé is of the same cloth as Fuller, demanding performance from materials transcending the past and giving maximum benefit to the populace. In a fashion similar to folding paper, he has folded sheets of metal to make buildings—some delicately, some drastically.

His exposition hall at Lille (1950) is a bent structuralist's dream of folded steel and aluminum, maximizing its structural and architectural potentials in concert.

**PUEBLO** Early megastructures of mud-brick in the Indian-American Southwest. Multileveled high-density housing, their simple detail and plastic form fascinate those concerned with such questions: whether the philosophy of Cubism or merely the concerns of simple mass housing. The Pueblo Indians are named after the urban structures they inhabit; and all is based on the Spanish word to describe their own colonial towns, later reduced in usage to those of Indians only.

**PUGIN, AUGUSTUS W. N. (1812–1852)** *English Architect* Son of France, he embraced Catholicism with a fervor that consumed his architecture; convinced that Gothic was good and of the true faith (and conversely creator and exhorter of that faith), he was also convinced of its structural truth and purity. His most telling work is his decoration of the Houses of Parliament by Sir Charles Barry, Gothic-decorated compromise on a Renaissance Revival body. Pugin not only encrusted the building, but also furnished its innards with tables, chairs, hat stands, windows, inkwells, and everything else portable.

**PULLMAN, GEORGE M. (1831–1897)** *American Entrepreneur* Pullman invented the premium transportation vehicle, attached to a regular train and paying its fare, and in turn, one paid an added fare for his facilities: berths, compartments, superseats. It is not very different from more stationary forms of real-estate development but had the advantage of no land cost to complicate the affair.

Pullman also was concerned with the stationary life, and at Pullman, Illinois, a suburb of Chicago, brought paternalism and architect Solon Spencer Beman to bear on the planned good life. It prospered, revolted, and went the way of many good thoughts: it was surrounded and absorbed by Chicago proper.

**PULPIT** The stage of preaching, elevated, allowing a projecting voice, and displaying him or them on it. A pulpit is the major humanistic object of a church, and one of its most elaborated architectural elements: architectural more than furnishing, because of its very scale; potentially a huge, heavy, elaborate, carved, gilded, gilt, encrusted place of God's agents.

**PURBECK** A Dorset Isle of England that gives a low-grade marble (high limestone) a distinguished name: polished, it is used to jazz up architecture by value contrast—dark pier parts or colonnettes in relation to Portland stone's lightness in a twelfth- or thirteenth-century Gothic place.

**PURCELL, WILLIAM GRAY (1880– ), and ELMSLIE, GEORGE GRANT (1871–1952)** *American Architects* Prairie School architects in the footsteps of Frank Lloyd Wright, their Bradley House on the Crane Estate (Woods Hole, Massachusetts) dominates the harbor, a geometric excursion into the shingle style raised

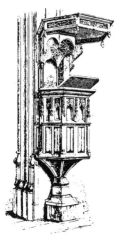

PULPIT *Fotheringay Church, Northamptonshire*

to its highest level, greeting the ferry voyager from Nantucket and Martha's Vineyard as he regains the mainland. Purcell and Elmslie's work includes the Merchants Bank (1911+; Winona, Minnesota), certainly equal to Sullivan's work at Owatonna (Minnesota), and the extraordinary Edison Shop (1912, Chicago).

**PURLIN**  The secondary members that span between trusses or girders to in turn support the boards or sheathing of a roof.

**PUTTY**  Any of variously composed plastic and doughy compounds that caulk and seal (particularly) glass into its paned sash. Linseed oil is its vehicle, which, when it dries, leaves the solids as a crusty joint.

PURCELL & ELMSLIE *Guest House, Bradley Estate, Woods Hole, Massachusetts*

**PYLON**  Those battered fortlike walls that flank the entrance to any Egyptian temple, capped with cavetto cornices, niched with sites for multiple flagpoles. They are major marks on the landscape of the desert, carved with bas-relief to relate their owner, purpose, or memory.

**PYRAMIDS**  The royal tombs of Old Kingdom Egypt west and south of present-day Cairo and across the Nile. Pyramids are triangles in profile, squares in plan (as opposed to the mathematically minimal tetrahedron, with a triangular plan as well as elevation, proselytized by Bucky Fuller).

The natural dead-weighted shape of a pyramid makes it easy to exist structurally, a simple engineering feat that, nevertheless, at the scale of Cheops, require a quantity of workers' effort beyond any *we* can consciously conceive.

When the imagined security of pyramids was breached, the Pharaohs turned to secreted tombs rather than other monuments: secreted in the Valley of the Kings, opposite present-day Luxor, tombs burrowed into solid rock, ornate places for afterlife— painted, carved, enriched, furnished; and concealed in a place that tried to reassume (at desert level) a status of undisturbed nature.

That didn't work either, except for lucky Tutankhamen.

Pyramids were savored by Roman architects for exotic Roman tombs, such as that of Caius Cestius at the city wall of Rome.

*Pythios*

**PYTHIOS (Fourth Century B.C.)** *Greek Architect in Asia Minor*
Designer and chronicler of the Mausoleum at Halicarnassus, that
tomb for King Mausolus, whose name sticks with us today for any
pompous tomb-monument. It was one of the Seven Wonders of the
World described by Herodotus. Grant's Tomb in New York City is
reputed to be an archaeologist's reconstruction.

**QUADRANGLE**  A four-sided rectangular place, enclosed and defined by surrounding buildings. A common term in college architecture to describe the grassed urban-suburban compromise that colleges savor (urban intellectual confrontations, with quasi-rural lawns for contemplation). They form scenic, and accidentally, picturesque places, photogenic with and without student occupants.

**QUADRIGA**  A four-horsed chariot, beloved sculpture object of monumental Roman memorials and their later admirers. Quadrigae crown neo-Roman triumphal arches in such diverse places as Brooklyn (MacMonnies's sculpture on Duncan's arch at Prospect Park), Berlin, and Buenos Aires.

**QUANTITY SURVEYOR**  The building accountant of English architecture and construction (a grave lack in sloppy America). The quantity surveyor determines how much of everything, and of what size and shape and description, a building's contract documents contain. The result is a list, which a bidder evaluates and upon which he bases his bid (tender). As a result, all bidders base their accounting on the same list, unlike many American equivalents who do everything from guesswork to making elaborately and redundantly repeated calculations.

**QUARRY**  A stone mine; place from which cut stone, sawn and blasted from the ground, can be taken for building.

Those at Carrara (Italy) are perhaps the most famous in the

QUATREFOIL

world, source of marble of the highest order; equal to the less famous but more important Pentelicus (Greece), quarry of the Parthenon.

**QUATREFOIL**   Four-leaved tracery of Gothic windows and voids.

**QUEEN ANNE**   The pre-Georgian style of Queen Anne's reign (1702–14). In American architecture it describes that odd late-nineteenth-century collection of inflated private houses made in large part from a kit of medieval and Classical parts, elaborate balloon-framed volumes, enriched, enporched, encolumned, white, off-white, or gray-shingled—the Tudor, Federal, and Greek Revival house grown fat, bulbous, rich, and encrusted. They are eclectic extravaganzas of delight.

**QUIRK**   The eased joint of mitered stone that prevents a sharp, angled tip from breaking off and gives corner shadow-line to the meeting sheets of stone.

**QUOIN**   Corner stones of a building that visually, if not structurally, anchor it. In Georgian architecture, white limestone quoins frequently gave cornered articulation to red brick.

QUEEN ANNE *Row houses, Brooklyn*

# R

**RABBET**   The groove for a matching tongue, rabbeted (i.e., incised or routed) out of the face of the receiving material.

**RACEWAY**   The route of water or electricity: a minicanal-like sluiceway, or a container for conduit of electrical wiring, a tubelike place for wires to be protected (by a metal shell) in their travels.

**RADBURN**   Radburn, New Jersey, experimental American garden suburb, only one toe of whose body was ever built. Houses served by cul-de-sacs surrounded central green parkland, commonly owned and used. Pedestrian circulation passed from house to green and under adjacent highways by pedestrian tunnel, allowing children to co-exist with the automobile without danger. Clarence Stein, Henry Wright I, and Lewis Mumford were the idealists involved. It was part of a whole series of ideal attempts, including Greenbelt (Maryland), Baldwin Hills Village (Los Angeles), and New York City's Sunnyside Gardens (Queens)—all created by the same (more or less) cast.

**RADIATOR**   Normal misnomer of convectors, the sometime cast-iron sculpture of pre-World War II America, piped with hot steam or water, warming the surrounding air and convecting it about the room, in turn warming you. A radiator, if it were fulfilling its physics, would radiate heat directly through the air to you. Such action is only possible where the body radiating is large in relation to the people warmed, like the whole concrete floor slab of a house or its

**RAMPARTS** *Walls of Pompeii*

249

plastered ceiling overhead. Such radiant heat is common and effective and allows the incidental air to be much cooler for breathing, a happy contrast of personal ecology for most people (warm bodies, cool lungs).

**RAFTER** A roof beam rising from eave to ridge, defining the roof's pitch.

**RAIL** A straight and horizontal structural part of a window or door, or the top connecting member of a balustrade—the latter when used for steadying travel is a *hand*rail; the former can be the top, center, or bottom rail of a paneled door, the meeting rail of a double-hung sash (window)—bottom rail of top sash, and top rail of bottom sash, and so forth.

Railroad rails are analogous: metal members across ties (wheel-rails as opposed to handrails, on a stunted balustrade).

**RAINALDI, CARLO (1611–1691)** *Italian Architect* He built the body of S. Agnese on the Piazza Navona in Rome, finished and façaded by Borromini. More telling are his twin churches that face the Piazza del Popolo at Rome's north entry (S. Maria in Monte Santo and S. Maria de' Miracoli; 1662+), defining the three great boulevards that sweep away from each other, impaling most of Rome's urban action on their routes: *the* Corso, Via del Babuino, and the Via di Ripetta.

**RAKE** The slope of a minor part that one normally thinks of as perpendicular: as in a funnel or ship's mast or Douglas Fairbanks's hat.

**RAMP** A sloping plane of travel, in lieu of steps or stairs, popular where vast crowds of people move from down to up and vice versa in a railroad station or airport, or on a ship's pier. Modern technology has made some ramps move, rubber membranes carting hordes of people up and down inclines, again as an alternate to the stair or moving stair (escalator). The latter is quicker but can only carry smaller crowds.

**RAMPART** A blurry word for defensive fortifications; or an additional bermed earthwork around a fortified place; or the walls and baseworks on which a parapet (plain or crenelated) is raised. (The

RAPHAEL *Detail from* Marriage of the Virgin

last version is recorded in "The Star-Spangled Banner": "o'er the ramparts we watched were so gallantly streaming": ramparts in question still preserved at Fort McHenry, Baltimore, Md.)

**RANCH HOUSE**  Wishful thinking equates a single-story suburban dwelling, on as little as a sixth of an acre, with ranch status. Ranch houses in the original were simple and pragmatic dwellings: office and staff dining halls combined. (But the more elegant were two stories, nevertheless.)

In real estate vernacular, building types have received unrelated stylistic code words: ranch for one story, colonial for two—even if the former is vertical redwood with sliding doors and the latter pink stucco.

**RAPHAEL (RAFFAELLO SANZIO) (1483–1520)** *Italian Painter and Architect*  Painter who moved later into architecture, his School of Athens in the Vatican (in the Stanza della Signatura, or Room of the Signers) concerned itself with architecture as much as painting (coffered vaulting in a dramatic perspective): a fresco in a single room, in an obscure part of the Vatican (Palace), has been singled out by art and architectural history as a birthing point of a painter's move to architecture.

His own house (House of Raphael) became a symbolic point of Renaissance design, perhaps best expressed in the later and still extant reality of the Palazzo Vidoni-Caffarelli (rusticated bottom with paired columns above, flanking windows). He helped Bramante (a fellow citizen from Urbino) at St. Peter's.

**RAPSON, RALPH (1914–    )** *American Architect and Teacher*  Student of and worker with both Saarinens, Rapson has headed the departments of architecture at the Institute of Design (Chicago) and the University of Minnesota. His built work ranges from his dry design for embassies of the U.S. in Copenhagen and Stockholm (with van de Meulen) to the ebullient Arts Center of Minneapolis.

**RATABLES**  That body of taxable real property within a city that can be assessed and taxed, as opposed to realty-exempt. The latter includes churches, nonprofit institutions, and, of course, parks, highways, public buildings—which usually comprise 40% of the land and a substantial portion of potential valuation. Cities dominated by colleges (Cambridge and Harvard, Princeton and Prince-

RAPSON *Humanities and Fine Arts Center, University of Minnesota, Morris, Minnesota*

RAYMOND *Reader's Digest Building, Tokyo*

ton, Palo Alto and Stanford) feel need to bite the hand that created them. Spawned by the college, they become more than a dog's tail, and hence wag the dog, demanding fees in lieu of taxes, since the land and buildings of the college are not ratables.

**RAYMOND, ANTONIN (1888–  )** *Czech-American-Japanese Architect* He went to Japan with Frank Lloyd Wright in 1916 to help design and build the Imperial Hotel, and stayed. With Lladislav Rado (Raymond and Rado), he built for Americans in the western Pacific, and particularly in Tokyo, where his Reader's Digest Building was one of the most short-lived modern monuments on record: built in the fifties, it was demolished in the sixties to allow appropriate exploitation of land values.

**REAL ESTATE** Somebody's state of mind claimed reality only for immovable objects, hence buildings and similar constructions and the land on which they do or might sit. Real estate, therefore, is that part of man's wealth (estate) that is thereby termed real.

**RECEPTACLE** That which receives, often a plug (an electric receptacle—outlet—receives the plug, although *it* gives the electricity and the plug receives).

**RECESS** A place away from the main; indention, alcove, apse, exedra—anything that is a small incision in the space in question to allow a person to withdraw, retire, or hide.

**RECTORY** The right place, or the place of him who brings us to "right"; and hence the residence of minister or priest or pastor.

**REFECTORY** A dining room for monks, and later, because monks created colleges, for college students. Refectories are spaces second only to churches in medieval grandeur: stone-walled, with timbered, hammer-beamed roofs, they were the secular meeting places of daily life, in concert with Christian devotions in church.

**REGENCY** The English style complementary to the French Empire in the era of archaeology's infancy: when each new discovery was in concert with its romantic political (real or imagined) context. The Regency of England began in 1810, when old George III was declared bonkers and his son, the Prince of Wales, was appointed regent. On George III's death in 1820, the Regent-Prince became George IV, a nasty, stingy, hated fellow; and the Regency was over.

Regency architecture is one of "taste," where the "upper classes" were allowed their rein in thumbing through the bibliography of possibilities: Rome, Greece, Egypt, fantasies, and reality—a kind of continuing stage-setting of ideas that allowed an economical urban design reality: Nash built Regent Street, the world's longest urban stage-set, and myriad suburban villaed garden complexes. Others covered the land with stuccoed economies of charm and diversion.

**REGISTER**   The baffling grill that can control the quantity and direction of air flow from a furnace or fan.

**REIDY, AFFONSO E. (1909–   )** *Brazilian Architect*   His most copied design is the sinuous eight-story serpentine building following approximate contour lines, the Pedregulho Housing Development (1947+, Rio de Janeiro). Even New York-on-the-flat has one: Kelly and Gruzen's Chatham Green (1961), twenty-one stories in red brick and open-access galleries built after B. Sumner Gruzen's trip to Brazil passed by Pedregulho: an elegant takeoff that more than does justice to its ancestor.

REIDY *Pedregulho housing project, Rio de Janeiro*

**REINFORCED CONCRETE**   Portland cement concrete is a strong material in compression (walls, piers, and foundations) but fails when flexed Tensed steel reinforcing makes with it a composite construction, each material a contributing part of a symbiotic relationship: steel pulls, concrete pushes. The two are economical in a labor-intensive economy, expensive in a materials-intensive one.

Foundations, dams, and highways are inconceivable without reinforced concrete, and the frames of urban high-rise buildings can either use it (apartment houses mostly) or merely use unreinforced concrete to fireproof (by encasing) steel frames. (See also *Hennebique, François* and *Perret, Auguste*.)

**RELIEVING ARCH**   A natural arch in masonry to relieve weight of masonry from whatever is below: sometimes a wood lintel unable to handle the situation by itself, as a steel lintel might; sometimes a vast opening where the weight of brick above is diverted by such relief. A wide arch at the bottom (as in Kahn's Capitol at Dacca) may, by such device, only hold part of the weight.

**RENDERING**   A pictorial illustration of a proposed building or structure, traditionally a perspective proto-photograph that appears to be as real as the finished product.

**RENWICK, JAMES, JR. (1818–1895)** *American Architect and Engineer*   As a youth he competed for the design of Grace Church, won it with a supremely competent English neo-Gothic country church design which sits today as a pivot on bent Broadway at 10th Street, New York City. St. Ann's Church (1869, Brooklyn), a multicolored Ruskinian Gothic, was a later and looser building containing a cast-iron interior space for mass preaching. St. Patrick's Cathedral (1858–79, with later towers) extended Grace, crossbred English and French Gothic, and was vaulted by lightweight terra cotta without any help of flying buttress—an engineering success and exterior archaeological oddity that confuses the purity of its neo-Gothic image.

The Smithsonian Institution in Washington is Renwick's too, a brick crenelated palace that became a kind of national attic of American artifacts.

**REPTON, HUMPHRY (1752–1818)** *English Landscape Gardener*   He made our suburban garden what it is today: trellised, arbored, terraced—a nearby formality of hard architecture and soft plants that then fades into woods and fields (in contrast to Capability Brown, who planted Palladian formalities in a sea of grazed mounds and picturesque trees). Repton anticipated the indoor-outdoor interplay of modern architecture: ergo, French doors.

**REREDOS**   A background for an altar; a screen of wood or stone, usually carved. A reredos was sometimes an object of art in itself, product of unrequited talent, as in that for Holy Trinity Church (1844, Brooklyn) by Frank Freeman (in a neo-Gothic church by Minard Lafever).

**RESERVOIR**   Place of reserve or storage, as of water for a house, town, or city, brought to it in aqueducts (sometimes plain pipes underground, sometimes the canal-bearing Roman remants). Reservoirs are concerned with neighboring pollutions and the status of ground water, and are therefore in most suburban locales densely planted with conifers all around and for some distance, to hold the water table and -shed free from incursions.

RENDERING

**RESTAURANT**   A place to restore the client to good health and spirits and, therefore, a place of food and drink. Restaurants in their own right are modern inventions, more than the eating services of inns or hotels, and cater to the physical and emotional fulfillment of men and women—who have found, not surprisingly, that the brain and stomach are connected, and the performance of one depends on the other, not only in the quantity of fodder supplied but in its quality, and even the grace with which it is served.

**RESTORATION**   The act of replacing the missing parts, and hence restoring that which was there first. Frequently, however, the process replaces what was never there as the enthusiasm of the restorer takes hold and "gives to airy nothing a local habitation and a name."

Viollet-le-Duc in France restored Carcassonne and Notre Dame at Paris; the Rockefellers paid for the conjuration of Williamsburg, Virginia, from foundation traces and rubble. It is not unlike the veneration of a saint through the possession of his feet. Restoration is a happy and worthy profession when constrained by reality rather than romantic wish or literary nostalgia.

**RETAINING WALL**   A wall that holds back (i.e., retains) earth adjacent and at a higher level.

**RETURN**   An extra right angle, as a buttress or recess or bay, meeting a wall.

**REVEAL**   The cheek of an opening, window, or doorjamb that returns, from the face of the wall, to the opening itself.

**REVELL, VILJO (1910–     )** *Finnish Architect*   Rational and unaffected architect in his early work (the Teollisuukeskus Offices and Hotel; 1952, Helsinki), he won the competition for the Toronto City Hall (1958), now built. The latter is, in contrast, an arbitrary formalist's form: two curved office slabs embracing the city council (the oyster shells containing a pearl), a self-conscious affair, particularly when it is realized that the office slabs are single-loaded, all offices facing in, corridors outside giving (in spite of potential spectacular views) their blank bottoms to the city. A stone English *perpendicular* fan-vault is also a visual, rather than structural, idea (cf. King's College Chapel, Cambridge).

RENWICK *Grace Church, New York*

255

**REVETMENT**  A veneer of flat stones over an embankment to prevent erosion. Particularly a military engineer's term, and hence somewhat old-fashioned, since forts are out of style.

**RIB**  Borrowed from the human rib cage, the Gothic rib is a rounded, usually structural member that carries the infilled cross vaults of a Gothic church. Ribs are also simulated structure—to give the vision of structure, but not its reality, depending on the time and place of the vaulting, as in, particularly, a plaster vault with simulated plaster-scribed ribs.

**RICHARDSON, HENRY HOBSON (1838–1886)** *American Architect*  Richardson was one of a chain of great nineteenth-century American architects, each working for the former and inspiring the further development of his successor: Frank Furness, Richardson, Louis Sullivan, and Frank Lloyd Wright.

Richardsonian Romanesque is a full-blown American style drawn from Richardson's fascination with utilitarian use of Romanesque arches, with rock-faced (super-rock) stonework surrounding. The Marshall Field Warehouse (1885, Chicago) is Richardsonian Romanesque on a super-Italian palazzo's form. The Glessner House (1886, Chicago) is a cold and brutal gray-stoned form of great internal elegance; and Boston's Trinity Church (1877) on Copley Square is one of the few church-plaza symbioses of America ever.

He also worked with wood (sticks and shingles), and his Watts Sherman House (1874, Newport) is one of the most extravagant constructions of all of Vincent Scully's magnificent roster in "the shingle style."

Richardson fancied himself as a medieval monk and had the gall to dress in monkly robes on occasion.

**RICKMAN, THOMAS (1776–1841)** *English Physician and Architect*  Rickman's *An Attempt to discriminate the Styles of Architecture in England* named the phases of English Gothic: Early English, Decorated, and Perpendicular. He then went beyond words to deeds, and consummated country Gothic at such unlikely name-places as Hampton Lucy (1826; he was 50).

He is known for his additions to St. John's College, Cambridge (the New Court), and the Bridge of Sighs (both 1831).

**RIDGE** The linear apex of two meeting roof slopes, a point for articulation and enrichment.

**RIETVELD, GERRIT (1888–1964)** *Dutch Architect* His "chair" has discomfited both lookers and sitters for two generations, a constructed plane and stick-wood sculpture, obviously not designed with the sitter in mind; very handsome on a display platform at the Museum of Modern Art.

The Schröder House (1924, Utrecht) is an overillustrated icon of the de Stijl movement that fractured the smooth closed volumes of Cubism, assembling a construction of white planes and incised volumes: an explosion of the pure box. De Stijl crossbred the early Wright with Le Corbusier.

**RISE** The height from spring to crown, boss, ridge, or apex; or the height from one level to another, as in a step (or riser).

**RISER** The face of a stair's step, rising from one tread to another.

**ROAD** A surface way to pass from one place to another, paved or packed earth allowing easy traffic on public land. A road is a rural conduit, as opposed to a street, boulevard, or avenue, which are urban and most often defined by the buildings that flank them.

**ROCHE, KEVIN (1922–    )** *Irish American Architect* Roche was the unpremeditated dauphin who ascended the throne at the premature death of Eero Saarinen (1961). Saarinen's romantic practice was continued in his name, then converted to Roche-Dinkleloo and Associates (New Haven). The facile virtuosity of Dulles International Airport, the T.W.A. Terminal, and the Yale Hockey Rink (plastic formal sculpture and space) gave way (under Roche) to the Knights of Columbus Building in New Haven and the magnificent Oakland (California) Museum.

**ROCKEFELLER, NELSON ALDRICH (1908–    )** *Businessman, Politician, Architectural Patron* The various Rockefellers created Rockefeller Center in their name; restored (or better, reincarnated) Williamsburg, Virginia, Colonial capital of that territory; contributed the site for the United Nations; and built the Albany South Mall (all a not too random sample).

Nelson Rockefeller has been at the heart of it all, as executive

ROCHE *College Life Insurance Company, Indianapolis*

257

leader or guiding spirit, largely through his relative by marriage, Wallace K. Harrison (architect). Unhappily, the projects are in descending order of quality, and (one hopes) in an equally descending order of influence: Rockefeller Center is the greatest commercial urban place ever built, anywhere. The South Mall is a vulgar extravaganza of tired creativity and nonurbanity.

At a personal level, Rockefeller has commissioned Philip Johnson (Rockefeller Guest House; 1952, New York City) and Junzo Yoshimura of Tokyo (Nelson Rockefeller House; 1974; Pocantico Hills, New York).

**ROCKFACE**  Stone-tooled to simulate supernature, more rugged than a cliff's face. Orderly stones, coursed and dressed on their sides, are sometimes rockfaced in Renaissance (and Victorian revival) architecture (cf. the Pitti Palace, Florence).

**ROCOCO**  A word popularly used to describe the ornate and romantic interior decoration of the eighteenth century, particularly that of France. It brings to mind the boudoir of Marie Antoinette and the painted cherubs, milkmaids, and cotton clouds of painters Boucher and Fragonard. In architecture, *Rococo* suggests ideas more serious, a culmination of the preceding Baroque. At its best, Baroque uses spatial dramatics, optical illusion, and a sequential set of mysterious and mysteriously lighted events. Rococo, in contrast, as at Die Wies by Dominikus Zimmermann, provides a totally comprehensible plastic space where white-and-gold plaster vaults, domes, piers, and arches are bathed in brilliant light through clear glass windows. Sequential mystery has turned to complex but obvious dramatics.

ROGERS *Tremont House, Boston*

**RODIA, SIMON (ca. 1885–1965)** *Spanish American Junk User* Rodia's remarkable works are his towers at Watts, a Los Angeles suburb later degraded by racial violence. He built from junk, metal, broken bottles, and pottery one of the great architectural statements of any untutored mind in all history, now happily preserved after much silly strife. Old Catalonian memories helped him (the church of the Sagrada Familia by Gaudí), but their translation into an airy filigree of steel, enriched with Pop mosaic (Pepsi Cola bottles and broken coffee cups), is Rodia's alone. When he finished, he left, apparently bored and uninterested, as if the making of a work was of sole importance, not its viewing or relish.

**ROEBLING, JOHN (1806–1869) and WASHINGTON (1837– 1926)** *German American Engineers, Cablemakers, and Contractors* The Roeblings spanned rivers with lacy networks of cables. They extrapolated the products of their Trenton, New Jersey works, through creative genius to elegant and monumental built-form, acts of building consonant with the great mid-nineteenth-century explosion of un-selfconscious aesthetic engineering (cf. Thomas Telford). The Cincinnati-Covington Bridge anticipated their most heroic moment: the Brooklyn Bridge (originally the New York and Brooklyn Bridge). Father John died in its construction (1869–83), his life taken by gangrene acquired from a crushed foot. Son Washington developed the "bends" in an underwater caisson and spent his thus-crippled life overseeing the bridge's completion by telescope from his town house on the adjacent bluff of Brooklyn Heights.

**ROGERS, ISAIAH (1800–1869)** *American Architect* In a country based on movement of population and trade, the hotel became an early and important building type. Isaiah Rogers built the elegant Tremont House (1829) in Boston, followed by the Astor House (1836) in New York, Greek Revival and very grand for those times.

**ROLLING MILL** The place where hot ingots of steel are pressed, formed, and rolled by pressure into shapes needed for the structural parts of buildings, bridges, and other incidental structures. Rolled-steel shapes and sheets are a vigorous, highly tensile iron product, whereas cast iron, poured in puddles into formwork, is a brittle affair, virtuous largely in its ability to exactly conform; good in compression, like stone or other masonry.

**ROMAN** The gregarious, business-oriented (sometimes Imperial) Romans developed an engineering to allow their places of commerce to develop, their pleasures place to be fulfilled, their traffic ways to circulate. The basilica, the bath, the aqueduct, the highway resulted—all still in large extent available in the original or near-original form. Roman architecture was an urban affair, a collection of collateral functions that together formed a place of public activity and interchange for the citizenry: cf. the Forum, as opposed to the remote religious place of Greece (the Acropolis). Roman aqueducts watered the city from distant hills; Roman *cloacae* (sewers) drained them. The circuses contained their most terrifying specta-

ROEBLING *Brooklyn Bridge, New York*

259

cles—of chariots, lions, ships, and martyrs (and the Colosseum was a special supercircus testing the imperially conquered races and creatures against each other: an empirical laboratory of gore and grief). The Roman ways of affluence and wealth were those of urbanity and colonization: urbanity to create the human reservoir of skills and soldiers to provide military force; colonization with those very soldiers to give land to the burgeoning population and resources and loaves to the homeland—a relentless and never-ending quest when unleashed.

**ROMANESQUE**   "Roman" in its use of arch and column: "Roman-esque" is the Christian architecture of Western Europe (as opposed to the Byzantine East) after the basilica was not enough for Christ and his troops, and greater spaces for religion and its servants were needed in both urban and monastic places: greater in size, scale, and symbolism.

The Romanesque arch was round, and so were its vaults, limiting the structure to one low in relation to Gothic but staggering in contrast to a timber-roofed basilica: Vézelay, St. Benoit sur Loire, and the apogee, the twin churches of Abbaye Aux Hommes and Abbaye aux Dames at Caen, are the great places of the Romanesque.

Austere when Cistercian, ornate when Benedictine, the abbey churches were all strong-boned structural statements—column, pier, arch, rib—that foreshadowed the more sinuous and elegant Gothic, but did it with a conviction and a relation to the common man-user that the Gothic could never match. The Romanesque seems peasant, the Gothic patrician.

ROMANESQUE *Nave, S. Michele, Pavia*

**ROOD**   Archaic English term for cross or crucifix, sometimes supported on a beam across a chancel's entrance (rood beam), sometimes on a screen (rood screen), allowing the screened clergy behind opportunity for mystical activity.

**ROOF**   The hat and cloak of a building, shedding the weather and sheltering it from the elements overhead, although the A-frame house, fleetingly popular in marginal modern architecture, is *all* roof.

A sloping roof is roofed with shingles or sometimes sheet metal (copper, lead, terne), largely because it is then visible and the material has major architectural status. Flat roofs, nominally unseen, are built up of sheets of fibered paper (felt) and tar; but high-rise American urban life makes most visible anyway (as opposed to those normally unseen rich top views of Italian urban roofscape, red-tiled all around, as from the lantern view of the Florence Duomo or the tower of the Palazzo Pubblico in Siena).

**ROOF TRUSS** An engineered arrangement of timber or steel sticks to economically and elegantly support a roof load across a wide span: it follows the network of stresses structurally needed (as if one carved away a solid planar beam to eliminate inert parts not working on the project of supporting the load).

**ROOT, JOHN WELLBORN (1850–1892)** *American Architect* Design partner of Daniel H. Burnham, he created with him the Monadnock Block and other great moments of the Chicago School; but he left the affair early, and by default (before *the* Fair, before the Flatiron, before the neo-L'Enfant plan of Washington, D.C.). Root was the Chicago School talent of the partnership, which floundered in the neo-Renaissance after his death.

In his early professional years he worked for James Renwick, Jr., and then John B. Snook, architect for *old* Grand Central Station (1876, New York).

**ROSE WINDOW** A round wheel of a window in the west (entrance) façade of a Gothic church, roselike in its petaled form, rose-colored in its spread of sunset light in a church's nave.

**ROSSELLINO, BERNARDO (1409–1464)** *Italian Architect* Alberti's legman, who executed for him the Palazzo Rucellai in Florence and the restoration of S. Stefano Rotondo in Rome. Garnering these thoughts, he built for Pius II a palace and cathedral at Pienza (throwing in parts of the Alberti façade from S. Maria Novella and the Tempio Malatestiano; in effect, creating a single-complexed collection of every built idea Alberti ever had).

**ROTH, EMERY (1870–1947) AND SONS** *American Architects* A pragmatist, the senior Roth crossed architecture with the realities of real estate economics at the Ritz Tower (1925; with Carrère and Hastings as his aesthetic bishops) and the Beresford (1928) and San Remo (1930) apartments, both twin-towered residential palaces on the west flank of New York's Central Park. Roth's children Richard and Julian (and later, grandchild Richard, Jr.) have carried the com-

ROOT *Reliance Building, Chicago*

mon sensibilities two more generations: they are the norm of real estate to which, occasionally, architectural heroes are attached in hopes of bringing architectural distinction: Breuer, Gropius, Belluschi, Barnes, and others have all needed Roth to make their packages credible. Occasionally, a Roth solo venture is surprisingly successful, as in the dormitory complex for the (N.Y.) State University Center at Stony Brook, Long Island.

**ROTUNDA**   A round built place, usually domed, as in *the* Rotunda of the Capitol in Washington, D.C.

**ROW HOUSE**   A house that shares the larger architecture of a city's block: the total form is the group, or row, each house only presenting its façade to the street. Row houses are more grandly termed town houses, for those who think of the former as lesser than middle-class accommodations; while, conversely, row houses can assume the grandeur of a Renaissance palazzo (Palladio's Palazzo Valmarana at Vicenza, Peruzzi's Palazzo Massimo at Rome, Otto Kahn's Fifth Avenue Town House, and so forth).

**RUBBLE**   Broken stone from nature used for wall construction, giving qualities very different from fieldstone (naturally rounded) or ashlar, which is stone dressed to give precise form.

RUDOLPH *Art and Architecture Building, Yale University, New Haven*

**RUDOLPH, PAUL (1918–   )** *American Architect* Exquisite draftsman, plastic and versatile form-maker, Rudolph was dean of the School of Architecture at Yale: his own client for his greatest building, a brutal concrete Piranesi-spirited space for nothing much more than its own abstract enjoyment, rather than any carefully programmed functions. (As the *carceri* were for Piranesi, except that Rudolph's is real and bears the burden of use.)

While passing through New Haven, Rudolph also left the Forestry Building (can you believe concrete trees support it?) and an Italian hill town transported to New England (balloon framing, brick-veneered; red terra-cotta Cubist Housing for Married Students—handsome, livable, but somewhat pretentious in imagery).

The State Office Building in Boston's Government Center and Endo Laboratories (Garden City, New York) are of elegantly striated and molded concrete block, with plastic, rounded, sinuous forms, more concerned with statement than use. (But who ever looked inside Alberti's Tempio Malatestiano, or tested the plumbing in the Parthenon?)

Rudolph is more concerned with the complexity of his advertisements than their usefulness or classic good looks. It is the case of the cat and mouse: he, the cat, worrying the mouse, the building, for the sake of worrying, a compulsive state of affairs.

**RUIN** The fallen remnants of a building, shrouded in romance in the Regency-Empire's beginnings of archaeological explorations that brought attention to Greece and Rome and Egypt, and hence simulated revivals of some of their superficial archaeological trappings; but also admired as ruins per se. English gardeners built ruins as original objects to decorate the eye's landscape and give a pictorial, painter's view to reality.

**RUSKIN, JOHN (1819–1900)** *English Writer on Art and Architecture* His *The Seven Lamps of Architecture*(1849) cited Sacrifice, Truth, Power, Beauty, Life, Memory, Obedience—enough to determine for Ruskin that the only architectural styles were those venerable and handcrafted, imperfect as only things made by man can be, picturesque, naturalistic, and of *real* materials. These constraints, coupled with his belief that because a good society had created the Gothic, the Gothic, revived, could revive a Good Society, drove him to *The Stones of Venice* (1851–53) and the proliferation of the Venetian Gothic, a strange polychromed stonework now extant worldwide by his missionary architectural zeal, from Oxford's New Museum (1858; Deane and Woodward) to Brooklyn's St. Ann's Church (1869; James Renwick, Jr., architect). Everyone has one on or near his side of the tracks.

**RUSSELL** The family name of the Dukes of Bedford, whose great estates near the City of London (now very much downtown London) were developed in a sophisticated land speculation that brought them profit (and still does) and gave urbanists elegant Georgian housing with a foil of streets and squares unmatched in what is still existing anywhere in the world: Bedford Square, Russell Square, and endless others joined their earlier and smaller scheme at Covent Garden, where their architect, the great Inigo Jones, conjured up a formal plaza and surrounding housing equal to the best of Italian urban design: a northern, and smaller, Piazza S. Marco (with its own church by Jones: St. Paul's).

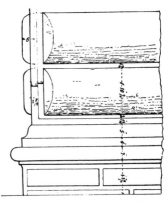

RUSTICATED *Detail from Strozzi Palace, Florence*

**RUSTICATED** An odd phrase for *urbanity* in architecture: the opposite of rural or rustic. But, nevertheless, it describes deeply articulated joints in bulky stone Renaissance building blocks. They look rockier and stronger, more massive, through such jointed exaggerations. Smooth rustications are jointed smooth stones (Palazzo Strozzi); rockfaced are those where stones are tooled to exaggerate an artificial cliff texture (Palazzo Pitti).

# S

**SAARINEN, EERO (1910–1961)** *Finnish American Architect*
Son of Eliel. Prolific, versatile, facile; each project seemed to demand originality for its own sake. The most serene is the General Motors Technical Center outside Detroit, loose Mies boxes, widely spaced and highly colored with glazed bricks. (Compare the compact and monochromatic Illinois Institute of Technology by Mies.) The clear and polychromed Cubism here dominates very elegant glass-walled detail, reminiscent of children's architectural building blocks.

SAARINEN, EERO *Yale Hockey Rink,*
*New Haven*

At the Yale Hockey Rink or T.W.A.'s Terminal at Kennedy Airport (New York City) he played with willfully plastic roofs, unrelated to the geometries of engineering: anticlassic, whimsical membranes, their stylish form becomes jaded for the more than one-time viewer. Also at Yale he created the rubble and concrete-stoned Ezra Stiles Dormitories, as meandering as collegiate Gothic, handsome, beloved by their residents, and caustically described by another Yale architect and sometime dean as an instant "stage-set for *Ivanhoe.*"

Before his early death, Saarinen made the Dulles International Airport (Chantilly, Virginia)—a hopeful foray into simplifying those great sprawling, fingered airport places. Instead of fingers to walk through or convey people from terminal to plane, superbuses ("movable lounges") collect the passengers at the gate and move them, en masse, to the plane. The place is a great hall under a slung, catenary roof, proudly propped by giant outsplayed concrete columns.

265

SAARINEN, ELIEL *Helsinki Railroad Station*

**SAARINEN, ELIEL (1873–1950)** *Finnish American Architect*
His Helsinki Railroad Station brought some Olbrich (cf. the Hochzeitsturm, 1907) to Helsinki: brick, spare and towered, and a grand space. Saarinen was invited to compete for the Chicago Tribune (building) competition, won second prize (Hood and Howells won first), and gathered such praise and admiration that he moved to America to enjoy it.

On the faculty of the Cranbrook Academy of Art, he built for it a symbolic place of austere Neoclassicism—gatewayed, columned portal going from nowhere to nowhere (garden informal to garden formal)—and some northern European brick neo-Gothic for its adjacent boys' school.

Saarinen, Swanson and Saarinen was a firm with son and second partner for early generation interlock and/or torch-passing: Crow Island School (Winnetka, Illinois).

**SACCONI, (COUNT) GIUSEPPE (1853–1905)** *Italian Architect*
The villain who gave Rome its white-marbled wedding cake (and that a product of an 1884 competition): the Victor Emmanuel Monument, which rough-shoulders the gentle, elegant, and magnificent Capitol on the Capitoline Hill and the latter's church, S. Maria in Aracoeli.

**SAFDIE, MOSHE (1938–     )** *Israeli American Architect* Safdie persuasively sold the administrators of Montreal's Expo '67 his architectural dream: Habitat, a Cubistic pile of prefabricated boxes arranged romantically, a modern reminiscence of primitive multiple dwellings that range from the cliff and Pueblo dwellings of America's Southwest to the hill and island towns of the Mediterranean— all with personal identity of dwelling place within an over-all system. The economics have not yet been conquered, and Safdie's proposals for Lower Manhattan, Puerto Rico, and Israel move sluggishly through the morass of their respective economic and political realities.

**SALAMANDER** Unlike that innocent miniature dragon, the builder's salamander spouts flame (internally) to create temporary heat for a space during construction—more to prevent the freezing of plaster or concrete than the people who placed them there. Salamanders are hot cylindrical boxes fueled by propane (gas) bottles.

**SALON** A formal social event, where conversation reigns, or the place where such events occurred. The salon of a house is often a special living room for special guests, vacant at most other times.

Debased, and with an *o* added, the word describes the drinking place of the American Wild West, the simple box building of a main street from which gunfighters erupted to duel; usually elementary wooden buildings that offered solace and sociability to a lonely cowboy or traveler. Hollywood created more as sets than the West ever owned.

**SANATORIUM** A place of health, or where health may be returned. Sanatoriums are the collective retreats of the mentally ill, chronically diseased, or the alchoholic, where slow rehabilitation can occur (unlike the expeditious hospital). Most famous sanatorium is that of Thomas Mann's *The Magic Mountain*. (The air of mountains—cold, clear, and crisp—was supposedly part of the remedy for tuberculosis, and hence the location suggested an architecture of mountain chalets.)

**SANCTUARY** The precincts of an altar; therefore, in more polite custom, inviolable, and place of personal sanctuary for one in danger or pursued by the police, army, gangsters, or anyone.

**SAN FRANCISCO** Hilly thumb (as if part of a resting right hand) that cuts off the sea to define San Francisco Bay. Its dramatic hills were urbanized, overlaid with a rectangular grid, to the horror of romantic and contour-oriented land planners. In fact, the clash of grid and topography brings great drama to the city in its precipitously rising and falling cable car routes, and the opportunity, down straight streets, continuously to glimpse *the* Bay from bay windows (impossible in a medium- to high-rise city terraced and planned as a spiraling, concentric ziggurat).

**SANGALLO, ANTONIO DA, THE ELDER (1455–1534)** *Italian Architect* Bramante inspired this Sangallo's church in the hill town of Montepulciano, S. Biagio. It should be particularly admired as the unique product of an architect in a provincial place unprepared for such monumental glories.

**SANGALLO, ANTONIA DA, THE YOUNGER (1485–1546)** *Italian Architect and Military Engineer* Palazzo Farnese, completed

SAFDIE *Habitat, Expo'67, Montreal*

(third story and cornice) by Michelangelo, a plain mass for the Renaissance, was his mark. He also, among many others, worked on St. Peter's (succeeding Bramante), preceding the same Michelangelo's moment of truth: the dome. Sangallo spent his many military engineering years working on Rome's fortified walls.

**SANGALLO, GUILIANO DA (1445–1516)** *Italian Architect, Military Engineer, and Sculptor*   Renaissance engineering was more usually a military than a civil affair, hence Sangallo's title. He created fortifications that are great architectonic structures. And so did Eiffel and so does Nervi create architecture in the name of engineering.

His Palazzo Gondi (1494, Florence) is a variation on a theme of Brunelleschi, used also by Michelozzo at the Palazzo Medici-Riccardi.

**SANMICHELI, MICHELE (1484–1559)** *Italian Architect and Engineer*   An active fortifier, he made bulwarks and ramparts for Parma, Piacenza, Legnago, Verona, Venice, and Corfu. The parts at articulate points (gateways and guardhouses) are lusty stonework, with Doric columns and scarifying faces (for emotional defense).

Palazzo Grimani, (1556+, Venice) is one of his glassiest non-forts.

**SANSOVINO, JACOPO (1486–1570)** *Italian Sculptor and Architect*   One wall of the Piazzetta S. Marco (Venice) (that link to the water from the main piazza) is Sansovino's Library and Mint, the single stretch of the containing walls of the piazza and its surrounds (excepting St. Mark's Church and the Doge's Palace, which are freestanding and participating buildings) considered important architecture for itself—not just more wallpaper (façade) of which the principal function is to define these great outdoor "rooms."

The Palazzo Corner on the Grand Canal is an aquatic Roman palace.

**SANT'ELIA, ANTONIO (1888–1916)** *Italian Architect*   The architect of Futurism, his visionary plasticity illustrated, with magnificent drawings, towered cities, laced with midaired transit tubes (remember H. G. Wells's *The Shape of Things To Come*—movie version —glass-tubed transit powered by steam? Trains were pistons in continuous cylinders).

SANSOVINO *Libreria Vecchia, Venice*

Sant'Elia, obsessed with movement, designed railroad stations, dirigible hangars, and other celebrations of arrival and storage.

He was killed in action in the First World War.

**SASH** The framework of a moving window, vertically sliding (double-hung), swinging (casement), outprojecting (awning), or in-tilting (hopper).

**SATELLITE TOWN** A dependent but largely self-sufficient urban place, held in orbit to a metropolitan core by attraction of superfacilities that only such a core can offer: universities, the stage's spectacles of opera and the theater, special shopping (availability of the rare or chic), libraries, records, resources; and most important, the intensity of life in such a communal confrontation. The satellite's residents, however, spend their *daily* lives at home, with local work and play, using the center city only for special trips, events, and purchases.

**SAWTOOTH** Formed like the teeth of a saw, whose profiles slope both gently and steeply at each tooth-face. Factory roofs, to bring in natural light, use such profiled sequential skylights: only the end view conjures such reminiscences, lines of "sawteeth" silhouetted against the sky.

**SCAFFOLDING** Temporary structure to support workmen and materials, raising them to the height, place, and position of their use (or application). Scaffoldlike structures to support arches, domes, and vaults while being built and until complete are called centering; those to support wet concrete until it sets and gains strength are forms or formwork. Scaffolding was first wood (small sticks) in Western countries, bamboo in the Orient; later, light tubular steel frames.

Frank Lloyd Wright built his 1954 Pavilion ("60 Years of Living Architecture"), on the site of the present Guggenheim Museum, of tubular scaffolding and plastic—a pleasant semipermanent space of great economy.

**SCALE** A loosely used word drawn from the Latin for *steps* or *ladder* and first used (in our area of discussion) for relative measure: *a* scale is that fraction of full size in which a drawing or model is represented (direct in the metric system, as 1/50th, expressed as

SANT'ELIA *Visionary railroad station*

269

1:50, and so forth; circuitous in the quaint English system, as 1/8 inch = one foot, architecturally expressed as ⅛″ = 1′–0″, where ′ = feet, and ″ = inches). Scale drawings are not intended to be scaled (i.e., measured with the scale, a proportionate ruler). They are dimensioned and are therefore only 98% exact, a practical affair for the eye, if the builder or artisan uses the dimensions shown.

But scale is much more: a state of the parts of the building in relation to the whole, or the whole in relation to *its* situation. To be "in scale" says that the relationship is successful and the proportioned hierarchy is well balanced.

A man is, of course, in or out of scale with a doorway; but the doorway of a cathedral, 25 feet tall, may not be out of scale with the crowds that use it. A 25-foot-square court is in scale with a family, the Piazza S. Pietro in scale with 100,000 present to receive the pope's blessing.

Scale too can be debated as an issue between two conflicting design attitudes. I am sure that Le Corbusier felt Wright's low sheltering house eaves a romantic toy and out of scale with the bare and vigorous Cubism he pioneered; and Wright thought the Villa Savoye an inhuman, abstract box without the friendly sheltering scale he himself sought. Both were building simultaneously, both were modern architects, both were great!

Le Corbusier had the special advantage of pursuing a whole canon of scale and proportion that he termed the Modulor (see entry).

**SCAMOZZI, VICENZO (1552–1616)** *Italian Architect and Writer*
A conservative fellow who picked up the torch of Palladio and became his verbal and graphic interlocutor. But on his own the Rocca Pisana at Lonigo is a Palladio-inspired, Palladian-catalyzing romance—the Villa Rotondo varied, impaled on a mountaintop, and given not only views but frames for them (cf. Prandtauer at Melk).

**SCANDINAVIA** The collective lands of Norwegians, Swedes, Finns, and Danes—cold, northern, ancient places. Their monolithic citizenry and maturity of culture allowed them confidence to be radical leaders in the arts, particularly architecture, in the thirties and forties; later they were bypassed when the nerve of less stoic peoples (combined with a natural showmanship) made the Italians group leaders of the fifties and some of the sixties. (All this excepts the individual leaders scattered hither and yon, such as Le Corbusier, Mies, Wright, Aalto, Kahn.)

The craving for architecture made it a populist part of Scandinavian culture, a matter for discussion in public, in cafés (whereas in the U.S. it's the product of a secret society). Masses became architects and filled the profession to more than surfeit, their excess energies and talents turning to furniture and furnishings, architectonic tools for life that reached a level of design unequaled anywhere else—not just for the elite or wealthy, but design for the common man. Among the leaders were and are Arne Jacobsen of Denmark (schools, houses, and chairs); Alvar Aalto (everything, and the best of all of Finland); and Sven Markelius of Sweden (planner and architect). Norway is the minor sibling and has not the same leadership as the other three.

**SCARFING** In joining two flat boards, as with a baseboard so long that one piece could never reach, each meeting end is scarfed, sloped to a razor edge in mirror image to the other, so that they can lap, their two surfaces glued, acting monolithically, with no danger of their joints separating. A cruder carpenter would butt the two.

**SCHAROUN, HANS (1893–   )** *German Architect* In the spirit of early Mendelsohn and Sant'Elia, Scharoun built and drew modest projects after the First World War. After World War II, a revival of interest in more plastic and romantic architecture brought renewed attention to him and gave him glory. He gave it back at the Romeo and Juliet Apartments (1955, Suttgart), and more than that at the Berlin Philharmonic (1963), a great grotto of a space, stepped and terraced for the troglodytic musicians to festoon, decorate, and sound the space: lovely, unique, a modern Rococo.

SCHAROUN *Berlin Philharmonic*

**SCHINDLER, RUDOLF (1887–1953)** *Austrian American Architect* Worker for Wright and later sometime partner of Neutra, Schindler crossbred Wright's romantic and picturesque massing with the cut white Cubism of Europe (cf. de Stijl). His Lowell House (1926; Newport Beach, California) is a reinforced concrete frame, slinging planes of activity within, jutting and receding, infilled with steel-framed glass walls. Schindler used Gunite (sprayed concrete) as early as 1924, and "tilt-up" slabs (poured in forms flat on the ground, and then tilted up) in 1922 for his own house. The Wolfe House (1928, Catalina Island) anticipates (in stuccoed wood frame)

271

the equivalent redwood houses hanging on Berkeley's hills in the 1940s.

In his latter years he returned to Wrightian use of rubble stone walls (thrown into forms with concrete) and varied ridge- and wing-roofed spaces, more histrionic than the strong Cubistic interplays of his earlier work.

A small man, with a thick short neck and a shock of Viennese hair, he posed for his recorded photographs with an apparent egotism that, happily, was only in the photographs.

**SCHINKEL, KARL FRIEDRICH (1781–1841)** *German (Prussian) Architect* Most remembered as architect of a spare Neoclassical Revival (as opposed to Greek Revival, which used incidental parts on another body). His austere monumental buildings (including the Old Museum; 1830, Berlin) were a prominent inspiration (of good proportions, clarity, and simplicity of form) for Mies van der Rohe. Schinkel was, however, an eclectic fellow, and also built neo-Gothic, Italian Romanesque, and Renaissance buildings. Essentially, however, his buildings foreshadowed functionalism, stripped down from those of his competitors to more practical and barer bones.

**SCHOOL** Originally the place of lectures; now any place of teaching anyone of any age, and the body of students that attends. The complex set of functions and forms that serve student life today are trappings subsidiary to the main point: intellectual communication, response, and development—with the incidental collection of knowledge only useful if the schooling process teaches the methodology of how to use the knowledge gained. More than half a school's building houses administration, gymnastics, swimming pools, social activities, dining facilities—the balanced parts of the life of a mind and body separated for whole days from a family: in loco parentis.

Historically, the rural box (one-room schoolhouse) was first multiplied into an urban tenement-like stack. When interplay of child and nature loomed large as new dogma, the school sprawled and opened its walls to the outside, bringing in sun and view, allowing the child out to grassy surrounds (cf. Maxwell Fry on Impington, or the Saarinens' Crow Island School). As a result, in-city schools have become low sprawls amid high-packed and -rise surrounds, an excision of space and dropping of scale with complementary openness for the child.

SCHINKEL *Casino, Potsdam*

**SCHUYLER, MONTGOMERY (1843–1914)** *American Architectural Critic*   In the beginning there was Schuyler (with some help from Russell Sturgis), then Lewis Mumford; now a widening set including Ada Louise Huxtable, Allan Temko, Grady Clay, Paul Goldberger, and others. Schuyler, the pure aesthete, led them all; an early and articulate outspoken crier in the wilderness, he praised with reason the Brooklyn Bridge, late Sullivan, and early Wright, raising, for two decades, architectural criticism to a height it had never before reached. (Architectural magazines are rarely critical in this incisive sense, acting more as public relations agents for those architects and movements their editors admire.)

**SCHWARZ, RUDOLPH (1897–1961)** *German Architect*   Church architect of maximum asceticism in design. His St. Fronleichman (1928+, Aachen) is a white box with a single incised side aisle and square windows of clear glass to light-wash the space: no mystical medieval grotto here, but a demanding northern verbal place for straight backs and rapt attention.

   Later, license creeps in and structural enrichment, if not luxury, takes hold at St. Antonius (1956, Essen) and the elliptical St. Theresia (1957, Linz). The Holy Cross Church (1957, Botrop) is one of the most elegant concrete structures ever built, with stained glass equal to the architecture it serves, lithe and powerful.

**SCHWEIKHER, PAUL (1903–     )** *American Architect*   A facile and romantic talent; Schweikher's Upton House (1950, Arizona; with partner Winston Elting) owes very much to Frank Lloyd Wright in its formed-rubble and concrete walls and its rough boards for banded fascias and decorative trellises. It is more regular and rectangular than Wright, and embraces a handsome walled courtyard. Schweikher was briefly chairman of the Department of Architecture at Yale; he later served in the same role at length at Carnegie Institute (now Carnegie-Mellon University).

**SCOTIA**   A concave molding—used at the base of Ionic and Corinthian columns, in particular; breast-shaped in section.

**SCOTT, (SIR) GEORGE GILBERT (1811–1878)** *English Architect*   Medieval revivalist: both restorer of Gothic churches and creator of his own vigorous neo-Gothic. Most prominently placed leftover is the Albert Memorial, alternately despised and beloved

SCHWARZ *St. Christophorus, Cologne*

273

crustacean monument, Victoria's own Victorian remembrance of her consort (still 37 years before her own end of reign and life).

Scott's most remembered client was Lord Palmerston, who reluctantly gave him the commission for the new Government Offices in Whitehall. Palmerston hated Gothic. Scott swallowed his pride, held on to his pocketbook, and produced a neo-Renaissance product, an exceptional interlude for an otherwise highly principled fellow.

**SCOTT, GEORGE GILBERT II (1839–1897)** *English Architect*
George, son of George. More big, bare Gothic.

**SCOTT, (SIR) GILES GILBERT (1880–1960)** *English Architect*
Liverpool Cathedral (1903+) is a heavy-stoned and -handed, bold, blunt free version of Gothic (this time not only revived, but crossbred: Gothic detail encrusts the heavy masonry of proto-modern masses). The central tower over the crossing inspired a similar affair (intended, not built) for the great Cathedral of St. John the Divine (1910+, New York City; as remodeled by Ralph Adams Cram).

Scott's Battersea Power Station (1934) brought a more severe and similar massing to the supersecular.

**SCOTT, JOHN OLDRID (1842–1913)** *English Architect* John, son of George I. Even more than brother George.

**SCREED** A guide for plastering along which a rod (plasterer's straight leveling stick) can be drawn as a guide to thickness and true level.

**SCRIBE** One scribes furniture and cabinetry to fit a perpendicular piece of wood against a molded wall; the profile of the wall is scribed on the wood, which is then cut to match and fit.

Scribing also is the making of plaster profiles by drawing a silhouette along a wet plaster ridge, forming it to the hard profile desired, as in the simple moldings of a Victorian ceiling.

**SCROLL** Carved in the form of a scroll of paper, as in the volutes of an Ionic capital, or the spiral scrollwork of a Renaissance modillion (bracket).

**SCULLY, VINCENT, JR. (1920–    )** *American Architect and Architectural Historian* Scully's bright mind codified the "Shingle

SCOTT *Foreign Office, Whitehall, London*

Style" in a book of the same name (1955): collecting work that was the apogee of full-blown, sometimes bulbous, often ugly, shingle-clad balloon frames, the wonderful fantasy castles of America's late nineteenth-century not so very rich. Many were at Newport (Rhode Island) and environs, a locale that gave cause for another elegant volume, *The Architectural Heritage of Newport, R.I.* (1952; with Antoinette Downing).

A more esoteric venture was *The Earth, the Temple, and the Gods* (1962), attempting among other things an explanation of the apparently casual placement of Greek religious buildings.

**SCULPTURE**   The shaping of material into designed form, with the conscious intent of art: a loose-ranging collection of possibilities involving stone, marble, wood, bronze, steel, and other materials; mined or found, carved, hewn, chipped, bolted, welded, and/or assembled.

Art is in the eyes and minds of a group culture, or those who tout for it, and opinion varies widely on what is or is not of the true faith. The sculptures of Meadmore, Rosenthal, and Tony Smith are far different from those of Praxiteles; as different as the buildings of Mies or Le Corbusier or Stirling or Kahn are from the Parthenon: but the press of all eras claim them all as "art."

In the beginning architecture and sculpture were one, and the interlock was guaranteed by the interchangeability of the creators. The Parthenon and Erechtheum were by architects who were sculptors, and vice versa; and, of course, the whole Italian Renaissance was the product of not multitalents, but the natural indivisible nature of those arts—they were not painting *and* sculpture *and* architecture: they were one.

Only in the nineteenth and twentieth centuries has there been a complete split, coincidental with the dispatch of engineers to their own corner of the ring. To bring together once more architect, engineer, and sculptor has proven yet impossible; a necessary armed truce of the first two was impossible to avoid, but the sculptor leaves his droppings scattered around the landscape surrounding a building, glued to its barren walls, or encrusting its lobby like postage stamps on an envelope, the afterthoughts of culture (often great or just good, but not part of any symbiosis). While the frieze and tympanum of the Parthenon were like the eyes and ears of its head, to be stolen by Lord Elgin and stored in the British Museum as head-hunted trophies, the body left for tourist jackals.

275

**SEAT** The sometime residence of a person of power, as the country seat of an English lord.

**SEAT** To firmly plant a building part. One can seat a brick but, more often, the sill of a window or a beam in or on a wall.

**SEIDLER, HARRY (1923–      )** *Austrian-American-Australian Architect* Vienna-born, American-trained, Seidler moved to Australia after work with both Marcel Breuer and Oscar Niemeyer. Seidler used both vocabularies well and with fresh thoughts of his own: his own house and the houses of many clients are based on a theme by Breuer; the Lend-Lease House in Sydney draws much from Neimeyer's white Cubistic, brise-soleil shaded South American work.

**SEMIOLOGY** The language of signs as opposed to that of words. In the process of a current reintellectualization of architectural history and theory, one body borrowed semiology not only as their process but their flag. Their renewed concern with the rationale of the Italian Renaissance and its full appreciation only through an intellectual process was the ground from which they extended research into the meaning of modern architectural signs, symbols, and form.

**SERLIO, SEBASTIANO (1475–1554)** *Italian Architect* Copybook author, his illustrated colonnade, with central arch and flanking columns, became the drawn reference for what is more popularly known as the Palladian window.

**SERT, JOSÉ LUIS (1902–      )** *Spanish American Architect and Teacher* Sert has served well as both ego and alter ego. His own substantial work is best exampled at the Hopkinson (Medical and Health) Center and Married Students' Housing, both at Harvard University (Cambridge). Both are notable excursions into the possibilities of varied rhythmic ways a complex can be subdivided by windows, louvers, and other openings.

Sert worked in the rue de Sèvres studio of Le Corbusier (Paris) and later served as his American "agent." The Carpenter Center for the Visual Arts (also at Harvard) is Corbu's only U.S. work (although he conceived the basic form of the U.N., its execution is far from his personal style). Sert made Carpenter possible by his overseeing of the client, construction, and legal problems. All the while he served as dean of Harvard's Graduate School of Design.

For a number of years Sert was in partnership with Paul Lester Wiener in the design of city plans for such major Latin American centers as Havana and Bogotá.

**SHAW, RICHARD NORMAN (1831–1912)** *English Architect*
Eclectic in his development, he progressed from Gothic and Tudor, through a romantic and picturesque variation on those themes, to protomodern, as in his glassy, bay-windowed New Zealand Chambers (London, 1872). The latter is prominent in all genealogies (history books) of the modern "movement." After New Zealand, Shaw turned to a pompous Neoclassicism.

**SHIM** A sliver of anything to fill space between two parts in the right place. A piece of wood on top of concrete or stone is shimmed (i.e., thin-wedged) to level, straighten, or align it.

**SHINGLES** The scales of roofing and sheathing, each one, like that of a fish or armadillo, overlapping the one below to shed water and weather; wood shingles, split or sawn from an oily wood, are of self-preserving cedar or redwood. Other shingles are slate or terra-cotta tile.

**SHINGLE STYLE** The high priest is Vincent Scully, whose book, so named, brought attention to a much-abused period of architecture that carried the balloon frame to an apogee, clad it with shingles, propped it with sticks, and gave America H. H. Richardson in wood (Watts Sherman House; Newport, Rhode Island; Stoughton House; Cambridge, Massachusetts) and the lesser but bulbously elegant works of Bruce Price (Emily Post's daddy), Stanford White, and a hassle of others.

The shingle allows a plastic form—shaped, rounded, porched, and eyebrowed—that clapboard or vertical siding could not accommodate. It is again another example of the "nature of the material," exploited and fulfilled.

SHINGLE STYLE *Cottage, Bar Harbor, Maine*

**SHIPLAP** Interlocking boards, each lapped behind another's opened (rabbeted) joint, usually with a space between to leave a designed shadow.

277

**SHOPPING CENTER**   The pilgrimage center of modern automobiles, replacing "downtown"; a cluster of pedestrian-surrounded buildings, in turn surrounded by a sea of cars, at first on a vast ground plane, later in dense stacked tiers as urban centers sought expensive land. The shopping center, in effect, is an alternate to anybody's Main Street. That profound realization has brought to them in later years the other services Main Streets provide beyond mere shopping: movies, town facilities, restaurants, bars and strolling people.

**SHORING**   The propping up of a structure that might collapse, as in a mine's tunnel, in supporting its natural earth and stone roof; or of a beam of a building that has been overstressed by too much unexpected weight.

**SHREVE, LAMB AND HARMON** *American Architectural Firm* Some firms are indivisible, yet of import for their group contribution to architectural history. McKim, Mead and White can be separated into the work of its individual partners, but Shreve, Lamb and Harmon is a group memory, most remembered for New York's Empire State Building, that behemoth in the fanatic competition for the tallest of American skyscrapers (1931; 1,250 feet). S.L.H. also participated in the elegant early-modern Hunter College (New York City); largely designed, however, by joint-venturers Harrison and Fouilhoux.

**SHRINE**   A boxed relic, and by allusion, the tomb of the saint where pilgrims pay homage. Shrines become *places* in turn by the suggestion of saintly neighbors and/or contents, as the Shrine of Lourdes.

**SHRUB**   A large woody plant with a structured form, common in domestic landscaping. Shrubs are land-based volumes punctuating a grassy place (or hiding an ugly foundation), while trees are the towers and umbrellas of a contrasting major scale.

**SHUTTER**   That which shuts (usually a window, sometimes a door) to limit access and light but allow passage of air. In tropical places shutters are all that is needed, glass or windows in fact inhibiting the needed natural circulation of air (until air conditioning changed all the rules). In New England, shutters are the protective closure of windows from the outside, to leaven weather or close an absented building. The French are so fascinated that they shutter their tenth-floor apartments (totally inaccessible save to a fly or a bird) when they leave for their August vacation: a ceremonial more than rational act.

Shutters festoon builders' eclectic everywhere in America, usually glued or nailed to the flanks of windows, immobile—and if they could move, too small to cover the opening they nominally serve. They rank with the plastic eagle over the door and the iron deer on the lawn as reflections of what affluence has accomplished with the untrained.

**SHUTTERING**   The Englishman's formwork, usually for poured concrete.

**SIDING**   That which covers the sides: in this case usually wood boards, vertical or clapboard (as opposed to shingles or brick or stucco).

**SILL**   The lowest supporting member of a structure—as the sill of a house, set on a masonry foundation, supports all the structure above. A windowsill is the underlayment of a window and the weather cover of the construction below.

**SILO**   Cylindrical container of fodder for cattle on your local farm, where it can settle moistly, fermenting its product (in at the top, out at the bottom) for the contented cows (or cows that become contented therefrom).

The silo is the campanile of Iowa, found-Cubism admired and painted by artists such as Sheeler.

**SINAN (1489–1588)** *Turkish Architect*   Facile copyist who translated the magnificent geometry of Christian Hagia Sophia for Islam's use in the Suleimaniyeh (mosque) (1556, Istanbul), more than 1,000 years after Anthemius of Tralles and Isidorus of Miletus made the original.

**SIREN, KAIJA (1920–    ) and HEIKKI (1918–    )** *Finnish Architects and Spouses*   The Students' Dining Hall at Otaniemi Technical College (1957) is timbered and trussed, bolted and nailed with

SIREN *Student Dining Hall, Otaniemi, Finland*

279

the vigor of very elegant packing-case design; an engineering of minimal wood, Finland's great natural resource.

**SITE**   The place of a building or event or town or happening.

**SITTE, CAMILLO (1843–1903)** *Austrian Architect and Planner* (Pronounced Sea-tay) The man who made "townscape" possible. His work *Der Städtebau* (1889) was resuscitated in the American thirties by architect Arthur Holden and recorded the accidental and incidental delights of medieval/Renaissance public town-spaces. Such possibilities caused others later (in the forties and fifties) to contrive such places for their peers, a mostly unsuccessful task, as the results were self-conscious, out of scale with the new-programmed buildings they served—plazas more for the abstract delight and amusement of architects than for any serious purpose for their users.

**SKETCH**   A drawn idea, quickly done, which suggests a final building, sculpture, or painting and sometimes becomes an end and art form in itself. Its crudeness or refinement is not the issue, but rather the intention for its final use: the sketches of Canaletto preparing for his painted scenes of Venice are some of the most precise architectural drawings ever.

**SKIDMORE, OWINGS AND MERRILL**   S.O.M., the foremost American organization of architects producing frequent, if not consistent, quality. Born from the New York World's Fair of 1939–40, the three named practiced in the modest success of a new partnership before the Second World War. Afterward, they covered the globe with their new-found mark: based on Lever House (1951, New York), first and most remembered success, elegant glass boxes have been placed in such diverse sites as Bremen, Bogotá, Sydney, and New Haven, the vocabulary of New York design partner Gordon Bunshaft.

Now a multiple personality, the New York branch is complemented by Chicago's Walter Netsch and San Francisco's Charles Bassett. Netsch, a near-fanatic in geometric formalism, has had opportunity to fulfill his most extravagant dreams on the campus of the University of Illinois at Chicago (Chicago Circle Branch), a license to experiment that may have ignored the nature and needs of its

SKIDMORE, OWINGS AND MERRILL
*Manufacturers' Hanover Trust, New York*

student body but makes fascinating drawings, if not a photogenic place.

Bassett has been the S.O.M. romantic, abruptly rejecting glass for San Francisco's John Hancock Building, clad in dark-gleaming granite with punched windows on an arched concrete base. Most recently his Regency Hyatt House Hotel makes an elegant plaza, exedra (subplaza or piazzetta) to St. Francis Square.

The secret of it all is a happy combination of organization client needing a complementary organization professional (Lever, U.S. Steel, and Continental Can—all needing S.O.M.) and a high quality control of consistent product, down to the carpeting, ashtrays, and paintings that have converted many an image of corporate stodginess (smelly spittoons and dumpy furniture) to high style. The empathy apparently works: business booms and executive life is more fertile.

**SKYLIGHT** A flat or tilted piece of roof allowing the sky's light to enter. A most accurate description when the plane faces north, as in a traditional artist's studio (garret); less accurate in other orientations, when the sun joins the sky (a sun-light?).

**SKYSCRAPER** To a city of four-story brick houses, a ten-story building must have scraped the eye's sky—a relative state, as nowadays even the World Trade Center's 110 stories brings an almost "so what" from the viewer. *Skyscraper* (word) became so common that its literal meaning was lost.

Skyscrapers became possible with the commercial development of elevators and the steel-framed building, since buildings of masonry ten stories and more were spatially consumed by the thickness of their supporting walls.

SKYSCRAPER *Irving Trust Company, New York*

**SLAB** A flat hunk of something, as stone or concrete; in high-rise buildings, the poured concrete floor is termed a slab. And the regular regimentation of tombstone-like public housing (Caracas, Cairo, or Cincinnati) is referred to as slabs.

**SLAT** A slender strip: of wood (named lath), it became the grounding of plasterwork; of metal, and slightly concaved, it is the separate part of a Venetian blind.

SMYTHSON *Wollaton Hall, Nottinghamshire*

**SLATE** A rock from schist that splits into leaflike layers, usable in its natural form as flagging. Slate, cut and honed, or cut and polished, or just split paves walkways and firehearths and serves as shingling alternate to wood (fireproof, handsome, and permanent).

**SLEEPERS** Shallow wood members over a concrete floor, to which wood flooring is applied, allowing flexure in walking and standing—less tiring to the stander and more pleasant to the walker. The space between was traditionally (in the twenties and thirties) filled with cinders for fireproofing.

**SLOAN, SAMUEL (1815–1884)** *American Architect* Longwood (1860, Mississippi) was Sloan's exotic octagonal mansion for planter-inventor Haller Nutt. Crowned with an onion dome on a clerestoried cupola, Longwood conjures nostalgia today as a hollow shell framed with Spanish moss-draped live oaks.

**SLUM** A crowded and degraded urban street. In modern usage, a social pejorative more descriptive of the people who live in a place and their way of life than of the place itself; for Park Avenue is denser than tenements, with equally sparse light and air, its buildings concerned more with their façades than their contents. Though dubious as housing, it has never been termed a slum.

Tenements can be places of relative delight when their inhabitants are trained to cope with urban life-styles, as those who live in the East Village (of Manhattan) or Haight-Ashbury (of San Francisco) or Limehouse (of London).

**SLURB** Sloppy urb. The sloppy suburbs, uncertain of whether they are at the edge of urban life or of country. Aimless and indecisive, they lack the delights of the city; nor do they gain the virtues of the country. They are all the anti-theses of Ebenezer Howard.

**SMIRKE, (SIR) ROBERT (1780–1867)** *English Architect* Greek and grandiose revivalist, he did the British Museum, whose face has more and bigger Ionic columns than anyone. (And whose contents are the attic of a whole civilization's transport of others' cultures to a place where the cultured, i.e., English, can observe them; for example, it has more mummy cases than you have baseball cards, and treats them a little like the latter.)

**SMITH, GEORGE WASHINGTON (1876–1930)** *American Architect* Part-trained as an architect, he turned painter (emigrating to Europe on the profits of successful business ventures). Returning to the U.S. at the outbreak of the First World War, he moved to Santa Barbara and was a leader in making the Spanish white stucco, plant-encrusted, tiled, and patioed world there—as it never was, but as everyone wished it had been. (He was the Addison Mizner of the middle-class Far West.)

**SMITHSON, ALISON (1928–     ) and PETER (1923–     )** *English Architects* The marvelous volumes within caged steel at the Honstanton School (1954, Norfolk) brought a sit-up-straight attention to them. Mies was source of the steelmanship, but the formal spatial interplay is theirs.

They defined Brutalism (Le Corbusier's late plastic concrete works) and then didn't try it. The Economist buildings in London, between Fleet and St. James streets, have all that intellect can gather and extrapolate from lessons of urban design and little of the charm such graceful bows to neighboring club buildings and townscape could afford. Their good intentions were here tripped up by their own overintellectualization.

**SMYTHSON, ROBERT (1536–1614)** *English Architect* Proto-Cubism with glassy planes, as at Hardwick Hall (1597+) and Wollaton Hall (1588+). His potent massing was portent of "modern" volumes (the innards contained compartmented gentry quarters). The Italians (of Florence and Venice) contributed by implication, i.e., the symmetric plans.

**SOANE, (SIR) JOHN (1753–1837)** *English Architect* Stripped and austere Classicist, Soane produced at the Bank of England a veritable megastructure and labyrinth. It has been demolished in the spirit of economy. His vast, flat vaulted (or skinned) spaces combined the edge of the Greek Revival with Byzantine, all suspended on cables, lath, wires, and faith from the spaces overhead (pendentives, domes, vaults, arches, and their varied intersections).

Philip Johnson used Soane's vaulting thoughts in his own bedroom building: annex to his glass house in New Canaan.

Soane's Regency came in his own fifty-eighth year, when the Regent (later George IV) took power. In those ten years (of Regency) Soane fulfilled himself, as at his own house in 1812 (now

SOANE *Soane House, London*

Soane Museum), avant-garde in its façade, wild in its interior space, light, and decor. The Dulwich Art Gallery, bombed and rebuilt, is a famous London of proto-Cubism event. Soane was prolific, spare, bold, ingenuous, ingenious, and facile.

**SOFFIT** The underside of any building's part, as in the soffit of an arch or lintel—the underside of overhanging or overbearing structure. Suburban American housebuilders have managed to subvert the word, so that the vertical filler panel between kitchen cabinets and ceiling is a soffit.

**SOLARIUM** Place of sun-absorption, a glassy room with conscious vitamin D in mind, as in a sanatorium. Nineteenth-century medicine believed that the sun's rays would erase and/or mollify congenital diseases, such as tuberculosis, and perhaps they did, more psychosomatically than by cellular conquest.

A solarium at residential level is a sun porch—south-oriented, small-paned addition to the small-holed and -windowed architecture of the anti-sun (and cold) house itself.

**SOLERI, PAOLO (1919– )** *Italian American Architect* Sun-worshipping guru and troglodyte (he has built "caves" in the western American desert). A man of passion, purpose, and direction, he has created an imagery of "organic" cities in literature and backed it with an urban desert construction that makes Wright seem "square" and his own fantasies possible. Arcosanti is the place, and student legions, as acolytes, come to worship with him at its shrine, lending their toil, passion, and architectural skill to him and it.

Soleri's domed piece of the desert—Desert House (1951; Cave Creek, Arizona; with Mark Mills)—was happily honored in the Museum of Modern Art's book and exhibition *Built in U.S.A.*

Egos need feeding, his through a summer-school student draft from architectural orthodoxies throughout the country, releasing students from their nine-month didactic bondage into his liberated and blindered romance—an act that nurtures his own social and aesthetic passions, but in fact is the stage of the most elite of elitist fantasy. He is a serious man, not to be taken too seriously.

**SORIANO, RAPHAEL S. (1907– )** *Greek American Architect* Anti-Establishment loner, he lives on a houseboat in San Francisco Bay and has housed the elegant suburban dweller in Lally columns,

SOLERI *Arcosanti, Arizona*

steel beams, and bar joists of an industrial building's normal parts.

**SOUFFLOT, JACQUES GERMAIN (1713–1780)** *French Architect* Catalyst of Neoclassicism, he made Ste. Geneviève, more remembered and known as the Panthéon (of Paris—as renamed after the Revolution of 1789).

**SPACE-FRAME** Framework of small members that covers, shelters, and spans a space: second-generation technology, of which the first is the truss. Space-frames work in four directions instead of a truss's two and could be thought of, simplistically, as a warp and woof of normal trusses, interlocked. In fact, such crossed structure is more powerful than the sum of its intersecting parts.

Some of Buckminster Fuller's Dymaxion geometry is reinforced by space-framing, as in the Union Tank Car Company's car warehouse in Baton Rouge, Louisiana, where a geodesic dome, spanning 384 feet, is made possible by a thick web of space-frame members that form its three-dimensional skin.

**SPALL** Fragments of stone chipped (by man's hammering) or split (by the action of freezing and other wet weather) from their rightful place on a building.

**SPAN** The open space or dimension freed by a beam, girder, arch, vault, or dome; the act of spanning allows the structure to jump, lean, arch, or spring across its space.

**SPANDREL** At first, the flat space between two arches and the column supporting them; a curvy triangle of masonry (which della Robbia so elegantly decorated with circular terra-cotta plaques at the Foundling Hospital in Florence by Brunelleschi).

Later, and currently, a spandrel is the opaque set of materials between the head of one floor's windows and the sill of the next in an office building (particularly one of curtain wall, glass, and sash). A spandrel beam is the beam at the edge of a multitiered building that supports the hanging curtain.

**SPECIFICATION** If drawings are the music, specifications are the words of architecture. They define quality and qualities, while drawings state place and quantity. Specifications describe what a material is—of what color, texture, manufacture, criteria, standard,

**SOUFFLOT** *Interior, Pantheon, Paris*

285

grain, strength, gloss, resilience, hardness, age—and the number of layers, processes, hours, labor constraints, legal questions, and so forth that constrain it. Specifications are more than the specifics, for those are largely drawn "details"; they are the undrawable statements of the quality of what is being asked for.

**SPEER, ALBERT (1905–    )** *German Architect and Minister of Armaments*  Speer, the released and retired "war criminal," wrote the best seller *Inside the Third Reich,* a rather flaccid and unconvincing bit of drivel that does justice neither to historical reality nor his own architecture. A hustler, he impressed Hitler in his (Speer's) twenties and rose meteorically (and sycophantically) to become, at his apogee, minister of armaments and second most powerful man of the fading Nazi war machine.

As an architect he built the German Pavilion (1937, Paris), a pompous bastion of marble. Later his Reichschancellery and the Zeppelinfeld (Nuremberg) remind us of Queen Hatshepsut's Mortuary Temple of the Egyptian New Kingdom. His maximum success was with staging rallies of superadulation, as at Nuremberg, with massed flags, lights, sound, and people that exceeded any opening Hollywood has dreamed up or of, and brought acolytes to a state of frenzy that made Hitler possible, if not plausible. Speer is much maligned in architectural history for his cold and dull supposed neo-academicism, but his dismissal is more political than academic, for he created buildings and spaces certainly equal to America's Washington of the same years, with a humanistic monumentality that was made gross more by the users of his talents, than by the talent itself.

SPENCE *Coventry Cathedral*

**SPENCE, (SIR) BASIL (1907–    )** *English Architect*  Coventry Cathedral, bombed to a ruin in the Second World War, became a romantic annex to Spence's competition-winning scheme (1952) for a new cathedral. Reclaimed in ruin, the tower serves the same purpose with the new building as the old, and the nave of the old serves as an open courtyard.

New Coventry is a slightly undulating and serrated box—a vast, brightly lit hall of little mystery or wonder festooned with art in its additive sense (appliqué, hung, attached, and placed—rather than part of it, as was the art of its neighboring ancestor).

**SPHINX**   A Pharaoh-headed lion sculpture; most famous is that of Cheops, near his burial pyramid at Gizeh, near Cairo. Sphinxes were the sculpted guardians of many religious avenues, as the many of Gizeh and Thebes that led from the Nile to the temple serving the burial place of the Pharaoh. At Gizeh itself, the funerary temple once was such a terminal: a landing stage on the Nile's normal bank led past dress rows of sphinxes to the temple, where priests could bring offerings to the god and Pharaoh.

**SPIRE**   A slender, tapered tower, conical or many-sided (polygonal), that ends it all—pointed lance against the sky.

**SPLAY**   Surfaces bent, turned, or warped from a right angle, as windowsills or reveals sloped down and/or out, to rid the inside of potential water and allow in maximum light. In a very thick wall, a splayed opening is a radiant device, gathering the rays of the sun and sky to its interior occupants.

**SPLINE**   To join two parts by a strip that interlocks with both; a key that locks two half-keyholes. A butterfly spline, in particular, is a beautiful sight.

**SPRING**   Where the arch, vault, or dome starts its leap across a bay or space; from a horizontal point (at the equator) that begins the half-circle of arch or vault, or in a dome the hemisphere of shelter.

**SPROCKET**   Radial tooth that participates in its group to pull a chain drive, as on a bicycle gear-wheel.

**SQUARE**   A corner, room, or part of a building is square if its two sides are at right angles to each other. *A* square is a four-equal-sided figure with all angles right (correct and orthodox, that is). A *square* is also the loose term for any building-contained public place (plaza, piazza, *place*).

SQUINCH *In Salisbury Cathedral*

**SQUINCH**   The corner "filler" of diagonal masonry that translates the geometry of a square building, by steps or stages, into that of a dome, using arches to support each tier of change: from square to octagon, from octagon to almost-circle (16 sides).

287

**STABLE**   A building for the standing of (in most cases) horses, who like it that way, awake or asleep. It is hard for the bed-snuggling human to appreciate such discreet manners in dumb animals, but it simplifies architecture: the stall of a stable provides proper space for eating, sleeping, and just wakeful musings.

**STADIUM**   A great stepped and seated enclosure for the viewing of spectacles and sports. Various in shape and design, stadia are sometimes elongated like a Roman circus, sometimes oval and high-rising, like the Colosseum. American sports-fields are contained by stadia, fields, and grounds (Yankee Stadium, Ebbets Field, the Polo Grounds)—all describing similar structures to support the audience of the same sport. And aside from baseball, stadia serve football, soccer, papal visits, and the immersions of Baptists.

**STAGING**   Place where materiel is assembled before use or transport, as in an army's staging area to which equipment is delivered and from which it is dispatched for use in battle. Staging areas equally serve building processes.

**STAINED GLASS**   Literacy was for the elite in the Middle Ages. The story of Christ and Christianity was told, therefore, pictorially, through stained glass that brought storytelling to its highest moments. Glass, fused with iron oxides, cut in both representational and abstract forms, was joined by lead; braced by first stone, then iron framework, to infill the great nave and clerestory windows of Romanesque and Gothic churches. For the less curious, it bathed and dappled the soaring stone piers, arches, ribs, and vaults in a light of both mystery and delight, diffusing form.

Modern stained glass was carried to extremes that made whole churches of it, a marvelous glowing skin for those worshipping, but lacking the mystery of the medieval stone carapace, punctured by light orifices. Best example is the Church of Notre Dame (1923) at Le Raincy (a Paris suburb) by Auguste Perret.

STAINED GLASS *East Window, Church at Raunds, Northamptonshire*

**STAIR**   The one universal architectural device that brings one through a tight and automatic routing, as does a Japanese garden (Katsura detached palace) or the fun (horror) sequence of an "amusement" park. A stair is a measured, rhythmic route controlled in direction and view, organized by the height and depth of its own treads and risers, the direction of its flow, the placing of its pauses: landings.

Special stairs to remember are: the Scala Regia (1678, Bernini) in the Vatican, bringing formal visitors from St. Peter's Square to the pope up a long and tapered tube that gives the illusion, through false perspective, of even greater length and monumentality; the Horseshoe Staircase at Fontainebleau (1634, du Cerceau); the grand place for social display created by Garnier, the stairs of the Paris Opéra (1875). The list is inexhaustible, stairs of importance and delight appearing in the simplest buildings.

**STANCHION**   Another term for a secondary, single-tiered supporting member: compare column, post, pier, prop, and so forth.

**STEAM**   Water vapor—hotter than boiling, usually white visible clouds—that powers engines (steam engines) and heating systems for human use: steam radiators that hiss with pneumatic bliss and knock as the water made from steam cools to its parent state and tries to crowd its way back down the pipery to the boiler. Steam made to power electrical generators (superheated steam for turbines) is sold to urban buildings for heating or operation of the compressors that air condition after the superheat consumed in electricity generation is exhausted and it is again merely a household variety of steam.

**STEEL**   The softer, and yet stronger, form of iron, made by reducing the amount of natural carbon it contains. Iron, good for casting, is hard, brittle, and weak in tension; after reduction of carbon, the resultant steel is softer, less brittle, and strong in tension—good for beams and columns, which must flex (as do your leg bones under stress) and take (as a beam) the impact of stamping tenants without splitting, cracking, or shattering.

**STEEL FRAME**   The columned, beamed, and girdered cage of steel, bolted or welded together, that forms the skeleton of a modern high-rise building. Strangely enough, steel is usually used for office buildings, concrete for apartments. In the latter, the flat underside of the concrete slab can be the ceiling of the apartment below, whereas an office building normally has a hung ceiling to contain and conceal ductwork for heating and air conditioning and wiring.

**STEEPLE**  A church's superfinial that scraped the sky before sky-scrapers and gave its church place and mark in a sea of lower buildings. The pre-Civil War skyline of New York, Chicago, London, Paris, Moscow—almost anywhere—was an array of steeples in silhouette, lances of God's temples that had infiltrated the city's body.

**STEIN, CLARENCE S. (1882–1975)** *American Architect* He worked for Goodhue and is said to have designed St. Bartholomew's Church (1919+, New York City). His great impact is in urban and *sub*urban design—Sunnyside Gardens (1924, New York); Greenbelt, Maryland; Baldwin Hills Village (1941, Los Angeles)—largely low-rise, relatively high-density housing, served by, but not subsidiary to, the car. The pedestrian began to have his first chance to dominate in these places—the buildings surrounding parkland, the cars moored in cul-de-sacs surrounding. See his own history of it all: *Toward New Towns in America* (1951).

**STEINBRUECK, VICTOR (1913–    )** *American Architect* His own house (Seattle, 1950) is a technological landmark: lapped cement asbestos sheeting clads a spartan box in a revival of thoughts tested years before by Maybeck at his Christian Science Church (Berkeley, Calif., 1910).

**STEP**  The basic human movement from place to place, whose namesake is the basic unit of a stair: a step, which rises (through risers) and accepts the tread (through treads) of the stepper.

A step is not a stair, but steps can become one in concert.

**STEREOTOMY**  Stonecutting and assembly, particularly where raised to a high art. The temples of Greece, built of precisely shaved marble blocks, were assembled without mortar (metal ties held the blocks invisibly). A slender knife blade coult not penetrate the joint. In contrast, the stonework of the Italian Renaissance sought visual bulk and/or a "rocky" quality: the result was rustication and rock-face walls as a basic palazzo ingredient. All are stereotomy with different visual intents.

**STERN, ROBERT A. M. (1939–    )** *American Architect* The discussion of abstruse design theories sometimes consumes the energies of architects more than building realities natural to their profession. Such is the case of the "whites" versus the "grays," a battle of the seventies that has pitted the neo-Le Corbusier formalists (and the neo-Renaissance formalistic theorists) against a relatively willful school of Victorian revivalists, illusionists, and theatrical virtuosos. (Whites, among others, are Graves, Eisenman, Hejduk, Gwathmey, and Meier. Grays are Stern, Moore, and Venturi.)

Stern's neo-shingle style has brought elegant summers to, particularly, the eastern tip of Long Island, in a renaissance of late "shingle-style" Victorian vocabulary in modern dress.

**STILE**  The vertical member of a door or window frame into which the horizontals (called rails) are pegged or mortised or let and glued.

**STIRLING, JAMES (1926–    )** *English Architect* Crystalline volumes and mechanistic form were the brash and yet unaffected product of Stirling and Gowan's (James Gowan, 1924–    ) landmark Engineering Building (1963, Leicester University). Stirling's canted glass thoughts have started a whole neo-greenhouse architecture and have enthroned him early for architects—a heady experience, well deserved, but difficult to cope with.

STIRLING *Engineering School, Leicester University*

**STOA**  A roofless and surrounding colonnade in pre-Christian Greek architecture.

**STOCKADE**  Superpicketry of contiguous logs set into the ground, lashed to each other, pointed on top to impale the incautious attacker. A stockade is a marvelous and natural defensive container for those with many trees available, as mud-brick serves the treeless mud-forted desert.

**STODDARD, GEORGE (1895–1967)** *American Architect* His stadium addition (1951) for the University of Washington (Seattle), a steel filigree for stands and weather roof, is served by giant concrete helixes for pedestrian access and egress: a powerful meld of architecture and engineering, functional and memorable. (Sigmund Ivarsson, engineer.)

**STOKES, ISAAC NEWTON PHELPS (1867–1944)** *American Historian* Stokes's massive six-volume *Iconography of Manhattan Island* is the most exhaustive record of a built place ever attempted, let alone fulfilled. He documents the physical history and development of Manhattan from its accidental discovery by explorers on their way to better things (i.e., the Indies: Block, Verrazano, Hudson, Gomez) to *his* "now," 1928. Almost every map, view, sketch, word, statement, scrap of evidence is reproduced, explained, and evaluated: a priceless historical record and a beautiful set of visual documents.

**STONE**   Cooled geology in the crust of the earth or compressed geology of a later age; the former hard (granite), the latter soft (limestone, sandstone and their variants: brownstone and marble).

Stone was the original, natural, universally available building material, cut into slabs, blocks, or obelisks. Sawn from the ground when soft (limestone, sandstone), sheared or split with wedges (and later, blasting) when hard, it simply formed walls, columns, and even "beams." In effect, although stone is a weak material for spanning a space, it is magnificent in compression (walls or columns).

Stone is the body of almost all remaining whole buildings and ruins of Egyptian, Greek, Roman, Renaissance, and Gothic architecture, and the remnants are remnant largely because the wood structures that supported floors and roofs went to dust.

From Sakkara in 2700 B.C. (a pyramid for Pharaoh Djoser's tomb —stepped, rather than sloping), stone architecture prepared itself for history and particularly the history of monuments. The architecture of the common people—mud, wattle, mud-brick, wood, straw, thatch, and whatnot—shortly perished.

**STONE, EDWARD DURELL (1903–    )** *American Architect* Talented and facile, he joined the modern movement at its font: the Museum of Modern Art (1937, New York City). Stone designed it with Philip Goodwin. "The Modern" is now the self-appointed arbiter of official and officious modernism, Cubism, neo-Cubism, Mies, Breuer, Le Corbusier, and expurgated Wright (and those old proto-moderns: Behrens, Berlage, Olbrich, Wagner, Loos, Mackintosh, et al.).

Stone's house for A. Conger Goodyear (tire and rubber) at Westbury is classic, a modern historian's dream: white sliced volumes of ice cream, black-laced glass, laundered purism.

Then, after an intermission of 15 years, in 1952 he blossomed with the idea for the American Embassy to India at New Delhi (the image was completed in 1958). The wall grillages there are re-

STONE *Stone House, New York*

nowned but incidental to the larger courtyard idea (compare Stone's later American Pavilion; 1958, Brussels World's Fair). Stone's obsession with light filtration produced a meshed overlay for that court (anti-bird, anti-sun dapple-maker).

Last, and hopefully least important, but bulkiest, are a bulging mass of boxes thoughtlessly cluttering the landscape, such as the International Hotel at Karachi; dormitories at Columbia, South Carolina; the State University of New York at Albany; and Pakistan's Atomic Energy Center at Islamabad. Like many good men, he fell from the grace of his profession but left an early mark of greatness that cannot be erased.

**STONEHENGE** Chief remnant of prehistory in Britain (*prehistory* doesn't suggest that there wasn't any, but that it wasn't recorded). Druids or some similar pre-Christians worshipped or prayed or sacrificed or conducted some mysterious rites at this very symbolic place, composed of open ground ringed with a series of stone monoliths, some still linteled. Too big to be called columns, they are history's greatest piers. They were erected about 1700 B.C.

**STONOROV, OSKAR (1905–1972)** *American Architect* One-time partner of Louis Kahn (1942–50), Stonorov admired Wright and even patterned his dress and hats on those of Wright; he managed a great series of traveling exhibitions (internationally) of Wright's work in the fifties.

Stonorov's own architecture did not ape Wright and had clear and simple form: housing of concrete balconied brick boxes, with the balconies handled as a major form, not glued on, as the petals of typical middle-class high-rise blocks. Schuylkill Falls (1962) and Westfield Acres (1938; Camden, New Jersey) are handsome examples. Architect for the United Auto Workers, he was killed in a plane crash with its famed president, Walter Reuther, a double tragic loss of talent.

**STOOP** The outside stair-structure of the urban middle class, allowing entry to their brownstones or grander town houses. A stoop is a platform, place, and object in the life of a street. The word (Dutch) comes from Amsterdam immigrants to *New* Amsterdam, where *stoeps* avoided floodwater and raised the classes above the masses. Without water problems, some complained that stoops were and are vestigial ornaments (like the Mercedes-Benz radiator

STONOROV *Schuylkill Falls Housing, Philadelphia*

finial, flaunted even after the water was capped under the hood with a matter-of-fact cap). But those complainers are just grumpy, demanding unswerving cause and effect: for stoops were simultaneously junior editions of the grand staircases of the Renaissance, like those of Fontainebleau (by du Cerceau) or Caprarola (by Vignola).

**STOP**  An architectural part that does what it says: stops a door at its closed position or keeps a double-hung window from falling out of its vertical track. A stop is a constraint that also aligns the moving part or plane that joins it.

**STORE**  Place of storage; here commonly stored for sale, and hence *a* store.

**STORY**  One tier of a building (the space enclosed, as opposed to the idea of a "floor"). Story-counting varies: in England, there is a ground floor where in America there is a first floor; and so the counting is off by one all the way to the top.

**STREET**  An urban place (including a way for traffic) contained by buildings that flank it, usually with sidewalks for the separation of pedestrian traffic, curbed to keep the cars in their place and allow for the drainage of rain water. Streets are the corridors of a city that lead (in more elegant ones) to the plazas, public "rooms" for civic meeting.

**STRESS**  The reaction of a structure to the weight (load) applied to it. A beam or column is stressed in ways that an architect or engineer can calculate in advance, allowing him to determine the proper size of needed parts to support the use for which the building is planned.

**STRESSED SKIN**  A structure whose skin works with ribs and members within to form a single working unit—as an airplane wing, some sea shells, and almost all American houses. The last named, sheathed with plywood, are strong and rigid from a symbiosis between studs and skin, each relying on the other for fulfillment. A fashionable but no more accurate use of the word is for prefabricated glued studs and plywood double-faced panels: there the skin is stressed before placement in or on the building; whereas a common builder's house is framed with studs and later skinned in place, full strength gained only at the end.

**STRETCHER**   The long face of a brick as laid in an exposed wall; as opposed to a header, its end (i.e., that of the same brick), that ties (bonds) two thicknesses of brick together.

**STRICKLAND, WILLIAM (1788–1854)** *American Architect* Student-employee of Benjamin Latrobe, he took the Greek Revival to levels, at times, of exquisite elegance and originality. He ranged from the orthodox "temple" building of the (Doric) Bank of the United States (1824, Philadelphia) to the nearby and exuberant Merchants' Exchange (1834). The latter takes a simple, pilastered box, adds a radial porched bay of elegant Corinthian columns, and crowns it all with another Choragic Monument of Lysicrates.

In the 1850s Strickland embellished the then western state of Tennessee with its Capitol (temple-fronted, lanterned with Lysicrates again) and built a number of country houses for the Tennessee gentry, among them Belmont and Belle Meade.

He was a bold eclectic revivalist and dared step beyond just formalistic aping of the past: the First Presbyterian Church (Nashville) has been described as Egyptian Revival, but its form is more from the vigors of Hawksmoor and Soane: elegant neo-Regency Brutalism.

STRICKLAND *Bank of the United States, Philadelphia*

**STRIKE**   The flat metal piece against which a door's latch strikes and then catches within a prepared slot or hole.

**STRINGER**   The edge-beam of a stair's treads and risers, springing from floor to landing, floor to floor, and carrying steps that may be notched (let) into its flanks or may rest on wood blocks fastened to those flanks.

**STRING COURSE**   A masonry lip, sometimes molded and profiled, which diverts the water sheeting down a wall from above and relieves the bare plane with shadows.

**STRUCTURE**   Anything built; including buildings, bridges, dams, aqueducts, kiosks, privies, and dog houses.

Structure is the system and materials that support a building, as one of concrete, steel, timber, or mud; built with beams, trusses, arches, domes, or shells. The materials and the system together are *the* structure. Structures, in the complex technology of the late twentieth century, have become so complex that their design as a subsystem of architecture is allotted to engineers (not surprisingly called structural engineers). Originally all facets of building design were the province of a single person or group; structural complication was a major factor in the profession's breakdown into subspecialties, and in the rise of organization architecture.

**STRUT**   A small stick that separates, braces, and supports others, as in a truss, or those that kept biplanes bi-.

**STUART, JAMES (1713–1788)** *English Architect*   Stuart and Revett's *Antiquities of Athens* (1762 and 1789) was a source, for the middle-class nontraveler, of the architectural wonders of the Greece about to be revived; a source book, particularly for the Colonies (America) in their new search for democracy through Greek design (both because of a romantic view of ancient Greek democracy and in sympathy with the modern Greek [1821] revolution against the Turks). He also practiced the architecture he preached, but none need be noted here.

**STUBBINS, HUGH (1912–    )** *American Architect*   The Congress Hall (1957, Berlin; for the Interbau Exhibition) is a saddle of concrete stretching between two concrete arches, a tour de force in West Berlin, in sight of the East.

Stubbins's more regular products are simple boxes, frequently with pitched roofs when they are houses: a kind of New England Protestant modern.

**STUCCO**   Outdoor plaster; usually of cement, rather than lime, to resist moisture. Bare stucco became the laxative against ornamental excesses in the later nineteenth century, raised to a level of remembered monumentality by Charles Voysey's bare white houses, slate-roofed, with narrow banded windows slotting their sides. More important for modernism, however, was the need of Cubist architects for sliced ice cream-like form (vanilla). Stucco on masonry or wire lath or anything: the Villa Savoye by Le Corbusier, the Steiner House by Loos, and a hundred others by Oud, Rietveld, Gropius, Mies, Mallet-Stevens, Gill, and others.

STUBBINS *State Street Trust Company, Boston*

**STUDIO**  A visual study, where an artist (painter, sculptor, or architect) may pursue his work, usually with natural light from north windows or skylights.

**STUDS**  Minitimber, that American invention of two by's (2 × 4's to 2 × 12's mostly) that standardized the small stick-stressed skin construction known as balloon frame: a cage of members sheathed and skinned, roofed and sided. Studs are the vertical walls and partitions, while the floors are supported by *joists,* the roof by *rafters.*

**STUPA**  In Southeast Asian architecture, a built mound, bare or veneered, that is a memorial, sometimes in the shape of a traditional beehive.

**STYLE**  A blend of two sources: *stylus,* or writing instrument; *stylos,* or column. The instrument (stylus) in man's hand made words (or recorded them), and the way of doing so was a *style* of writing. In painting, sculpture, and building, it describes the ways and manners of a culture's art and architecture, the materials and systems it employs, and the visual product resulting. Styles are more the conscious ways of an intellect than the gross, slowly evolving natural product of ancient or primitive culture. Ancient Egyptian architecture had style but wasn't one; even the orders of Greece and Rome are scarcely styles—they are the long-evolved products of slow movement and thought, far from whim.

But, in contrast, the Renaissance produced styles, in many plurals, even within a single Italian city-state (Florence, Venice, the Papal States), and evolved a spectrum of short-lived styles (short-lived as compared to Egypt, or even Greece): Mannerist, Baroque, Rococo, Georgian, Federal, Greek Revival. By the time broad cultural products were revived, styles had descended to whim, one architect building in sequence (without blushing) Greek, Roman, Egyptian (style, only when revived), Chinese, Japanese, and just plain ruined buildings.

STUPA

**STYLOBATE**  The platform on which a temple stands, and/or the top step of a crepidoma.

**SUBDIVISION**  The act of dividing land for "development," that unblessed euphemism describing profit by cutting the cake and decorating each piece for sale to the ultimate consumer. Development implies the subdivision of land, serving it with access roads and providing water, sewage, and utilities (or reasonable promise of them). Subdivisions usually bring more profit to their entrepreneur when house and land are sold as a package, rather than independently; for the fact of reality, in place and ready for use, is important for the purchaser, and the inflated price of land, or building, is concealed in a combined sum.

Rarely, subdivisions are places of quality and/or delight, as Radburn, New Jersey, or Forest Hills Gardens, New York. There their very merits tend to draw a description as a satellite town or garden city, rather than the pejorative: subdivision!

**SUBURB**   Annex to the city (sub-*urb*), that somewhat indecisive space between city and country, swallowing available open land and space near the center of things and pushing true country beyond the reach of the normal city-dweller.

In Renaissance Europe, a city was contained by its walls or its site (mountain, island, river-bound), a discrete place surrounded by open country, nature used for farms of city-farmers. In pre-auto America, suburbs were the semi-rural retreats of the rich, or those aspiring to be.

But in post-World War II America, autos, cheap energy, and an antipathy to planning as a socialist plot (or integrationist blather) have leveled the countryside and made discrete houses (as opposed to the discrete city) the absolute culture-goal to be sought as the ultimate escape from a city on its way to dirt, crime, waste, costs, and social oblivion.

Ordinary contemporary suburban houses are rarely architecture, seldom even good building. The exceptional places designed by architects are usually for the very upper middle class and the rich.

SUGER *Choir and Ambulatory, St. Denis, Paris*

**SUGER, ABBOT (1081–1151)** *Abbot, Architectural Client, and Regent of France*   Abbot of the Abbey of St. Denis, north of Paris (now an industrial suburb), Suger was present at the birth of French Gothic: the choir added to his church brought together at a single orchestrated moment the elements we now consider should be called Gothic. While Louis VII was off fighting the second crusade, Suger subbed for him as Regent of France, a brilliant administrator, excellent businessman, and consummate materialist for the Crown and Christ. The Church of St. Denis (1144, choir) is an historian's touchstone, that valuable moment of record where one can start the Gothic lecture (or book).

**SUITE**   A following! and therefore a set, matched, as in a set of pearls. A set of furniture or set of rooms, as in the ephemeral world of hotels.

In furniture, it is mostly the vulgar and cheap that is termed *suite*: a cover of elegance for a bunch of junk sold at extortionate cost to impoverished residents of urban jungles, on time (payments).

**SULLIVAN, LOUIS H. (1856–1924)** *American Architect*   Saint of the Chicago School of architecture, where the skyscraper was born and where its aesthetics was refined to fulfill a building type (elevator-served steel cage) totally new and without precedent.

Sullivan attended M.I.T. and Vaudremer's atelier at the École des Beaux-Arts in Paris. But on his return to Chicago he joined Dankmar Adler, a successful engineer, and became his partner in 1881 at the age of 25. They immediately produced a major monument, the Auditorium Building, a multipurpose office building with a concert hall seating 4,000, now happily restored by Harry Weese.

The Garrick Theatre (now gone) in Chicago, the Wainwright Building in St. Louis, the Guaranty Trust Building in Buffalo, the Condict Building in New York City—all remain as vertically soaring articulations, ornamented with the quasi-Art Nouveau decoration that Sullivan invented and developed himself.

His most exciting building is the Carson, Pirie Scott Store (1899; built as Schlesinger and Mayer), a direct aesthetic development of the steel cage, clad in sleek glazed terra cotta, the windows infilling almost a whole bay of cage-edge space.

After the World's Columbian Exposition (Chicago World's Fair of 1893), his practice declined, for the corporate clients of America were overtaken by that fair's neo-Renaissance architecture. He mused in writing in his *Kindergarten Chats,* built a few handsome, small-town midwestern banks (National Farmers' Bank; 1908; Owatonna, Minnesota; restored by Harwell Hamilton Harris), and drank a lot.

SULLIVAN *Great Hall, Auditorium Building, Chicago*

**SUMP**   The collection basin for any draining place, as a cellar sump to collect the wet effluents that tend, on unhappy occasions, to fill it.

**SUNDECK**   Platform for the sun-drenched human; a wood, plat-formed stage of ultraviolet bathing.

**SUPERBLOCK**   City blocks assembled from smaller ones, to eliminate streets and the bother of traffic, and assemble great spaces for residential life and pedestrian domination.

**SURVEYOR**   He who overlooks and then defines by visual engi-neering the edges (called meets and bounds) and levels (contours) of a property, locating objects, buildings, trees, and points of inter-est for engineering and legal purposes.

**SWAG**   Carved relief of draped cloth hanging between and over-lapping two supports.

**SWALE**   A natural, continuing shallow place between rises that drains water from the surrounding topography: a mild minivalley, at the scale of single lot or property.

**SWEDEN**   The largest and most populous place of Scandinavia (see also *Scandinavia*). A middle-class and unadventurous place, Sweden has a monolithic social consistency that permeates its archi-tecture: invariably acceptable and of reasonably good taste, it rarely "sings." Denmark reaches a higher style, Norway is stodgy, and Finland soars over them all.

**SYMMETRICAL**   Mirror-imaged flanking a dividing plane or line; a state of literal balance demanding exact duplication. Faces are not, of course, symmetrical, although they seem to be. Buildings, how-ever, frequently are. The subtlety of physiognomy far exceeds that of anybody's architecture, at any time, anywhere.

The formal symmetries of the Renaissance are tempered by hu-mor and the understanding that literal symmetry means nothing unless it can all be observed at one instance. That the park at Versailles is symmetrical is of no importance except to a balloonist; that the four principal chambers of Palladio's Villa Rotondo are symmetrical in interior arrangements is of no meaning, as one can only *be* in one place at one time. But the *idea* of symmetry is compell-ing and gives a state of mind and stature to a place or building grossly different from conscious asymmetry or, even more ex-tremely, the picturesque.

# T

**TABERNACLE**   A portable Jewish place of worship, of cloth and wood members, that was carried through the Sinai on the way from Egypt to the Holy Land. A temple is sometimes termed a *tabernacle*.

For Christians, it is the ritual box, container of the bread and wine of Communion.

**T.A.C.** *American Architectural Partnership*   T.A.C. (The Architects' Collaborative) was created in the search for a renaissance of medieval craftsmanship by groups, where the making of the end product was entwined with its design: a premise developed at the Bauhaus under Walter Gropius, T.A.C.'s founder. It survives vigorously today as a vehicle for architecture of distinction, without the needs for self-conscious originality so prevalent in the reporting of architectural magazines.

**TANGE, KENZO (1913–      )** *Japanese Architect*   He learned his Brutalisms from work in the office of Kunio Maekawa, his senior, a former attendant at the rue de Sèvres studio of Le Corbusier. The Japanese, as we all know, do everything with a thoroughness and gusto matched by no other race; at first in drawing from the talented direction of others, and then in outdoing their teachers (cf. the Second World War "Zero," television sets and computers, and traditional wood architecture: all drawn, then improved, from German, American, and Chinese models respectively).

Maekawa was no exception, and his block at Tokyo (Harumi) is

TANGE *Yamanashi Broadcasting Company, Tokyo*

301

more brutal (in the elegant concrete architectural sense) and better than Le Corbusier's own at Marseille or Nantes.

Tange's Brutalism matured at the Kurashiki City Hall (1960). His early works, including the Peace Memorial Museum at Hiroshima, are in the cartoonlike spirit of Niemeyer, diagrams of architecture without substance or detail. Some of these qualities persist even in his Tokyo City Hall (1957), but are overcome in his powerful concrete architecture (based on wood forms and visions) at the Kagawa Prefecture Office Building (1958).

For the Olympics of 1964 (Tokyo) he built stadiums for running and swimming as elegant as those of Nervi's for similar activities in 1960 (Rome). The Swimming Stadium is a happy space for the spectator, light and form well scaled to the audience size and swimming pools. Lastly, his master plan and main Theme Building for Expo '70 at Osaka let him play with some of the ideas he jointly flaunted with his allies, the Metabolism Group (who have suggested floating, entubed, futuristic cities that skirt dangerously close to the ego-trips of Niemeyer, those soft, crayoned, willful, quick drawings given to society by the largesse of "genius").

His modeled plan for Tokyo's extension into Tokyo Bay is also of this order—handsome, fascinating, and visionary architecture, and a potentially oppressive place to live as a human.

TECTON *Penguin Pool, London Zoo*

**TANK** Deep, stationary water, as in a pool, a pond, or a swimming tank. Tanks more often are the artificial containers of liquids stored for future use, whether water tanks atop tall buildings or gasoline tanks to store a *tank*er's deposits.

Tanks are frequently round wood (superbarrels), their contents maintained without leaks by their own wetting and hence swelling of wood. Steel bands in tension surround them (silos are sometimes similarly made to contain fermenting corn). But tanks can be any shape and, when other than round, must rely on steel and concrete for their structure. One of the art forms of flat lands are the water tanks of towns, distant objects more important than the spires of a Gothic cathedral—signal of commerce, civilization, and water. (Compare the elegant tank of Saarinen's at the General Motors Technical Center and Hans Poelzig's Water Tower at Poznan or railroad water tanks at prairie sidings for thirsty steam engines in transit.)

**TATLIN, VLADIMIR (1885–1953)** *Russian Painter, Sculptor, and Architect*  One illustration of his one proposed building defines Constructivism in architectural history books: his great spiral steel Monument to the Third International (1920), a quarter of a mile tall.

**TAUT, BRUNO (1880–1938)** *German Architect*  An early modernist, he presented orthodox modern buildings to the Werkbund Exhibition (1914, Cologne) and the Stuttgart Weissenhof experimental housing group (all the stars of modern architecture attended) in 1927. His words and drawings were much wilder than his deeds.

**TAX**  In itself the word indicates assessment of value. Taxes are the fuel of government, drawn from proportionate assessments on the wealth of individuals and corporations. Taxes on buildings and land were nominally to pay for the physical services that supported and protected them (streets, lighting, sewers, police, fire departments, and so forth); but they have come to be just another cog in the myriad spectrum of tax devices supporting governments at large. In urban sumps like New York, their burden is exacerbated by the huge costs of education and welfare, a disproportionate drain on the residents resident.

**TECTON**  A joint venture of architects (team, to some) that achieved photographic immortality through their London apartment houses (Highpoint I, 1933; Highpoint II, 1938) and, more romantically, the Penguin Pool (1933) at the London Zoo. Berthold Lubetkin organized it, Denys Lasdun was present.

**TELFORD, THOMAS (1757–1834)** *Scottish Engineer*  Although he built some churches, he is known for great engineering feats (in daring, not in size): bridges, aqueducts, docks (St. Katherine's Docks), and warehouses. The Victorians had nerve with their new technology, and Telford suggested a new London Bridge, a single span of 600 feet of cast iron leaping the Thames. A lovely suspension bridge by Telford (1826) connects Castle Conway in Wales with the mainland, steel cables straddling neo-Gothic towers, recalling the towers of the castle proper (visualize the doughty Welsh defending their bridge from its crenelated battlements).

Architecture wasn't left behind by brilliant engineering, but took

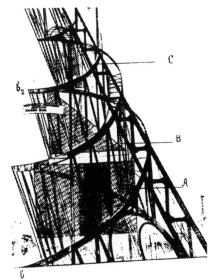

TATLIN *Proposed monument to the Third International, Moscow*

a different route through revivals and eclecticism (a pinch of this, a little bit of that), using engineering facility secretly (underground knowledge) to frame the finery it wished to display. Only when architecture and engineering rejoined (the Chicago School of architecture) did they both become overt and unselfconscious parts of a greater whole.

**TEMPER**  To mollify, relieving the internal stresses of a material that has been made hard and brittle by its working. Steel and glass, when drawn, rolled, and pummeled, are internally stressed, then relieved by heat treatment: ergo, tempered. A hot bath for an aching, stressed human is not dissimilar.

**TEMPLATE**  The profile which guides hand or machine to make a part. A cut simulation of the final part or object.

**TEMPLE**  A building for worship of God (gods). Egyptians, Greeks, Romans, and Jews built what we call *temples* in retrospect. Synagogues, mosques, churches, chapels, cathedrals are all other names for generic places of worship. Common usage decrees one or another for the use of a particular religion, rather than there being any strict rules about it all; and the usage varies from time to time.

TEMPLE *Roman Temple, Vienne, France*

**TENANT**  Holder and user of property. A tenant rents or leases a dwelling or commercial space from a landlord, using it as if it were his own, save for restrictions of the lease agreement. A tenant-farmer rents his land and dwelling from the plantation by giving a percentage of his produce to the owner rather than cash; but the principle is the same.

Development of cities is based on future tenancies, both because most buildings since the Industrial Revolution have been built to *rent* and because bank mortgages are based on the dollar value of leases and the financial stability of the leasing tenants. A good developer can build a building or complex with a set of leases, the resultant mortgage, and no money of his own: capitalism without capital.

**TENEMENT**  The nineteenth-century urban mini-apartment house. Before steel framing allowed taller buildings and elevators made them plausible, *tenement* was the term for masonry bearing-walled apartment houses, often on the lot previously occupied by a row house, but much deeper and taller, and hence more profitable. At their worst, tenements filled 90% of a lot, leaving little light and air for the back rooms and apartments; and they were as much as seven stories tall (six flights of stairs).

The avalanche of immigrants that invaded New York—from, first, Ireland, then Italy—were the fodder for the Civil War and cheap labor, but those seemingly sad fates in retrospect were better than the potato famine left at home in Ireland and the poverty of Sicily. Their housing, instantly needed and in large quantity, was the tenement, speculatively built—maximum exploiter of dense urban land —crossed with, and served by, the newly developed elevated train service, three of the five boroughs joined as warehousing for the arriving masses (Manhattan, Brooklyn, and the Bronx).

The "railroad flat" (American apartments were *flats*, in the English terminology, when they were tenements; *apartments* when they became respectable for the middle class!) was named for the half floor of a tenement house (split longitudinally from front to back), each room behind the other in a chain, like a railroad train, some internal without light, some narrow with light shafts, and the caboose overlooking a narrow (10- to 20-foot-wide) rear yard. Only the front room (the decorated engine) gained full light and air.

In retrospect, the apartment houses at Ostia, ancient Rome's suburb near the sea, are tenements, there also seven-story walk-ups of brick, anticipating, but with more gracious rooms and light, the congested late nineteenth century.

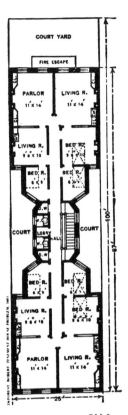

TENEMENT *Old Law Tenement plan, New York*

**TENON** The fingertips of a board, which interlocks with a mortise, its negative counterpart; mostly for cabinetry, furniture, and fine paneling.

**TENSILE** Pull, as in a tug-of-war. In the structured bones of architecture, tension is that tug within a member, inflicted not only by end-to-end pulling, but in a beam by weighing it down: as it bends, its bottom is in tension, its top in compression (the exact opposite). Try it with your own stalk of celery.

**TERMINAL** The end of it all, and, in turn, a beginning, where tired people, trains, buses, and planes all halt, rest, and return on a voyage to the (or an-) other terminal. Pennsylvania Station in New York City was a terminal of its railroad until, in 1910, a daring and bold urban act was consummated: a tunnel driven under the Hudson River, continuing the trackage uninterrupted onward to Philadelphia and southward; a terminal became a station (or stopping point in transit).

**TERRACE**  An English word for a group of row houses designed with a larger architectural image than the sum of their parts, as in John Wood's Royal Crescent at Bath or one side of Bedford Square, London.

**TERRA COTTA**  Baked land (and hence fired clay) and, not surprisingly, earth-colored, from yellow through brown to red. Terra cotta is the raw material of pots, tiles, roofing shingles; and for two whole generations (1840–1920) the encrusted ornamentation of buildings, simulating, through a machine process, the carving of older "labor-intensive" cultures. Terra cotta is glazed, an act that sheathes, colors, and protects the body within. Examples range from the innards of buildings (James Renwick's vaults at St. Patrick's, New York City; Minard Lafever's entire Gothic interior at Trinity Church, Brooklyn) to their bumpy skins (Cass Gilbert's Woolworth Building, 1913).

**TERRAGNI, GIUSEPPE (1904–1943)** *Italian Architect* Architect of modest formalism, he battled the absolutes of the International Style with the same plain white forms of his opponents, used in a decorative way to create light and shadow (such a minor deviation that one wonders what all the shouting was about). His most famed work is the Casa del Fascio (Fascist Party Headquarters; 1936, Como).

TERRAGNI *Fascist Party Headquarters, Como*

**TERRAZZO**  Ground and polished marble chips bound with cement, mostly for floors; a relatively cheap and multicolored, multipatterned marble substitute.

**TESSERAE**  The cut parts of a mosaic (of wood or glass or marble or anything) that participate in the final picture or image like the painted dots of Pointillism.

**TEXTURE**  The quality of finish of anything (taken from the word meaning "way of weaving") and its textural result. The texture of a wall or floor or fabric is an indication of its smoothness or roughness, flatness or bumpiness, and, on occasion, the specific design of that state.

**THATCH**   The hairy head of a primitive reed- or straw-roofed building, woven (thatched) to shed water and weather, aging quickly and delightfully, whether in the Cotswolds or Yucatán.

**THEATER**   A place or building where dramatic events are enacted or reenacted before an audience, usually in terraced or bowled seating surrounding or facing the participants. Greek or Roman theaters were half-round bowls, serving an open stage (Greek) or a permanent quasi-building set (Roman). (E.g., Theater at Epidauros, 350 B.C.; and Theater at Orange, France/Gaul, A.D. 50).

The modern theater is an elaborate technical device that places simple seating before a framed stage (proscenium) that in turn is served by wings, lofts, and towers, storing and supplying scenery as needed.

Movie theaters became the ultimate populist monumental building of the 1920s through 1940s: great eclectic and ornate palaces for the common man's vicarious delight, not only in the movies displayed but in the place displaying.

Modern urban events provide no such places of fantasy, excepting the extra-urban pilgrimage sites of Disneyland and Disneyworld, and their lesser copiers.

**THERMAE**   Latin: "warm places." Baths of A.D. Rome—elegant urban amenities in which citizens could assuage their senses (and do business at the same time). Antidotes to the stress of Christian confrontations, the largest, most memorable and copied are those of Diocletian and Caracalla, the former now partially a church (S. Maria degli Angeli, as remodeled by Michelangelo), the latter a ruin now used as a stage-set for opera. Their scale is, to us, almost inconceivable, vast 25-acre complexes of great buildings, spaces and events, indoors and out.

Bath, England, is where the Romans built a great one for their own provincial occupation and use.

TESSERAE *Mosaic, S. Apollinare Nuovo, Ravenna*

**THERMOSTAT**   The control that measures and then supplies or shuts off heat or cold; a proselytizing thermometer.

**THOMPSON, MARTIN E. (1789–1877)** *American Architect* A whole family of Greek Revival buildings serves as his Sailors' Snug Harbor (1831+; Staten Island, New York), former hostel for the old salt in his old age. Thompson, as befits a revivalist of note, worked in a variety of styles seemingly appropriate to a program: his New York State Arsenal (1848; now the headquarters of the Department of Parks) in Central Park is crenelated Gothic, to offer symbolic defense of the symbolic ammunition within.

**THOMSON, ALEXANDER ("GREEK") (1817–1875)** *Scottish Architect* He kept Greek remnants alive after their nominal revival had waned with a later Victorian vigor that made pale the purist temples of the twenties, thirties, and forties. His Presyterian churches might convert the heathens by overwhelming them (if not impressing, scaring, or subduing them by visual brickbats).

**THORNTON, WILLIAM (1759–1828)** *English American Doctor and Architect* He won the competition for the Capitol, Washington, D.C. (1793). As at St. Peter's, a series of architect-superintendents continued the building (surprisingly faithfully): Hallet, Hoban, Latrobe, Bulfinch, Walter (work, work, work—new interiors—work, and the Dome respectively).

Thornton also designed Octagon House (1800), now part of the national headquarters of the American Institute of Architects, an elegant Federal palace.

**THROAT** A narrow, special and/or critical passage, as in that of a human, allowing breath, food, voice, and gas to (intermittently) pass in both directions. The throat of a fireplace is the constricted place of control, where the damper (a smoke door) sits on the way to the flue, or void, within a chimney.

**THRUST** The shove of a building outward, tending to topple its walls and let fall its vaults or arches, which by their very nature create the thrust. Buttresses, attached or flying, are the antidote, balancing the forces.

**TIE** A tensile member to hold together parts of a building that tend to separate. A Gothic vault (see *thrust*) was sometimes tied instead of buttressed, and so were Renaissance vaults, like those of

THOMSON *Church of St. Vincent, Glasgow*

the Cathedral (Duomo) in Florence or the Hospital of the Innocents (foundling hospital) porch by Brunelleschi.

**TIER**   Layer of a layer cake, floor of a building, terrace of a series, slung level of an opera house; a grand and gross word for layers of action and activities, or layers from which action and activities can be viewed.

**TIFFANY, LOUIS COMFORT (1848–1933)** *American Artisan and Entrepreneur*   Notorious for Tiffany glass (churchly "stained"-glass and secular leaded-glass lampshades), Tiffany's ultimate material reached its greatest aesthetic heights in the muted, translucent pastels of vases in sinuous shapes now aped in "Venetian" commercial glassware. His works thus decorate, light, and give form and color to myriad turn-of-the-century (Victorian-Edwardian) interiors.

The Tiffany Studios were contractors (designers and builders) for interior architecture similar in function to Lebrun at Versailles.

**TILE**   The second module. The first was brick from prehistory's sun-dried river bottoms. The second was fired clay that floored floors or veneered walls and domes, a sheet rectangle rather than the squared lump (brick). Tiles are now used for roofing (terra cotta) and flooring (terra cotta glazed and unglazed, asphalt, vinyl, linoleum, cork, marble, wood, glass, ceramic, plastic, stainless steel, or anything that serves the same purpose modularly.

**TIMBER**   Big wood, at the scale of whole trees. Fibrous (think of asparagus or celery), it can support weight as a beam, a bridgelike action from here to there. Timber buildings are popular not only because they are intrinsically handsome and economical where trees are prolific, but because they provide a building that can't easily be burnt down. Thick wood will char to a certain depth, and then combustion can no longer be supported: the building stands, ruined in its charred members, but the people sheltered can escape, as nothing falls or collapses upon them. Conversely, a steel building of the same arrangements would buckle, as steel goes to taffy under heat and fire (and hence the need for fireproofing steel-caged buildings by encasing their members in concrete or spraying them with asbestos).

**TIN** A precious element (close to silver in value and rarity) that is used in alloys with other metals to improve the lot of both, structurally and visually (bronze = copper + tin). Tin cans were the tin-plated steel containers of preserved foods, vacuum-packed, the tin preventing corrosion and hence contamination; now replaced internally by plastic, externally by a plating so thin as to be unmeasurable.

Tin got a bad name because of cans (tin shacks, tin lizzie, and so forth), which belies its true worthiness.

**TOILET** At first the place (and act) of dressing, then grooming, later washing, and last defecating, a sorry degeneration of the word. A toilet (fixture) in America is more properly and pompously called a water closet (and even the French, importers of it, call it a W.C.).

But Marie Antoinette's toilet was the grand act of dressing, grooming, and assembling her portable costumery, that crust of polished social shielding that converted the wet nymph of the bath into a regal leviathan.

**TOMB** The place of one dead, buried, or coffered in sepulchral splendor, a tomb implies a building, or at least a cave, that contains under or above ground the remnants of life; if it were a pompous or a grand one, it would be a mausoleum.

TOWER

**TONGUE** A linear tendon, lip of a piece of wood that fits to its female counterpart in an adjacent piece. Boards so fitted can clad a building's exterior or be its paneling, the interlock aligning them all and preventing the warping of each. Within the tongue, a nail can be nailed "blind," so that the finished assembly will appear all wood, without hardware.

**TOPOGRAPHY** The conscious knowledge of landform's shape, height, position, and characteristics, recorded on maps and charts. And, more specifically, the graphic knowledge of a place however expressed: three-dimensional photography, contour mapping, computer graphics can all participate in the act of topography. Most common examples used by the public are the U.S. Geodetic Survey Maps, a record of every bit of the country, its buildings, routes of travel, hills, vales, and edges.

**TORROJA, EDUARDO (1899–1961)** *Spanish Engineer* Concrete shell man, in spirit (and consonance) with his peer-engineers, Nervi and Candela (and the late work of Freyssinet and Maillart). Torroja's Zarzuela (1935) racetrack-shed at Madrid anticipated Nervi's later wonders.

**TORUS** A doughnut shape, a fat round band of a molding, usually at the base of a column. A scotia, or concave molding, adjacent makes it all the more articulate and plausible: negative reinforcing positive.

TORROJA *Stands in the Madrid Racecourse*

**TOWER** A man-made structure usually much taller than it is wide, and usually relying more on proportions than sheer size. Towers tend to be places of viewing or defense and place man high in space for those efforts: round, polygonal or square; brick, stone, and wood, towers are varied and handsome remnants of special events in a culture.

The Tower of London, however, is a squat one, a castle with two lines of battlemented walls, each with subsidiary defensive bastions and a moat; and within it all a keep (the French *donjon*) termed the White Tower (the only real tower present), which is squat, barely taller than a cube. Those Saxons must have had vertigo or thought things proportionately taller than they were.

The Eiffel Tower more than fills the bill, a soaring spire for viewing the urban arrangements of Paris, built for the Exhibition of 1889 by Gustave Eiffel, great French engineer, and named in his memory.

**TOWN** An Anglo-Saxon urban center where farmers came to market, and later an urban place of modest size, more than a village or collection of houses, but less than a city. In some American states the title "town" or "city" is unrelated to size or qualities: e.g., New York State, where the town of Hempstead is a major city, in fact, while Garden City is a suburban town. The confusion hence multiplies.

In New England, a town is a section of land equivalent to other states' counties and comprises, on occasion, hundreds of square miles; there it is also a system of government, where the legislature is the whole voting population, assembling as a "town meeting."

**TOWN HOUSE** The town dwelling of the country gentry in England's balmier days, word-surrogated to the tightly sited row building of modern times: America's brownstones, England's terraces (Royal Crescent at Bath), France's *places* (Place des Vosges), Italy's palazzi (no royalty necessary for an Italian palazzo). Town housing implies high density and tight geography, where the pedestrian can circulate without the aid or hindrance of a car. Modern planners and architects have brought town housing back to the middle class, as at Reston, Virginia, by Whittlesey, Conklin and Rossant, or Cumbernauld, Scotland. The Latins (French, Italians, Greeks) have not rediscovered what they themselves started and did so well—the anonymous hill and island town architecture of simplistic town housing at Míkonos, Volterra, San Gimignano, Rapallo, Gassin, and so forth—and have borrowed the superbuilding and superblock from America and England to create unfortunate highrise, free-standing Mediterranean worlds (look at the nontourist outskirts of Paris or Rome).

**TRABEATED** The formal word for post and beam, as opposed to arched and vaulted (arcuated) architecture. Greek architecture is almost universally trabeated—Roman mixed, as is that of most of the Renaissance. Current building is neither trabeated nor arcuated: it is mostly of *continuous* structures (balloon frames, stressed-skin wood; concrete beam, slab, and shell—all monolithic; and/or steel, welded or bolted). Both trabeated and arcuated imply the principal effort is contending with weight (gravity), not in the flexured strength of the material and its connections.

**TRACERY** Both ornament and structure in and for stained-glass windows. Tracery of stone was the armature of glass for Romanesque and Gothic. In later days, technology supplied cast iron, plus reinforcing bars to stabilize vast and fragile expanses. Plate tracery was that cut, like cookies, out of a single sheet of stone.

**TRACING** The translucent paper of architecture from which one can print an image on other opaque paper, originally by sunlight exposure, now by artificial machine-fed light. Developed with ammonia, it can produce blueprints or whiteprints (with blue or black lines). Tracing paper allows the designer and draftsman to draw over his previous work, refining its development, or to transfer rough sketches onto a neat working drawing (which is the document of contractors and building).

**TRANSEPT**   The crossed arms of a Christian chruch, where the extra (brethren) clergy sat—the lay population in the nave, the operating clergy in the chancel (choir). The transept offered not only form and space but also alternate entrances to the congregation when crowded.

**TRANSIT**   Latin: "it goes across." A movement spanning a space, as in a train's transit from city to city, or a subway's transit from stop to stop within one. Transit can apply to things as well as people, but most commonly now it refers to the short-ranged public conveyance of commuters and businessmen on their way to and from regular and irregular places of work. *Rapid* transit is a wishful conveyance that hopes to attract passengers by claiming rapidity; but rapid transit frequently has nothing to do with speed and concerns style of travel, as in the subways of New York and San Francisco, the Metros of Paris and Montreal, the underground of London, or at a larger scale the Tokyo–Osaka express that makes the space between those cities seem like a commuter's adventure rather than the 300 miles of reality.

Transit can save the urban world from the car. In a world congested by traffic, polluted by effluents, and starved by energy shortages, transit can solve all three problems while maintaining the possibility of urbanity for city residents: leaving city space for people, not autos, and allowing graceful concentration of architecture, rather than sprawled blurbs of anti-country.

**TRANSLUCENT**   Passing light, but not vision, as in frosted or stained glass or natural amber filling the window lights of ancient architecture. Clear glass, trans*parent*, is a relatively new affair, only possible for the upper classes in the eighteenth century, for the common man in the industrially revolting nineteenth.

**TRANSOM**   That bar that separates door from window or fanlight, fixed or movable, above.

**TRAP**   An indoor manhole (trap door) that gives access to cellars, attics, and roofs.

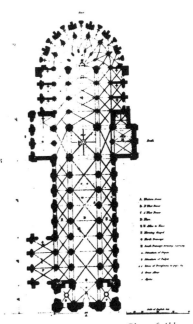

TRANSEPT *Plan of Abbaye aux Hommes, Caen*

**TRAP**  An S-curved pipe beneath a plumbing fixture that serves to prevent sewer gas from backing up into a room. Water fills the S and, in effect, corks the pipe.

**TRAVERTINE**  Cousin of limestone, brother of marble, travertine is the mineral deposit of water at and near great springs. All three stones are calcium carbonate, and sources of lime and the makings of Portland cement.

Travertine is naturally pocked when sliced and bears hues from beige to rust, sometimes striated when polished. A popular material for floors, it has clad great clustered urban complexes, as at Lincoln Center, where it is the most expensive outdoor wallpaper ever used. Its texture gives it an apparent quality of age when almost new (the pits and pocks collect dirt and spread patina like instant history).

**TREAD**  The step of a stair, where feet tread, spaced in height by the vertical risers between.

TRUMBAUER *James B. Duke House, New York*

**TREE**  Trees have been meeting places for teachers and gurus, outdoor sheltered classrooms with a sense of place, a naturally domed schoolroom. They have often been trained rigorously, espaliered against walls in medieval cloisters by monks who savored their fruit in the early spring (the walls faced south, and the cloister protected all from the cold winds). As elements in the larger design of buildings and cities, they were banned from the city walls (except as occasional fruit gardens) until the Renaissance ordered them into masses to define the outdoor spaces of formal gardens, and then later used them as sculptured objects in informal landscape (cf. Le Nôtre; Olmsted, Capability Brown). All trees bear fruit, but only some of their fruit is coveted by man.

**TREFOIL**  Three-leafed cloverlike void in stone Gothic tracery.

**TRELLIS**  A place for vines; slats, straight or woven, that will allow the firmly footed wandering of grapes. Trellis and vines jointly are termed *arbor* and are frequently built and grown for the natural dappled shade they produce for a lunch of wine and cheese beneath.

**TRENCH**  A ground slot, dug, with the diggings piled as an earthy parapet, most commonly for the protection of a passing embattled army; a dirty bastion for temporary fusillades. More ordinary trenches are those slots temporarily cut for installation of the pipes and wires of utility services.

**TRIBUNE** The platform from which a gathering or group is addressed and, similarly, newspapers performing that symbolic function (the *Chicago Tribune*).

**TRIFORIUM** The free space between sloping aisle roof and its vaulting in a Gothic church, opened, frequently, to the main nave by arched and traceried voids. At times, the triforium becomes a gallery for spectators and participants in churchly services. At other times, it is a spatial attic.

**TRIGLYPH** The slotted panel that alternates with a plain or sculptured metope in a Doric temple's frieze, as at the Parthenon in Athens (432 B.C.). Two full half-rounded slots trisect the panel, two half-slots ease each end or edge.

**TRIM** The neat pieces of architecture that cover joints and conceal the natural imperfections of materials meeting and joining. Functional participants, they became decorative elements as well: baseboards (they also divert abuse from a soft wall), door trim (which covers the structural frame bearing the force of a door's swing), and so forth. Classical architecture, through Renaissance modulations, has given us Federal and Georgian trim in America (and of great elegance): molded and embellished as an end as well as a means.

**TRUMBAUER, HORACE (1869–1938)** *American Architect* The Edward Berwind House at Newport (The Elms, 1901) and the James B. Duke House (1912) on New York's Fifth Avenue are two French châteaux (although a château is hardly feasible on Fifth Avenue, the Duke house aspires to that state by standing free). Trumbauer owes a lot to Hardouin-Mansart.

**TRUSS** A collection of structural parts on their way to higher purposes, such as the span of a great space; a truss of stiff members (steel, concrete, wood) allows by its arrangement for the most efficient use of material supporting a load or weight: a network of structure. A skeleton beam without an overweight body.

TRIFORIUM *Gallery, Lincoln Cathedral*

315

**TUDOR** Mostly sixteenth-century England, with a bit of the fifteenth and a touch of the seventeenth, including Henry VIII and Elizabeth I (Tudor was their family name). Tudor memories include Elizabethan and embrace the end of Gothic and the beginning of the Renaissance (the English always were late starters).

Most memorable image is that of half timbering—timber-framed buildings infilled with stuccoed masonry, white and black (the black from aged wood, the white from freshened whitewash). Monumental buildings of brick, gabled, but with formally planned elegance include Compton Wynyates, Hampton Court Palace, and Sutton Place (home of Jean Paul Getty). The *common* memory is that of and for the middle class, inns and houses abounding for the arch artifice of tourism.

**TUFA** The porous volcanic rock from which much Roman architecture was made; soft, carvable, light, it allowed a greater flexibility than that possible with limestone, travertine, or marble.

**TUNNEL** An underground tube, in natural or built masonry drilled through rock, as a train's tunnel under a river (Rotterdam) or through a mountain (Simplon Pass).

**TURKISH** The Turks were another in the sequence of Hittites, Romans, and others who lurked in Asia Minor. The Ottomans (i.e., the Turks) made their own empire in the fifteenth through twentieth centuries, absorbing Arab lands as well as the late eastern Roman (Christian) Empire and all of its remnants. Byzantine great-domed churches are thought of, in retrospect, as Arabic or Moslem but in fact were the legacy of the Roman Christian emperor Constantine and his followers. Under the fifteenth-century architect Sinan, that architecture was revived 1,000 years later.

**TURRET** A little tower on a fortified building, usually medieval, and usually the equivalent of a wall's bastion: later, a remembrance of fortifications, used for decorative purposes on Tudor buildings, as Hampton Court Palace.

**TUSCAN** The smoothed and rounded (no flutes) Doric of later Roman architecture, popular in Victorian times; a more facile set of parts, with less rigid proportions; easy participant in a Renaissance hierarchy where columns are only background components and the

TURRET *St. Mary's Church, Beverly, England*

larger formalities of plan and proportion are the question; or where the columns are incidental to the building's greater glories (Tigbourne Court, 1899; Sir Edwin Lutyens).

**T.V.A.**   Tennessee Valley Authority; architectural patron for the great works of engineering that dammed Tennessee's rivers, generated its power, and provided contained water for irrigation—all part of President Franklin Roosevelt's New Deal.

**TYMPANUM**   The sculptured pediment, triangular end crest of a Greek or Roman temple; and the later arched, sculpted space over Romanesque and/or Gothic doors. The tympanum is the available space as opposed to the sculpted contents.

# U

UNWIN *Hampstead Garden City, cul de sac*

**UNDERCROFT**  A vaulted or timbered cellar, under a church, useful for live activities, as opposed to a crypt, similar in structure and placement, which is a container for the dead.

**UNDERGROUND**  The people-mover of London, trains moving through deep-driven tubes lacing an underworld; the elegant, cellared rat-travel that makes urban life urbane (by avoiding the space-devouring car and getting one from place to place rapidly and pleasurably).

New York has a subway (very efficient, but scarcely pleasurable), Paris and Montreal metro(politan)s.

**UNDERPINNING**  Those props that hold a neighbor stable when one builds a building deeper, below the foundations of that pinned and propped: a ticklish affair, almost inevitably inviting movement and cracks in the older building.

**UNWIN, (SIR) RAYMOND (1863–1940)** *English Planner*
Ebenezer Howard's vision was applied by Unwin (and his partner Howard) first at Letchworth (1903+), then at Hampstead, (1907+). Romantic plans—meandering, with separate places for carriage, car, and pedestrian—and a common denominator of architecture (here neo-Tudor) combined to make a comfortable middle-class image that was later embraced by America from Bronxville (speculative) to Forest Hills Gardens (1913+; group-planned speculation: Frederick Law Olmsted and Grosvenor Atterbury).

**UPJOHN, RICHARD (1802–1878)** *English American Cabinet-maker and Architect*  Upjohn built the second Trinity Church (1846, New York City), finialed end of Wall Street's canyons today, built when the finial dominated. In neighboring Brooklyn, he made the more spare but plastic-formed Church of the Pilgrims, a carved ashlar volume, and elegant town houses facing the harbor's view.

**URBAN**  Citified; a state of large-scaled and dense living and life that suggests concentration and may also cause congestion. In a happy city the first can exist without the second. An urban place may become urbane (i.e., with the best and suavest components of urban-ness that become urbanity) by elegance and the elegant life that fills it; and by elegant life and the elegant place that life demands and commissions. Both components are necessary, as neither can exist without the symbiotic other.

**URBAN DESIGN**  The implementation of planning (that first act of allocating resources and the priorities of expenditures). Urban design embraces the logistics of execution and the architectural act of arranging large parts of a city: in effect, weaving together the needs of neighbors and the public life of a city with its circulation, sanitation, light, air, urbanity, and politics. Urban design sometimes is miscast as the business of ornamenting public streets and plazas and arranging buildings to make those outdoor spaces elegant (as those, particularly, of Italy). That is a necessary component of a much larger cake of activity.

**URBAN, JOSEPH (1872–1933)** *Austrian American Architect and Stage Designer*  Urban used his training in stage design for architecture and produced results much happier than those of most architects: country houses for the so-called robber barons of Long Island (the nouveau riche of those times) and, more importantly, the New School for Social Research (1930), an early modern monument. Its banded brick façade has graded spacing between its alternate stripes that, in the Renaissance fashion of false perspective, makes the building appear tallest when the observer is directly opposite. Urban was an eclectic stylist; his other buildings, such as the old Ziegfeld Theatre, were modern in the way a Cadillac is modern: stylish, willful design using decoration invented for that one job and not part of any tradition or development (the antithesis of classic).

UPJOHN *Church of the Pilgrims, Brooklyn*

319

**USURY**   Nasty interest that is unreasonable, illegal, and probably the fringe activity of Mafia or other ethnic gangsterism to maximize its cash—put it to work without need for stock, banks, real or unreal estate. Money with a low profile, ill-gotten, can demand much interest from those desperate.

**UTILITY**   Useful thing; arrogated by the merchants of power—natural gas, electricity, steam—to describe their work as "public" utilities (in fact they are private utilities for public purpose and private profit, supposedly regulated to benefit the recipients and general public and minimize the noxious effluents or pollutants that harm us all). One should rename them "public usefuls" and then demand they fulfill their own semantics.

**UTZON, JORN (1918–   )** *Danish Architect*   His serene rectangular (sometimes almost Japanese) house-pavilions gave way to the phantasmagoria of Sydney, the Opera House won in open competition. It is analogous (from afar) to a series of ballooning spinnakers on a man-made spit at the harbor's entrance, containing many music and drama spaces, as well as the Opera itself. Utzon withdrew under fire, as the cost rose exponentially to make it one of the most expensive buildings ever built. Disappointingly, the contents bear little relation to the exterior form.

# V

**VALADIER, GIUSEPPE (1762–1839)** *French Architect* He arranged Rome's Piazza del Popolo (before 1820), fountains, obelisks, gates, and bric-a-brac.

**VALLEY** The V-shaped intersection of two inwardly sloping roofs; a natural gutter that sweeps away joining rainwater to the ground.

**VAN ALEN, WILLIAM (1883–1954)** *American Architect* Van Alen's glory has been shunted aside in that statistical race for the tallest spire of New York: his Chrysler Building (1930) held title for only months. But the building remains a true landmark of orientation: the eye can place the viewer in the city by its sight of the Chrysler and the Empire State (a function church spires and domes performed in high-density, low-rise anywhere before steel and elevators created tall buildings).

The Chrysler Building displays elegant and early uses of stainless steel as a building material and some of the more bizarre ornament of modern America, including ten-foot-high inflated radiator caps and a needle-finial suitable for impaling King Kong (which no doubt explains why that stalwart climbed the Empire State instead).

**VANBRUGH, (SIR) JOHN (1664–1726)** *English Spy, Playwright, and Architect* England's Baroque, at its best, was Vanbrugh's, particularly Castle Howard and Blenheim Palace. Blenheim, the nation's gift to the Duke of Marlborough, a present for his presents

VANBRUGH *Blenheim Palace*

321

of British victories, had unlimited budget and the fertile mind of a romantic and theatrical architect. Hawksmoor helped and contributed some of his proto-Cubism (at least to the kitchen wing, if not the front door). Winston Churchill was born there, a suitable stage-set for his entry (plumbing, comforts, heat, and other suitables were minimal).

**VAN DEN BROEK, J. H. (1918–   )** *Dutch Architect* See *Bakema, Jacob.*

**VAN DE VELDE, HENRY (1863–1957)** *Belgian Architect, Painter, and Designer* Art Nouveau proselytizer; his art school at Weimar (1906), chunky white stuccoed masonry blocks, held curved skylights that are suggested later in Sant'Elia's Futurist drawings. This is the building and school that Gropius later directed and moved to Dessau, renaming it the Bauhaus.

Van de Velde had decorated four rooms in the shop l'Art Nouveau, in Paris (1896), and his recognized leadership in the development of this abstract sinuous ornament placed him among Art Nouveau's elite.

VAN EYCK *Children's Home, Amsterdam*

**VAN EYCK, ALDO (1918–   )** *Dutch Architect* Architectural student's folk hero of the sixties, whose Children's Home (1960, Amsterdam) is a multicelled accretion, where a human's unit is one of a factorylike set (336 11-foot-square spaces), honeycomblike when viewed from the air, lovely and humane at the user's level.

**VANVITELLI, LUIGI (1700–1773)** *Italian Architect* The palace for Charles III, King of the Two Sicilies, at Caserta, near Naples, is a giant Late Baroque 1200-room block, banal from the street, extravagant at moments in its interior stage-settings.

**VASARI, GIORGIO (1511–1574)** *Italian Painter and Writer* His *Lives of Architects, Painters, and Sculptors* (1550) boosted Michelangelo. On his own he built that much-toured and -photographed court of the Uffizi Gallery in Florence, a private street to the Arno, with ornamented flanks of arcades simulating those of Serlio at the Library in Venice.

**VAUDREMER, JOSEPH-AUGUSTE (1829–1914)** *French Architect* His bulky Romanesque revivalisms are commonly thought to have inspired America's great Henry Hobson Richardson.

**VAULT**  A warped plane of arches that spans and roofs a space, essential in societies that had no wood but could provide brick or stone (i.e., Mesopotamia). Barrel vaults are the linear continuous arches of Rome and the Romanesque, groin vaults the crossed vaulting of the same times that allowed windows and light into the central space (Basilica of Constantine, St. Benoit sur Loire). Ribbed Gothic structures relieved vaulting of some of its burdens, relying on a cage of ribwork to carry loads, within which was an infilling of masonry panels. Such vaulting allowed more light and air, less weight, more linear elegance.

**VAUX, CALVERT (1824–1895)** *English American Architect* Vaux (pronounced Vawx, not Voh, and hence English, not French) was sometime partner of Andrew Jackson Downing and Frederick Law Olmsted, supplying the architecture that punctuated their parks, as the Bethesda Fountain in Central Park. He also contributed New York's alternately beloved and behated Jefferson Market Courthouse (preserved now as a library).

**VENEER**  The skin material, a thin layer laminated to the parent body, as fine-grained and exotic wood on a plain furniture framed box, or plastic (melamine) on a kitchen counter.

**VENT**  A place through which air moves, exhausting the polluted smoke of a kitchen, the gas of a bathroom, the cigars of a smoker. Vents may work by the natural convection of air, gases, or the force of mechanical ventilating fans.

VENTURI *House, Chestnut Hill, Pennsylvania*

**VENTURI, ROBERT (1925–    )** *American Architect* Theorist in both words and practice, Venturi's second built work, a house for his mother in Chestnut Hill (Philadelphia, 1962+) staggered the international stylists (those locked into Mies and Gropius, in particular) in the sixties, a punch from which they have never, happily, fully recovered. His first work was a visiting nurses' headquarters (North Penn Visiting Nurse Association, Ambler, Penn., 1961) stylistically less startling than the Venturi house. His writings have explored the architecture along America's highways (Hollywood's Brown Derby and the incredible visual anarchy of signs, wires, and parking lots all cities now enjoy) and the tendency toward artificial oversimplification and/or a forced volume/form relationship between a building's space and shape. "Where simplicity cannot work, simpleness results. Blatant simplification means bland architecture. Less is a bore."

**VERANDA**   An Indian word for the great shaded porches of summer and the tropics, where indolent life served by menials reached an art form. The veranda was imported to late nineteenth-century America, and is the wide active porch of a shingle-style or Queen Anne house.

**VERDURE, MORDANT (1899–1934)** *French American Landscape Architect*   Verdure came to America as field superintendent for landscaping the grounds of John Barrymore's summer castle (the Log House) at Banff. He stayed to carpet the landscape of the wealthy in and around Palm Beach (he was a sometime protégé of Addison Mizner).

**VERMICULATED**   The apparent worm tracks tracing some of the rusticated stone work of Renaissance buildings; naturalistic imagery, but far-fetched for worms.

**VERNACULAR**   Common speech as used in common communication. A vernacular implies reality and the way things happen for the mass man: and as borrowed for architecture it describes the ordinary mass-built and -served architecture of semiprimitive societies, as that of the Greek Islands (Míkonos) or the pleasant carpenter Gothic of the nineteenth century in America.

**VESTIBULE**   The changing room of a building where outer and inner garments are juggled in transit from artificial to natural climates, and vice versa. One is vested, or unvested, in a vestibule.

**VESTRY**   Room or place of robing (and hence vesting) for the clergy, whose garments are sometimes quick-changed in the process of liturgy.

**VIADUCT**   A many-footed roadway across a valley or gorge (as opposed to a bridge that jumps across). Viaducts are in a league with aqueducts, those arched, high-piered Roman carriers of water.

VERNACULAR *Stucco and masonry buildings, Capri*

In later times wheeled traffic was carried in a similar way: all possible with simple brick and stone.

**VICTORIAN**   Of the age of Queen Victoria (1837–1901). Modern (i.e., post-Victorian) architects and critics felt, until recently, that "Victorian" architecture was usually impure, florid, and a sort of Protestant gimcrack Baroque. In effect, in America, everything after Federal and Greek Revival is "Victorian" (who else can claim a whole century qualitatively?)—i.e., those styles loosely called Queen Anne, General Grant, Romanesque and Classical Revival (as opposed to Greek Revival), Renaissance Revival, and Gothic Revival and even late forms of Greek Revival itself (neo-Grec) are the myriad faces of a profession wandering through its own history, abetted by its new tools of technology and the Industrial Revolution.

**VIGANÒ, VITTORIANO (1919–   )** *Italian Architect*   The Italians' Brutalist: his Istituto Marchiondi (1959, Milan) is a powerful, almost histrionic exposed concrete structure with big and cumbersome bones.

**VIGNETTE**   An artfully cropped drawing or photograph (view) showing a small piece of a whole composition.

**VIGNOLA, GIACOMO DA (1507–1573)** *Italian Architect*   The Palazzo Farnese at Caprarola (the Pentagon of the Renaissance), with a circular center (reflectively imitated by Guy Lowell's New York County Courthouse in New York: a hexagonal plan with a circular center). Caprarola is now the summer residence of the presidents of Italy.

More telling is the great church, Il Gesù, which, with Alberti's S. Andrea (Mantua), was the father-image and genetic imprint of Baroque churches all over the world. An early Latin cross, it housed a preaching congregation; later (as you see it now), it was gilt and ornamented to a state of the highest Baroque decoration.

**VIGNON, PIERRE (1762–1828)** *French Architect*   The Madeleine of Paris is Napoleon's super-Roman monument to himself (and incidentally a church); the Corinthian columns surrounding honor and ornament it, atop a grand pedestal. Vignon officiated.

VIGANO *Marchiondi Institute, Milan*

325

**VILLA** A more than middle-class country house near a city—a thought to boggle the mind at first, until one realizes that suburbs are a relatively modern affair, and one could once (and can even now in Italy) live in the country next to the city. Villas are a Latin thought, implying respite from urban pressures: as one has a villa at Cannes or Capri or Alexandria.

**VILLANUEVA, CARLOS RAÚL (1900–     )** *Venezuelan Architect* Literal translation suggests his name was prophetic ("new house") for the leader of modern architecture's maturity in Venezuela.

The Aula Magna is the most spectacular and satisfactory of a whole campus of buildings at the Caracas National University (1950; along with the Olympic Stadium). Art as a complement, not part of the integer, is everywhere: Henry Moore, Jean Arp, Alexander Calder, and others have left sculpture, mosaic—and even the floating acoustical "clouds" of the Aula Magna (Calder).

Villanueva participated in some of the spectacular housing built by the Workers' Bank (i.e., Social Security System) between World War II and 1958. El Paraiso (with Celis and Mijares), of exposed concrete-framed eighteen-story slabs, has access corridors to the duplex apartments incised every three floors. Their exteriors are matter-of-fact multicolored painted structure.

**VILLARD DE HONNECOURT (Early Thirteenth Century)** *French Architect* Master mason and hence, in terms of his day, an architect in an age when architects were usually without public ego, honor, or recording (not necessarily a bad idea). He was contemporary with the work at Rheims, Laon, and Chartres, and is best remembered as the first professional who drew and wrote it all down, in an early manuscript of instruction to his assistants and followers: to be viewed at the Bibliothèque Nationale in Paris.

**VIOLLET-LE-DUC, EUGÈNE EMMANUEL (1814–1879)** *French Architect and Restorer* The great Romanesque church at Vézelay, the lacy glassed Sainte Chapelle, and Notre Dame itself (Cathedral of Paris) were face-lifted by Viollet-le-Duc, who may have "improved" them in the process, making them "purer," "better," more perfect examples of the medieval periods they represent but could not in their own times fulfill (he said).

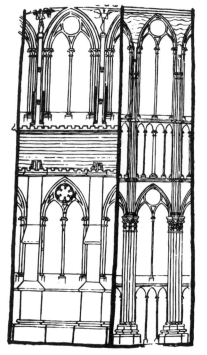

VILLARD DE HONNECOURT *Sketch of the interior elevations of a Gothic church*

Viollet-le-Duc was passionately concerned with the articulated sculpture of medievalism, analyzing the ribs and vaults of Gothic as if they were the incipient iron of his own age; and when he got to iron itself, he canonized it, used it, promoted it. His words fascinated the young Frank Lloyd Wright, who always recommended V-L-D to students and aspiring architects.

**VISTA** An arranged, or framed, view; the prescribed experience of a designer of land- and building-scapes.

**VITRUVIUS POLLIO, MARCUS (First Century B.C.)** *Roman Architect and Verbalist* His extant words (*De architectura*) gave heart to the Renaissance and, apparently, any lessons they cared to read into his words, which were generous, general, and without the constraints of deeds (i.e., drawings or buildings). Like an oracle, his writings were used as the quoter saw fit to support any truth, sophistry, or hypocrisy under promotion.

**VOLUTE** The ram's horns of an Ionic capital, scrolled crest and cushion of its loading.

**VOMITORIUM** The superscaled opening through which architects (particularly Le Corbusier) describe mass migrations of people (particularly at stations of transit): an unhappy analogy for the queasy, but certainly a graphic description of hysterical movement.

**VON GÄRTNER, FRIEDRICH (1792–1847)** *German Architect* Architect to Ludwig I (of Bavaria) and embellisher of Munich's Ludwigstrasse (to the glory of Ludwig), with a major church (Ludwigskirche), state library, university, and Feldherren Hall.

**VOUSSOIR** The wedge stone of an arch, radially cut to fit its circle.

**VOYSEY, CHARLES F. ANNESLEY (1857–1941)** *English Architect* A cosy plastered vernacular anticipated the hard ways of Cubism. Tempered with the scale of Tudor: domesticity, white volumes, slate roofs, slotted windows. He designed wallpaper, furniture, and all the furnishings and fixtures, frequently inspired by

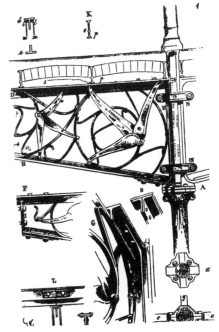

VIOLLET-LE-DUC *Drawings of architectural iron details*

327

the Three Ms: Mackmurdo, Mackintosh, and Morris. But his own plain forms, foiled with carefully preserved nature (particularly trees), became a movement on their own, much admired and copied.

# W

**WACHSMANN, KONRAD (1901–    )** *German American Engineer*  Conjurer of great steel space-frames (like aircraft hangars), he started in Germany as an engineer-architect of timber structures, switched to concrete in Italy after he won the German Rome Prize (1938). Later he moved to the U.S. and became partner of that other German American, Walter Gropius. With Gropius he developed the General Panel Corporation, an early attempt at prefabrication of simple suburban houses for the post-World War II housing boom. (Two of these, built as a sample exhibit on New York's Flushing Meadow, were later moved to Stamford, Connecticut, and joined to form a single country residence.)

His grand engineering ideas have remained largely theory—as the Chicago Convention Center (1953; with Mies van der Rohe), while he was professor at Mies's School of Architecture at Illinois Institute of Technology.

**WAGNER, OTTO (1841–1918)** *Austrian Architect*  In at the creation, father-image of Hoffmann and Olbrich and Behrens and Gropius and Mies. His Post Office Savings Bank (1906) is light, white, glassy—a translucent rather than crystal palace. The wildest detail, however, is that of the aluminum bolts fixing the marble skin. His earlier work was eclectic.

**WAINSCOT**  The partial paneling of a wall to protect and decorate it: from floor to chair rail.

**WALKER** *New York Telephone Company Building*

329

WANK *Dam, Tennessee Valley Authority*

**WALKER, RALPH (1889–1973)** *American Architect* For one brief period, Walker delivered an architecture of exotic brickwork to the telephone companies of America: the Barclay-Vesey Building, next to the World Trade Center in New York City, is an early experiment in an aesthetic piling to take advantage of the then new zoning resolution (setbacks became an aesthetic tool). In Brooklyn, the telephone company's Long Island headquarters still bear a graded palette of brick color and value washing the face of the building vertically, a subtle action that deceives the eyes of the beholder.

Walker was party to various firms: McKenzie, Voorhees, Gmelin and Walker; Voorhees, Gmelin and Walker; Voorhees, Walker, Foley and Smith; and so forth. He was at the heart of it all when performance was high (and even, occasionally, when it was low). The torch is now carried by successor firm Haines, Lundberg and Waehler.

**WALK-UP** The pejorative term for a tenement, building type born before the elevator. In a walk-up, one walks up to an apartment.

**WALL** The barrier and membrane between two spaces, sometimes infilling without participating in the structure, sometimes the structure itself. Walls enclose, define, and support buildings, cities (Carcassonne), and regions (Great Wall of China). Most surprising wall is Wall (portable human of *Midsummer Night's Dream*), friendly separator and joiner of lovers.

**WALLBOARD** Prefabricated sheet; skin of a wall's bones; on studs (wood or metal).

**WALLPAPER** The papered veneer over plaster that provides color, pattern, and texture to a space and makes the wall smooth and reinforced. At first this Victorian printers' mass product attempted simulations of the third dimension, but William Morris and Mackmurdo and Voysey, in England, made it first a patterned Arts and Crafts participant, then a flowery vehicle of Art Nouveau.

Wallpaper now, released from all discipline, provides everything, from blank papered color, to small patterned texture, to psychedelic space-boggling, to placid mural scenes.

It is a rich, relatively inexpensive parlor art in the ephemeral environments of our mobile life-styles.

**WALTER, THOMAS U. (1804–1887)** *American Architect* His crown is the Dome of the Capitol at Washington on Thornton and Latrobe's body, of cast iron and stone, an industrially possible quick-Gargantua that dominates the city and is the box within boxes (dome within domes) of the Renaissance: the interior skin for the space and eyes of its beholders, the exterior higher, bolder, and grander for the scale of the city (compare the drawings of Thornton's timid dome).

Walter also made the Roman temple known as Girard College.

**WANK, ROLAND (1898–1970)** *American Architect* Principal architect for the Tennessee Valley Authority's great powerhouses and dams, early adventures in modern architecture far from the urban tastemakers of the East and West Coast cities.

**WARD** A political piece of a city, its geography served by and serving the local chieftain (i.e., politician). A ward is the precinct of a councilman. In older ways, it was the courtyard, or bailey, of a castle.

**WAREHOUSE** Storeplace of goods for sale; wares; a reservoir of availability for the consumer. Warehouses have always been the no-nonsense buildings of all periods of architecture, from Telford's St. Katherine's Docks (1825) in London to Brooklyn's Empire Stores (1846). Modern warehousing is a high-rise filing system of heavy loads and giant elevators, now being replaced by containers carried by ship or train, drawn by trucks (with wheels added), and stacked on open land—part of the portable modern default architecture of our latest civilized steps.

**WARNECKE, JOHN CARL (1919—    )** *American Architect* With his father, Carl (as Warnecke and Warnecke, Architects), John Warnecke first received attention for the Vista del Mar School (California, 1951). A simple set of pavilions stepping down a hillside, it was a fresh venture into a sun- and light-filled schooling place for children. Later, Warnecke's political and selling talents brought him to bigger things through the attention of those in power, Jack Kennedy most prominent among them, for whom he remodeled

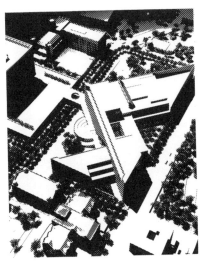

WARNECKE *City College North Academic Complex, New York*

Lafayette Square (the public plaza–park opposite the White House), preserving its local scale and shoving the bulk of programmed federal office buildings away from this nineteenth-century "English" place to streets behind. Current Warnecke work includes the monumental megastructure for New York's City College (1977+).

**WASTE PIPE**  The drain of waste (the swill of human eating and washing), usually cast iron for durability and large enough to carry off the wasted solids (food mostly) that join the flushing water.

**WATER CLOSET**  Toilet derived from the attached privy (a windowless bay (closet) on the rear of an urban town house).. At first water sluiced the stuff into cesspools buried in the garden, and hence the *water* closet. The flush toilet was a derived invention, causing what was unwanted to disappear, leaving crystal water in a white container, supply water stored in a tank. Strictly speaking, a water closet is the place, not the implement.

**WATER TABLE**  The diversionary ledge near the base of a building, throwing water to the ground, away from the foundations, which have a hard enough time, without water, keeping dry.

**WATT**  A unit of power or work or energy available, named after the steam power of James Watt's steam engine, but most common today in describing the electrical needs of a house, piece of equipment, motor, and/or their consumption for the utility's monthly bill, usually expressed in kilo*watts* (thousands of watts).

A 100-watt bulb is only by habit so called, for its light capabilities don't relate only to wattage (a fluorescent tube of 40 watts produces more light): "100 watts" is more a price tag (leave it on for a month at 9 cents a kilowatt hour, and you will spend $6.48).

**WATTLE AND DAUB**  Thin natural or sawn sticks were plastered with mud or clay, a naturalistic and primitive outdoor stucco, to fill voids within a timber-framed building: a cheap substitute, in rural half timbering, for brick and stucco.

**WEATHERING**  The aging of materials due to weather—rain, cold, freezing, sun—that bleaches, cracks, splits, spalls, and gives to the surface a patina of age: a happy and romantic affair with solid

WEESE *Sketch of the American Embassy, Accra*

materials in mild climates (England) and a disaster with shoddy materials in unhappy places (Congo, Amazon, Siberia).

**WEB** The stretched membrane between two sticks, posts, fingers, or toes: in a frog, an umbrella-like taut skin; in a steel beam, the vertical spacer that separates top and bottom flanges, articulating the acts of tension and compression.

**WEBB, PHILIP (1831–1915)** *English Architect* Prime housemaker to the middle class, imbued with Gothic virtue, but, in fact, a modern simplifier, clearing away the decorative debris of his time and peers and retaining plain but sophisticated remnants of brick, slate; plain and spare interiors. His first house, for William Morris (Red House, on Bexley Heath), is a saintly relic of the modern movement.

WEBB *Red House, Bexley Heath*

**WEEP** The tears from a building's innards, allowed out through weep holes, draining hollow masonry walls and other contained spaces in the same spirit as modern ship: there, since leaking (and shipping) of water is inevitable, everyone relaxes about it and maintains floating status and dryness by getting the water out as fast as it comes in (bilge pumps = weep holes).

**WEESE, HARRY (1915– )** *American Architect* His Walton Apartment House (1956, Chicago) nestles next to Mies's 860 Lake Shore Drive—delicate steel bay windows glimpse Lake Michigan. An elegant and restrained understatement in comparison to Mies's bald and well-publicized prisms next door—and more important to architectural history than Weese's monumental Time-Life Building (1972, Chicago).

His own house, of the same era as the Walton, is a latter-day shingle-style place with folded roof planes and intricate space complete with nooks and attic crannies.

His Columbus (Indiana) School is a revival of the handsome brick industrial aesthetic of pre-steel nineteenth century, brick arched openings in a giant square doughnut surrounding a central play court.

**WELL** The first community built-form, and an impetus to urbanization. Originally wells were dug to ground water, as children still do on a beach, then lined with timber or stone to prevent cave-ins.

When deep, water was raised by bucket or animal skin, cranked on a drum or raised in a swoop by a well-sweep, a counterbalanced log or tree trunk.

The well is still the meeting place of many primitive societies, as in India, where it (with the washing area adjacent and the Panchayat —platformed shelter for the meeting of village elders) forms the village center. Drilled wells are the deep probe of steel technology, allowing water for even a residence to be tapped from hundreds of feet below grade. An artesian well, strictly speaking, flows to the surface by itself, driven by underground pressure; other wells have to be pumped.

**WESTERN FRAME** The way stick houses are made in America today, each floor framed separately and sheathed with, usually, plywood subflooring. Sticks mean studs, joists, and rafters of 2 by's (2 × 4 to 2 × 12 mostly). Each tier is stacked on the floor below, as opposed to the original stick-style *balloon* framing, where studs were the full height of a building and notched in their height to receive a girt (belt) of wood from which intermediate floors were hung.

WHITE *University Club, New York*

**WHITE, STANFORD (1853–1906)** *American Architect* One of the greatest and most facile architects of all time. He was rich, and of the rich; gourmand, gourmet, lover, and bon vivant: peer architect for peer clients.

Most important of his products are the Low House at Bristol, Rhode Island, demolished by a nouveau riche dwarf, and the Newport Casino, happily still there, and worth as much as a score of modern "monuments."

White worked for H. H. Richardson, savored his shingle style, seriously contributed to its elegant advancement (Low House), and then wandered into Queen Anne eclecticism, collecting and redistributing delicate classical parts (Renaissance). His own house at Saint James, Long Island, is the most ingenuous exponent of his thoughts.

**WILLIAM OF SENS (1111–1178)** *French-English Proto-architect* Imported French master builder of the choir of Canterbury Cathedral (replacing a burnt earlier one) who boosted the phlegmatic Saxons with his experience at Sens and knowledge of the avant-garde (which he led) in the Île de France. The elegant ribbed choir is similar to that of Chartres or any equal French Gothic.

**WILLIAMSBURG** Williamsburg, Virginia. A place of America's colonization that has affected the state of mind of architecture, its history, and the morality of architectural styles in America ever since. John D. Rockefeller's magnanimous gesture to cause the rebirth of Williamsburg (major buildings were merely buried foundations) brought back, with more than a dash of imagination, the seventeenth century—one we never knew and hoped to reconstruct, both in its buildings and its affairs. Today, the urban stage-set remade is a handsome place of nostalgic delights, bearing a simulated life-style that may or may not ever have in reality existed.

Romance has many merits, and the romance of history many more: but the burden of it all includes the responsibility for those who ape it, copy it of plastic, and use its innate and solid virtues for superficial affairs. Nobody has built a governor's palace in such fashion, but they have extrapolated the history of nothing into something and made of a privy a roadside inn, of a farmer's shack a local monument—all in the name of virtue, and the spirit of profit.

**WILLS, ROYAL BARRY (1897–1962)** *American Architect* Archaeologist of beloved Early American architecture (mostly houses) who cared about the whole and *all* its parts, rather than the normal watered-down stage-sets that are called Colonial (a term in fact most frequently applied to architecture created when America was no longer a colony).

Wills cared not for functionalism nor modernity. His Achilles heel was his very perfection: too perfect, too manicured, too intricately fulfilling a theory of history, rather than history's sometimes casual and imperfect reality. (But that is the falseness of all restorations, whether Viollet-le-Duc's at Notre Dame in Paris or the Williamsburg restored by Rockefeller.)

WILLS *House, New England*

**WINDER** Radial steps, allowing a greater vertical rise in a compact space: the steps replace a landing, pivoting about the newel post that anchors the stairs' change of direction.

**WINDOW** A hybrid hole, serving (these days) several purposes: light, view, ventilation (or nonventilation).

The principal design element in anonymous or primitive architecture (American-European division). Consider the placement of windows in Italian hill towns, among Greek island villages, in Cotswold cottages, in the cliff dwellings of Mesa Verde.

335

Modern windows are double-hung, casement, or the more specialized French, awning or hopper. Double-hung are two overlapping framed planes of window that bypass one another, allowing either the top or bottom to be open at a given time, or half of each. Casements are hinged on one side, as doors are, and open either inward or outward. Most European windows in history are casements, save for the Dutch, who exported their double-hung invention to England and America.

**WING**  A big but secondary building part—at the scale of a whole building on its own, but subordinated to an even larger body.

In English country house architecture (literary and/or novel department), one is a weekend guest "in the west wing." Palaces, hospitals, churches, schools all have wings (even wings have wings).

**WIRE GLASS**  Steel mesh reinforces clear or translucent glass, strengthening it against shattering from impact or fire, as in a small window in a fireproof stair or a skylight.

**WIRE LATH**  The metal filigree that (stretched across a structured frame, usually of metal or wood studs, joists, or hangers) offers an armature for bearing plaster: a modern replacement for wood lath (slats).

**WOOD**  Sliced trees in sheets (plywood), sticks (joists, studs, rafters), beams, and girders (rectilinear, formalized logs). Wood is a linear fibrous material and can range its services from fishing or flag-poles to the gilt paneling of Malmaison, an endlessly grown source of architectural detail and services.

**WOOD, JOHN, THE ELDER (1704–1754)** *English Architect*
He dreamt of a neo-Rome at Bath, one-time Roman provincial city (and site of great baths). The Circus (1754+) was his first great gesture and used imperial grandeur for elegant row housing, a cylinder of building that forms a circus (traffic circle) of traffic in its void and gives an urban space of urbanity to the city's pedestrians: a great moment in the history of urban design.

**WOOD, JOHN, THE YOUNGER (1728–1781)** *English Architect*
He finished father's Circus, and added to the grandeur and elegance of Bath's urban design with the Royal Crescent, confronting a park as in the manner of a Baroque palace (cf. Versailles or the Villa

d'Este or his father's Prior Park, which confronts Capability Brown's verdure).

**WORKING DRAWINGS** The drawings used for the work of building buildings: and hence part of the contract between the owner (or developer) and the contractor. Working drawings are essential in a society where the building function is separated from design and a rigid description of the end product is necessary to accomplish the designer's intent.

In the Middle Ages, on the contrary, the master was just that: the master of the total design and its translation into reality; to an extent, a design is the act of reality, the design model also the end product.

**WREN, (SIR) CHRISTOPHER (1632–1723)** *English Anatomist, Mathematician, Astronomer, Member of Parliament, and Architect* Contemporary of Bernini, Le Vau, and Mansart, he worked into architecture by dabbling (building at Oxford while a professor of astronomy) and abruptly was in charge of it all as surveyor general to the king. The Great Fire of London (1666) so destroyed the wood medieval city that the materials and methods of building and the stylistic attitude of a new crop of designers provided a clean slate, both a gruesome event and awesome opportunity.

He offered a Baroque plan for reordering the city, both functionally and visually, which was rejected. But undaunted, he built 51 churches in 16 years (with 30 under construction at one time), all elegant, some suffering from the sketchlike nature of his involvement. He ended with St. Paul's Cathedral, modest peer of St. Peter's, Rome. (Churches were the responsibility of the state, and Parliament passed an act to build, rebuild, and finance them, as a normal duty after the Great Fire.)

Wren was a cartoonist and idea-generator, but had remarkable control, nevertheless, for one so thinly spread.

**WRIGHT, FRANK LLOYD (1869–1959)** *American Architect* It is hard to separate reality from wishful fantasy, but Wright was, and is, the greatest American architect, even though he said he was! Victorian-born and -bred, Celtic romantic by inheritance, he was steeped in architecture by his mother, who hung etchings of medieval cathedrals over his crib!

Wright worked for the lesser shingle stylist J. L. Silsbee, briefly attended the Engineering School of the University of Wisconsin,

**WREN** *Cross section of St. Paul's Cathedral*

WRIGHT *Guggenheim Museum, New York*

then nested in spirit with Louis Sullivan, great leader of the Chicago School, whom Wright called, romantically and in retrospect, *Lieber Meister.*

His life-style advertised architecture, complete, in later years, with twin matched Jaguars, white cape and beret, and the grand and patronizing feudalism of his great teaching estates, Taliesin and Taliesin West, where food, wine, and music were part of the apprentices' rights and duties. (Anyone who imagines himself the soul-heir of the Welsh poet Taliesin has, at the least, a substantial ego.)

He lived so long and worked so productively that he should have been a series of men—the whole practice of the Woods, father and son, spanned 27 years; Wright's alone spanned 70. First there was a natural search for direction, where his own shingle house in Oak Park stood forward. Then the great Prairie Houses, culminating in the Robie House (1909), horizontal, ground-hugging, decorated and roofed Cubism that so drastically influenced young Europe (Rietveld, Mies, van t'Hoff, and others) in their own early formative years (they were 20 years younger than Wright).

Best of all are the great monumental buildings of those early years: the Larkin Building (1904, Buffalo) and Unity Temple (1906, Oak Park), intricate Cubistic forms housing lush space that unfolds before the viewer, never fully revealed, always suggesting a little more. Unity Temple still brings Unitarians to its fold, but the Larkin Building (a mail-order house) was unhappily demolished in favor of that great American institution, the parking lot.

The Imperial Hotel (1916+, Tokyo), an exciting sprawl of urban building containing its own gardens, an experimental earthquake-proof structure of concrete, lava, and brick, devoured his seven middle years (ages forty-seven to fifty-three). He left other, more modest buildings in Japan (which remain today), but the Imperial has been demolished in tribute to high-rise hotel "progress."

Last of his phases is his most renowned, most spectacular, but with more superficial and flamboyant merits: Falling Water, the cantilevered house over a waterfall in western Pennsylvania; Taliesin West, his timber and canvas-roofed desert camp near Phoenix, Arizona; the Price Tower in Bartlesville, Oklahoma: the Guggenheim Museum in New York City; and a hundred others. They are brilliant, clever, original forms and space but lack the solid, consistent classic quality of his early work. They are stylish and already are out of style, while the Larkin Building was avant-garde for all time, and is gone.

**WRIGHT, FRANK LLOYD, JR. (1890– )** *American Architect* Son of Frank Lloyd Wright, called Lloyd. The Wayfarer's Chapel, a Swedenborgian crystal house of redwood and glass, sits on the handsome California coast at Palos Verde, its decorations the waves and bluffs of its site.

**WRIGHT, JOHN LLOYD (1892–1972)** *American Architect* Son of Frank Lloyd Wright and inventor of Lincoln Logs, those notched toys for child-built log cabins.

**WROUGHT IRON** Iron worked with heat and banging (the village blacksmith) that both hardens and tempers, producing a linear material for gates, railings, and horseshoes stronger than its source material.

**WURSTER, WILLIAM WILSON (1895–1973)** *American Architect* Master of understatement: his planar, boxed architecture in the San Francisco Bay Area, a latter-day New England. Redwood houses, clerestoried, with low pitched roofs, are in sharp and humble contrast to his attempt at Something Monumental: the Bank of America Building (1973, San Francisco), with S.O.M. (Skidmore, Owings and Merrill).

**WYATT, JAMES (1747–1813)** *English Architect* The greatest neo-Gothic extravaganza of all time was Fonthill Abbey (1796+), a stage-set for the wild romantic megalomania of William Beckford, millionaire dilettante. A park surrounded by 8 miles of 12-foot walls; a house called abbey to suggest medieval connotations, never to serve religion or its workers. Its 276-foot octagonal tower crowned a hall (read *nave*) 120 feet high, larger than any Gothic church, but for the house of a single man. Hundreds of men worked around the clock, frequently by the light of bonfires, to make it quickly, much of it of lath and plaster. Hollywood would never have dared to suggest it; only reality made it plausible.

**WYTHE** A single brick-thick wall, usually part of a laminated set: as in a cavity wall, where two wythes are spaced apart with air space between, propped and braced by wires or other spacers. Cavity walls allow drainage of the rain that penetrates the outer wythe, escaping to the world outside via weep holes at the bottom of the void.

# Y

**YAMASAKI, MINORU (1912–    )** *American Architect* First renowned, and rightly, for the great vaulted St. Louis Airport (1951; Yamasaki, Hellmuth and Leinweber), Yamasaki paradoxically turned to a decorated architecture, based on a delicate and eclectic pseudo-structuralism: the Science Center at Seattle's Fair of 1965 (neo-Gothic) and the World Trade Center for New York's Port Authority (1973–74).

The airport at Dhahran, major Arab stop on world-circling flights, is a more straightforward structuralist's posture; but the idea of structure and its embellishment seems more important than the structure itself. To pursue such ventures in Gothic architecture was to develop attitudes over centuries and generations. Here is unilateral "creativity," or just plain willfulness.

A handsome space is the hollow-cored, skylit Reynolds Metals Building, in Detroit's auto-dominated suburbs. A fancy gold grill on its exterior can't detract from the rare drama of its six-story skylit interior and balconied central well.

**YEON, JOHN (1910–    )** *American Architect* The Watzek House near Portland, Oregon, is a plain, spare, and luxurious viewer of Mount Hood: crisp, prismatic, low-pitched shapes surround a courtyard. Unconscious Cubism (or by default).

**YEVELE, HENRY (d. 1400)** *English Master Mason (Architect)* Designer-builder of the naves (main bodies) of Westminster Abbey (1375+) and Canterbury Cathedral (1390+), of which the choir had been designed by the imported Frenchman, William of Sens. One of the few warm-blooded identities documented and identified in the architecture of the Middle Ages.

**YORKE, F. R. S. (1906–1962)** *English Architect*  An early English modernist, he was partner of Marcel Breuer (1935–37) after Breuer fled Hitler's Germany and the Bauhaus and before Breuer went on to America to join Walter Gropius at Harvard.

Gatwick Airport (1958, London) is an articulated Mies(ian) volume of crisp black steel, a podium of white concrete and brightly colored innards.

YORKE *Gatwick Airport, England*

**YOUNG, AMMI (1800–1874)** *American Architect*  Boston's elegant four-faced Doric Greek Revival Custom House was Young's entrée (1837+) to Federal establishment architecture. Like Robert Mills, whom he replaced, or the later Alfred Mullet, he became architect to the U.S. government, as close to the role of national architect as ever existed in the United States.

**YUCATÁN**  Flat former sea bed of limestone that bears a sparse tropical forest, its thin lamination of soil supporting modest trees and dry brush. No lakes or flowing surface-water are available to support life, but the cenote (well-like natural or man-opened incision in the land exposing underground rivers) became the urban and religious waterhole, allowing the watering of Mayan-Aztec-Toltec-Spanish civilizations: their great ruined remnants left for our romantic reflection today at Chichén Itzá, Uxmal, and so forth.

# Z

**ZEHRFUSS, BERNARD (1911–   )** *French Architect*  Joint venturer (to provide national flavor for the glory of France) with Marcel Breuer and Pier Luigi Nervi for the U.N.E.S.C.O. Building (1953+, Paris). He was (with partners Camelot and de Mailly) designer of the great ribbed shell exhibition building (Centre des Industrie et Techniques; 1958+) at the new commercial center of the Place de la Défense, Paris.

**ZIGGURAT**  The mud-brick stepped pyramids of the Tigris and Euphrates valleys (where Assyria and Babylon occupied what is largely present-day Iraq). Not tombs, as those of Egypt, but rather processional holy places, as those of the Mayas in Yucatán. As a result they were served by ramps from tier to tier or, alternately, the whole series of tiers was a square spiral, continuous from ground to templed crest.

**ZIG-ZAG**  Sawtoothed profile decor used on Norman architecture as continuous banded decoration.

**ZIMMERMANN, DOMINIKUS (1685–1766)** *German Stuccoist and Architect*  Die Wies pilgrimage church (1745+, Bavaria) is a stucco Rococo, a magnificent light, bright interior for populist grandeur (the French Rococo was a style for the king and his court; Wies is for the townspeople and peasants). Zimmermann is thought of in the same breath with Neumann, his greater contemporary.

**ZINC** Element metal that participates with copper to make brass (an alloy) and is used as a coating to protect steel from corrosion —either electroplated, when it is called galvanized, or hot-dipped.

**ZONE** A geographical place with special qualities, as the Temperate Zone or a fire zone, but used most commonly to describe areas of a city where particular constraining laws are applied controlling use, height of buildings, and density of people resident, as in zon*ing*.

**ZONING** Zoning is the legal constraint of urban landholders from excess, preserving light and air and view for extant neighbors and limiting uses, particularly noxious ones. Zoning usually limits amount of construction, number of inhabitants, height, shape, and uses of a building or group of buildings.

**ZOOPHORUS** Early Greek cartoons; bas-relief animals in procession on a frieze; most famous at the Parthenon (but on anyone else's frieze as well).

ZIMMERMANN *Die Wies, Bavaria*

## A NOTE ABOUT THE AUTHOR

Norval White is Chairman of the Department of Architecture at the City College of New York, where he teaches courses in the history of architecture. He has his own firm, and has designed a number of important buildings. He is author (with Elliot Willensky) of the definitive *American Institute of Architects Guide to New York City.*

## A NOTE ABOUT THE TYPE

The text of this book was set, via computer-driven cathode ray tube, in a typeface called Baskerville. The face is a reproduction of types cast from molds made for John Baskerville (1706–75) from his designs. Baskerville's original face was one of the forerunners of the type style known as "modern face" to printers—a "modern" of the period A.D. 1800.

The book was composed by Compucomp Corporation, New York, New York; printed by Halliday Lithograph Corporation, West Hanover, Massachusetts; bound by The Book Press, Inc., Brattleboro, Vermont.

The book was designed by Earl Tidwell.

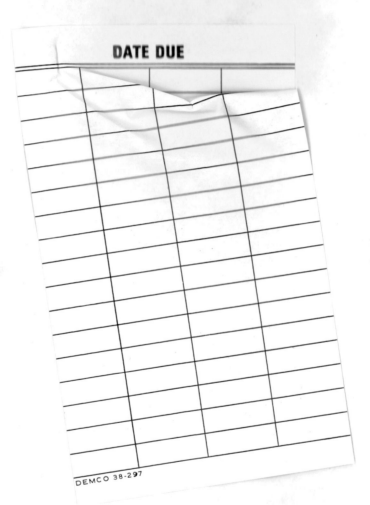

**DATE DUE**